BEHIND THE BOARDS II

BEHIND THE BOARDS II

The Making of Rock 'n' Roll's Greatest Records Revealed

Jake Brown

HAL LEONARD BOOKS

An Imprint of Hal Leonard Corporatio

Published in 2014 by Hal Leonard Books
An Imprint of Hal Leonard Corporation
7777 West Bluemound Road
Milwaukee, WI 53213

Trade Book Division Editorial Offices
33 Plymouth St., Montclair, NJ 07042

Printed in the United States of America

Book design by Leslie Goldman
Book composition by Kellner Book Design

Library of Congress Cataloging-in-Publication Data

Brown, Jake.
Behind the boards II : the making of rock 'n' roll's greatest records revealed / Jake Brown.
    pages cm
ISBN 978-1-4803-5060-1
1. Sound recording executives and producers--Interviews. 2. Popular music--Production and direction--History. 3. Popular music--History and criticism. I. Title.
    ML3790.B7763 2014
    781.66'149--dc23
                    2014007444

www.halleonardbooks.com

This book is dedicated to the late, great Mike Shipley (October 1956–July 2013). Thank you for blessing the world of rock 'n' roll with the great gift of your ear. RIP.

CONTENTS

CONTENTS

ACKNOWLEDGMENTS

Project Thank-You(s): I would first and foremost like to thank John Cerullo and the fantastic staff at Hal Leonard Books for the opportunity to continue this series into its second volume, and to thank the producers, both for the music you gave us and for sharing the behind-the-scenes studio stories of their creation in the pages of this book: Ken Scott, Bill Szymczyk, Nigel Gray, Howard Benson, Danny Kortchmar, Jim Gaines, Narada Michael Walden, Mike Shipley, Keith Forsey, Mike Flicker, Bill Bottrell, Nick Raskulinecz, Frankie Sullivan, Chris Kimsey, Joe Blaney, and Chris Tsangarides.

Personal Thanks: James and Christina Brown; Sgt. Joshua Brown (Ret.); Carrie Brock and little Hannie, and the best dog buddy ever, Scooter; Bill and Susan Brock; the extended Brown and Thieme families; Alex, Ellen Jackson, and Wilhelmina Schuchard; Andrew and Sarah McDermott; Cris Ellauri; Adam and Shannon Perri; Sean Fillinich; Bob O'Brien and Cayenne Engel; Alexandra Federov and Larry Jiminez; Richard, Lisa, and Regan Kendrick; Joe Viers; Paul and Helen Watts; Aaron Harmon; Freddy and Catherine Powers; Kenny Aronoff for the friendship and literary collaboration; Melanie and Jim Choukas-Bradley; Glenn Yeffeth et al. at BenBella Books; Joe Satriani and Mick Brigden; Tony and Yvonne Rose / Amber Books for giving me my start; Jack David et al. at ECW Press; John Blake Publishing; BearManor Media; Cherry Red Books; Ed Seiman et al. at MVD Music Distribution; and anyone and everyone else who has contributed to my personal, professional, and creative well-being over the past thirty-seven years.

CHAPTER 1

The Long Run–Bill Szymczyk

*"I am not a musician, I approach record production from the board,
the console is my weapon."*
—BILL SZYMCZYK

When *Billboard* magazine spotlights a record producer as "one of the greatest . . . of his time," you need a greatest hits collection to back that stature, and in both skill and sales, few measure up to Bill Szymczyk's track record. Whenever you tune in to your local classic rock radio station, you hear Szymczyk's sound, whether jamming out to Joe Walsh's greatest hits, from "Rocky Mountain Way," "Funk #49," "All Night Long," or the seminal "Life's Been Good to Me So Far," to the bulk of the Eagles' biggest #1s, including the legendary "Hotel California," "Life in the Fast Lane," "New Kid in Town," "One of These Nights," "Take It to the Limit," "Already Gone," "The Long Run," "I Can't Tell You Why," "In the City," and "Heartache Tonight." Szymczyk shot to the top of the charts with other rock 'n' roll pop culture staples including Rick Derringer's "Rock and Roll, Hoochie Koo," B. B. King's "The Thrill Is Gone," Elvin Bishop's "Fooled Around and Fell in Love," the Who's "You Better You Bet," and Bob Seger's "Against the Wind" among others that the producer proudly attributed to a by-product of his ambition from the very start of his career to pattern myself after two engineer-producers, Tom Dowd on the American R&B side and Glyn Johns on the bombastic rock 'n' roll side, and I tried to do a combination of the two. I grew up in Muskegon, Michigan, which is way up in the northern part of the state, and one night I discovered WLAC in Nashville, and they were rocking R&B and the blues, and up in Muskogee, it was all white-bread, so I'd never heard anything like this. So I started sending away for their *Midnight Blues* special, "six singles by Jimmy Reed, John Lee Hooker, B. B. King," stuff like that, and that's when my musical education started.

Not the typical child tinkering with electronic devices around the home, Szymczyk didn't discover his talent for auditory arts until his later teens. Unlike those who popped their heads into a studio out of curiosity one afternoon after school or wound up in one for the first time courtesy of a band they were playing in that wanted to cut their first demo, Szymczyk and his fate first found one another after

I joined the Navy when I was seventeen. This was 1960, so at that time, the biggest threat—according to the Pentagon—was Russian submarines, so they placed a high priority on sonar operators to track down subs. So everybody that went into the Navy, every enlistee, was given a (audio) test, and no matter what you wanted to do in your Naval career, if you scored in the top 5 percent of your test, which was basically pitch-perception, then you were going to automatically be sent to Sonar School in Key West, and I scored high and away I went.

I got out of the Navy in 1964, and three weeks before I got out, I was in a car driving down from Newport Island to New York City, where I knew I'd be relocating when I got discharged, and I heard "I Wanna Hold Your Hand" for the first time, and went "Holy shit! What's that about?" And then three weeks later I was a floor sweeper in a recording studio. It couldn't have worked out better.

Indeed, *Sound on Sound* magazine would report on his foot in the door that

a friend got him an interview at Dick Charles Recording, a studio heavily used by the new generation of songwriters that came up as the old Tin Pan Alley faded in the city. Don Kirshner was running Screen Gems Music, with staff writers like Carole King, Gerry Goffin, Neil Sedaka and Neil Diamond, who were using the studio to cut demos to acetate . . . For seventy dollars a week, Szymczyk made the acetate copies of the demos that were being churned out on Dick Charles Recording's mono machines at a furious pace, in the days before the singer-songwriter undercut the notion of the professional pop composer. Within a year, though, he had worked his way into the engineer's seat, cutting some of the demos by ping-ponging back and forth on a pair of mono tape decks. The next serendipitous occurrence took place in 1967 when Szymczyk met Jerry Ragovoy, producer for R&B artists like Paul Butterfield, Dusty Springfield and Dionne Warwick, who was preparing to open the Hit Factory studio at its original location at 701 Seventh Avenue.

Working as the Hit Factory's first lead engineer under the tutelage of Ragovoy, Szymczyk worked for several years as a freelance engineer, recording many of the studio's early albums by groups including the Fifth Estate and others. While a promising gig, Szymczyk's true make-or-break moment to step out as a producer in his own right came in the late '60s when he took a massive pay cut from $1,000 a week to a $300-per-week salaried gig as a staff producer for ABC Records. Excited by the opportunity to work as a staff producer for a major label, the producer would soon see his gamble pay off when

after I was hired by what was ABC-Paramount at the time in New York to be a staff producer, my initial first gigs were artists who were already signed to the label, "We need an album by this band, so go do that, this, etc.," and I discovered B. B. King was on the label. He was signed to Bluesway, which was a subsidiary, and I was a big fan and *really* wanted to produce him. I had an idea, and I kept bugging the powers that be at the label to let me produce him, and they said "No, you can't do that, you're too white and you're too young," and I kept bugging them until finally one said "Okay, look, B. B.'s coming to town next week, and we'll set up a meeting between the two of you, and if he says it's okay, then we'll let you try it."

Walking into the meeting with a vision for the new direction he wanted to take B. B.'s sound, rather than play it safe the first album out and stick with what had been King's approach to recording in the studio up to that point, Szymczyk put it all on the line in a gamble to sell the blues legend on a new producer and approach to recording, recalling that as he confidently walked into

that first meeting with B., I explained what I wanted to do, and going in with this pitch, I was very aware—having been a freelance engineer before I got the gig at ABC and having tons and tons of records with all the best session musicians in New York—and I told B. B., "Look, this is what I want to do: I want to take these young, energetic session guys and surround you with them," because at the time the Brits were bringing the blues back to us and pretending it was theirs. So I said, "It really started with you, and your ilk, and we got to get it as energetic as what's coming from overseas."

So he agreed, but he hedged his bets, and said "We'll do half the album your way, and half the album with my band," his road band, and I agreed. So we set up a recording gig out at the Village Gate, and recorded a couple of live shows, and from that, I called half the album *Alive and Well*. That was the live portion, and the *Well* portion was I booked guys that I liked, players who were young and energetic, and we made the *Well* portion of *Alive and Well*, and one of those tunes was a really energetic thing called "Why I Sing the Blues." It was real up-tempo, and a lot more energetic than his previous records had been, and that not only broke blues, but it broke the R&B chart pretty big, and made the pop charts, which was the first time he'd ever been on the pop charts.

Repackaging the punch of King's rhythm section for a new generation of listeners Szymczyk knew were waiting to embrace King, the producer found B. B. even more receptive to expanding on the approach with their next studio collaboration, *Completely Well*, where the producer remembered

> with that next album, he said "Okay I like this," and was all for it, and we did the whole album with my musicians, and one of those tunes was "The Thrill Is Gone," which became one of his biggest hits.

A Top 6 R&B singles chart hit for King, the true peak of the song's influence is still being measured by rock historians, with *Billboard* arguing—in a nod to the producer's decision to shake up B. B.'s rhythm section—that "the song's overall groove that is the star here, giving the overall piece a definitive atmosphere. This is, in fact, the lesson that he had been teaching all of his students from Michael Bloomfield to Eric Clapton in the '60s, and although many of their records preceded his on the charts, it was this exquisite piece at the dawn of the '70s that defined the blues movement." In breaking down the fundamentals of that groove musically, the legendary rock publication would add that the pair's studio experiment worked because "using a blues-rock basis for the main melody, King (cast) . . . the entire song in a very heavy jazz feel and flavor, attacking each verse with a world-weary vocal and some radical and sinewy guitar arpeggios. The feeling of breaking free from a possessive lover is the main basis for the lyrics, and King's use of blues imagery is perfect for the song, which indeed provided real release."

Amazed from lick one by King's hypnotic serenade of Lucille as the guitarist set about laying down one of the most recognizably haunting lead solos in modern blues, the producer—taking fans inside the studio for a firsthand look at the song's physical tracking—began with a spotlight on what he felt was King's greatest strength as

> a lead player, B. B. can play chords, no question he can do that, but he's known as a lead player, so one of the people I hired was Hugh McCracken, who was one of the best rhythm guitar players ever. So as they tracked, Hugh was filling in all the chordal passages, which left B. free to play lead. I think B. B. was playing Lucille through a Fender amp, and he recorded vocals while he was playing guitar, I think I only overdubbed him vocally on one cut, and that was years later on "Hummingbird," but "Thrill Is Gone" was a live vocal. On B. B.'s vocal for "The Thrill Is Gone," and others, I tended to use some echo, some reverb, nothing like we would do nowadays with delays and this and that and the other thing. Ahead of the session starting, we'd sat down in the

studio with the players and worked out the arrangement. When we started recording "The Thrill Is Gone," the basic track for that was cut as the last tune on maybe a 7-11 PM session.

Seeking to push the pop envelope as far as he could knowing they were onto something truly special in terms of its crossover potential, the producer pulled another surprise for King out of the air when

as I was just flipping out over that, at 2 o'clock in the morning, I called him and said "I want to put strings on this," and he went "What?!" Then he said, "Well, okay, I'll try it," because by that time he believed in me. So I arranged for *Bert Decoteaux*, who was my arranger at the time, to write a nice string chart for it, and the only thing I told Burt was "I want it to be dark, I want it to be not joyful in any way, the thrill is gone, I want it to be a dark string chart," and he brought it in and it was hypnotic. And B. B. said, "I want to come to the session," and I said, "Of course, come," and I'm engineering the string overdubs, and just kind of glanced over at him, and he had a big smile on his face the first time he heard the first rundown. I thought "Okay, I'm good now." Working with B. B., I was thrilled at being able to record a legend, and have success doing it!

Walking out of his collaboration with King packing a Top 10 hit whose reverberations would be felt for decades to come, the ambitious producer was eager to spend his newfound capital wisely in selecting his next project. Rather than take the safer route of working with an established star, the producer was eager to discover and develop his own. Riding off into what was at the turn of the decade truly rock 'n' roll's Wild West, where a producer with a bona fide hit could not only find and sign a diamond in the rough, but also help that star find and shape his or her sound in the studio from the ground up, Szymczyk's boomtown would be Cleveland, Ohio, recalling that his real gold rush began

once I'd had success with B. B., the record company said, "Oh, well maybe you do know what you're doing," and I kept going, "Well, I want to sign my own band, because I'm not just a blues guy, I want to make a rock & roll record." And they said, "Okay, well go out and find somebody and sign them." So I had a friend of mine who used to be a roommate in New York named Dick Corn who had moved to Cleveland, and was working as the manager/head bartender at this rock club called Otto's Grato, and it was in the basement of the Statler Hilton Hotel. So he said, "Man, there's a bunch of great acts coming through here, you gotta come out and check some of them out!" So I started going to Cleveland, and in the course of three or four visits, a band called the Tree Stumps—which was an awful name—came through, and the lead singer was Michael Stanley, and I really liked his tunes and his voice. So I signed them and changed their name to Silk, and the next group I signed was at the time a three-piece power trio called the James Gang.

The James Gang was fronted at the time by a 6-string axe played by Joe Walsh, who would go on to become classic rock's original cowboy—ranked #54 on *Rolling Stone* magazine's list of "100 Greatest Guitarists of All Time." In discovering Walsh, the producer was keen to hitch his wagon to the then-unknown star. Recognizing Walsh's immense gifts stylistically and substantively as a player, in celebrating the range he first witnessed that night onstage and subsequently in the studio, the producer felt from note one that

> Joe was a completely unique player: he can play the blues, he can play serious rock & roll, he can windmill with Townsend, I think he covers pretty much all the rock bases. So I made records after that with both groups I'd signed, and while Silk barely cracked the charts, the James Gang got played immensely, and that was the beginning of their career.

While the band's debut studio LP, *Yer Album*, released in March, 1969, was well received by critics, fans, and rock radio, it was via their second collaboration with Szymczyk, *James Gang Rides Again*, that Walsh's star was truly born courtesy of his lead riff work on the now-legendary "Funk 49." Rocking the kind of monster opening hook that left listeners stunned, this was the smash hit that made Popmatters.com observe that "Joe Walsh . . . proceeded to make a name for himself as one of the most important rock voices in the genre . . . With equal amounts of stridency and overblown self-indulgence this album introduces the world to Walsh's song writing . . . (and) arguably the greatest guitar boogie tune of all time. Chugging through a riff to end all riffs, Joe Walsh belts out the most incoherent and, more importantly, stupid lyrics ever uttered on tape." For as epic a classic as the song would become, Szymczyk revealed that its writing was far simpler, stripped down to

> six lines and a great guitar riff (laughs), that's all there is to it. On that one, I remember he just played me the riff, and I asked "Well, what's the song about?," and he says "I'm not sure yet," but we had to track it. A lot of his early, early writing was almost nonsensical, or it didn't make a whole lot of sense. There weren't any "story songs" per se, it was more images. He would bring in the riffs, and I'm not a player, he is, but as far as how to record it, that would be left up to me. So I would offer suggestions, "Well, I think this would really sound good if we doubled this," or "This would go good against this," it was all a collaboration once he brought riffs into the studio.

Producing three wildly successful albums with the James Gang that would establish a blueprint of sorts that Popmatters.com argued would "serve as important signposts to an as yet unwritten history of how the Midwest often defined the central aspects of American popular music." Adding the important summary note that the albums were "milestones in the winding history of Middle American music into the seventies," Walsh and Szymczyk's partnership would continue thereafter without the James Gang after the producer recalled

> I was in Cleveland, and the James Gang came through, Joe confided in me one fairly drunken night that he was thinking about quitting the James Gang, and I said "Well, move here, and we'll start your solo career," and that's basically what happened.

The first gem in the priceless collection of classic rockers that followed came with the making of one of Walsh's signature hits, "Rocky Mountain Way," which would serve as a roundabout ode to the studio location they picked to record the bulk of Walsh's first solo LP, *The Smoker You Drink, the Player You Get*, a title as colorful musically and lyrically as the personality it contained. When Szymczyk and Walsh set up shop at Caribou Ranch in scenic Nederland, Colorado, the producer knew they'd picked the perfect backdrop for recording, one Szymczyk had first become smitten with after

> I'd moved to LA for slightly over a year . . . when an earthquake happened in '71, and that did not register in my book, so I quit my job along with another guy who worked at ABC named Larry Ray, and we went to Denver to start our own record company. So at this point, I became an independent producer and started doing other acts, and there was no place to record in Denver, per se. So I would live in Denver and then obviously fly to LA or New York or San Francisco or wherever, and then we heard Joe Walsh moved out to Denver just shortly after I did, he actually moved up to Nederland, and we heard Jimmy Gercio—who I had met a couple times but not gotten to know very well—was living just outside Nederland on a huge ranch and building a studio.
>
> So we went over there, Walsh and I did, and were astounded at how it looked, it was under construction and not quite complete, and Jimmy was about to go off and direct a movie called *Electra Glide in Blue* with Robert Blake, and was going to let the studio sit until he got back. So we begged him, "No, no, no, no, put a temporary board in, please, and we'll use it." So he did, and we had a little MCI 400 console and a 16-track reel machine, and he went away to make his movie, and we proceeded to make Joe's *The Smoker You Drink, the Player You Get*, and did Rick Derringer's *All American Boy* up there, and overdubs on Michael Stanley, and other things like that.

Taking fans inside the studio and the creation of an album that *Guitar World* magazine would say "became ubiquitous on Seventies FM 'Album Rock' radio, buoyed by the signature track 'Rocky Mountain Way,'" the producer revealed of the latter classic's characteristically out-of-the-box recording journey that on the day Walsh showed up to start work on the song,

> he had already done the drums, he'd done this shuffle track that eventually turned into "Rocky Mountain Way" by himself when he was producing himself at Criteria, and I forget why I wasn't involved in the initial recording, but he brought it back and basically we stripped everything off except the drums and started over again, and did all the bass, kick, piano, the guitars, and everything. See, by then, he'd had the words, but when he first cut the track, he was thinking "Let's just do this blues-shuffle thing," but two, three months later when we were working at Caribou, he had the song done, so then we knew exactly how to go about finishing it. So we stripped that initial Criteria Studios take down to the drums and bass, and everything was done up at Caribou.
>
> Joe liked to layer his guitar tracks, lots, there's like six or seven guitars on there of various kinds, and the talk box. Joe was playing through a pretty small amp, either a Champ or a Princeton, and I had a 57 on it, and away we went! There wasn't a lot of planning, thought, chain, anything like that, it was like plug in, put some mics on it, and start playing. Back in those days, it was usually strictly one mic on an amplifier, so the thickness of the guitar sound is how Joe played it.

Working a typical rock star recording schedule where the team—which also included drummer Joe Vitali (Crosby, Stills, and Nash, the Eagles) and bassist Kenny Passarelli (Elton John)—kept largely nocturnal hours, Szymczyk confirmed that

> Joe and I usually worked 2-2, 2 in the afternoon to 2 in the morning. Caribou's live room was fairly big, and not as live as what we like nowadays. It had a drum booth, but nobody ever used it, we'd put the drums out in the middle of the room and have everybody else gather around it. Joe would cut his rhythm guitar tracks live off the floor with the band, but his lead vocal was overdubbed, 99 percent of the time we did it that way because when we were cutting the track, he wasn't done with the song yet. So it was a lot of working it out in the studio, but he would almost always have—even if the song wasn't written lyrically and we were doing rhythm tracks that the lyrics would be written to later, which happened quite a bit—a pretty good sense of what he was going to do as far as additional overdubs. "Now if I do this here, I can do that there on an overdub," and his parts would really complement one another.

Spending the better part of two years camped out up at Caribou Ranch churning out many of what would become the 1970s' most rotated and celebrated rock radio hits, including Rick Derringer's *All American Boy* LP, which featured his biggest hit, "Rock & Roll Hoochie Koo," the producer recalled that the project first came to him in the mid-'70s, so it was long before there were many producers on one album—which is kind of prevalent nowadays—but at the time, he and his manager had a great idea, and they were gonna get five or six different producers, and each producer was going to do two songs, and that's how it started. And I was the first producer to say, "Sure, I'll do that," which led to the recording of "Rock & Roll Hoochie Koo."

Throughout the recording of the album and aforementioned classic hit, Walsh would serve as Szymczyk's unofficial coproducer of sorts on the album, demonstrating the tireless currents of creative chemistry running back and forth between the two. Capitalizing once again on the instinct for groove he had first demonstrated during his collaboration with B. B. King, Szymczyk knew with Rick Derringer that he already had this base covered, explaining that

> because I was living in Colorado at the time and working out at Caribou, when Rick came out, I put him with Joe Vitali and Walsh and Kenny the bass player. Basically, I put Rick in Joe's band, because we all lived in Colorado and we cut two tunes, so Rick goes after that to England to work with some other producers. Well, a few months go by and they call me up and say, "Look, we can't get this together, we like what you did and want to finish it up with you." So he came back to Colorado and we finished the rest of *All American Boy*.

As they created what would become a Saturday night cruising anthem for the ages, in describing his process for constructing the wall of guitar tracks that would become one of Szymczyk's most celebrated production signatures throughout the decade, the producer shared his memory that

> there were three or four different guitars going on that song, basically that song was done with Rick playing rhythm guitar, then he overdubbed the bass, and overdubbed the other guitar rhythms and leads, track by track, pretty much building it up by himself. We had a real good time doing the vocals on that song. Rick likes to keep it light in the studio.

As the mid-1970s rolled around, though Bill had settled comfortably into life in Colorado working out of Caribou, the producer remembered a rude awakening when he found himself in the unique position of being among rock's most in-demand producers suddenly working without a studio after

> about a year and a half or so when Jimmy, the studio owner, came back once his movie's done, and he finished the studio, and he'd been waiting on this gigantic

olive board that never really did work, but he put it in, and then he starts working with Chicago and the Beach Boys, and once again, I'm out of a studio (laughs). It was his studio, so I couldn't kick him out, so there was about a two-year run where I was up there where it was just fabulous, it was like inmates running the asylum because there was nobody around. If something broke, we had to fix it—me and my assistant—and whoever the band was.

Feeling the time had come for a change of scenery, Szymczyk's next serendipitous twist of fate with shaping the 1970s rock 'n' roll landscape would come in 1974 when an ambitious band of Southern California rockers on the rise calling themselves the Eagles came circling the producer's services. Of a group whose musical influence cannot be understated, let alone really fully measured, the Rock and Roll Hall of Fame reported that when Don Henley, Glenn Frey, and company came under the producer's wing, they graduated from "wide-eyed country-rockers on the fertile Los Angeles music scene and evolved into purveyors of grandiose, dark-themed albums about excess and seduction. The Eagles were defined and bounded by the Seventies." Szymczyk's first collaboration with the group would be a clean-up effort of sorts with their *On the Border LP.* He recalled that

they had gone to England for the first two records, and went and started the third one, *On the Border*, and had probably seven or eight tracks that were in some form of completion, and that's when they decided, "No, no, no, this wasn't working with the producer they were working with at the time," and were looking for a new producer. Most of the band—meaning Glenn and Don—wanted to rock more, and Glyn Johns did not see them as a rock band, his comment was "The Rolling Stones are a rock band. You're not a rock band, you're a vocal band," and that of course rubbed them the wrong way.

Recognizing immediately and instinctively that the group's rock 'n' roll sensibilities were the stuff of superstar potential, the producer found himself on the same production page with the band from the time of their first meeting. Sharing the details of their history-making dialogue as vividly as the very night it took place, Szymczyk fondly recalled that

Irving and Joe at that point set up a meeting between me and the band, and we had dinner one night, and they asked me questions about rock, and I was even hesitant about doing it because I didn't want to do a cowboy band. I wanted to do a rock & roll band, and so when they said "We wanna rock," I said "Well good, if you wanna rock, I'm your man!" So one thing led to another, and we started working together.

Rescuing the band from their country roots just in time, according to *Rolling Stone*, for the Eagles to realize their "potential for bigger things," once he was officially hired, the producer was put through a trial-by-fire in his first studio session with the group. In deconstructing the recording that would become the album's biggest single, "Already Gone," Szymczyk began by highlighting some of what he felt were the group's central musical assets that both he and the band were equally eager to bring off the bench and put into play with

> that very first cut I did with them. That was a Jack Tempchin song they brought in, and said, "We've been playing around with this for a while," and it was just a case of "Well, let's just turn it up and go!" Glenn Frey had the opportunity to play lead guitar, which Glyn Johns previously would never let him do, because it was always Bernie—Bernie was the country player, and Glyn Johns gravitated toward that, as opposed to Glenn Frey. Frey was not as gifted a musician at the time as Bernie was, but he really had the desire to rock, so I took a lot of time with Glenn Frey on the guitar solos, and the sounds of the rhythm guitars and stuff, and we were off.

Szymczyk tapped the considerable talents of the band's newest member, lead guitarist Don Felder, to help round out the group's reinvented guitar sound; the producer felt Felder added the extra musical muscle needed to fully flex the Eagles' potential as a rock 'n' roll band with real radio credibility. Feeling the meat on the band's musical bones was the strength of their guitar sound, the producer's secret sonic formula involved

> using one of three different mics on guitar amp: an SM57, an AKG 414 and a Sennheiser, and basically I wasn't double-micing anything in those days.

Employing an old-school concept that had worked wonders for B. B. King's band a few years earlier to shake up the Eagles' groove, Szymczyk recalled that throughout the recording of *On the Border*,

> it was everybody in the same room, but I would gobo the amps off from one another, and we were recording at Record Plant Studio A in LA, the 3rd Street Record Plant, the original one. We were recording on a Quad 8, which was a 16-channel console.

Knowing he was on to something once tape was rolling, as the group worked through a reinvention with electrifying their sound for the first time, in a less dramatic context than Dylan had gone through with the same process, their producer could hear an equally real awakening happening within the sound of the record. It was one the band welcomed with open ears and arms as they spread their rock 'n' roll wings, with Szymczyk singling out a particularly fine example with a song he saw take flight

> during the making of that record that I was real pleased with. It was they had done a version of the song "On the Border" with Glyn, and it was pretty just straight-ahead

kind of country acoustic guitar/vocal, and I said, "Well, man, let's make this into a real R&B record," and we funked up the rhythm section—the drums and the bass—and when we were doing the vocals, it was almost like doing a Temptations kind of record where everybody gets one line thing, at the end there, "Just show us your name . . ." So everybody got a line or two in that last verse, and it was, to me, patterned totally on Temptations records.

Another famous skill the Eagles shared with the Temptations that Szymczyk capitalized on heavily throughout the rerecording of their first collaboration was the group's gift for blending vocal harmonies. Showcasing them loud and clear in radio waves around the country on "Already Gone," the producer felt the band excelled in this department on one musical malefactor, that of

one word, BLEND, that's all it is: they have an incredible blend, and that's something they came in with. The blend initially of Don, Glenn and Randy, and to some degree Bernie—but he was more of a player as opposed to a singer. So the three-part harmony was basically Glenn and Don and Randy Meisner, and then later on, obviously Tim would fill the high role, because with both Randy and Tim, it's play low, sing high, play bass, sing high.

After the producer proved both his and the band's potential to themselves as a rock act following the crossover success of "Already Gone" on rock radio, in 1975, with the Eagles eager to head back into the studio to build on the momentum they'd started rolling on turntables around the country in homes and radio stations alike, "One of These Nights" took shape as an effort to expand on everyone's strengths within the band, including for Szymczyk the shot at pushing drummer Don Henley vocally more front and center to share the stage with Glenn Frey. Szymczyk reasoned that the move made sense based on Henley being

one of the best vocalists I've ever recorded, just natural, and our nickname for him was "Goldenthroat," because the guy would just start singing and it was fucking brilliant. Initially, when we first started "On the Border," which he sang lead on, and "One of These Nights," it was pretty quick. It wasn't till we started *Hotel California* and we all discovered vocal comping together that they started to become extreme nitpickers, but nonetheless, it would still be a matter of three, four completed takes, and that's where 90 percent of your performance comes from. Then you labor over the little 10 percent.

As a drummer, the producer found the multitalented Henley once again to be a dream to work with, crediting him as among the most naturally gifted skinsmiths—let alone vocalists—he'd ever recorded. Henley's talent translated so naturally to tape that all the producer needed to do to match the drummer's spot-on delivery with the appropriate number of attentive microphones, and Szymczyk recalled to that end that

> one of the first things Don asked me when they interviewed me was how many mics I'm going to use on the drums? I said "Probably seven, or eight or nine, something like that," and that's exactly what he wanted to hear because Glyn Johns was more of an organic three-mic deal, and I had only ever done it that way early, back in the early '60s in New York as an engineer. But when we went from 4-track to 8-track, and you listened to a couple Beatles records, it was like, "Well God, I gotta mic everything now!" So for Don's drums, I was using a D-12 on the kick drum and probably RE-20 on the foot, and usually the 57 on the snare—of course everyone tries everything different and then goes back to the 57—and I didn't mic on the bottom of the snare, I would just work with the top. I did that because I didn't like the sound of snares rattling, and that's what you get with a bottom mic.
>
> For overheads, I would have various things. I remember 87s, and then I went to some Swedish mics called PMLs that are no longer around, back and forth. I was all over the map. We didn't really have room mics in those days, most the rooms I was cutting in were relatively dead rooms, so it wasn't until we got into "Long Road Out of Eden" in 2001 where we had live rooms, Henson Studio A and a couple others out there where you really get a killer live drum sound.
>
> On "Heartache Tonight," on that snare sound, we were using the very first Senair, an electronic snare that one of the local bands in Miami had in their kit, and when I'd first heard it I said, "Ooh, I've got to borrow that." So I borrowed it, gave it to Don, and said, "Come on, we can use it," and he said, "Oh yeah, I like that."

Signaling Henley's early willingness to be cutting edge with the use of programmed/ electronic drum elements back in the mid-'70s when few others in rock were, the Eagles were breaking new ground with each hit that drove their knack for perfectly executing each concept commercially in the form of another hit single a notch higher on the charts. Taking fans back into the studio for the making of one of those hits, the beloved "Take It to the Limit" was a Top 5 anthem whose musical momentum is centered around a gorgeous piano sound that was captured on tape using

> a pair of 414s, and it would be blanketed off, but still in the room, oboed off and somewhat blanketed, but it would be live 99 percent of the time.

In sum, "One of these Nights" would succeed in broadening the band's fan base based on "the Eagles' ensemble playing" on songs like the aforementioned hit, which *Rolling Stone* felt was "unprecedentedly excellent," positioning the band at "the apex of post-Byrds Southern California rock" heading into what would be their next studio LP, *Hotel California*, the biggest-selling rock album of the 1970s.

The album's musical mythos would revolve around everything one could expect from the making of an epic, beginning with the expectations that naturally hovered over the band heading into its recording, a unique form of pressure only a producer of Szymczyk's skill was suited to help the band relieve. Beginning with the decision to take their time recording the album so the group's principal writers, Don Henley and Glenn Frey, had time to flesh out a concept record based around a title track spearheaded by Henley, Frey in a conversation with *In the Studio* radio show host remembered that it marked "the first time that Don took it upon himself to write an epic story." Afforded this luxury of time courtesy in part of a lavish studio budget that allowed the band to lock out studios including Criteria and the Record Plant, Szymczyk detailed a recording routine where

> we'd do the track, and then work for three weeks, then take a month off, and during that month off is when Don and Glenn would write lyrics. They had innate talent as songwriters, and fed off each other brilliantly, much like Lennon/McCartney. They'd go to each other's houses, and then come back to the studio for the next session with "Well, here it is," and Glenn and Don by that point both knew who was going to sing lead on what song pretty much, they would always have decided that prior to cutting the lead vocal.

Another strategic development came with the band's decision to infuse their musical personality with one of rock's most colorful, longtime Szymczyk collaborator Joe Walsh. Of this key addition that the Rock and Roll Hall of Fame reported "added even more of a hard-rock edge to the Eagles' sound," Szymczyk remembered that

> the whole band was happy to have Joe's musical input, most assuredly, because Joe brought energy to the band, and it's easy for me to describe the dichotomy between Don Felder and Joe Walsh as players, because Felder was and is a great technician, he's technically one of the greatest guitar players I've ever recorded. Whereas Joe is free-form, and more impromptu-spontaneous, and that's what made the two of them work.

Felder would shine in his own right as the group member responsible for the musical genesis of the album's title track, a gem the producer remembered first discovering after it

> came in on a cassette of a bunch of Felder riffs, Felder ideas, and Henley picked up on that, and didn't have any idea what the song was going to be about, but said "Let's work on this riff for a while." I think the only song on the whole album that was

finished before we started was "Try and Love Again," but everything else was constructed in the studio, as with "Hotel California."

The album's road to its eventual Grammy in 1977 for "Record of the Year" would wind on for a year and a half and with the creation of the #1 hit title track, several evolutions that Bill Szymczyk remembered involved "a long history," translating to

> our recording that track THREE times! The first time we did it, it was too fast, but you're doing a track, and you have no idea what the words are going to be or where they're going to be, and then when Don would start to get an idea about what to write about here, he'd say, "Well, this is going to be too fast, we gotta cut it again." So we'd cut it again, and then he'd progress further with the song's writing, and next decided it was in the wrong key, so the third time's the charm, and that's the version that everybody knows. By then, by the third time we cut it, he pretty much had 90 percent of the lyrics done by that time.

Inviting the band's fans inside the studio for a look at the recording of the legendary song, beginning with Don Felder's mysterious acoustic guitar opening, Szymczyk describes this signature prologue that

> starts with Don Felder playing a 12-string, which I recorded with three mics: my go-to acoustic guitar mics for recording acoustic guitar was a Neumann KM-84, and I've used the same one since before in "Hotel California," and I still use it to this day. But then, Don had a pickup in his guitar, and he widened off to a pair of small orange amps, and I miced them in stereo, so the initial opening guitar intro, that's what that is—it's acoustic guitar in the middle, and an amp on both sides with a chorus that is flowing back and forth between the two amps.

Szymczyk was excited to introduce the interplay between Felder and Walsh to tape with the song's lead solos, a creative by-product of what *American Songwriter* magazine would call "the smartest move the Eagles ever made." This resulted in "Felder and Walsh guitar-sparring off each other and helped confirm the Eagles as one of the world's biggest bands, with the duel repeatedly voted one of rock's greatest guitar solos—despite it being played by two people." Capturing that lightning was not work left to assistant engineers, but a process where Szymczyk proudly shared that

> for the guitar recording, I was on-site constantly watching the two of them work. Then when we did the leads, every one of them was constructed—whether it be Don or Joe—with their amp, and their favorite guitar for that part. We could play five different guitars during the course of making that song, and we had maybe sixty guitars at our

disposal in the studio. We were all over the map at that point with amplifiers as well, so we had thirty amps.

An intimate process that culminated with the song's blaze of outro solo glory, this monumental musical triumph the producer still considers "one of the highlights of my career" came together during an inspired marathon recording session that unfolded over

> a two-day period working at Criteria Studios in Studio City, and I got Joe on one side of me, behind the board. We ran lines out to the amplifiers in the studio, but they were both performing in the control room, so I was in the middle and Joe Walsh was on one side and Don Felder on the other side, and we just attacked this ending blend of solos. So during that two-day run of leads, there was a lot of stop/start, and "Let's try this," and "That didn't work," "Well, if we did this with that, maybe that would work," piece by piece by piece until it was done. They were equal gunfighters, Joe and Don.

Truly a team effort all around, when the time came to construct the song's haunting chorus vocal harmonies—a gift within the group that *USA Today* would describe as "spine-tingling"—Szymczyk was excited to collect the members' combined vocal talents around one magic microphone he recalled was

> an 87 I opened up all the way around, omnidirectional, and then had them gather around one mic, and then I'd be moving them in, moving them out, depending on each vocal part. That stayed stationary throughout our collaboration together. I was always a one-mic guy for harmonies, and those guys would have to balance themselves in the room around the microphone. Anywhere—depending on who was singing what part—you would have one guy maybe six inches away from the microphone, and another guy who was booming maybe two feet away, that's what I mean by balancing them out.

Sharing other highlights from the tracking of other smash hits from the album including "New Kid in Town" (#1 on the *Billboard* Top 100 singles chart), the producer said that as a special touch,

> on "New Kid in Town," I thought it would be real neat if we had an upright bass, but Randy couldn't play an upright bass, but he could play a guitarrón, so I had him in an isolation booth in Record Plant Studio C, and he would play that in there on the basic track, and it just added that Spanish kind of ambience to the track itself.

Pulling his compositional weight with the writing of one of classic rock radio's most famous lead riffs, when Joe Walsh first presented the riff "Life in the Fast Lane" to the band's producer, Szymczyk remembered recognizing the song's potential instantly, as he recalled Henley did as well the day

Joe brought that lick in, and Henley wrote the words. By that point in my working relationship with Joe, when I heard a riff of his, I could tell when it was a hit riff, and we all jumped on that one. Most of the lead solo overdubs were done in the control room, but the original basic track would have been done with everybody in the studio, and then once we started overdubbing guitars, they would come in one at a time. But for "Life in the Fast Lane," that's all Joe, even though Felder played some rhythm parts and doubled the lead lick an octave higher, it was all support to what Joe was doing on guitar. I don't think Joe was dying to sing lead on that one, because when you have someone like Henley, it's about who's the best person for the job. That's pretty much how that band delegated who sang on what. On Don's lead vocal, I had a Cooper Time Cube Delay on him, which I still have and still use.

As recording finally wound down after more than a year of tracking, *Sound on Sound* reported that the record was "mixed in Criteria's Studio C . . . (and) was released in December 1976 and spent a total of eight weeks atop the *Billboard* 200 en route to selling more than sixteen million copies in the United States alone. "New Kid in Town" topped the singles chart in February 1977, followed by the title track that May, which shifted a million units within three months of its release." At the 1977 Grammy Awards, the Eagles would be acknowledged for multiple musical achievements, including "Record of the Year" for "Hotel California" and in a nod to their producer, "Best Arrangement for Voices" for "New Kid in Town." Ultimately selling thirty-three million copies worldwide, the success of *Hotel California* would prove to be a double-edged sword when the Eagles regrouped two years later with Szymczyk to record their final studio album.

Shedding light on some of the divisions the band's superstar status had begun to create within the group that he'd have to navigate for the first time in the studio, the producer began with the band's general state of steadily splintering camaraderie, confirming that while

they were friendly initially in the studio, very much so, when I started working with them on *the Border* it was all for one/one for all, all the way through *One of These Nights*, other than Bernie was getting a little less interested in the band because we were rocking more, and he didn't really want that. Then when he left after *One of These Nights,* all the way through the making of *Hotel California*, everybody was getting along pretty good. But coming off the heels of the success of *Hotel California*, among the band, there was a lot of expectations, everybody was like, "Oh my God, how are we going to top that?" And according to the critics, we didn't, but in my mind, *The Long Run* was a very, very good album, it just took forever to get done.

At that point, the pressure was seriously high, and everybody was getting a little antsy with each other, and that's when the dissension in the ranks started, instead of the old all-for-one/one-for-all, instead it was "What about me?," a lot of that attitude. They were still a team, but instead of everybody riding in the same car, eating together, and staying in the same house, it was two or three different houses, everybody had their own car, and it was more standoffish, if you will, than up until that point. But when they got into the studio, 90 percent of the time, we all got along good and did our work. We would always track together, and we may replace one thing if it didn't fit later on, but we would do five-piece live off the floor all the time. My M.O. was to try and keep everything light, happy, and moving forward, and eliminate as much hassle as possible from outside the control room and inside the control room.

Seeking a change of scenery from Southern California, Szymczyk set up shop on the opposite coast in Miami, fulfilling every producer's dream of owning their own recording studio. For Szymczyk, that oasis was Bayshore Recording, which he proudly recalled was

the first one we'd recorded at my studio. Right as we were finishing *Hotel*, I was building my studio, Bayshore Recording. My studio had a relatively dead room, it was about the same size at the Record Plant Studio A, and not a huge room, but worked really, really well for how I wanted the studio to sound, regardless of who I was recording. Studios are people's personal taste, and at that time, in 1976, we weren't doing a lot of live-room stuff, things were still pretty much dead. It wasn't until about ten years later that the big live-room drum sound came into being, and everybody was changing to that. The studio had all the equipment I wanted as far as outboard gear, which included a bunch of LA3s, a bunch of 1176 mic pres, a couple Eventide digital delays, which were really, really new at the time, and my old trusty Hooper Time Cube, and harmonizers, and an MCI 500 Series Console, and I had a little help in designing that one, because MCI was right up the street in Ft. Lauderdale.

Employing many of the same technical applications he had mastered on *Hotel California* in recording the band, beginning with Don Henley's drum sound and vocal track for "The Long Run," arguably the album's biggest radio hit, the producer confirmed that "I used the same drum micing setup I'd used on *Hotel California,* and I had Don singing through an 87 mic." Dividing up lead vocal duties among the band's various members,

Timothy Schmidt sang lead on "I Can't Tell You Why," and Glenn Frey sang lead on "Heartache Tonight." Joe sang lead on "In the City," and he and Don Felder were still sharing lead guitar duties throughout the album. I dug them for two entirely different reasons, one Felder being more of a technician and on the money, and Joe being more of a loose, free-spirit jam kind of a guy, and they worked really well together, and that's what each one of their jobs was as the band's lead guitar players: to complement one another.

The thing I remember most about *The Long Run* was, initially when we went in, it was going to be a double album. They figured, "How do you top *Hotel California*? Well, what if we give them a double album, and really stretch out?" So we could cut track after track after track, and the songwriting modus operandi was: the tracks would come first, the music would come first, and the lyrics would come later, to be written to the track, and we had about eighteen, nineteen, roughly under twenty tracks, but they were in certain stages of completion, and by the time we were into this album about a year, they realized, "Well, hell, we're never going to get a double album," so they just concentrated on the ones that were the most fully lyrically done, and that's what turned out to be the final track listing. So there's about eight or nine tracks that are floating around left over.

Szymczyk would wind up the '70s adding one more crown jewel to his catalog of decade-defining rock radio smashes when he teamed once again with studio soulmate Joe Walsh to produce what would become Walsh's greatest hit, "Life's Been Good to Me So Far." After this literal party on tape that longtime fan *Rolling Stone* would conclude was "the most important statement on rock stardom anyone has made in the late Seventies," the producer was eager to get back into the studio with Walsh and what he felt was

one of the best bands that we ever put together. That was Joe Vitale on drums, and Willie Weeks on bass and Jay Ferguson on keyboards, and Joey Murcia—who was an R&B player from Miami—playing the second guitar to Joe. Joe, at that point, having been in the Eagles, felt it was nice to have another player to bounce off of at the same time, instead of him having to do everything overdub-wise.

Seeking to surround Walsh and his band with the spirit the song celebrated in literal scenic terms as they got down to work, as the team kicked off recording,

to get the album underway, we'd rented like a seventy-two-foot yacht out of Miami, and had gone down to the Keys with a 4-track machine and all their instruments, and we spent a week down in the Keys hashing these tunes out, and pretty much everything on the *But Seriously Folks . . .* album was rehearsed down on this boat, and "Life's Been's Good" was one of them.

The project boasted an episodic arrangement that *Mix* magazine later observed was "approaching the symphonic, with individual movements and a recapitulation of the main theme that would bring the song back to its original light reggae vamp after an extended middle section." As they started work on its tracking, "Szymczyk looked at it as a project in parts." Beginning with the construction of the song's famous foundational wall of rhythm guitar tracks, the producer remembered there being

> six or seven layers of guitar on the song, and to get that sound, there would have been a couple of Tweeds, a couple Fenders, and a Princeton amplifier. He had four or five he'd bring to the studio, and then depending on what the song called for, he'd experiment and say, "Let me play through this, no, no, let me play through that . . . Okay, that's it," and we'd mic it up and go. I recorded the acoustic guitar breakdown on that song with a KM-84 through an 1176.
>
> Vocally, an 87 was my basic go-to vocal mic at that point. To me, it was a very high-quality microphone, and mostly I did not have access to the old 47s and the classic Neumanns from the '40s and '50s and '60s, I just never had any of those, but an 87 was basically a 67, just with transistors instead of tubes. That's what I went to, liked on vocals, and it worked great with Joe. There's a bunch of effects on his vocals for "Life's Been Good to Me," for instance, on the verses, there's a digital delay that's left and right that is maybe forty milliseconds on one side, eighty milliseconds on the other, and then I take that off on the choruses and put a time-cube on him. Then of course there's some reverb.

In what could have become among rock's greatest travesties—a gem left on the cutting-room floor—the producer revealed that the song almost didn't make it to the finish line after

> we got back to my studio, which by this point was set up at Bayshore in Miami, and worked on this, and though he had the song, all the way through making the record, he was getting more and more hesitant about putting it out, because he thought the public would take it the wrong way lyrically. I was the one who was just on him constantly, "No, no, no, no, you've gotta finish this," because at one point he wasn't even going to finish it. And I told him "You MUST finish this, this is a killer record! You've gotta finish it," so finally he agreed, and the rest is history. I did change a couple of melody lines in it, so it made it easier for him to sing, and gave it more of a light-hearted thing, because initially (singing in low, slow tone) "Life's been good to me so far," real kind of down and dour, and I went "No, no, no, no, no, you've gotta be exuberant there: LIFE's BEEN GOOD TO ME SO FAR!"

Indeed, life had been good to Bill Szymczyk by that point in his storied career, and heading into the 1980s, his status as one of rock's most in-demand producers would continue, his next call coming from Bob Seger to work on the singer's 1980 hit "Against the Wind." Jumping at the opportunity to work with Seger, the producer joked he'd taken the gig first and foremost because he's another Michigan boy (laughs). I'm from Michigan, he's from Michigan, and in fact, Glenn Frey was from Michigan as well and had been in one of Bob's first bands way back before any of them had left Michigan and gotten famous. So they were still friends, and Glenn had actually played on the *Stranger in Town* LP while we were making an Eagles LP, which is how I first got to meet Bob. So as time went on, when he was in the middle of working on what turned out to be the *Against the Wind* LP, I was a big fan of his when I got the call to do that record. He asked me, "Do you want to do three or four songs?," and I of course said "Sure!" I had my studio open by then, so we recorded the title track, "Against the Wind," and "Betty Lou's Getting Out Tonight," "Her Strut," and a couple others.

Once he got to work in the studio with Seger, noting the singer's famously meticulous and hands-on nature in the studio, the producer remembered that

Bob was very particular, but it was pretty effortless. He's one just like Henley who's a natural talent, the two of them to me are two of the best vocalists I've ever recorded. I used to take a lot longer with other vocalists who weren't as good, but he was a natural. For the acoustic guitars on "Against the Wind," I used a KM-84 which I still have, and use on every acoustic guitar to date. I like that mic because it's bright and it projects what I think acoustic guitars should sound like to my ear, and luckily everybody dug it.

Another of Szymczyk's high-profile collaborations came when he worked with legendary rock band the Who on their *Face Dances* LP, a more delicate affair considering the fact that

this was the first album after Keith Moon had passed away, so Kenney Jones was the drummer, and so he and I were the new kids. There were the usual band rifts going on, for instance, the band didn't want to be around when Roger was doing vocals, and Roger never showed up when we were cutting tracks. So I'd have to do each one of them individually almost.

That was the hardest record I ever had to produce, I worked my ass off on that, and I'll be honest with you: to this day, I'm not real happy with the mix of the whole album. So it was tough, just because of a lot of the dissension, and there was some serious drinking going on, not by me, but by the band members, so it was a rough record to make.

Pete brought songs in, but he did not have a cohesive *Quadrophenia* or *Tommy* vibe to it, it was strictly: "Here's a bunch of songs." So there was no story line to follow, per se, but unlike the Eagles, he had the songs finished, and for instance, that bubbily loop in "You Better, You Bet," he brought that in and we basically overdubbed everything to that. Pete was impressive as a guitar player, songwriter, visionary, and just all-around really good guy. He had five or six different amps to go to, and we'd put up some mics and away we'd go. As a player, he was the epitome of a slash-and-burn guy, he would attack it, and it was fun to watch. I still am in communication with him to this day. He was the reason I was doing that album, he's the one that wanted to hire me.

Another of Szymczyk's favorite hits to come courtesy of an invitation from the artist was his collaboration with Elvin Bishop on the 1975 smash hit "Fooled Around and Fell in Love" (#3), which the producer recalled was actually

sung by Mickey Thomas from Starship, who was already in the Elvin Bishop band, and their manager Phil Walden called me and asked if I wanted to produce Elvin, and I said "Sure!" Before that, I had engineered some things for the Paul Butterfield Blues Band back in the '60s in New York when I was just engineering and not yet a producer, and Elvin was in that band. So we'd known each other from way back in the '60s. When we were recording that song, we recorded at Criteria Studios in Miami in Studio C, and I probably had a little bit more reverb than usual on the drums on that one.

Elaborating on his knack for producing hit singles, while his track record would suggest that it's a conscious talent on Szymczyk's part as a producer, in fact, he revealed that throughout his career,

I've very seldom had a preconceived notion about something being a hit or not, because I learned on that you can say about a song when it's coming together in the studio, "That's a SMASH!," and then it comes out and absolutely nothing happens, and then others where I thought a song was just okay, and it turns out to be a hit. So I have no clue, and still don't.

Either way, his whirlwind success at producing a double-album's worth of classic rock's greatest hits between the late '60s and early '80s afforded Szymczyk "the luxury of relaxing a bit from the industry," according to *Billboard*, throughout the rest of that decade and much of the 1990s. As his catalog began to filter down via regular rotation on rock radio stations, television, film, and commercials to a new generation of fans, *Billboard*, the music industry's most followed weekly periodical—which had documented the impact of Szymczyk's hits throughout their consistent reign at the top of their albums and singles charts—added that "even in his absence, Szymczyk . . . (remained) a class act whose work is felt through the younger producers and engineers he has inspired."

Bringing the conversation chronicling his amazing career full-circle, while the legendary producer acknowledged that "I don't have the desire to be in the studio 24/7 like I used to," he added that from the purest place he ever first desired to produce, the same fiery passion has never gone out

> for my love of the creative process itself, that's what I still love about it. Doing what a producer does: here's your script, the song; here's your actors, the players; and you've got to guide the whole thing through to the end where it's a great-sounding record. It's a drug, number one, and it still jazzes me when something I have a vision for works and turns out good.

Reflecting back in closing on whether any favorites stand out among his astonishing catalog of classics, Szymczyk offers an understandable—and extremely common—answer among hit-making producers of his stature that

> most of what I consider my favorite records were not hit records. So James Ferguson's first solo record, called *All Alone in the End Zone*, I thought that was one of the best records I ever made, and there's a Mickey Thomas record—after he left the Elvin Bishop band, I signed him to a contract with Elektra, and cut a solo album with him I think is just brilliant. Then to go way back, there was a very weird jazz record by a guy named Howard Roberts that I did with Ed Michel called "Antelope Freeway" that is one of my favorite records. Joe was definitely one of my most kindred collaborations, I found him, I signed him to his first contract, and we still work together. So those are the babies, and the other kids grew up, went out, and made money! (laughs). I'm just very, very happy that I grew up in the business when I did. I'm blessed, and I thank God every night for the wonderful life he's given me.

CHAPTER 2
Rocket Man–Ken Scott

"An album should take you on a journey, and to do that, you have to treat each song as an individual."
—KEN SCOTT

It's not that uncommon for a young recording engineer to be thrown to the lions in being asked to work a studio session when he's never actually sat behind the console in that role before, it's just not often it happens to be with the Beatles. That's precisely how fate unfolded for eighteen-year-old Ken Scott when, one serendipitous day in 1964,

> the very first time I saw any of the Beatles, it was a couple of weeks after starting at EMI, and I was walking along the corridor and coming toward me were the two Georges—Harrison and Martin—and I wanted to scream just like all of the girls out front! It was "Oh my God!," and so obviously, at that point, I was completely starstruck. Then I actually got to go into the studio with them when they were recording one of the tracks for *Hard Day's Night*, and I got kicked out very quickly by George Martin because I wasn't supposed to be there.

Flipping back through his memories to the time when he first began to discover the innate love of recorded music that would soon enough lead him to start *recording* sounds, Scott began as a fan, sharing that

> as a small child, I had an old wind-up Gramophone, and a bunch of 78s, now those 78s happened to be Elvis Presley, Bill Haley, Eddie Cochran, and as I started to play those, was completely enamored with that style of music and would lock myself away in the room with that wind-up gramophone for hours on end. Then when I was 12 ½, I got a tape machine for Christmas, and totally got into recording everything from records off of the radio and also doing radio plays. So friends would come over, we'd record those radio plays, and that kind of served two purposes: firstly, I enjoyed recording, and secondly, it was also great because we could take the tape recorder into our English lesson in a couple months when we'd finished it, and we played the Radio Play for the class, which got us out of learning things like adverbs and pronouns and that kind of thing, so everyone in the class was happy with that break.
>
> So that's what got me into recording, basically, then a year and a half, two years later, I was watching an English TV program called *Here Come the Girls*, and it took place in a recording studio, and I saw at one point when the camera pulled up to this large window this grey-looking desk with someone sitting behind it, and my immediate reaction was: that's what I have to do. I have to be what that guy is, and I eventually found out that it was #2 Studio at EMI Recording Studios, what later became Abbey Road, and that the guy sitting behind the desk was Malcolm Eddy, and he eventually became a mentor of mine and a good friend. So I was already enjoying the science of sound before I got to Abbey Road, experimenting with it to a point.

An "Ed Sullivan" moment of sorts for Scott, who thereafter set his sights on the studio as a professional path he wasn't willing to wait years to begin walking such that,

> a couple years after that, at sixteen, I was fed up with school, and one Friday evening, I wrote to about ten studios in London, and there weren't many recording studios around at that point, so I wrote to the BBC, maybe a couple of film companies, any place I thought might need a recording engineer. That was maybe ten letters, and I mailed them out on Saturday, and heard from one on Tuesday, had the interview on Wednesday, was accepted by them, left school by Friday, and started work at what became the most famous recording studio in the world that following Monday. So within nine days, everything completely changed for me.
>
> The first session I was assistant engineer was starting on Side 2 of *A Hard Day's Night*, the non-film stuff, and I was still starstruck at that point, but maybe one of the saving graces was that EMI at that time only had two 4-track machines for three studios. So the four tracks were in completely separate rooms and could be patched

through to whichever studio needed them, so I would be in the control room when the Beatles were actually rehearsing a number. Then when it came time to start recording, I was down the hall a bit, so I was sort of broken in and managed to get through my starstruck stage fairly early on.

As essential adjustment for any engineer to make who hopes to gain the respect of the artists he'll be working with day in and out as colleagues, Scott would do just that even as the Beatles' stardom outside the sanctuary of their beloved Abbey Road Studios continued to rise throughout the mid-later '60s to heights only seen previously with the popularity of Elvis Presley. As the group transitioned into their most free-spirited creative period as the 1960s progressed into its second half and the group helped normalize experimentalism within rock production, Scott's comfort and confidence grew in the same time, such that

by the time I was sitting next to them as the actual engineer, I was too busy learning my gig to be starstruck, and I'd gone through it and spent so much time with them, because I'd worked with them as a second engineer on side two of *Hard Day's Night* all the way through *Rubber Soul*. So I'd spent an awful lot of time with them, and I think that was actually my saving grace because I had no idea what I was doing that first time I sat down at the board to engineer for them. I really had no idea what I was doing, but they continued with them, and my feeling is that was because of the relationship we'd built up over those other albums as second engineer. They gave me the chance to prove myself.

Scott's true step up to the major leagues of engineering would become among the Beatles' most celebrated albums of the later '60s, *The Magical Mystery Tour*. Following the success of an album that shifted the direction rock rolled in forever after, the effect—in the esteemed opinion of *Rolling Stone*—was a double-edged sword in that *Sgt. Pepper's* (introduced) . . . an incredible (and soon overused) dimension to rock and roll." One that by the time of their follow-up LP, the Beatles were well aware of and already trying to get away from as quickly as possible, as Scott remembered witnessing firsthand in the studio:

On that album, the Beatles didn't want anything to sound the same way twice. Beginning with the way the studio operated, the Beatles were the ones who started to change the hours. They started their recording sessions later on, and because EMI had very strict session times, 10–1, 2:30–5:30, and 7–10 in the evening, that's the way most artists were recording, including the Beatles from the beginning. But then as the band became more popular and more powerful, making more money for the record company, they started to come in later and later. I've been asked numerous times why Geoff Emerick would be put on their sessions after only engineering for sixth months, and I was put on their sessions having never engineered at all, and the reason was that the old-time engineers—there were four incredible pop engineers working there at EMI at the time—and they were old-school and used to the hours, and most of them had families they wanted to get home to. And because the Beatles were starting later and later, and going till later and later, those older engineers hated to do that. They just wanted to go in, record the orchestra, and get home kind of thing, that's why Geoff and I were put on those later night sessions, because we were the youngsters and didn't have families, and didn't mind getting in late because we had no other life really. So as they started to do it, then the studio started to become more used to the strange hours, and other bands started to do the same thing.

Bringing a youthful energy and enthusiasm as rock fans to the sessions, the young engineers were free of some of the constraints of convention that likely would have proved problematic for his older counterparts at EMI had they been engineering the same sessions. With Ken Scott, the Beatles found an ally eager to experiment with throwing tradition out the window entirely, such that

there were occasions when I would go into the mic room with Paul, and he'd say "Okay, I'd like to look at that mic, let's try that on something," but it was purely on how it looked, not how it sounded. Now, for me, as a trainee engineer, it was the most perfect setup that I could possibly have gone through, for a couple of reasons: #1, most engineers, especially back then and especially at EMI, when you first started, you would do recording tests. Then when you got into actual sessions, you had to record like three songs in three hours, and so there was no time to experiment, to find your own mics that you liked, all of that kind of thing. Whereas, I was working with a band that would take three days to record a basic track, so there was plenty of time for me to mess around and try different placements of mics and different mics, because they wanted different mics.

So I didn't have to totally fear mistakes sound-wise, because always at the back of my mind was: let's say I was recording a piano, and I could use completely the wrong mic in completely the wrong place, completely screw up the EQ and compression, and there was just as much likelihood of them coming up and listening and saying "That sounds awful, we'll use it," as there was of them saying "That sounds too nice, we don't want to use it." So the freedom to experiment and find my own road was amazing working with them, and there was no other band I could probably have learned as much as I did within engineering.

The results of taking such chances allowed the Beatles to break down barriers the business hadn't even been aware of previously as the band were making discoveries in real time, rewriting the way the rules of record production worked in the process. Pioneering examples of these sonic shifts that Scott had a direct hand in recording included such staples as "Hello, Goodbye" and the legendary "I Am the Walrus," which *Billboard* hailed as "one of the strangest and most avant-garde Beatles songs," adding that it was "the densest and most symphonic track from the Beatles' psychedelic period, with so many layers of sounds and effects that it takes quite a few listenings to get to the bottom of them." Beginning with the tracking of the aforementioned symphony sound, Scott recalled that

> back then, with violins and violas, it would have always been Neumann U-47s, cellos tended to be AKG C-12s, for brass, it would generally have been a Ribbon mic, SPC 4038s back then, and then of course, the old standby as always was the U-67, which would have been used for saxes, woodwinds, flutes, that kind of thing. Typically, whoever wrote the song would always come in with an idea of how they wanted it to go, but then, more often than not, at least in the basic track, they would work through and get it sorted out altogether. Always the one who had the final say was the writer of the song, but they would collaborate trying to come up with parts and all of that kind of thing on the basic track. Then, a lot of the time, it would be whoever wrote the song was there more than anyone else, completing it.
>
> With the writing of string arrangements, generally speaking, Paul quite often would sit down at the piano and tell George Martin, "I want this kind of thing," and then George would go away and write. John, I don't know that he got too specific, other than probably strange requests, knowing the way he was, he wouldn't say, "I want this to be more like Brahms," or something like that. It would be much more esoteric coming from John, and the way George Martin tended to do the arrangements, especially John's, was he would overwrite. George was well aware that it's easier if someone turns around and says, "I don't like that, get rid of it," easier to do that than to say, "Oh, I want something there, put it in," when you've got a room full of musicians. So George would tend to write too much, knowing that they would go through "I like that; I don't like that bit, get rid of it; Oh, I love that bit, can we move that bit to there?" That kind of thing.

Rolling Stone would conclude that "Martin composed a masterful orchestral arrangement that felt like vertigo," while reporting in their review of "I Am the Walrus" as #33 on the 100 Greatest Beatles Songs of All Time that "Lennon asked for as much distortion on his voice as possible—he wanted it to sound as if it were coming from the moon." In revealing how the team in fact achieved that aspiration in the studio, Ken Scott remembered that

> vocally, we ran John's voice through a Fairchild limiter, heavily limited. Sometimes John would do a double, but he didn't like having to do that, which is why he'd first mentioned to Ken Townsend one day, "I wish there was a way of doing this electronically," and Ken came up with the whole ADT thing. As far as vocal effects in general,

Abbey Road had three chambers, and they had I believe three plates, and the chambers were specific to the studios generally, and the plates were: you requested a plate and you were given it. So there was never really "We want this particular one," because they were all set up in the same way, if I remember correctly, so they all sounded fairly similar.

Turning to the recording of Ringo Starr's drum sound, where *The Telegraph* recognized "genius in these grooves," beginning with his reverence for Starr's skill as a skin-hitter, before delving into the technical side of harnessing what became over the course of *Sgt. Pepper* and *Magical Mystery Tour* the signature sonics of the band's drum sound for the remainder of the 1960s, the producer felt hand's down from session one that

Ringo was one of the best rock 'n' roll drummers ever, and a certain amount of that came from his lack of being a technician. I'm sure that a lot of the fills he came up with were purely because he would start off a fill and then not quite know how he was going to get out of it. So he'd have to come up with something completely unique to get out of the fill. His timing was excellent, like I say, one of the best rock 'n' roll drummers ever!

When we were recording Ringo's drum kit, very seldom did we use room mics because there were other things going on at the same time, so we didn't want to get the pickup of the other instruments, so it was all relatively close-micing for Ringo. The mics changed a little, we experimented with things once we were going, but invariably we would put him through a Fairchild limiter, that was something that Jeff started to do, he was the first one to really limit the drums heavily through the Fairchild. That became known as sort of the Ringo sound, it was the tea-towels on all of the drums, they'd been tuned very low and very dead, and then putting it all through the Fairchild limiter gave Ringo that later sound completely, and I did that as well with his drums when I was recording them.

Underscoring one of the most important roles a producer plays with a group whose creative talents don't require coaching in terms of performances, composition, experimentation, or any of the other key elements within the Beatles' creative formula as they worked creating in the studio, Scott pointed to lead producer George Martin's wisdom to know when to stay out of the way.

George was not the kind of producer, as I'm not, that would go in and say "Okay, it's going to be this way or forget it." He wasn't dictatorial, as I am not. You allow the talent in the studio to put across their ideas, always knowing that if they go too far afield, you can always sort of nudge them back a little to more the way you're thinking of it. But they have to be able to find their own path, it's their record, it's not yours, and you have to allow them to do it. It took me some time to actually realize what I'd learned from George. There was an interview that David Bowie did for BBC, and apparently at some point during the interview, he was asked about working with me, and he said I was his George Martin, which at that particular time I took offense to.

There were a lot of times when I was sitting next to George, but really working with him came when the Beatles didn't need him as much. So I saw a lot of the early stuff where he was obviously important, and helping with arrangements and all of that. But then when I was sitting by the side of him, I didn't see him do that much, and didn't quite understand it, so I'd be sitting there, thinking "What the hell is he doing? He's not doing anything, I don't get it." And it's only looking back on it, I've realized that he was setting up a major learning experience for me, because I was thinking for a long time that the Beatles were in complete control. And they certainly did have far more control towards the end than they did in the beginning, but in looking back, once that statement had been made by David, I started to look back on George, and by this time, I'd walked in his footsteps a lot more as producer, and I realized that what I'd learned from George was: what he did, and what I later did, is to allow talent to do what it is supposed to do in the studio, and that is create.

That license would lead the Beatles in 1968, following a tumultuous period in the wake of the tragic passing of their manager Brian Epstein, to regroup in the studio for the making of what many critics still consider to be their greatest artistic accomplishment to date, *The White Album*, so much so that in 1968, *Rolling Stone* declared it "the best album they have ever released." Providing a bit of background to the band's mood heading into sessions for what would become the two-disc opus that produced hits like "Back in the U.S.S.R.," "Ob-La-Di, Ob-La-Da," and "While My Guitar Gently Weeps," according to Scott,

once Ringo left, and then came back, after that, they were very, very much a band. They'd realized what they meant to each other, so they were playing a lot more togeth-er at that point than they had done before. They were getting on really well, and they'd been getting along okay up to before that, but once Ringo left and came back and they told him how much they loved him and all of that, and probably told each other, then you couldn't pull them apart basically.

It felt like more a group effort with that record, even for probably the one who least liked being in the studio, which was John. He liked the more instantaneous thing, I wouldn't classify John as being a perfectionist. He liked to sort of get it over and done with, whereas Paul would keep on pushing and pushing and pushing. They had both proved themselves, so I wasn't expecting anything less from them at any given time. They came up with great songs, and kept coming up with great songs, so you got used to that, and I came to expect it as the norm.

Pushing their desire to escape the creative chains of *Sgt. Pepper* even more aggressively than they had with *Magical Mystery Tour*, as Scott observed,

> what they were striving for from the beginning of the *White Album* was that "We want to get away from the over-production, if you like, of *Sgt. Pepper*, we want to get back to basics." So the *White Album* was a stripped-down concept.

Arguably among the most celebrated of these stripped-down productions would be the legendary psychedelic shredder hijacked by Charles Manson in the late '60s, "Helter Skelter." Of this counterculture anthem that would also become among the most covered rock songs of all time, tackled by later generations of rock and metal superstars including U2, Motley Crue, Aerosmith, Siouxsie and the Banshees, Oasis, Pat Benatar, Phish, and Soundgarden, among others, listening back, Scott seemed to be most proud of the fact that

> it has been stated to me that it had to be the loudest, most raucous recording ever! The guitar sound on that song came a lot more with what the band was playing through their amplifiers than what we were doing with the board. They were all set up in the studio all live, and with the Beatles' guitar sound on that album, the guitar amplifiers were varied all the time, I believe on "Skelter" they were Fenders. There were some small baffles around the amps, but nothing much. We didn't have isolation booths or anything like that. As far as guitar leads, throughout the album, if it wasn't sorted out beforehand between John and George, then it was sorted out fairly easily during the recording.
>
> For Paul's bass sound, I remember there were some tracks on the *White Album* where Paul wasn't even playing bass, and others where there'd be two basses both played at the same time, by him and George, and one of them would be playing 4-string bass and the other one would be doubling the line on 6-string bass. There were a couple places on the album where it was a vocal bass, where Paul would do a bass line vocally, and we'd make it sound as much like a bass as possible, so it was all over the place.

Turning to a lighter side of Paul McCartney's songbook for the album with the recording of "Birthday," Scott highlighted it as a fantastic example of the Beatles' talent for writing as they recorded, a no-no for most producers. Naturally an exception to that or any rule, as Scott remembered witnessing firsthand in the moment,

> "Birthday" was just started off in the afternoon, almost literally written in the studio by Paul, and we started it, got the basic track, went around to Paul's to watch an old rock 'n' roll movie that happened to be showing on BBC, and that infused everyone and we came back and finished that song that evening. It was similar with the recording

of "Julia." John came in at the last minute at that song, and I think it was the last one we recorded for the album. John did "Julia" live, recording both the vocal and acoustic guitar at the same time. He tended to do that more than anyone.

A fan throughout his collaboration with the Beatles of Lennon's freeing flair for favoring what happened in the midst of recording vs. working take after take to find a song's perfect moments, Scott pointed to "Yer Blues" as one such inspired example, where

John sang that live along with everyone playing behind him, and he messed up the lyrics at one point, and that's why, about halfway through the song, the sound completely changes, and it's because we had to go and punch in where he'd screwed up the lyrics. And of course, suddenly we didn't get all of the instruments coming back in, so the sound changed, and John just said, "Okay, it's messed up anyway, let's go completely mad," and we put a tape echo on the voice, and all that kind of thing. We recorded that in a very, very small room by the side of #2 control room, and they were all in there together, and they could just about fit. So the amount of pickup, between like the bass onto the drums, and drums onto guitars, it was just a mish-mash, and we just had to sort of mix together to get the best sound possible. We weren't overly concerned about leakage.

Serving as yet another brilliant reminder to the producer throughout his engineering tenure working with the Beatles of the constant importance of keeping performance at the center of his sonic sights at all times, Scott reasoned that

to me, it didn't matter what came out of the speakers because I was working with the biggest band in the world. You had to be excited about that, and there were times when some of what they were doing didn't necessarily make sense and it could be as boring as hell. But what kept me always going was the thought of what it would be like in the end, because it was the Beatles, and you knew it would be good in the end.

Graduating from his collaboration with the Beatles before his twenty-second birthday, heading into the 1970s, Ken Scott was among the most in-demand first engineers in the business. Leading him to his next charmed assignment, Scott would soon find himself recording across the coast in France, working alongside producer Gus Dudgeon creating what would become one of Elton John's biggest hits, "Rocket Man (I Think It's Gonna Be a Long, Long Time)." Setting up shop out of Chateau De Raveau in France, the producer remembered a feeling of fantasy as he arrived

just outside of Paris at the Chateau De Raveau where we were all staying, and it was the first time Elton was recording outside of Britain. Gus Dudgeon was producing and I was lead engineer. I was there for preproduction on, and the way preproduction would go was that, in the evening, fairly early, Bernie Taupin would go up to his bedroom and would come back down at breakfast time. Now, this was communal living, so we were all sitting around the breakfast table, and Bernie would come down with sheets of paper, hand them to Elton, and while eating breakfast, Elton would go through these papers, and he had two piles, one much bigger than the other. The smaller pile were lyrics that Elton liked, and he'd take those, go over to a Baby Grand in the main room where we all hung out, and just start to go through them.

Witnessing rock 'n' roll's greatest songwriting team in action, Scott was watching genius in action, pointing to the real-time writing of what would become among Elton John's greatest hits while everyone was still eating breakfast during one such morning, revealing that

I actually saw him write "Rocket Man" in ten minutes! Once everyone had finished breakfast, everyone would rehearse and try to work out the arrangement for the song, or however many songs he'd written and was cutting that day. Then the same would occur the next day until we had enough material for the album, and then we'd start recording across the way.

Giving fans a firsthand look inside John's inspired recording process once the team was set up in the studio and recording the legendary rock hit, Scott recalled that given the dual assault of John's power behind the piano and vocal mic, the two instruments were tracked individually, wherein

Elton tracked his vocals separate from his piano tracks. We had to have a special thing built to go around the piano because we were used to working at Trident Studios, where there was a drum booth located immediately under the control room, so we had really good separation between the drums and the acoustic piano. But when we went to France to record at Chateau, there was no drum booth, so the way we got around it was: Gus Dudgeon got the studio to bring in a couple of carpenters, and they built a box which was basically the shape of the piano, which went down over the piano and completely engulfed it, except for a couple of holes where the mics—which were a 87 or 67 combined with a KM56 or 86—would go in to record it. That's how we got the separation on the piano, and that allowed Elton to give to do rough vocals when we were recording, or just give instructions as we were going, but Elton always recorded his lead vocals later.

Complimenting Gus Dudgeon and Ken Scott from behind the boards for giving Elton John's newest material "a warm, relaxed feel which complements both the sincere and the ironic songs," the BBC would reference Scott's most noted collaboration to come by comparison in their note that the singer-songwriter was "clearly indebted to (David) Bowie's Space Oddity" in the creation of a song whose "melodic power and sadness are undeniable." As he focused on harnessing the considerable emotional weight John brought to the song's lead vocal, in drawing a stylistic studio contrast from Bowie, the producer remembered that

> Elton was not as quick as David. We had to do a little more, but he was still very good. It was down to the performances, and Elton always gave great performances. I would have recorded Elton using a U-87, and one very special thing I noticed about Elton as we recorded him was that he'd obviously grown up listening to the Everly Brothers and their type of harmonies, because he would come up with harmony parts instantaneously. It was almost as if he'd written the melodies with harmonies sort of already in mind because he got to them so easily.

Acclaim would follow the album's release, not only for Bernie Taupin and Elton John's achievements in songwriting, but equally—in the opinion of Jon Landau, *Rolling Stone*'s most historically respected rock critic, who, when summing up why *Honky Chateau*'s songs shined, began with a nod to its production staff, noting that "the bogus over-production that marred both of the earlier releases at crucial moments is never in evidence, and the album sounds more intimate and personal than either of its predecessors. John and associates are obvious creatures of the studio and so shy away from nothing in terms of technique—there is plenty of vocal double tracking, but their use of it is more natural than ever before."

Scott would lend his ear's excellence to polishing John's sound on another of the rock legend's most timeless classics, "Tiny Dancer," which the producer mixed along with the rest of the *Madman Across the Water* LP, an assignment whose sad circumstances Scott recalled:

> Robin Geoffrey Cable—who had engineered all of Elton's early stuff—had recorded *Mad Man*, but unfortunately had been in a really bad car accident before he got a chance to mix it. We didn't even know if he was going to live, it was one of those type of accidents, it was that bad, but obviously commerce continues, and not knowing if he was going to be okay to come back and finish up what he started, all of the songs he'd recorded were divided up between the other three engineers that were there at that point. Because I'd worked with Gus before at EMI, I was put on the sessions that included *Mad Man Across the Water*. So it was tough, because it wasn't a particularly nice situation. There I am coming in and taking over from a friend who had been in a major car crash, and I don't know if we even knew at that time if he was going to survive, because it was that bad. So it was a strange project to work on.

Modest about taking credit for his role in crafting the final sound of a record that—

including Scott's other John collaborations—the BBC would later argue amounted to "albums (that) . . . for many, are Elton John's best years," the producer shared the credit

for all of the early Elton stuff, anything that was recorded at Trident, for that incredible Trident piano. It was a Beckstein that was built in the 1800s, and was the hardest piano I've ever heard, the most amazing rock and roll piano. A classical musician would absolutely despise it, but it was incredible. Everyone who played it just fell in love with it, and it became a problem with the later Elton John stuff that we recorded at Chateau, trying to match up to that piano sound, which wasn't easy.

So that's one of the things that always comes through, and you can't mask that in the mixing, and then you come to Gus. Gus had been an engineer himself at Decca, and Gus loved to get his hands dirty within the mix, and the way we'd always set up, Gus would be looking after the rhythm section, so he'd have the bass, the drums, maybe some rhythm guitars, and I'd have the vocal, quite often the orchestra, piano, and we'd just work in tandem. Gus always liked, whenever there was a tom fill, he would always goose the drum mics up and then pull them back down again as soon as the fill was over, just that kind of thing is what I remember for songs like "Tiny Dancer."

When we were mixing those records, it's always, and Gus was like this, it was whatever felt right for the song. If it felt right that the vocal was in your face, then that's the way we'd mix it. If it felt better sat back a bit, that's the way we'd go, it was all down to the individual song, and it shouldn't be that it's one setup from beginning to end of an album. An album should take you on a journey, and to do that, you have to treat each song as an individual.

With Scott's stock on the rise, he would soon join another star in the making on a voyage that would transport the production team of Ken Scott and David Bowie to another dimension of record making that rock fans hadn't heard before, and one that would alter the course of alternative rock 'n' roll forever after. Qualifying the true measure of the new territory the pair would cover in the course of making the albums many credit for pioneering "art rock" as a genre, *Record Collector* magazine recognized *The Rise & Fall of Ziggy Stardust & the Spiders from Mars* as "a seminal moment in pop music history, transforming David Bowie into a worldwide superstar and cultural icon on its release in 1972," adding that "its predecessor, 1971's *Hunky Dory*, is as much of a musical landmark in Bowie's career."

Rolling Stone would spotlight the producer with their five-star conclusion that *Hunky Dory*, Scott's first album as head producer, "not only represents Bowie's most engaging album musically, but . . . Ken Scott's production is quite splendid—delicious little flourishes of the sort that the casual listener will not detect but that one who gives the record a few serious spins will find thrilling abound, like, say, Mick Ronson's guitar suddenly beginning

to echo distantly at the onset of a solo." Tracing the roots of his and Bowie's kindred con-
nection in the studio, the producer began by recalling that

> we'd started to work together when I was staff engineer at Trident Studios and was
> put on the sessions working with Tony Visconti for the *Space Oddity* LP, and that sit-
> uation happened again with *Man Who Sold the World*. Then David took a break, and
> came in one day to produce a friend of his, Freddy Burretti, and I had at this point
> in time decided I wanted to move more into production, and during one of the tea
> breaks, I happened to mention this to David, and he said, "Well, I just signed a new
> management deal and they want me to go in and record a new album. I was going
> to produce it myself, but I don't know if I'm capable of doing it, will you co-produce
> me?"
>
> So naturally, I jumped on it immediately, and said, "Yes, I'd love to co-produce it
> with you," and a few weeks later, he came around my house with his wife Angie and
> publisher Bob Grace, and we were going through material for what turned out to be
> *Hunky Dory*, and it was at that point that hearing his demos, I realized he was a hell
> of a lot more talented than he'd gotten credit for up to that point and that he could be
> huge. And so here we go again, I'm being thrown in the deep end again with an artist
> that a lot of people might actually hear that product, so that was how it all started.

Billboard would hail *Hunky Dory*, which showcased Bowie's imagination as a songwriter, as "a kaleidoscopic array of pop styles, tied together only by Bowie's sense of vision: a
sweeping, cinematic mélange of high and low art, ambiguous sexuality, kitsch, and class."
Heading into production, Scott remembered feeling equally as dazzled by the demos David
had played him, feeling it was clear that

> he had his own musical ideas which he could bring forth. I feel very strongly that one
> of the reasons he moved to me after Tony Visconti was that Tony was one of the mu-
> sicians, and he and Rono (Mick Ronson) worked out all of the arrangements. David
> didn't seem to have too much say in the musical side on the records before our col-
> laboration as co-producers began. And I think he, obviously insofar as how he wrote
> the songs—what style the songs were in—that pushed Tony and Rono in a certain
> direction. But on those early studio albums before *Hunky Dory*, David came in, did the
> vocals, and that was it basically.

Eager to cut Bowie as much slack in the studio as he required to properly realize
the brilliance waiting to burst, Scott felt his star shined on the album's opening serenade,
"Changes." This legendary rallying cry on behalf of rock's youth would become famously
quoted as relevantly as ever fifteen years later in the opening scene of the iconic 1985
John Hughes film *The Breakfast Club* with "and these children that you spit on, as they try

to change their worlds, are immune to your consultations, they're quite aware of what they're going through." Arguably, Bowie was seeking the same sense of independence with

> *Hunky Dory.* I think he had ideas that he wanted to see if they worked or not, and wanted to sink or swim under his own guidance. Generally speaking, David's demos were either him and an acoustic guitar or piano. So that first night he and his manager came over, we went through his demos, decided which material would work, and from then on, it was in the studio and sorting it out with the band. As I'm not a musician, I would not get in there and say "Look, why don't we play a C flat here as opposed to an E diminished 9th," or something like that. I wouldn't get involved in that way, and David knew that, and so it worked perfectly.

Detailing the physical process of recording "Changes," which Bowie came into the studio eager to get down on tape, Scott—beginning with his micing approach to the song's famous lead piano track—recalled that

> for the piano, I would have miced it with a Neumann U-67 on the low end and a Neumann KM-56 on the high end, which has remained consistent from that point on to today in how I mic pianos in the studio, the only difference being, I now also use another Neumann U 87 or 84 in the mix as well. Alongside "Changes," on "Life on Mars," Rick Wakeman played his ass off, probably one of the best piano parts he's ever played, and I think he's in agreement with that. The ending is kind of strange, the way the strings sustain and it fades out, then you hear the piano come back in again with this weird bell thing going off.
>
> What transpired was, we'd started an earlier take, and it got interrupted by a public phone that was in the bathroom in the actual studio, so we stopped, and it was a great take so Rono got really pissed and was swearing his head off when we had to stop it because of the phone going off. So then, okay, we're gonna do another take, and typical, I'm not one of these people who likes to keep everything. As far as I'm concerned, if it's not the master, we record over it. It's making decisions, that's what it's all about, that's what needs to happens today. It's ridiculous when you get something to mix and it's got seventy-six guitar solos because no one could make up their damn mind which one was best.
>
> Anyway, so we're back, we're recording after all this, and finally get the master, start to do the overdubs and come to the final overdub, which was the orchestra, and their sustaining at the end there, and it was the first time we'd let the tape run that long, and suddenly this old piano comes in and then the phone goes off. And we just loved it so much that we had to keep it! But I had to fade it out really quickly, because then you hear Rono start saying "Oh fucking hell, fuck this!" So we had to get it out,

and if you really crank your stereo loud enough with headphones, you can just about make out what he's saying. That's a remembrance of "Life on Mars."

Working on a hurried schedule that was truly amazing given the complexity of the material contained on both *Hunky Dory* and *Ziggy Stardust*, Scott and company kept an energized pace in the studio, reflecting that spirit in performances the producer revealed were

> always tracked live off the floor by David and his band, and for me, using that approach vs. overdubbing depended on the act. For David, it had nothing to do with the sound, it was to get it down quickly, for two reasons: a) we didn't have much time, because we had two weeks to record for EACH album. So we had to be quick, and b) the other thing was, as I said, David got bored, so we needed to get things going quickly, otherwise, he'd get fed up with the song and want to move on to another one, so the songs all went down quickly. We would generally start around 2:30ish in the afternoon, and go till whenever we finished.

Ultimately an album that was liberating for both Bowie artistically and his critics commercially, the BBC said *Hunky Dory* was "very much a songwriter's work (that) . . . finds Bowie for the first time finding his own voice after scrambling around stylistically for the best part of a decade." They concluded that "this album finally demonstrated David Bowie's enormous potential to the listening public. It became a huge hit after Bowie broke through and became a household name."

When Bowie came knocking again a year later to follow up his breakout success, he came packing a nuclear bomb's worth of ambition with what would become the most storied studio album of his career, *The Rise & Fall of Ziggy Stardust & the Spiders from Mars*. The BBC would beam their rays of praise toward Bowie's coproducer, recognizing that "it was, in fact, with his previous album *Hunky Dory* that DB found the perfect studio partner for this phase in his mercurial career. The pairing of Bowie with Ken Scott at Trident Studios allowed him to finally nail a simple format of guitar, bass, drums and piano into the place where the New York nihilism of the Velvet Underground met a quintessentially English way with a tune and a vocal. *Ziggy* represents the peak of their achievement."

Indeed, though Bowie was absolutely the conceptual captain of this visionary journey, the producer was quick to point out that the singer-songwriter had surrounded himself with an exceptional crew to help steer the Starman's musical rocketship toward the eventual heights the album would reach. Following a philosophy he'd adhered to throughout his remarkable recording career, Scott reasoned that

> I'm a firm believer that almost all good things come from a good team, it's not just one individual, and the team that we had together of Woody on drums, Trevor on

bass, Rono doing the guitar and backing vocals, and then David and I, we just worked so well together. It was difficult to tell, at times, where one sort of left off and the other one continued. It just flowed perfectly, and there were times when David and I were talking, like "Okay, it's time for the guitar solo," and we'd call Rono, and he'd say, "Okay, I'm going to go down and do the guitar solo," for whatever song we were talking about, we didn't even have to tell him and what he came up with was exactly what we were after.

Rono was a nice guy, incredible guitarist and did great arrangements, unlike most arrangers would ever do. You can't ask for much more. He wasn't that great a singer, so a lot of the backing vocals were David, and at times, Rono would join in with David just to give a bit more depth to it, but his guitar playing strengths—knowing what would work for a particular song—one didn't have to guide him that much. It was great teamwork, and we were just all feeding off of each other and having fun, and making albums that we liked. And it just so happened that other people liked them as well.

David always had an idea of what he wanted, he didn't always know quite how to get there, is probably the best way of describing it. There were very specific ideas that he knew he wanted, as an example, "Moonage Daydream," the solo on that—which is a baritone and a recorder—he knew exactly what he wanted there, and it was borrowed, shall we say, from the B-side of a single by the Hollywood Argyles called "Sho' Know a Lot About Love." All the way through that, there is a line that's played by a baritone and a flute, and David really loved that sound and wanted to try and emulate that sound on the solo for "Moonage," so that's what we did. So there were times like that where he had very specific ideas, and then times where we had to work on it some more. It was such a team effort that no one had to tell anyone quite what to do.

Arguably alternative rock's first true anthem, the latter title track was one where Scott showcased his gift for creating what became the dazzling tapestry of vocal effects the producer wove with Bowie's voice throughout songs like "Ziggy Stardust" and "Moonage Daydream," a process that always began with the recording of

David's lead vocal tracks, which I always used an AKG 414 for. David came in knowing exactly what he wanted with vocals, he's an amazing vocalist. Of the four albums I coproduced with him, 95 percent of the vocals were one take from beginning to end, and first takes. He would sing a bit so I could set the level, we'd go back to the beginning of the song, record from beginning to end, and that was the record. We usually recorded David with a double of his lead vocal, and David already had a lot of that kind of thing worked out in his mind. He already knew the concept of when it comes time for the chorus, you need to give it a bit more oomph, and so quite often, a double track on the chorus gives the vocal that much oomph.

Effects were generally left to me later. David wasn't fond of the studio, he got bored very easily in there, and that led to him not coming to any of the mixes, I think he came to two mixes over the total of the four albums I did with him. So all of those decisions were totally left up to me. The effects I used mixing David's voice varied on songs, so sometimes it would be a single repeat, sometimes it would be a long reverb, sometimes it would be a short reverb, it was totally dependent on the song.

In capturing the cosmic crunch of the guitar riff that opened the "exhilarating collaboration . . . (of) Mick Ronson's terse phrasing and skewering distortion igniting David Bowie's sexually blurred confrontation," as *Rolling Stone* would rave of *Ziggy Stardust*, the producer recalled that

with Mick Ronson's sounds, it was always the same: he ran through his 100-watt Marshall and used his Les Paul, and the way he got those tones you hear was he'd always be going through a Crybaby wah-wah pedal, and he'd go through the top and slowly go through it to the bottom and we'd find the tone we wanted, and he would just leave the pedal at that point. Very simple, but he had such unique sounds, because he never got it from the amp. He always got that weird wah-wah sound, but it was just a constant sound, and that's what you hear—for instance—on "Ziggy Stardust." If we did to D.I. on guitars, it was very rarely and for a specific effect if we did do that.

With the drum sound, the setup remained the same, so it was either a D-12 or D-20 on the bass drum, a Sony C-38 on the snare, Ribbon mics for overheads, either 40-38s or Bayer M160 mics, but definitely Ribbons over the top, and it was 67s on the toms. More than the microphone selections, I always felt the drum sound we got on that album was more the tuning of the drums. I'm a believer that everything starts in the studio, from the sound to the performance, and we in the control room are there just to add the finishing touch to what's coming from the studio. I don't look at my job in the control room as being the person to take a shit sound and make it sound incredible. It has to sound great in the studio to start with, and from there, I will hopefully make it incredible.

Turning to the recording of one of the album's most poignant production achievements, with "Starman" —Bowie's first hit single (#10) since "Space Oddity" —the producer revealed that the song almost didn't make the record's final cut, stating that "it was thrown in at the last minute, purely because RCA didn't hear a single, and originally the track it replaced was Chuck Berry's 'Round and Round,' and what would that be doing on a concept album about a space alien(laughs)?"

The song would ironically play a key role in rounding out the "Ziggy Stardust" storyboard, with Bowie explaining to *The Guardian* in an interview on its last-minute composition that, "Ziggy is advised in a dream by the infinites to write the coming of a starman, so he writes 'Starman,' which is the first news of hope that the people have heard. So they latch on to it immediately. The starmen that he is talking about are called the infinites, and they are black-hole jumpers. Ziggy has been talking about this amazing spaceman who will be coming down to save the earth. They arrive somewhere in Greenwich Village. They don't have a care in the world and are of no possible use to us. They just happened to stumble into our universe by black-hole jumping. Their whole life is traveling from universe to universe." Once Bowie had finished writing the song, Scott remembered the team hurriedly reassembling to

> record that song about two weeks later, and it was done in two days because we had the orchestra and all that, so Rono couldn't have done the arrangement before we'd done the recording. With regard to string arrangements, it was left totally up to Rono what the orchestra would be doing. He always had this habit, he always ran out of time, and would have started the arrangements the night before, and according to Suzie Ronson, he would do the arrangements in the bathroom, which coincides with exactly what always happened whenever we recorded orchestra with Rono. He would come in about fifteen minutes early, before the session was due to start, and would immediately go running upstairs to the bathroom on the first floor in Trident, and he'd lock himself away. Then he'd come out after about a half hour, fifteen minutes into the session, with a whole sheath of manuscripts and a big grin on his face, and he'd just finished up the arrangements, would walk down to the studio and hand out all the parts, and it worked the same way every single time.
>
> On the Bowie albums, I still was recording the orchestra along the same lines as I had the Beatles, but by that time, it was more likely the AKG-C12As on cello, because I don't think Trident had any of the original C-12s, and it would have been U-67s as opposed to 47s on violins and violas. Quite often, we wouldn't know how many tracks the orchestra was going to take up on the 16-track until we'd recorded everything else, that was one of the things that being the coproducer/engineer, that I was constantly aware of: making sure that I could always do whatever David wanted. So one had to keep one step ahead.

The album was more than a few of those steps beyond its competitors as it took the world by storm upon release in June 1972, delivering a masterpiece that became so wildly popular that, according to the BBC, "to an entire generation this album has become a yardstick by which to measure all others." Amazingly, ahead of its release, Scott revealed of the title track that "when Ziggy Stardust was recorded, I don't know that we knew that that was the album title!" Having headed into mixing knowing he had something very special in his hands with the master tapes, the producer shared that this phase of the album's production was one where he and Bowie had almost intuitive vs. spoken creative rapport. Scott recalled that

> I never sat down and listened to *Hunky Dory* or *Ziggy Stardust* with David when it was finished! I never got a single comment from David about that or ANY of the albums in the mixing. I accepted that if we moved on to the next one, then he appreciated what I did.
>
> One of my favorite aspects of working with David was just being given the complete freedom and having no one around for any of the mixes, I was the arbiter of good taste for the mixes. It all came from me, and just being given that responsibility was amazing. While I was always—and still am—very conscious of is depth, I like certain things to be to the forefront, and other things toward the back, and it was almost a surround-sound sort of thinking, before there was such a thing as surround sound.
>
> When I was mixing David, or anybody, each song is its own individual entity, and I mix according to how I feel that song should be. A good example of that is a track called "Watch That Man" off the *Aladdin Sane* album we did after *Ziggy Stardust*. My feeling on that one was, the vocal should be more like an instrument, it shouldn't necessarily be featured. So on that particular track, the vocal is sunk so far back it's ridiculous, but at the time, that's how I felt it should be, and as it turned out, the management company also felt it should be that way, and the record company felt it should be that way once they heard mixes where the voice was further forward. I bring that up just to show that that was the only track I ever mixed with the vocal way back, because it's how I felt that song worked best.

Ultimately, the record would go on to sell eight million copies worldwide, becoming a touchstone for the 1970s fledgling alternative rock scene he helped found, delivering with #35 on *Rolling Stone*'s *Greatest Albums of All Time* list a record that the legendary rock rag hailed as "David Bowie's most thematically ambitious, musically coherent album to date." Concurring, *Circus* magazine celebrated the album "from start to finish" as "an LP of dazzling intensity and mad design . . . At times one is almost mesmerized by the tumble of images and the sheer force of Bowie's performance. A stunning work of genius."

After working so closely with Bowie on the making of their epic records, in taking a step back to appreciate what he felt made the collaboration among the most enjoyable and exceptional of his career, the producer mused that

> what made working with David stand out—his talent, his songs, and most especially, his vocal performances. It was the combination of all of those. My three favorites among the songs I made with him, and it sort of covers from my end through David's end through just the way they work, and the bottom line for me is always: does it work or not? So my favorites are "Life on Mars," "Moonage Daydream," and "Time," one from each of the three sort of *Ziggy* albums.

Another of alternative rock's founding anthems Scott was responsible for recording came when he found himself sitting behind the console at Trident Studios manning the board for Lou Reed's seminal breakout solo hit "Walk on the Wild Side," ironically produced by David Bowie and guitarist Mick Ronson. Still in regular rotation on classic rock radio forty-plus years after it first took the airwaves by surprise (#16 peak) with a melodically infectious base line and a shockingly provocative lyric the *New York Times* confirmed "elevated him from a minor cult figure to one of the best known and most talked about artists in rock & roll, with its incisive portrait of the demimonde and the distinctive hit single." Beginning with the creation of the single's legendarily catchy bass line, Scott offered the bulk of the credit to

> Herbie Flowers, who was one of the top session musicians in England . . . (and) played bass on that song. We laid it down with drums, and Herbie played an upright double acoustic bass, and then overdubbed an electric fretless bass on top of that. I would have miced his acoustic upright with an AKG C-12 or a Neumann U-67. It's funny, because at the time we were recording the song, I didn't consider it to be a lead instrument—as the song later turned out to be known for—so for that session, I probably would have just put up a mic quickly. In those days micing bass, in general, there were other things I would sometimes do for an upright bass, but that's more when it was a lead instrument with someone like Stanley Clark from Jeff Beck's band.

With the song's famous baritone saxophone solo, Scott dished out another heap of praise on respected jazz sax master Ronnie Ross, who previous to his work with Reed had first met Scott playing on the Beatles' *White Album* (on "Savoy Truffle"), along with stints as a member of the Modern Jazz Quartet and alongside fellow jazz greats like Tony Kinsey, Ted Heath, Don Rendell, Bill Le Sage, Woody Herman, John Dankworth, Friedrich Gulda, and Clark Terry. By the time he made his way into Reed's session, as Scott set up his favored mics in front of Ross's sax, he explained that

> you're going to learn fairly quickly that my favorite microphone is a Neumann U-67 or U-87, I use them on everything, and I would most definitely have used one of those on Ronnie Ross, who played the sax solo on that track. Around that same time, I worked on a Harry Nilsson album called *Son of Schmilsson*, and during the recording of that, I got to work with Bobby Keys on sax, and Bobby taught me an amazing thing that I've used virtually ever since. He said, "Have you ever tried recording sax with two mics?" I'd always used the one mic, which was over the bell, the standard way, and he said, "Put one there, and put one up the top as well closer to the mouth," and I tried that, and loved the sound of it. Now, whether I did that for Ronnie Ross or not on "Wild Side" I'm not sure, but what I always found happened was you get the full sound from

the bell mic, but you get a much airier sound up near the mouth, and blending the two together, I really loved what that gave.

While the song would peak as a Top 10 hit on Britain's Pop singles chart, going on to become wildly popular on radio around the world, the producer put the song on the B-list when it came to picking from among his favorites, confessing that

I'm not a fan of that record, not particularly, it's a nice record, but I don't see it as being outstanding, but "Walk on the Wild Side" definitely is, that is a phenomenal track, it just works on so many different levels. But the rest of the album is . . . yes, it's different, it's okay.

Though through his collaborations with the likes of David Bowie and Lou Reed he could have become pigeonholed as a certain style of producer, Scott considers himself fortunate to have avoided being classified as such, arguing that, throughout his career,

my sanity was saved because I jumped all over the place. It didn't necessarily help my career, because A&R guys tend to pigeonhole, and because they couldn't pigeonhole me, I was never the first one they would think of. I would sooner keep my sanity, and be broke than insane with stacks of money. I look back on my career, and I think the training that I had and all the limitations were the best I could possibly have imagined. I give lectures at universities, and one thing I say to every instructor is: your students should spend at least three months working on 4-track.

When I give out advice to the younger generations of engineers and producers, one of the things, for me, as I said earlier, is *make decisions*, no one—and this isn't just in the music business but in life—seems to want to make decisions these days. And to me, the only people it would hurt making wrong decisions are maybe a brain surgeon or pilot, if they make wrong decisions, people can die. But other than that, so what if you make a bad decision, it doesn't make that much difference, especially recording guitar, he plays a great guitar solo and you've erased it, fine, do another one, it will be different but people put too much importance on it, as far as I'm concerned. And it's about learning to use mistakes. As an example, "Glass Onion" on the *White Album* starts off with a bunch of snares going "blat, blat," and when we put the initial track down, we knew that the single snare wouldn't be enough that Ringo played. So we overdubbed a whole bunch of others, and were on 8-track by now, so we bounced all of the additional snares over to say track 8, and we then started all of the overdubs.

We came to what at the time we thought was the last overdub, which was Chris Thomas and Paul playing recorders, but the trouble was: we didn't have a track to put them on. So someone came up with the idea of dropping them on the snare track, and to cut a long story short, I was doing the punching in, and after lots of takes, I punch in early and erase the last lot of "blat blats." And these days, it would have been easy, just cut and paste, and it's fixed, but back then you couldn't do that, so my immediate reaction was that I was going to lose my job. I was petrified, but John was standing by the side of me, and said, "Hang on, take it back and let me listen again," and I played it for him, and he said, "You know, no one would ever think of coming from the biggest part of the song to the smallest part of the song like that. I like it, we'll leave it like that." That wouldn't happen today, and if it hadn't been for my mistake, a moment like that wouldn't have happened. Mistakes are good, so make decisions and just live by them.

One of my bitches, if you like, about today's recording is—I don't know if you'd put it down as there are too many choices—but the way it goes, I've seen so many times how someone set up a mix within Protools, and they have a separate reverb on every single solitary thing. If you go back to the good old days, if you want to call them something, generally speaking, we had one reverb, and that had to suffice for everything. So obviously, for say the orchestra, we would want a fairly long reverb to make it more concert-hall like, so as we only had the one, that's what we'd have to use on Elton as well. There was no "Oh, it would be better if we used a different reverb on Elton," we didn't have that opportunity, we only used the one, and *IT WORKS*! In those days, that was the EMT plate, and so you find what works for everything, and you make it work.

Taking that point back to the age of modern-day record making, my overall take between recording in analog and digital is that it doesn't have to be just one or the other: they both have their good points and they both have their bad points. Under the best of circumstances, I will use both, I will record in analog and get what I need to get out of the analog recording, and then transfer it to Protools and get what I need out of that. I do think that the struggles that we used to go through to get sounds and effects led to the invention that came out of it, which was superb and we wouldn't be where we are today without that invention. These days, it's too easy, it goes along with everything else—it lacks soul, the choices. And it's led to this whole thing of "You don't have to get it in the studio, you can get it in the control room." So you can have a shitty performance in the studio, and then you can patch it together in the control room, and to me, that takes the humanity out of it all.

There are certain types of music where all of the effects and everything are, I won't say necessary, but they're not necessarily a bad thing. But most of recording, especially if it's rock 'n' roll or pop, you don't need all of that stuff: *simpler is better*, as far as I'm concerned. When I was writing my book, my co-writer Bobby Owsinski asked me if I'd engineer for him some music he was producing, and I said "Yeah" and jumped on it, because as much time as I can spend in the studio, I will. And he has worked with some of the great engineers, and once we were in there working, he was absolutely floored by how little I did to anything. Be it EQ, be it effects, or anything, and I tend with the way I record, to get it in the studio in the first place, so I don't need to use all those things, all those gimmicks.

CHAPTER 3

In Step—Jim Gaines

"Do you yearn for a simpler time, when you could load 63 D-cell batteries into your boombox and cruise the beach for babes with piles of feathered hair? When music videos were punctuated with so-so sight gags, and the No. 1 record in the country was dripping with saxophone and synthesizer? (Just listen to) Sports—the monumentally successful 1983 LP from San Francisco's Huey Lewis and the News."
—THE NASHVILLE SCENE

Rock 'n' roll has an ironic tradition of stars crashing to earth before their time, even if their music shines on forever after like the sky above. If there really is a heaven, *Entertainment Weekly* once mused, then "someplace, somewhere, Stevie Ray Vaughan is probably teaching God how to boogie." Hailing *In Step* as Vaughan's "comeback record," the album became a touchstone for the guitar legend's legacy, winning the 1990 Grammy for "Best Contemporary Blues Album." According to *Rolling Stone*, "before his untimely death in 1990, guitarist Stevie Ray Vaughan had become the leading figure in the blues-rock-revival he spearheaded in the mid-'80s," while the *LA Times* added in 1989 that on the album, Vaughan had "processed a whole history of styles into his playing: On those twangy bass notes you hear

Duane Eddy or Link Wray, on those voodoo-ish high squeals there's a Hendrix spirit riding in for the overkill," succeeding—in the opinion of the BBC—in "retooling the blues" so authentically that he "made it relevant to a new generation." Looking back, producer Jim Gaines agrees that

> when I think about all the stuff I've done, those records were talked about the most. Stevie would go out there at night in the studio and play Hendrix, and you'd swear Hendrix was in the building. I'm telling you, I've worked with some heavy-duty cats, and Santana's one of my favorites because he can take two notes and make you cry. Stevie was like a ball of energy, and that's how he played, when he played, you felt every ounce of his energy level coming through that guitar. That's what I loved about it, because I'd never heard anybody play like that. Being around Albert King in his young days, and Steve Cropper, and Stevie was on their level, he had a passion and fierceness when he played. First, he was a very energetic person, he was fun, he had a big smile, and was the nicest guy. If you shake hands with Stevie, it's like shaking hands with a blacksmith! I mean, he had one of the hardest hands I ever shook, because his hands were so strong, which is another reason I think he could pull some of that stuff off on the guitar.

The pair's first meeting revealed Vaughan's vision for the album's ambitious sound that would have been daunting for even a producer as experienced as Gaines, who leading up to his collaboration with the guitar giant had already racked up multiplatinum tours of duty behind the boards with Steve Miller on "Fly Like an Eagle"; Huey Lewis and the News' most popular and best-selling albums/hits, including radio staples like "The Heart of Rock & Roll," "I Want a New Drug," "Jacob's Latter," "The Power of Love," and "Workin' for a Livin'"; and Tower of Power. With Stevie Ray Vaughan, the latter is precisely what the 6-string Shaman was seeking:

> When I walked into the Sunset Marquee for our first meeting, we all get introduced, and about the second or third thing out of Stevie Ray's mouth was "How do you feel about recording ten amplifiers at once?!!" And my reply was: "Well, I just did six with Ronnie Montrose, Santana we've used two to four, it sounds like a good count, sure, I'm in." Now, this at the time was an unheard of question, first of all, ten amplifiers at once! Well, next, I haven't heard any demos, and I'm told "First of all, we're going to look around for a studio," so we met up and checked out a studio out in Northern Florida, it had just been built out in Tallahassee, and it just didn't feel right, it was too new and just felt too cold. So we checked out a couple other studios, and Stevie decided he wants to do the record at the Power Station in New York. So we go to New York to rehearse for three days, and then we go into the studio, and we were booked for six weeks there. I'd never worked at the Power Station, and had no idea what I was

getting myself into. So I'm at rehearsals, and am trying to see how this ten-amp thing is going to work, because this was a combination of everything, man. So we're in the studio, and I'm in the smaller room at Power Station, where they had an ISO-station that was fairly dead I'd set Stevie up in, and it's not very big, so I can't hardly get ten damn amps in this room, much less record them! Well, now suddenly Stevie's also not feeling very good about this thing because he wants those ten amps live. Okay, so we get set up, and it takes a while to get all this mess set up, and when you think about it, we were still working on 24-track analog at that point, because the 32-track Mitsubishi machines were out and available by then. So I'm thinking, "Man, I really need that extra eight tracks on that Mitsubishi," but it's digital, so I thought, "These guys aren't going to go for it.'

Realizing the answer to their dilemma lay back in the blues' hometown, Memphis, Tennessee, Gaines knew he needed to let Vaughan's experiment run its course before he'd go for moving the entire operation down South. The producer recalled that

we screwed around for a couple days and try to get something cut, and Stevie's not happy with his guitar sound because it's not live enough, so I said to Stevie, "Man, this room's not going to work for your amps, it's just not big enough. Here's the deal, man: I just worked at this studio in Memphis called Kiva Studios, and they have a huge tracking room and a huge ISO room, and they will give us a week to come down and experiment, and I'm sure it will work better. If it doesn't, I think we might need to go somewhere else. But first, I'll tell you what, let's do this: I want to try and record on digital, because I really need that eight extra tracks." So I set up at Power Station with an analog machine and a digital, and we recorded the same thing at the same time, so you play it back, and hit one button and the analog version's playing and I hit the other and the digital version's playing. And I didn't tell them which is which, and said "Y'all listen back, and if this digital really bothers you, then I won't go digital." But in the meantime, I knew from working in digital a little bit in the past that if you don't go through some tube gear getting there, coming back you're going to hear it. So I went through some tube gear going in and coming back, and when they played both back, they picked the digital! I was shocked, and was so happy because now I could spread my tracks out a little bit, and knew I was going to need ten or twelve tracks for drums, and I got organ, and bass, and ten amplifiers to go there.

Relieved he was being given the proper space in which to construct what would become a sonic monument to all things glorious about amplified rock 'n' roll, Gaines joked that among all the hats a producer is called on to wear in the course of producing an album, with his latest assignment, he was wearing that of a scientist of sound because man, just to hook up ten amps, man, that's like a scientific feat within itself! So I'm trying to figure out a way to set them up, and we've got double 200-watt Marshall major stacks, a 150-watt Dumble Steel String Singer, a vintage 1959 Fender tweed Bassman, all kinds of stuff. So I end up renting the whole studio, and they have a B studio right next to A studio, and I remember I'd told the owner, "I need this whole building, I don't need anybody in here but us," and had put the big amps in the big ISO booth, and put like the Fender Vibratone, and a stereo Gibson amp, which I ran around the corner in this other little studio for isolation. The big room, the first day we cranked up, the ceiling was rattling, they had these big round baffles that were rattling, so I had to bring in a carpenter to tear open these damn things and fill them with foam, tape up the ceiling, and then we had to start over again. Now, we discovered pretty quickly that this room, Studio A, had a hum in it, and it's not an A/C hum, but the kind of hum that, if you went and stood underneath a big power line, you'd feel this hum coming at you, the magnetic kind, but it was in the room! And I have ten amps and two Tube Screamers going, and I'm thinking "What the hell am I gonna do?"

So I told them I needed some time to experiment there, and called my friend in New York, and said, "Man, I can't figure out where this is coming from, but I got a feeling it's a train-switching complex across the street, that's got some kind of microwave or something coming through this building, what am I gonna do?" Well, he told me, "We had this problem in New York, and had this copper mesh all over the control room to break up the signal," and I said, "I can't copper mesh this damn room, it's huge." So I went out, and got some chicken wire and conduit, and built a like a batting cage with an open front, like an open cage with chicken wire, and put Stevie in it with his guitar, and about 70 percent of this hum went away. So I'm known as the crazy som'bitch that put Stevie in a chicken coop! But finally we got it working, man, and the whole idea of this record was: we want to do live solos, and we'll overdub rhythms, so in this ISO booth with ten amps going, including a double and a Marshall live, I have a vocal mic—a 57—and then I have the rest of the band in another big room tracking out there. So that's how we started the session, and I'm telling you: it was a test from God for me to pull this off.

Once the RF interference was cleared up, Gaines got down to the complicated task of matching microphones to appropriate amplifiers to create a master mix for Vaughan's guitar sound so that

the way it worked, I had to mic the room as like a room mic, and use it as a blend, because I was running eight or ten tracks, which is another reason I wanted to work in digital, because I knew I was going to have to run eight or ten tracks just as one pass of guitars. So I miced all the cabinets separately, but in some cases, I put them together as a unit, so some I wanted to keep separated, but then have the room mics going on, which was so loud in this room we called it the "Room of Doom!" You almost had to beat your assistant with a whip to get him to go out there, and Stevie was running through two Tube Screamers and two wah-wah pedals, that's his normal setup, so if you get those sons-a-bitches cranked up, and TWO doubles going, and that's the loudest amp ever made! So I had our guitar tech, Cesar Diaz, constantly changing out speakers and fixing things, and I had set up Studio B as our spot to fix guitars . . . it was a mess man!

With his little amps, like the Deluxes and stuff like that, you can only push them so much, especially when you've got a big-ass Marshall sitting beside you with everybody up. So I had to separate things out, and combine things that I thought later I could deal with and mix, even though later I had planned on really dealing with them even more than when I was recording, because you can't go in there and start individually dissecting each one of these tracks while they're going down on tape. You have to treat it as part of a general sound, and if, for instance, I needed a little more brightness somewhere in a song, I'd pull up this end; need a little more bottom and I'd pull up that end. But that sound really comes from the tonality of the amps, and that's what he wanted.

As Vaughan strapped on his Fender Stratocaster, he made his own adjustments to the amplifier sound based on what his ear felt each individual track called for, an arena where Gaines felt the guitarist's talent as a coproducer shined. He recalled that Vaughan

would go out there for each song and adjust things that he wanted to adjust, and we may adjust it six times for a certain track, because we don't have to do that many takes. Again, we're doing takes to fit the solos and the feel of the track, so he may go out there and screw around with this amp or that amp after a playback, and say "I need more of this, we need more of that," and hell, man, I spent fifteen hundred dollars in one day on speakers, we blew speakers out like crazy one day! And when you change speakers, guess what, tones change, so you have to reset things, because these were some loud damn amps going on!

With that band, the impression I got right away was Stevie's the leader, and they are the followers, so wherever he went, if the tempo went up, they went up, if the tempo went down, they went down. It's just one of those things where, usually, I don't cut to the click unless I really, really have to, and with (Vaughan's group) Double Trouble, we even tried cutting some of these songs down a little bit more, and because of the tempo changes, we couldn't, so it was like "Forget about it." They were a band who, again, because they'd started out as a Texas bar band for all those years, had the mentality of: "We are a band, and we follow each other," and they are great players!

Turning to the techniques he brought to the party as the band rumbled through "The House Is Knockin'," "Tightrope," and other rockers that showcased what *Rolling Stone* recognized as a "live intensity" that "made them . . . legends," the producer remembered feeling equally wowed as he listened to the band track live in the studio, reasoning that

> Chris is probably the best Texas, blues shuffle guy I ever met in my life, I mean: he can LAY IT DOWN! That's his forte, so when you get into those realms, you don't care about the tempo moving a little bit, because that's the way it goes. When you go and see them live, that's the way it is, and I was trying to make the record sound like the band, not like somebody else. So there's a lot of forgiving little things that went on in the studio, and there's some things I wish I could have done differently as a producer, but my goal there was just trying to capture the band.
>
> Basically, Chris is the kind of guy who doesn't really tune, tune, tune every drum. They're kind of tuned, but remember, this was a Texas blues band, so they didn't really get into the heavy tuning that other styles of drummers I'd worked with would get into. With Chris, just as long as it sounds like a tom-tom, he's happy, so I just miced his kit with my normal micing situation for that album. I think I used 421s on the overheads, and on the floor, because I wanted a floor sound that was a little heavier, I think I miced over and under on that. I usually only bottom-mic the snare if I need more brightness out of the snare drum, but I find most guys that use it, they've got it so far down in the mix that it's like "Why did we even go through this?"
>
> On Chris's kick, I had a D-12 on the kick, and the problem when you start using condenser mics close to those floor toms, because the kick drum isn't that far away, you're going to get some of that in there. I think in his case, Chris doesn't play with a heavy foot, so I blanketed the kick drum a little bit and used a D-12, and at that point, I think we were using a Phet 47 or a condenser as well for his kick drum. With the snare sound, fortunately, Chris brought like fifteen snare drums, maybe even more, so we had a good selection of snare drums, and we used different ones for different songs on the album. We tracked in a big live room, and again, since we were going for kind of a rock sound—and being really a rock guy—I was using some room sounds, and they had some 67s there I used for room mics.

When his eyes and ears were focused on bassist Tommy Shannon, who *Guitar World* said "had a solid reputation for his work with Johnny Winter, playing not only Woodstock, but also with B. B. King, Freddie King, and Little Richard" even before hooking up with Vaughan a decade earlier, Gaines remembered the bassist not only for his stellar playing, but also for

> another thing he was going through when we were making that album: those guys had just cleaned up. In fact, one of the reasons I was hired was the band had just cleaned up after Stevie almost died in London from an overdose, so they didn't want

anyone around him after that who did drugs. Well, here I am, Mr. Squeaky Clean, and the whole band was going to AA meetings, and a lot of the crew, they all had quit smoking so I was dealing with Nicorette hell. Matter of fact, we had the famous Dr. Nick come in at one point, because in those days, they only gave you two months of Nicorette and that was all they gave you, so Dr. Nick came in and he loaded the band back up. Tommy Shannon was chewing those things back to back, and had this little stand he kept his old gumball things in during recording, and I saved them all and toward the end of the sessions, made this big, giant softball-looking Nicorette ball, wrapped it up in ribbon, and said, "Tommy man, I just want you to see how much you chewed in the last three weeks!" But we had a good time.

When his attentions were turned to tracking Stevie's rhythm and lead tracks, the process was challenging from the start because each take was tracked *live* with the band off the floor, a technical juggling act for Gaines working in a time predating the digital age of infinite virtual tracking—and given the reality that

90 percent or more of Stevie's solos were *live*, so solos were not overdubbed! The whole idea of recording that way was Stevie's, and that's one of the reasons he approached me. He said, "How do you feel about doing solos live?" And I'd replied, "If you can pull it off . . . We may have to do fifteen takes till you get the right solo," and he said, "I'm going for the solos live," and I said, "Perfect, perfect, no problem with me." So most of those solos were recorded live, and we may have gone back and added rhythms underneath it as an overdub.

On top of that, with the rhythm guitar tracks, on a pass, each pass was eight to ten guitar tracks, because we had eight to ten amplifiers going. That's exactly why I needed those thirty-two tracks, because if that got eight tracks of just one pass of guitars, and I want to do an overdub, that's eight more, that's sixteen! Well, if you're recording on a 24-track, good luck, you're gone, you're over with, so that's what saved my ass, was being able to go to 32-track digital, because I could make it without bouncing him or anything else. I didn't want to have to bounce, because again I was trying to record them as live as possible, so though we're only talking about two passes, it's sixteen tracks of guitars going down.

While we were tracking his lead solos, delay in the mix was the only thing as playback. The only thing that he would let me put on his guitar, two effects: the Roland Dimension D, which is a little box that's a chorus unit with four little buttons on it, and delay. Now his pedal setup was strictly two Tube Screamers, two wah-wah pedals, that's it. He might be using both of the Tube Screamers at once, but that was it.

With "Number One"—his affectionately named Strat—and with Double Trouble, as Stevie Ray set about tracking his lead takes, Gaines remembered catching Vaughan off guard initially as the producer insisted on holding the guitarist to a standard of excellence commensurate with his potential as a player by objecting when he felt a given take wasn't good enough. A strategy and style that he realized was a first for the guitarist up to that point in his rapport with producers, nevertheless, he felt it was the necessary approach because

any producer will probably tell you this: it's about gaining the confidence of the band that when you say "No, it can be better," that they believe you after a while. Because up to that point, they don't believe a damn thing you're saying and to trust you. There's a whole psychology that goes with cutting with artists, and I'm a street psychologist in a lot of ways, I know how to make people work and not even know they're working. But you have to be that guy who can convince the people you're working with that you understand what they're going for and are trying to capture it for them, #1, and #2, at the same time, you want to give them the best record that they've made up to that point, which means I need to have a little bit of control and be able to say "That's not good enough, that needs to be better, let's work on this sound."

Well, the interesting part about that collaboration was: working with Stevie in the studio, he was relaxed in a way, but in a way, he was a little nervous because I was the first guy outside of Texas to work with him, and all the Texas boys would just go with the flow in the studio, "Play it, great, okay let's go," I was the first guy to say to Stevie, "No, that's not good enough, we gotta do it again." So it kind of was a little tense for a while, because I would at times say to him, "No, man, I mean you're playing good, but it's not good enough yet. We gotta do another take," so things were a little tense because I felt like I was the first guy to say "No, it ain't good enough," and so we had a rough couple of moments there, but after it was all over with, it was worth it. Once Stevie saw I got that, we got that trust factor going, and I could say things to him in the way of suggestions, and he knew exactly what I was talking about, vs. "What the hell do you mean by that?" That's what a good producer does.

Applying the same general concept to producing Vaughan's vocals, Gaines took on a bit more gentle bedside manner as, while the guitar master was rock-solid in his confidence as a player, as a singer the producer quickly discovered it was a different matter entirely

once we started working on Stevie's vocal overdubs. He hated his vocals, so therefore he didn't want to sing. So to get him to sing, he would come into the studio, and on a little stand next to the vocal mic out there, I had every Hall's cough drop known to man: I had lemons, I had limes, I had juices, whatever it took to get over that insecurity. And he would pace back and forth in the control room before each song's vocals, back and forth, back and forth, and of course, he'd quit smoking and missed that I think. So finally, when he was ready to sing, he'd go out into the live room, and during those takes where I'd tell him "We need to do it again," once again, because no one had ever told him "No, it's not good enough," here we go again with a little tension, BUT, I got vocals out of him. I knew how to speak vocal talk, like "Man, that word needs a little more hot sauce on it," or "grease," I use that word a lot and people know exactly what I could talk about.

The best thing to do, I've found over the years, when you're doing vocals is, first, you gotta get me to believe what the hell you're singing. First, you got to get them to believe what they're singing, but you gotta convince me they believe what they're singing, that is one of the toughest calls, because a lot of time it's words, just words. And it's not words, it's got to be words with emotion, with soul, the phrasing's gotta be right, "Stretch this word out," "cut this word out," "put these two words together and make it one . . ." There's all kinds of tricks, man. Later, after the record was finished, he told me, "Man, I never worked that hard in my life for vocals," and I replied to him, "Well, do they sound good?," and he said, "Man, they sound good. I appreciate you pushing me," and I remember I told him, "That's my job, that's what I get paid to do," and the critics LOVED his vocals on that record.

When we tracked Stevie's vocals, I could use a little delay and a little reverb, and I used to use Plates, but I didn't want to get it too wet. I just wanted it to sound a little live without getting like reverby, especially since we were mixing for *presence*. I wanted those guitars up, I wanted the snare drum up, I wanted it to be very present.

One of the pair's finest accomplishments in this delicate arena came courtesy of the recording of what would become one of Vaughan's most celebrated vocal performances, "Life by the Drop." Inspiring *Billboard* to declare "the touching survivor-story ballad" as among "the most moving moments in Vaughan's oeuvre," Gaines revealed that the guitarist brought the song in at the last minute after principal tracking for the album was largely completed:

That particular song we didn't end up cutting in Memphis. We ended up going to Los Angeles to do vocals and mix, and so we get there, and Stevie says, "We're going to save this song, 'cause it's just a little acoustic song for LA," because we didn't need all the crew and everybody there. So once we were in the studio, he played it for me in the control room and said, "This is how this's gonna go," so since it was only him and guitar, I just wanted to get a nice big guitar sound. They had great mics out there, and I used a U-67 close to the whole so I could get the bottom-end warmth of the guitar, because it's a warm mic. And actually towards the bridge is where I put a condenser or 451, and I also used a dynamic mic so I could get close and get the picking out of it without a lot of vocal leakage. I think I had a room mic going on a separate track, so I think there were three or four mics involved at least. As an engineer, you try to separate that a little bit, but you're gonna be able to get it entirely. I've seen guys actually put like cardboard over the mic so the vocal didn't get in there, and that's NOT the whole idea: the whole idea is to play and sing it live at the same time.

We recorded that song in maybe four or five takes, and it was done entirely live. He had a vocal mic hanging right in front of his mouth, and that was all done live, no overdubs. I think Stevie was a great guitar player who had to sing because it was his band, and here's the sleeper: he HATED his voice, he hated it. He was a guitar player who was forced to sing, and half the guys I've worked with over the years are like that, and whenever we got ready to do vocals in LA, again, he was just pacing, pace, pace, pace—back and forth in the control room, and finally I'd say, "You about ready man?" And he'd say, "Okay," get out there, and he was nervous about doing vocals, because he felt like that was kind of a test for him. Playing guitar was the easy part, where doing vocals is a very sensitive thing, so to get him to do vocals, I had to kind of pat him on the back, "come on man, you can do it." I saw a lot of critical reviews of my work with him that said it was the best vocals he'd done, and I'm not going to say it was difficult, but it wasn't easy either. With that song, it did work to our advantage I think that he was playing and singing at the same time on "Life by the Drop."

Another of Gaines's favorite recording moments with Vaughan during their collaboration came during the recording of "Riviera Paradise," with the producer sharing

a famous story. We're in the studio, and first they won't play me the song in rehearsal, because when I asked about the song, I had a list, and said, "What about this 'Riviera Paradise'?" And they said, "Well, it's a little instrumental ditty," don't worry, Jim, we got it down cold. We'll just cut it, it's like a free-form thing, so don't worry about it." So I say "Okay." We're in the studio cutting around 1 in the morning, this was a late-night song, so you start off during the day with up-tempo stuff and you wind your way down to late-night stuff like this. I remember Stevie had told me "This's one of those very moody songs," so I'd turned all the lights down in the control room and studio, and Stevie's out there, kind of with his back to me. And I'd made sure there was nobody in the studio, so people weren't going to walk around and trip over anything, so I ask him, "How long is this thing?," and he told me, "Oh, it's about four minutes long."

Well, at that point, I had a roll of tape in the machine that had maybe 7 ½ minutes of tape on it, so I figured, "Well, okay, we'll only get one take on this and then I'll change reels." So I start recording, and it's magic right away, like "Holy shit, this is one of the moodiest things I've cut in a long time," but it's going on and on and I'm watching the tape counter, thinking "I ain't gonna get this song," because the tape's gonna run out. So I jumped up and start running around the control room like crazy, and thankfully, Stevie can't see me because he's playing looking down. I run around and get Chris's attention, and point at the tape machine and give him the throat-cut motion with my hand across my neck, and he nods at me. Well, in the next moment, Stevie just happens to look up at him, and he gives Stevie the cut sign, and I swear to you, they stopped that song within maybe five seconds of the tape going "click, click, click," making that sound it does when tape has run out!

I mean, I *BARELY* got it on tape, and we tried to cut it again a night later, got halfway through, and Stevie stopped the band, said "Nope, what we've got's fine," but that song barely got on tape. That's one of my favorite Stevie stories, and we all knew the take was that special because the only thing I overdubbed was one little keyboard part to fix something, and the only thing Stevie redid was: he had this rainstick someone had given him, and that damn thing was six foot or eight foot long, it was huge, and he wanted to put this thing on there. So, I'm thinking "I don't have enough room at the end of the cut," so we had to kind of make do splicing some extra tape on so this rainstick could end the song, and the damn thing lasts forever, so when you turn it over, it'll go on like ten minutes before all its sound'll drop out, but that's what he wanted to put on there, and that's the famous "Riviera Paradise" cut.

With "The House Is Rockin'," among Vaughan's most popular radio hits upon release and for decades since, in capturing the "dynamite boogie" *Billboard* felt the song projected out of the stereo speakers, back in the studio, Gaines revealed as a final production note that as they laid the song's signature parts,

we had a B3 set up in its own little ISO booth, and the piano was overdubbed on that one only because there was so much noise in the room with the drums.

Upon release in June 1989, *In Step*—Vaughan's first studio album in four years, and ultimately his last with Double Trouble before he passed away the next year—was embraced by critics and fans alike as the guitarist was triumphantly welcomed back to the radio waves with hits including "Tight Rope," "The House Is Rockin'," and "Crossfire," with MTV raving that "the magnificent thing about *In Step* is how it's fully realized, presenting every facet of Vaughan's musical personality, yet it still soars with a sense of discovery." That was Gaines's as well as he wrapped work with one of the greatest guitar players ever to strap on the 6-string, finding that as he looked back in later years on the collaboration,

I've been fortunate to be involved in several classic records, and I have to say Stevie Ray, because first of all, it was such a challenge, and to pull it off and it to end up being a "legendary" record, it made me a "legendary" producer, because after that record, I was a blues god for a minute. I think Stevie and I elevated each other in our respective crafts through the course of making that record together.

Turning the page to another of his favorite studio chapters in a truly storied catalog, Gaines pointed back to a pivotal period in his career that saved him from quitting the business before many of what would become his most celebrated albums had even been recorded. Flipping through his memories back to 1981, the producer revealed that it was in fact Huey Lewis who had placed the call that brought him out of his first—and only to date—retirement from record making, following a difficult period at the turn of the decade that ironically had been preceded by

> my getting passed over for production gigs with three artists in a three or four month period, Tommy Tutone, Pablo Cruise, and then Huey Lewis, and I'm not kidding, it was strange to me because I'd had a lot of hit records at this point, so it wasn't like I was some unknown som'bitch out here. So I said "You know what, I'm done if the record companies have gone so political, that they're not going to give me a chance, I'm not staying in the business." What had happened was, prior to that, Huey Lewis's manager Bob Brown, I knew him, and because he managed Pablo Cruise, and Pablo used to open up for us some with Steve Miller. So at first, Huey had this band called "Huey Lewis and the American Express," and they had to change their name to the News because they thought they'd get sued by the credit card company. They played a lot at George's Club in Marin County where I lived, and one night I was invited down to see them. Well, that night his manager asks me, "Look, would you be interested in cutting some demos with them?," and I said okay, and we cut some demos at Automat Studios, and the record company Chrysalis came in, and the A&R guy sat right beside me in the control room and said, "I want to do this band with Jim Gaines at this studio, it's a done deal." Okay, well a month later, they were in Los Angeles working with Bill Shnee on what became their first studio LP, the self-titled one.
>
> Well, at that point, I packed up my family, moved to Oregon, bought two businesses and couldn't have cared less, and while I'd started my new life up in Oregon, they release the album, and it doesn't do anything, I mean literally anything! See, there really wasn't a Huey Lewis and the News record before *Picture This*, nobody ever knew about it, because the label had taken them down to LA, and turned the band into this slick LA sound, when Huey had initially wanted me for my R&B background and rock background, and that's what the band really was. So I'm up in Grants Pass, Oregon, living for about a year when out of the blue, I get this call from Huey, and he says, "Jim, man, they've given us five guys to check out for producers on the next record, and we want to produce it ourselves, but you have to come back out here and engineer it. We've gone through five or six people, and you're the only guy who understands this band and what the hell we're trying to do here, out of all these people." And my initial reply was "I could care less man, I got screwed over and I ain't coming back," and he says, "Please, please, I promise you, we'll work together on this thing.'

Sensing there was something special about Huey Lewis that was worth taking the gamble at one more shot that would turn out to be a make-or-break moment for both artist and producer, Gaines said, at that point in time, Huey and I were kind of in the same boat. He had a one-truck failing yogurt business, and I'm in the windshield repair business and I had a diet center, so I'm fixing Mercedes windshield cracks and we're just on the phone laughing the whole thing off about our shared predicament. So I decided to take a chance and give this thing one more shot, said "Okay," and decided to stay living in Grants Pass, but to fly back out there just to do the *Picture This* album, moved into a hotel in San Francisco, and we cut it at two different studios.

Once he was back in the pilot's chair behind the console, Gaines was keen to capitalize on the band's secret weapon as far as their niche on the '80s pop chart went, being one of the best live rock bands playing in the business.

First of all, the way I saw Huey Lewis, when I'd seen them live and was going to be recording them in the studio, the whole idea was to capture their essence as a live, good-time band. When you see them, they have a lot of fun, big smiling faces, Huey's out there working the crowd, plays great harmonica and breaks things up, and so I was just trying to capture what I saw at the band, and undoubtedly that's what they saw being captured in the way I recorded them. As a producer, I'm a raw energy guy #1, groove and raw energy are the first two things I'm looking for, I'm not looking for everything to be *Picture Perfect*, pardon the pun.

All I can say is this: when we did those first records, especially the first two, we were kind of creating a new sound. I didn't go about in the front of my mind saying "I'm going to this session to create a sound," but once you get into the session, and you hear those songs coming up, then you start as a producer to say, "Well, we need to do this to make that work," and the band at that point had gone and done their first record with Bill Sney in LA, and Bill is great at engineering, but I have a different concept and approach to engineering than he does. I'm a little more loosey-goosey, it's gotta-make-my-ass-wiggle kind of thing, so I'm not as much into the technical side: "We need to add 2B at 3K here to make this work," no, to me, it's like: "Does it need to be bright?"

So the first thing I wanna do is: "Can I get it from the amp, if it's a guitar thing? Or if it's an organ, can you change a few of those drawbar settings so we can get a little bit more of this?" Then we let the mics do the work, and then we get through the console and can do the EQs and whatever we want to there, but my approach when we were doing those records was I just wanted to create some fun, good-time songs, all of us did. That's the way the band was, and we were all in synch at that point in time, we were literally all on the same page. That's why they brought me out of retirement, because they felt like I understood what they were trying to go for.

In the studio, Huey's a take-charge guy, he runs the band, they're a democratic band in a way, but at the end, he's the leader of the band. He's a morning person, so we get going before other people do. I became a producer because being an engineer first, I understand the band, so therefore, I look at everything I produce as a coproduction with that band, that artist, whatever. It was easy with Huey because we were friends, we just enjoyed each other, and most of that band's from Marin Country, so we would all hang out together and have a good time, and even when we were working hard in the studio, we were still having a good time because the band was making the record they wanted to make this time.

With the same vision in mind for the sound they were creating in the studio, Huey was doing it his way this time around, seeking to overcome criticism following the band's previous album release that "the debut suffers from an uneven selection of material and a somewhat stiff production," as *Billboard* had observed, whereas on *Picture This*, the magazine felt "Huey Lewis and the News sound considerably more focused." The producer recalled his own sonic ambitions as he began designing the studio layout for the band's various instrumental sections.

I had a blueprint in my head for those records as far as the sound goes, because I'm one of those old-school guys, so as I'm cutting, I'm making the mix right there, I'm cutting to a mix. One of the funny things that a lot of the maintenance engineers used to talk about me was, you could pretty much take my monitor section, cut straight across, and you've got a half-ass mix going on, and that's kind of how I worked, even today. As I'm cutting, I'm cutting to a mix in my head already, I'm starting the song knowing what the mix is going to sound like on the end. I know that sounds weird, but I think any engineer will tell you that, that when you're starting a song, you know where you're trying to go and you're cutting to the level, the sound, the dimension of the song, where you want it to be, I'm cutting to that level at all times.

Highlighting the recording of "Workin' for a Livin'" as an opportunity to showcase one of what would become among the most recognizable signatures of the band's run of hit singles throughout the decade to come, when he turned his ear to capturing the band's world-class horn section, Gaines said that

recording the horns for that song is a funny story. I had done the Tower of Power, so they were friends of mine, and so Huey says to me one day, "Man, I think we need horns on 'Workin' for a Livin',"" and we can't get it out of the synth," because some of the horn stuff did come out of the synth, "Do you think Tower of Power would play on our record?" And I said, "Well, Hell yes, they just live across the East Bay," and that floored Huey at the time, because back then in 1982, to him and the band, Tower of Power was this unreachable band. So Doc comes in, who is the funniest guy, and Mimi comes in and Greg, and asked Greg if he could arrange the horns. Johnny

Colla on the record also plays sax, so we cut the horn section, and Huey and the guys thought it was the greatest thing in the world! They became friends, and went on to cut more stuff. When Huey sang his vocal on that song and the rest of the record, I used an M-49 as much as possible with him, just because of his voice character. He actually ended up buying an M-49, and that's what he records with every time, he brings it in with him.

Turning to the creation of another single, the album's biggest, *Billboard* hailed "Do You Believe in Love" as "a stunner, a tight set of polished, anthemic hooks that is one of the best mainstream pop singles of the early '80s." For Gaines, the addition of the second single was a welcome bookend to what had been an album written and recorded on the band's terms, but still lacking what the suits felt was a homerun hit record to launch Huey and the News up the charts and into the pop stratosphere.

"Do You Believe in Love" was one of the last songs that came in, it came from Mutt Lange, and BAM, we were a Top 20 single. That is a very catchy song, and it came to us at the end of the session when we were kind of wrapping up but were still looking for another song, and that one, when it came in, the way Johnny Colla and the boys set up those harmonies, that melody just really stuck out at me. All those guys in that band sang, and when they sang harmonies—especially when we put Chris and Bill and Johnny and Sean together—they're all good singers, but Johnny Colla did a lot of specifying what he wanted on it. So it sounded very young, and very summertime sounding, that's what made that song work. Huey's also a great singer, he gets in there, and does what he does, and knows how to deliver a hit vocal.

As a producer, there's certain things about a single, you've got to remember, a single's played on radio, and so there's certain things about radio that you just have to be a little careful of: you don't want the solos too long; you don't want it too congested so that the clarity is not there, and I'm talking about what I know as singles; the melody has got to be very dominant; the hook line needs to be repeated, not over-excessive, but quite a few times, so is the hook line catchy? Here's one of the main things—can you sing along with it?

By the time he'd completed work on the album, as he prepared to check out of his San Francisco hotel/studio residency and return home to Oregon, lightning struck a second time when

as I'm getting ready to go back to Oregon, I get this phone call from Santana's people saying "Can you come over and cut with Carlos for two days, and we're going to bring another guy in for two days, we want to get away from the CBS guys, and want something fresh?" So I go in with Santana and cut the first day, and they say to me, "Well, what are you doing the next six months?," and I replied, "I don't know," and they said, "You're hired," the other guy never even got a chance.

Hired back in the same fashion for his sophomore outing with Huey Lewis and the News, Gaines and the band would fire back at the one-hit-wonder tag with a thunder of hits that came to in many ways define the decade for fans, beginning—*Rolling Stone* reported—"in an era when 'radio-friendly' was the coin of the Top 40-dominated realm, *Sports* was a veritable radio reach-around, spawning five Top 20 singles."

By design, the production team of Huey and Gaines had begun masterminding the album that would take pop radio by surprise in 1983 coming off the heels of the success of their first collaboration, back in the studio within a year working on what would become their most popular radio hit ever with "The Heart of Rock & Roll," with Yahoo Music News saying that "Huey Lewis and the News may best be known for their nationwide ode to rock . . . The crisp lyrics and kicking beat are an anthem for the rock 'n' roll eighties." Beginning with its now-legendary intro, the producer remembered its creation as a complicated, cutting-edge combination of live and programmed drum parts that

we spent a minute on, that heartbeat intro. We were working at Fantasy Studios, and I remember we were all sitting there trying to figure out, "Well, what the hell does a heartbeat sound like?" So we tried a kick drum, and "Naw, that ain't working, that's not going to work," so Sean and I were dicking around with some sounds, and we took a synth sound from this Jupiter 8 he had and I tricked it up. We spent about four or five hours just working on that sound, because we thought in our heads that there was a lot of low end associated with a heartbeat, and knew we had to get the right low end, and again, that kick drum wouldn't give it to us. It was too straight, and I think a heartbeat almost has a little delay to it, so I ran the sample through a little bit of delay so it's kind of got a little bit of slap to it, like you hear on the single. So Sean Hopper, the keyboard player, and I came up with that sound out of a synth sample with some tricks on it.

The drum sound on that song—and the entire album—at that point in time, I was using 87s for overheads, and sometimes—depending on what mics I had—I used 421s for toms because I liked the attack and the way it projects the midrange, for kick drum, in those days, they didn't have a D-112, so we used RE-20s, and I might use two mics, an RE-20 and something a little more bottom-oriented. I liked the RE-20 because it could take the impact and give you the attack. There are times I like to use a 414 on the tom, if I can get by with it, especially the floor tom, because it just makes the floor tom whip, and the 414's just got a great, smooth bottom end. It depends on how close that ride cymbal is to it, whether I can get by with it or not, and the other big thing is having a live room you can work with. So, with *Sports*, we recorded some of the tracks at Fantasy in their big room, but basically, I didn't have any room mics going on, I just had the drums miced. Then we ended up cutting the rest of the record at the Record Plant Studio B, which was my room basically, where we cut *Fore!* too.

I kind of ran the Record Plant for a while, I was their #1 client, and it was my room, and when I didn't want it, they could book it, but back in those days, they'd always have to clear it with me, because I was doing so much stuff in there. And recording Bill, he's one of those drummers who, first of all, comes from a rock background, but the Huey material had a lot of R&B feel to it. All the guys in that band—Johnny Colla played with Sly for a while—and all came from an R&B/rock hybrid background, and Bill's one of those guys who, as a player, just kind of lays the groove down on that backside, which, if you're an R&B guy, that's where you want it. He plays to the song, that's what I like about him, is you're not trying to play a drum part, he's playing to the song, and a lot of drummers don't get that, but he did.

"I Want a New Drug" was another of the album's Top 10 smashes that Gaines and the band banged out during the *Sports* sessions. The song again represented all of the now-signature elements of a Huey Lewis hit, including an irresistibly melodic hook, a power horn section, a Hammond B3, Lewis's booming lead vocal backed up by the band's R&B harmony blend, and the famously ripping guitar riff that opened the song. Beginning with the latter opening pitch, the producer recalled that

Sean Hopper came up with a great riff on that, that synth riff that sounds like horns. The synthesizer sound throughout the *Sports* album was a Jupiter 8, and we did have some DX-7 stuff going on too. In those days, this is when the Midi world is starting to kick in, so we hooked up a couple of things, a Super Jupiter 8, which was this extra module you could get, and an organ, that's what we were using. Sean is a GREAT organ player, and we would go D.I. with his sound.

When we did that song, the record company had this whole big thing about "No drug lyrics on the radio," and we're thinking "Well, they might not even want to release this thing because of all this anti-drug stuff that was going on at the time," Nancy Reagan with the "Just Say No" deal, all of that, even though Huey's talking about love. So when we were cutting it, we just wanted to make it fun, and up with these cute little effect things on it, but we didn't know what was going to happen with it. And the damn thing almost got pulled because everybody was so concerned radio wouldn't play it, but when it became a big hit, the whole thing became a snowball because of the amount of plays it was getting, and then the video became successful, MTV helped a lot with that one.

"Heart and Soul" would round out the band's amazing run of hits off *Sports* LP, peaking at #8. Gaines shared the story behind how the song first arrived on the band's doorstep, coming after

> Bob Brown, who was Huey's manager, and his wife split up, and Bob didn't have a place to live and I had a spare bedroom, so he came to live with me for a while. So one morning I get a call from Huey, knowing Bob was in the room, and he says "Man, I've got this song I want you guys to hear, I think it would be good for the next record," and he's playing me "Heart and Soul" over the phone. Bob Brown is strictly an R&B guy, said "I don't get it," but I said, "I love it man, it sounds like pop-R&B," and had been written by Mike Chapman and Nicky Chinn, and had actually been recorded at the time—we didn't know it—by the group Exile, and by the Bus Boys. So we get to the studio, and are in the middle of tracking this thing, and the assistant from next door walks in and says, "Oh man, you're cutting 'Heart and Soul,' Exile did that, and Suzi Quatro," so we come in the middle of tracking to find out that four people have already cut this thing! We thought we were making a brand new song out of this, so then it became "Oh, now what do we do?" So we decided to keep working on the band's version, and to make it fresh vs. feeling like a cover, we just treated it as a Huey Lewis song, and that's an important lesson: you still gotta treat it as yours, even if it's a cover. It's like, "This is our baby, and God forbid if it's going to sound like those other folks.'

By the mid-'80s, *Rolling Stone* joked that "Huey Lewis was so famous in the mid-Eighties that when Pepsi signed Michael Jackson, Coke felt they had little choice but to reach out to Huey," while CBS News more seriously affirmed that "in 1985 Lewis was among the biggest names in music, literally." You can remember an era in band-specific terms if they were as successful as Huey Lewis and the News had become by then with eight million albums sold and seven hit singles/videos under their belt, a singular achievement for a band who was self-made in their sound and style, a blend that the *Village Voice* would admiringly observe "had a sort of family-friendly optimism and their big sax solos and Lewis's scratchily soulful soliloquies served as an anesthetic to Reagan-era recession-related depression. It was a unique quality that they captured best on their multi-platinum 1983 record *Sports*." As they looked ahead toward *Fore!*, Gaines and the band headed back into the studio in the interim to record some holdover hits, including the wildly popular "Back to the Future" film theme "The Power of Love," "Back in Time," and the ballad "Stuck with You." Beginning with the story behind the #1 *Billboard* Hot 100 singles chart smash, the producer revealed

> an interesting story with that song, because here we are in-between *Sports* and *Fore!*, and we get a call from the record label that "We need a single to tide us over till the next record comes out," so we went in the studio and cut that one song basically, just

so they could have something for radio to prepare for the next album. So that's how that song even came about, was because we needed a tide-me-over song, and when it became a hit, it was like "Holy Mackerel, the damn thing's on the air!"

The only thing is, and this is one of the things you get wrapped up in when you have a hit record: when you have a hit record, you've got X number of songs that were hits, and I think we had five singles off *Sports*, so heading into *Fore!*, the pressure was "Okay, we've got to make another record, and it's got to be good or better than *Sports*," so we need one like "Heart of Rock & Roll" and one like "I Want a New Drug," and you can't think like that, you have to take the next record and it's got to stand on its own. You can't A/B them, because a lot of the songwriting had changed a little bit between those albums—and I'm gonna say this but I probably shouldn't—I don't think they were quite as fun songs as we had on *Sports*. I think when you listen to *Fore!*, there's not as many "Heart and Soul," "Heart of Rock & Roll," so some of those elements weren't quite in the next record, but you try to make what you've got as fun as you can get, at the same time.

Still, in spite of any internal concerns on the producer's part, as their attentions turned to the epic "The Power of Love," which dominated both the radio waves and movie theatres in the summer of 1985, there was no denying Huey and the boys were at the top of their game. Hailed by *American Songwriter* for being "not only well-crafted and catchy, but were superbly produced and performed," as was the standard for all Huey Lewis and the News material under the watchful eye and ear of coproducer Jim Gaines, as the gang headed back to the Record Plant to knock out a song that would eventually land them an Oscar nomination for "Best Original Song." Cowritten by Lewis, Johnny Colla, and lead guitarist Chris Hayes, the song began with Hayes's guitar chain. Gaines recalled that

Chris Hayes didn't have a big rig, but I figured out a way to use two amps at once, which I still like to do. Basically, with Chris, we just worked with the sound. The Record Plant's Studio B had this little room that was originally meant to be an echo room or an ISO booth, it had a tiled floor, and was a little live, but I put a rug down, and put his amps in there, and it's a short room, so you get a little liveness out of it. I also liked to double-mic amps, that's another thing that created that guitar-sound, because when you double-mic an amp, it gives you more lower-mids, like 300 cycles or 400 cycles, it just builds up, and so your presence just comes forward another couple inches in the speakers. I'd been doing that quite a bit by then, so we'd just work with Chris on sound, and he was just a cool guy to work with, because he'd say, "Okay, let's try this." We'd use a few effects, and he's a very clean player, so I wanted to get more distortion on some things, so that's how that worked with Chris.

We cut that at the Record Plant in Studio B, which again, when I'd first moved back from Oregon to work with Huey and Santana, the Plant had called me and said "Would you be interested in working out of our studio if we could work out a deal with you?" And I'd said, "Well, here's the deal: I don't want you to pay me anything because that way I am locked in to you, and I may have a client that wants to work at another studio, so I can't do that." So the deal I made them was: "Supply me with housing, and I'll bring you my business, that's all I want," and that was the deal we made, so after we'd finished up *Sports* there, we came back and did "Power of Love" there.

That B Room was my favorite tracking room, it was live enough for me, and another thing I did there that helped create my drum sound for that record and others, was I had a riser built, because I don't like putting drums on a flat floor any more than I have to, so that gives me liveness. When you put drums on a really hard-surfaced floor, what happens is the toms don't have that after-ring, it kind of just dissipates, a kick drum, the same way. So if I put Bill Gibson, Huey's drummer, on a riser and raise it up six inches or eight inches on something that's not solid, you get a whole different drum sound.

It was amazing, and so we heard the bottom end come up drastically, so I had a special riser built that was built out of 2x6's, and it was heavy and open, and when I wasn't using it, it just laid up against the wall. But when I put it down on the floor and had a rug put on it, that's how I created a lot of the drum sounds in that room. I remember when Rod Stewart's road guy come in there, and he just said, "Oh, that will never work," and when he listened after we'd set it up and tracked, he said, "WOW," because the toms took on a different atmosphere. They had more of a sonic low-end boom that rises above, and the kick drum was not so dead, and the snare had an extra-low mid-thing that generates with it, and it's just a simple little trick, but was part of my sound in those days.

The success of the song, as *USA Today* chronicled, would launch "the band truly . . . into orbit," sending them to the top of the charts with their first #1 single, and set the stage brilliantly for the band's highly anticipated follow-up, *Fore!* Commanding a massively increased budget from Chrysalis commensurate with the success of *Sports* and "The Power of Love," the producer remembered that

heading into that album, we had a little more time because of those budgets. In those days, our recording budgets allowed us basically ten weeks of recording and two weeks of mixing, that was how most of the contracts were: basically three months of recording. And our normal sessions the way I worked back then was 5 ½ days, so we'd work 5 days, and the 6th day we'd come in and work a little, just on minor tweaking and miscellaneous stuff, and everybody could have Saturday night to blow it out, recoup on Sunday, and we'd be back to work on Monday. That's kind of how it worked.

Discussing the sonic side of his and the band's vision for the record, rather than experimenting with any major facet of their sound, they opted to stick with an "if it ain't broke, don't fix it" approach that the producer reasoned made perfect sense at that point because

> when we headed back into the studio to do *Fore!*, we had established a sound with the band, and that's why I was brought back in, because they felt like I knew what the band should sound like. One thing I always did was record Huey and the News live off the floor as much as possible, and we're talking tape days, so there was no comping, so you cut till you got it. Whether it was two takes or fifteen takes, or even twenty, whatever it took, and sometimes, some of these songs were being written and finished off the floor! So songs would come in as a part, and we would work it up and cut it, so it's not like these things were heavily demoed out, but Huey and the News were tight enough of a band that someone could come in and say, "Well, I've got this idea I've been working on a little bit, let's work it up in the studio and cut it." So it may take a day or two days to cut it, and it may go through different forms as it's being worked up and different parts were being experimented with: "I feel this," "Let's try this," "It's too fast, it's too slow," etc.
>
> Basically Huey and Johnny and Chris were like the arrangers in the band. You have to remember, some of these songs were worked out live before we got to the studio, and some were done in the studio live worked up from demos.

One such example was the band's first massive hit from the new album, "Jacob's Ladder," again a #1 hit on the *Billboard* Hot 100 singles chart, a gift that the producer recalled

> actually came from Bruce Hornsby. I knew when I heard it that it was one of those songs that could be set up a little differently, first of all, because it's a kind of unique song. The arrangement we all came up with was like "Wow, it works for this song," because it was such a different style from everything else they were doing, and I didn't look at that song at the time—to be honest with you—as a radio-friendly song, like I did say "Happy to Be Stuck with You." With that song's live sound, one thing about the way I produce is I try to capture a little bit of liveness to the music, and that's the concept they wanted, which is always what made it work. So you look at a band like that, and I do it today with a lot of bands that work with me, is: I look at it as if you're going to see a live performance.
>
> That's kind of the sound I want to hear, except with us in control, so visually, if I hear that music, I want to actually kind of see a live performance going on, and I Just approach my engineering like that. So as a producer, I try to get the engineers working for me to get that same concept, and it has nothing to do with a bunch of room mics, and in fact, I don't remember having room mics for that band. It's just the way I miced Bill Gibson's drum set and the way we approached the guitar sounds, so we didn't have a lot of big giant amps, and we had a nice little room for them.

That was an important thing because they're not the kind of band where you drag out the big stack of Marshalls and kick their ass on power sounds. Most of the sounds were self-contained kind of rhythmic sounds, with little solos, and Chris Hayes is a great player. He's not like a heavy-duty rocker, but is more like a jazz rock player in a lot of ways, and so one of my tricks is: I double-mic an amp. If it's got one speaker, or no matter how many speakers it's got, I use two mics on it, and it gives me a lot of lower-mid stuff, but it also gives me a different presence than you can get. And of course, you gotta work with the tones on the amp, and we had a great little room at the Record Plant that kind of had a slate floor, and it was weird because it had actually been set up to be an ISO booth or a live echo chamber, and it was roughly 12 x 14 feet, and it was kind of a pie shape, but not real pie shape. I would set the amps up in that room.

For Mario Cipollina's bass, in those days, I had an amp set up, so we would go both D.I. and amp, and that was another coloration situation, because if I want the attack, like Mario played with a pick, so if I wanted the attack sound, I'm going through the amp, because if you take one of those big old rock and roll amps, man, you can hit that bass string with your fingers, and there's a lot of midrange that comes at you in the attack. So if I'm wanting some of that attack, say for instance on a song like "Jacob's Ladder," I go more to the amp and jacked up the amp so I get that 2k, 3k coming off of it, because there's a pluck sound that comes out of that speaker on the amp that you cannot get out of the D.I. The only thing about some of those amps is the consistency of notes is not as even as a D.I., so you kind of need both sometimes.

Covering radio from coast to coast when it was released in January 1987, both "Ladder" and the follow-up single would come to define what Yahoo Music News celebrated as "a time when nerds were all the rage . . . (so) who can forget a tune like "Hip to Be Square," a masterpiece of a song." Quintessentially Huey, "Hip to Be Square" became an anthem for the height of the yuppie era, boasting such autobiographical lines about the band as "I got my boys in business suits, you watch 'em on TV, I'm working out almost every day, and watching what I eat." *American Psycho* author Bret Easton Ellis would even review the album through the voice of his book's lead yuppie serial killer Patrick Bateman in 1988, arguably offering the best summary of precisely why "Hip to Be Square" became "the key off *Fore!* . . . a rollicking ode to conformity that's so catchy most people probably don't even listen to the lines, but with Chris Hayes blasting guitar and the terrific keyboard playing, who cares?" Taking fans inside the micing technique he applied to Hayes's latter guitar lead throughout the album, Gaines began by sharing his memory that

on Chris's guitar sound on *Fore!*, in those days, I double-miced, and would use a 57, of course, which you can't go wrong with, but if I was looking for coloration, I would pick a condenser mic, and might use a U-87 or might even put a Ribbon mic like a 77 DX. If I was looking for a brighter sound, I might have put a 414 on his amp, it really depended on the character, so I always have a 57 on him, but that second mic, it could be different character because of whatever character I thought the song needed, or that we were looking for out of the amp. It was just another coloration.

Sean Hopper plays great organ on that song as well, and we did use a real B3 on those, and in micing the B3, I still, if I have my druthers, like to use a couple of 87s on the top, and then whatever you want to on the bottom. We used to use an RE-20, or if you want a really live low end, you can use a condenser down there, but the problem with using a condenser on the bottom is the wind noise, because that rotor generates a lot of wind noise, and so it's better to use something that's a little tight. So basically, that's how I mic the organ.

On the drum sound throughout the record, along with his usual micing setup, the producer remembered having fun with

this thing called an AMS we had in those days. It was the gated reverb sound that Bob Clearmountain made famous, I bought one and one day, these people at Guitar Center called me and said, "Jim, we'd got this reverb unit we'd love for you to try out, just tell us what you think." It was called the Yamaha RB90, and had these reverbs in it, so I got this gated reverb sound out of it, and this thing cost $350, and I'm thinking, "Well, this is stupid, I just paid $10,000 for the AMS, this is stupid." So I ordered three of the Yamaha, sold my AMS, and I used those a lot for my drum sound as well.

Gaines's favorite memory from that particular hit's creation came from the compositional side, in that it had been brought to the band by an old and trusted friend, such that

"Hip to Be Square" is actually Doc from Tower of Power's song! On the horns for the stuff on that album, I went for a little flatter sound with the horns because we were trying to create a new sound as well, which I guess we did, we kind of did, didn't we? That's a special song, man, because that's a Tower of Power tune, and he presented it and Huey said "God, that sounds great, we can cut it with the horns," and I think some of the 49ers were hanging out in the studio, and we got them to sing some of the background parts, so it was just a fun song to record.

Upon release, *Fore!* debuted at #1 on *Billboard*'s Hot 200 albums chart, producing five Top 10 singles with the aforementioned "Jacob's Ladder" (#1), "Stuck with You" (#1), "Hip to Be Square" (#3), "Doin' It All for My Baby" (#6), and "I Know What I Like" (#9). Cementing the band's "superstar status worldwide," as PBS would report years later, the album's massive success also helped the band reach more than "30 million albums and . . . (a ranking) in the top . . . selling groups of all time."

Reflecting back on other studio highlights from his amazing catalog, Jim Gaines proudly points to his role as head mixer on Steve Miller's seminal hit "Fly Like an Eagle," and specifically the creation of many of the song's atmospheric overdubs, which the producer remembered as being

a special, special project to me because Steve would let me experiment and try out-of-the-norm things like cutting vocals in the control room right beside me, and cutting guitars with a Fender Princeton amp at my feet under the console, I was allowed to do those things. When Steve Miller had originally called me, I'd never worked with him, and he was in the studio at Capitol Records in LA, and I remember he said, "Jim, this is Steve Miller," and I said "Hey Man!," and he says, "I'm working on my record in Los Angeles, and I hate this place. They're running tours through my session, do you have any time?" And I said, "Well, I can give you two weeks," and he says, "Okay, I'll be there," done deal. So he shows up, and Mike Fusaro actually recorded most of that album at CBS San Francisco, but Steve had a little studio at his house, so he did a lot of work there as well on overdubs.

So he shows up with his tapes, and we proceed to overdub stuff and mix, and so he will tell you we did in seventeen hours, but we really did it in seven days basically, because we were redoing a lot, for instance, all the wind sounds in "Fly Like an Eagle." We had this little $90 Casio thing he bought at Macy's, and all the little flute sounds, oboe, that all came off that damn thing, and we were also recutting some of his lead vocals. In fact, some of those vocals we actually did live in the control room with an RE-15 with a Shure "level lock," that's why you hear all that lip-smacking going on. The Shure "level-lock" is a semi-pro piece of gear, and if you put that compressor on 10, you can hear a fly fart, basically.

So as I'm mixing "Fly Like an Eagle," if you know the way that record works, there's a lot of segues from one song right into the other, there's no "breaks," so the way it worked with "Fly Like an Eagle" is it's coming out with the spatial sound through wind, and then the wind's gonna duck underneath the start of the next song. Well, we're working on 24-track analog, and in the old days on tape, you put a piece of white leader tape after your cut so you separate the cuts, find them real quick, and so I'm getting to the end of "Fly Like an Eagle," and I realize I don't have enough wind to create enough wind to get me underneath the next song, so I thought, "Okay, I'm going to get a blank tape and create some more wind," because his little Casio wind machine was right there. So I took a piece of shop tape, which is what they set up these machines with back in the day, picked up a bulk eraser, and kind of erased it. Well, if you don't erase enough, there's going to be some wind left over.

I must have spooled out about thirty seconds of tape into the floor, sliced it, sliced it into "Fly Like An Eagle," put some wind across so I had another twenty seconds of wind, and as I pull up one of the faders off this new piece of tape, it's got tones on it that didn't get erased. And if you don't erase enough, it sounds like a thumping sound, but the tones were still left, so somehow I had cut this piece of tape where the tones were in time with the song that's left over. So Miller's half asleep on the couch, I pull up this tone, and am thinking, "God, this sounds great," so I shove it in like two echo chambers, and Steve wakes up and says "What the hell is that?" So I told him, "Man, you ain't going to believe what happened . . . What do you think?" And his reply was "I love it," so when you hear those sonar sounds at the end, that's exactly what that is, is pure accident, and I used the accident to use the sonar sounds, otherwise it would have just been wind going out.

So I'm mixing and doing overdubs with Steve, and was actually was running two rooms while this was all going on: I had him maybe doing a few overdubs in one room while I was mixing in another room with my assistant, and that's how we finished "Fly Like an Eagle." I mixed that album on my new API console, and he got the mixes home, called me, and said "Man, I want to tell you right now, you hit it on the head brother, I love these mixes!" And because of that, I ended up working on *Book of Dreams*, and wound up going to work for him exclusively for two years on retainer, so anytime he hollered, I came, and ended up moving to Oregon for a while after he built a studio on his ranch up there. I also ended up going out and doing some live stuff with him and recording a bunch of shows.

Turning to another of his beloved best-of moments of collaboration over the years, Gaines points to his decades-long relationship working with another guitar great, Carlos Santana (including on his Grammy-winning comeback LP *Supernatural* in 1998):

With Santana, just working on him because his passionate guitar playing is one of the finest in the world! I'm telling you, man, I've worked with a lot of cats, but he could play two or three notes and make you cry. He's one of those great, great artists that . . . it comes from the heart, it really does, and it's hard to find players . . . I mean, I've worked with guys that play lots of notes, they can play with notes all day long, but to play consistently with that kind of passion, and I've done hundreds of shows with him because I used to be the guy to go out and do all the live radio and TV shows, and man, I've seen in every show that he played with that same passion.

It was funny, in the early days working with Carlos, I could tell his mood by fashion, so if he wore the white leathers in, we were having a good day, but if he wore the black leathers in, God knows what's gonna happen! He's just one of those guys who can hear minute, minute things, he and Stevie were both that way by nature as players. So it's a matter of knowing that Carlos hates high end on his guitar, #1, hates it, so brightness is something that I had to constantly deal with, and try to pull it down from midrange down, that's where he wants it. But yet, we need the brightness for some attack, so it was a matter of finding that delicate balance with him, and there were times working with other engineers where guys just didn't get that concept, and if you didn't get that concept, you were only in there a day or two and you were gone.

Bringing that relationship full-circle through *Supernatural,* here's the deal: by the early '90s, I'd moved back to Memphis, and was kind of out of the San Francisco scene, but Carlos would still bring me out to do some live stuff, so for instance, I worked with him on *Spirits Dancing in the Flesh* in 1990 and *Sacred Fire* in 1994. Then a few years later, toward the end of the '90s, I get this call, and first of all, at that point, he'd had no record deal for about five years. When he and CBS had parted ways, I didn't hear anything for about a year or two, and then I get this call from his manager while I was out making a record in Texas, and he says, "Look Jim, we just signed with Clive Davis, we're doing this record, and we've got this kid out here we're working with in San Francisco, and things are falling apart, and I mean *fast.* Do you think you could find time, like tomorrow, and come out?" And I said, "No, I'm tracking right now, I can't come out," but I told them I could give them a week a few days later when I was done in Texas. I fly out to San Francisco, and they'd started the record and the way it had been set up was: Clive got X number of songs, and Carlos got to choose X number of songs.

A brilliant concept that would earn Gaines a Grammy for "Album of the Year" when "Supernatural" won that among four of nine Grammy nominations in 2000, including other coveted grabs like "Best Rock Album of the Year," in elaborating on his role in the recording of the album, Gaines began by explaining that with

Clive's X number of songs, he'd wanted all the new young guns to come in and play on it, and I was being brought in for Carlos's part because, the way it worked for the collaboration songs was: with the other producers, writers, engineers involved, we'd get a track in from them that was completely done except for Carlos's guitars, and maybe CT playing keyboards, and Carl Raoul playing percussion, but by and large, the backing track would be done when we got it. So it was my job to get Carlos's parts recorded on all those songs that came from Clive.

Now, on the songs Carlos had picked, we cut those in Fantasy Studios in Berkeley, and Carlos was another guy who loves to cut live, as much as possible. Now, getting his amp separated from the rest of the band is another problem, so most of the time we would overdub his lead parts, just to get through, but the band—whatever they were cutting live with Carlos playing rhythm was pretty much going to stay that way. That's just the way he works, so he could cut with the band, and even attempt solos if I had the right room set up for him, because some of these rooms were not set up good for us because he plays very *loud.*

He plays with a Dumble Amp and a Marshall, so if I can't get that leakage situation controlled, I would have to have him get me through the track and we'll overdub. And he likes to do his solos later and concentrate on them, because when he's cutting with the band, he's directing the band, and has to be listening to their parts as well as his parts, and in most cases, he would rather do the solo later.

As far as his guitar sound, this was my normal setup—and by this time, he was again going through a Dumble and a Marshall and the Boogie—so the Dumble amp was miced with two mics, a Royer and a 67. Then we had these room mics, which were C-24s, and the Marshall was a 57 and the Boogie was always then a dynamic mic, because it just has that edge, and if you'd put a condenser mic on there, it would rip your head off. So the dynamic mic was ideal for that amp because it has a lot of midrange on it.

So I loved working on those records, and then working with Albert Collins, that's another great, great player, and I was so lucky I did those last records before he passed away. We became friends, and as a matter of fact, I talked to him a few nights before he died, and his manager wrote me this beautiful letter about how much joy I gave him, just talking, and saying, "Look, you need to get well, come back, we got some barbecue for you, and we need to finish this record . . ." Because I was in the middle of a record we didn't finish, so there's a lot of special things that are emotional attachments as well.

Now seventy-one, Gaines still gets up every day and sits down behind the console with the same perspective he's kept throughout the entirety of his fifty-year career in a business, one where his legendary successes came not from talent as much as, he says,

just being a lucky guy. I'm just a hardworking hillbilly from Arkansas. And I've just been very lucky throughout my career to be involved with all these great artists, that's the way I look at it. I'm just a hardworking guy, and most people who survive in this business are hardworking guys, and I've been fortunate to work with people where those collaborations accelerated their career to a point.

With Blogcritics.org hailing him in 2012 as the "legendary Grammy-winning blues producer," Gaines's rare breed of soundman is something akin to the bluesmen he's spent years recording from his hometown of Memphis, Tennessee. Still working today as energetically behind the boards as he did decades ago, his touch hasn't grayed at all, spotlighted by *Premier Guitar* magazine in their review of Royal Southern Brotherhood's 2012 self-titled debut when the "cool union" of "two musical lineages (intertwined) . . . in RSB, a new quintet headed by the mighty Cyril Neville. As a member of The Meters and Neville Brothers, the Grammy-winning vocalist and percussionist helped pioneer New Orleans funk, and at 63, he's still a force of nature. Les Paul-wielding Devon Allman, whose dad is Gregg Allman, represents the other, equally potent bloodline. Allman and blues-rocker Mike Zito trade fiery leads and sweaty riffs throughout the 12-song set, and their contrasting Gibson and Fender tones are a treat for anyone who has OD'd on mushy, high-gain guitar sounds. Producer Jim Gaines (SRV, Steve Miller, Santana, Albert Collins, John Lee Hooker) deserves credit for this . . ."

Still schooling assistant engineers today as he has for years, in offering closing points of wisdom, Gaines begins with his general thrill at the opportunity to

> talk to a lot of young engineers, and what I tell them is: you gotta keep this concept, because, see, a lot of young engineers, once they have some success, they think they're God, and that the band's working for them, when really it's the other way around. They're paying you, see, so you're working for them, and I love teaching young engineers because I've got all these old-school ideas and things I do and I feel like, with all the young engineers I work with, they're all my little kids. And they'll tell ya, I'm "Uncle" Jim, and will often say "Uncle Jim taught me something today I didn't know existed." I also like to work with young artists because a young artist has that enthusiasm, like "Man, let me in there Jim. Can you please work with me and show me how you do this?" "Okay," and seeing them grow and their success grow, and go from one day nobody knows who they are, and the next day, they're like the hot new item on the charts, I love that! It's not the money, it's the success rate that I can help give back. Some guy asked me in an interview not too long ago, "What's your role?," and I'm seventy-one years old, man, I shouldn't even still be doing this, first of all. But my role is to give back as much as I can, to artists and engineers, tell them what we experienced, "Here's how we used to do it, and you can use it or throw it out, whatever you wanna do." Or you can use a piece of it, that's how I learned, so go ahead, take a piece of this, take this micing technique, whatever it is, and use it, just don't abuse it.
>
> A lot of these younger engineers, with all this technical stuff we got going on, forget about the true meaning of trying to capture feel, emotion, groove, and think, "Oh, we can just fix it later with Protools." Well, there's some things you can't fix, for one instance, I'm pretty tough on singers in the studio, and will tell them "Sing it to me, sing it in tune, I don't want to go to this damn tuner for every little note." But a lot of these young guys would say, "Oh, don't worry about it, we'll take care of it later." Well, if you have a singer singing ten tracks of bad shit, you still got bad shit, where if you just get the singer singing where the passion is coming out, because I bust singers all the time for sounding like they're reading the words off a paper when they track, and when they are, I can tell it in a heartbeat.
>
> I know exactly when they're just reading the lyrics instead of feeling the lyrics, and I'll go out there and take the paper away from them, because if you don't know the damn song by now, go home and learn it! So I've sent singers home, I've sent two or

three girl singers home in the middle of a record, and told them "I have no time to waste, I'm not wasting your money, the record company's money, and definitely not the studio time that's costing a fortune." So it's one of those things where I think the young engineers, if they love the old stuff, there was a reason it came out like it did. It was *about performances*, and we didn't get into every technical nuance, and we brought out the music so it sounded like you were seeing the band live, where when you listen you get that feeling like "Wow, this is a great performance!"

CHAPTER 4

I Wanna Dance with Somebody–Narada Michael Walden

Whitney Houston defined '80s R&B-pop, period. Madonna may have had the monopoly on dance-pop superstardom, and in the early '90s, Mariah Carey started to eat into Whitney's airplay turf, but by and large, between 1985 and 1995, Whitney was the Queen of R&B-pop radio and record sales, racking up two hundred million record sales worldwide during the height of her career. The producer behind the console for many of her most popular hits—"I Wanna Dance with Somebody (Who Loves Me)," "How Will I Know," "So Emotional," "Where Do Broken Hearts Go?," "All the Man That I Need," and "I Belong to You" (which won Houston a Grammy for "Best Female R&B Vocal Performance")—was the one and only Narada Michael Walden. A student of the radio growing up, Walden mused that

> I use this phase, I was always "charmed by radio," and what that means is I was always listening to radio and a student of radio, and still am really, and being a student of hearing hits on the radio, you know that certain things just come out and do grab you. So being a producer and trying to be good at my craft, I always wanted to be competitive with things I always loved, so I studied what made those things pop out. I was raised up on jazz like Jimmy Smith, the Sermon, Cannonball Adderley, This Here, Dave Brubeck, "Take 5," and all the Motown music when it came out: Smokey Robin-

son, "Shop Around," anything the Marvelettes were on, Stevie Wonder, all the Marvin Gaye music, the Supremes, and out of Chicago of course there was Curtis Mayfield music, Johnny Matheson was big, "Chances Are," Patti Page, "Old Cape Cod" when I was really little. See, in Kalamazoo, Michigan, you heard everything, that's what was so magical about Michigan, you heard every kind of music. So I'm very blessed to say there was no music that ever escaped me, I could hear it all, from classical to every kind of music, but I always drawn to jazz because I liked the drummers. I was always drawn to drums, and so the music that had the most excitement with drums would be like Max Roach vs. Buddy Rich, and my dad had a collection of all the great jazz drummers, so I would hear them all when I was a real, real little kid.

My mom is the oldest of six, so all her siblings were into music, every kind of music, and the twins could play flute and clarinet, and my Uncle Travis, who was five years older than me, played piano, I played piano with him when I was a little boy coming up and we'd win talent shows together, playing either "Moon River" or things that would sound like "Horse Silver," those astanado type feeling things. I'm just a fan of music, so my love of music and artists come through in what I do because I've always had a real love for them, almost like a kid's passion. And quite frankly, most of the artists I know, they're all big kids, music keeps you young, and the part of it you love when you're a kid never dies. So that's what keeps you like a big kid, which is in fact the fuel to go forward and keep pursuing higher heights in music, is that kid love you first had.

A gifted drummer in his own right whose skill got him into the record business and eventually producing, according to *Billboard*, Walden's "proficient drumming skills have made him a first-call session musician playing on countless recording sessions. Walden has played on all kind of sessions from rock, jazz, pop, R&B, to fusion, sharing the recording and concert stage with the likes of John McLaughlin, the Mahavishnu Orchestra (a twenty-one-year-old Walden replaced drumming legend Billy Cobham), and Jeff Beck (his *Wired* album) to name a small few." Looking back on a talent that began to bloom at a young age, Walden fondly recalled that

I always loved drums, and played boxes and tins and all that kind of stuff, and got toy drum sets when I was five and six years old for Christmas time that I would break the heads on in about twenty minutes. But my first real drum set came when I was ten years old, that my Grandma bought for me with a $100 bill, it was a Ludwig bass drum, snare drum, cowbell with block and cymbal, and that following Xmas I got a hi-hat. So when I was ten years old, I had my first real drums.

At Christmas time a couple years later, maybe eleven or twelve, my dad got me a small tape machine, a little tiny reel-to-reel, and I remember the first thing I recorded off the radio was "Downtown" by Petula Clark, and just listened to it over and over and over again. I was also a fan of all the records I had, so the B-side of "Chances Are" was this beautiful intro called "A Certain Smile," and I record and play that intro over and over again. Or I'd come home from school and listen to a song by King Curtis called "Soul Serenade," or I'd rush home to hear Ray Charles's "That Lucky Old Sun." I was always rushing home from school to hear things I loved. I think all of that showed up later on in my sound, everything that's in my heart.

Speaking from his longtime home base, Tarpan Studios, more universally on his production philosophy and approach to producing the countless gold, platinum, and multiplatinum hits that line his studio walls, Walden emphasized that

as a producer, I'm not trying to make a stamp of my sound on anybody, I want their sound to be the predominant thing, but making that sound, off the fabrics of things I've learned and loved for my whole life, and then primarily it's the quality: making sure things are in tune, making sure things all fit lyrically, making sure you have the right tempos—things that are so small are the biggest things. Should the tempo be 98 beats, or should it be 99 beats, or 96 beats per minute? What's best for the singer: G, or G Sharp, or go A, or A sharp, B flat? Find the small things and that sky can open up, and those are always things I've learned from listening to all the best records that were ever made, from the British Invasion with the Beatles and Jimi Hendrix, all that stuff, just trying to make good-sounding records that had energy and spirit that just jump off the damn needle and out of the speakers!

Walden's storied collaboration with Whitney Houston began in 1985, just as his production career was beginning to take off, and together, the pair shot up the charts straight to #1 with "How Will I Know," their first collaboration that helped launched Houston's career. Taking fans back to the song's creation from the ground up in the studio, Walden—also the song's cowriter—began with his construction of the song's driving drum track, which *Rolling Stone* called "irresistibly danceable."

I did the drum track for that song on my Simmons electronic drums, which I loved because you could sample any sound you want, so at that point in my life, I really wanted the big fat snare drum, like what Prince was doing in "Purple Rain" or Don Henley on an Eagles record. You have to know what planet you're on, and at that time, planet Earth was very much into fat snare drums, and you could pop in some handclaps on it if you wanted to, but they had to be fat. That's what drove the folks to the dance floor, that fat snare drum. So the fat snare drum, I could find exactly what I wanted, and the bass drum as far as that goes too, and of course, add live cymbals and live hi-hat, and everything else would be all machine, I would just play. I would play them along with a programmed handclap and a programmed percussion track, and a shaker, or tambourine, something like that. With the synthesizers you hear throughout the track, back then, we mainly used the Oberheim and the Prophet, that was the main synthesizer because you could get a lot of cool sounds on it, also the DX-7 was very popular because it had cool vibes, we used that in a lot of our songs. It wasn't that we were so sophisticated, we just brought soul, and if you bring soul, you don't always have to have a big, old arsenal of stuff, it's more about how you play it and how you tune in.

Once his attentions turned to capturing what the *New York Times* in 1985 hailed as an "exceptional vocal talent" on tape, the producer remembered finding himself impressed with the fact that

Whitney never did warm-ups, she just comes in and blows, never warms up, just blows. She had it like that, that was her gift. She would just run, and she sounded so good doing it that you'd go "Damn, alright, let's just go!" I liked again a C-12 or SM-7 microphone on her, Whitney would sing for about three hours at a session, and then I would get as many takes as I could get out of her before I could see she'd gotten tired, and given me her best stuff, then she'd go home, and I'd comp the best bits together. Then when she'd come the next day, and I'd play it for her, and she'd say, "Wow, that sounds like a smash record," and I'd say, "It is. All you gotta do is maybe add one more line here, a harmony here," double certain things if you need, and you were done with it. We always used slap echo, "How Will I Know" has a lot of slap echo on Whitney's voice.

Released in late 1985 as a single, "How Will I Know" rocketed to the top of the *Billboard* Hot 100 singles chart, was later voted #12 on VH1's list of Greatest Songs of the 1980s, and won the MTV Music Video Award in 1986 for "Best Female Video." Teaming up with Houston once again in late 1986 to work on her sophomore LP, *Whitney*, Walden was involved in producing the majority (seven of eleven) of the record's tracks, including "I Wanna Dance with Somebody (Who Loves Me)," a #1 smash that won the singer her second Grammy for "Best Pop Vocal Performance, Female." Another of those massively popular hit singles was the dance-floor craze "So Emotional," a song where *Rolling Stone* would rave "Walden covers all the bases" in crafting the quintessential pop hit, an art that the producer reasoned begins with the fact that

I go into every session thinking I'm going to make a hit. I do my very best work on every song, thinking it could be a hit if it's given exposure, given airplay, it can be a hit. Everything we do we think is a hit, that's why we're spending time: to scratch our heads, and open the sky up on how to make it a hit, how to make it sound like a hit? For example, Clive could find a demo which we all think could be a hit—as was the case with "So Emotional" —but then how do you actually manifest that into being a hit, and so then you've got to really put your thinking cap on, how to do that. Now, when you're working with a singer like Whitney Houston, she can sound like a damn hit any time she sings, so with her, it's not about convincing her, but just having fun, and then when she starts opening up and singing on it, then she'd get excited because they hear how they sound doing it, and that excited starts spreading. It can happen within a matter of seconds, and you know you have a hit. It happens really, really fast.

When I'm working, I also like to keep it me and the artist because I get nervous, people watching me, being so intimate with someone, it gets me nervous. I personally don't like to have people watch me produce, because the things you have to say to someone to get them to go beyond themselves, things you might have to talk to an artist about to get them to go beyond themselves, can be intimate things, and it's no one else's business. So I get nervous when people are watching me do that, it makes me break out in a cold sweat, and adds pressure which I don't need, and the artist doesn't need it. Much less entertain people who want to watch you and then they want to add their two cents, and I don't need any of that. I think there's a time or place for it, but the truth is, until we get what the vision is on tape, everything else is a distraction. Now, after we get it on the tape, and I know it's good, and someone wants to add their two cents, no problem, but until I get it on tape, don't interrupt me, because it's hard to get a focus and concentration and a great performance. Once I get that performance, I'm good about it, and anyone can say whatever they want to say.

So when we were doing vocals, it would be just my engineer, myself, Whitney, and maybe her assistant Robin or CeCe or BeBe Winans, or her mom or father might stop by, but they were always closed sessions. But after we recorded a vocal, and she was all happy, then she might let other people hear it. One time in New York, Mick Jagger ran in the studio to hear "So Emotional," and he was jumping around because he was just flabbergasted at the sound, because at the time it was a new sound! He was awestruck, and she was all happy to see him be so awestruck. But in the making of the record, when we were recording it, it would always be closed session, that way she could just focus on me, I could focus on her, and we could get down to it. I don't want to be distracted by anyone else looking at her, and she looking at another person, I want her to look right at me and really focus on what we need at that time, and then move quickly. Because don't forget, doing a session with Whitney, you had to move fast, especially because she was doing a lot of TV, a lot of travel, a lot of touring all at the same time, so time was of the essence, so you had to smash it in a three-hour window.

It's a combination of what she does, she's a brilliant artist, a genius artist, just to hear her sing that chorus would give you a chill, and then it's a real production, because there are backgrounds in there, and they track against machines, and I quantized my machines, first I played them live then hit a button where it quantized it over the 4 and ½ minutes worth of time. At the time, that was revolutionary, because with one of the Oberheims we had, I would play my drums into the computer, into the drum machine itself, then I would hit a button, and it would quantize them, and then take that quantized performance and put it into tape. Then I would overdub onto that the bass, which Randy Jackson played, actually playing a bass synthesizer with one finger, he played it like a bass guitar would. Because the basses that I had, they sounded bigger and huger, and nastier, and this growl sound effect, letting you know something was about to happen, and Randy was an excellent bass player.

Walden would also enlist Jackson to play bass on what would become soul legend Aretha Franklin's first platinum album, *Who's Zoomin' Who?*, featuring among the biggest airplay singles of 1985, "Freeway of Love." Winning the singer her twelfth Grammy for "Best Female R&B Vocal Performance," it was a thrill for the producer, who remembered being especially energized

when it was my turn to produce Aretha Franklin with "Freeway of Love," in thinking about "How do I make her a modern-day smash?" To accomplish that, I took elements of old things and developed some new things. We all know her music, so you're very much aware of her legacy, and all those records: "Dr. Feelgood," "Natural Woman," "Chain of Fools," "Respect," all those songs are part of her bible. So I'm very much aware of what she does and what people expect of her, but that's why I know in producing her and having a smash, you want elements of what people are going to think "Oh, it's legendary, it sounds classic." So you borrow from Motown, you borrow from Stax, you borrow from Atlantic, those records that people already associate to, but you bring something new to it too.

So, for example, even though she was never signed to Motown, the fact she was living in Detroit, Michigan, I borrowed the Motown sound. On those drum fills, rrrrrr-rap, a lot of early Motown drummers like early Stevie Wonder stuff, Marvin Gaye, they always had Benny Benjamin on the drums. They also used tambourines and vibes, so I used to put vibes on her records, so immediately you think something old from Aretha, but NO, it sounds so fresh because it's cut brand new with modern sounds. So Old-Meets-New is always something kind of something I liked in having a hit record, because you can't beat what those cats before us put down, you can't beat it. You can't beat what the generations before us have done, but what you can do is borrow from it and put a new spin on it.

Aretha comes from a school where she's not used to recording a whole lot of takes, she warms up singing down an octave about four times, she sings the whole song through three or four times way down the octave. When she's warm, she says, "Okay, let's cut it," and that first take is a smash, her second take is a smash, and her third take—if you can get a third take out of her—is a smash, so much so, that she'll say, "Okay, let me give you one more outro so I have all the fireworks," she'll give you that, bam, killer, and you have a smash record.

Winning a Grammy for "Producer of the Year" in 1987, Walden—sitting on top of the world with the juice to pick whomever he wished to work with—chose to pair Franklin with pop-soul superstar George Michael on another of what would become his greatest #1 hit, "Knew You Were Waiting (For Me)." Appearing over the years on countless best-of lists from the 1980s, Walden was later hailed by *Billboard* for producing "crisp, synth-heavy soul-pop" that "remains bright and cheery, having aged particularly well." As he began assembling Michael's pop masterpiece from the ground up, Walden began as always with the song's groove, recalling that

> I make decisions really quick, and let my spirit dictate the things I put down on tape: a handclap, a bongo, or tambourine programmed, so I can play to it, even a bass drum pattern if I want to. Then I'll play along with those machines with my live drums, and then find the combination of whatever I like as I put my live drums on top of those machines. In there will be some kind of combination I will love: either the machine kick or my kick, or the machine kick and then my live snare drum, along with the programmed handclaps and my drum fills and my live hi-hat. That kind of combination in there is gonna work, or if I don't want acoustic drums, then it's going to be me playing on electric drums, where I can put the sounds in there I want. But I have to move really quick, because if I take too long, then you can get really confused and beat up on your enthusiasm, and then your decisions aren't sharp. The best record decisions come really fast.

> I also have a few cats around, with a bass, a synthesizer bass, or guitar, or keyboard, where I can talk to them as we're recording and say, "Play this now, lay out here, come in strong here, add this part there." If I can do that really quickly, it will become a hit really fast, but if you take too long, you lose the hit. And it goes on now for the singers too, if you take too long with a singer, you can blow it too, you've got to jump on it and seize it, because I'll tell you, if you fool around, you lose it. The singer's got to feel like, "Oh my God, something really important's happening," you almost have to move so fast that their mind can't participate. "Do another take here, please do another take here, do it again, do it again, that was great, wonderful, one more take please," and it goes so fast that it springs this genius out of them. But you go slow, it becomes tedious, like work, and now they're not into it as much, and don't sound into it. But if you can go really quick, out can slip the spirit and the soul, and you know you're getting things that are really dazzling, so I find the baddest shit comes when you're fast, and efficient and inspired! And they feel that heat of inspiration, and before you know it, it's just flowing out like diamonds, but if you take all day to do it, they can't hang on that long. Don't forget singing is a muscle, so when you're sharp, you've got to jump on it!

> I put that nasty, kind of street chicken grease on that bass line, so it sounded like Motown would have done, or Steve Cropper would have done, or Gerry Germont at

Atlantic would have done, but not pretty. We had that kind of skip in the front, those little skips make a person think "Oh, it's R&B, it's old R&B meets now," so those little things trigger the mind to think "Oh, it's a smash!" Especially when you have a strong hook: "I knew you were waiting, I knew you were waiting for me," but what makes it new are the guitar parts, because I had the guitarist playing guitar bits that were kind of a new European kind of a thing, and we sampled chimes so you'd have chimes ringing in the song. Then the drum track itself isn't just drums, it might be Simmons drums or electronic-triggered drums, so it sounds old but new! I always had this combination of kind of old-meets-new, that way you really can't fail, because you've got something that you already love with a thing that's new to it. What is that? That means you're going to shock them a little bit, because they don't know quite what it is.

While the producer had a well-established working rapport with Franklin from their previous studio successes together, with George Michael it would be the first time for both and, the producer would soon discover, among the first times George had been produced by anyone other than himself. Highlighting a common challenge for producers working with veteran artists who have established recording routines, in having to coach a specific vocal performance that might challenge those norms, Walden found that

George is such a perfectionist that, on his first day of recording, he wasn't used to having a producer tell him anything because he produces his own records, and I think the only other time he'd had a producer was on the "Save the World" Christmas song. So here I am trying to tell him, "George, try this, try that," and he wasn't used to having a producer, so he says, "Go back over my early track," and I said, "No George, your earlier tracks are the keepers, what I really love, and I'll comp the best bits together and make a smash." And he looks at me like, "Who are you to tell me what you're not going to do, I'm saying go over those earlier tracks," and I said, "No, I'm not going to do that." So we had a little bit of a struggle, but then he said "Okay, you're the producer, go ahead and I'll trust you."

So he went home and I comped together the best bits that I loved from his earlier tracks, which were flawless, his early takes were badass. But you know, when you're going into the studio to sing with Aretha Franklin, you get nervous, so you think "The more you do, the better it's going to get," but that's not always true. There's a thing called "diminishing returns," where you think you can do better, but you really know your early takes were your best because they were fresh and flawless. And without those early tracks, the song wouldn't have been the same as it was, so I'm so glad I stuck to my guns on that, and I'm sure he's happy about that too.

I think a producer is a coach, there's different kinds of producers, though, but the kind of producer I am is definitely a coach. My job is just to record things and get things on tape, and recognize when "God walks through the room," as Quincy Jones always says, because you want to catch that magic, and if you get the magic early on, then recognize you get the magic early on. If you're not getting the magic early on, get it, do whatever you have to do to inspire that person to go beyond themselves, to let the sky open up, where now something magical's happening. And that will happen pretty soon within your first hour or two if you just let them go crazy, and I've learned a technique: you record the ending first, the scat and crazy things that you really need to get going, get all that stuff first before you get too technical on a verse. Because when you start getting technical on a verse, then the spirit kind of calms down, and then if you want to get the outro, you won't be able to get it the same way. So get anything you need, the fireworks, get that pretty fast on, and then from that firework, you can kind of take that same spirit and energy and put it anywhere else you need, but if you wait on that kind of thing, you may never get it.

The vocal mics on that song were primarily an SM-7 and the C-12, the SM-7, a Shure mic, the reason I liked that mic was because it was a Michael Jackson mic that Quincy Jones used on Michael, and I also used it for Whitney Houston stuff. It's not a very expensive mic, but it can handle dynamic range for that person that wants to do that kind of soft, whispery verse stuff like "Like a warrior that fights, and wins the battle, I know the taste of victory . . ." So it can handle light, but can also handle when Aretha starts screaming, it can handle it and doesn't get all distorted. So I like the SM-7 for that, and the C-12, it's an old tube mic, and the C-24 because it has dual capsules, that mic can also handle dynamic range, which you have to have for Aretha Franklin, Whitney Houston, George Michael. Those are soul singers that want to get intimate, but also then can explode at any minute, so you don't want distortion to happen.

I recorded Aretha first, just doing her basic bits, but not doing any of the ending stuff yet, then George flew in from London to do his basic bits, and then the third day, they came into the studio and met each other for the first time, and then did the outro bits to the song together. Those were done together, and Aretha was trying to be all nice, kind of not scaring him, and then all of a sudden I remember she rears back and sings this shit that just floored him, where he couldn't sing anymore! He was stunned, like a knockout blow in the boxing ring, and I kept them on the record.

Delving a bit more deeply for fans into his master songwriting craft for writing/producing hit singles, Walden began with some simple pointers, starting with the fact that

whenever I'm writing, back then or now, I keep a tape recorder and when a song idea came, would hit record on the piano right then, or guitar and sing it out, whatever you can do, before you forget it, because if you sleep on it, it will go away. I also tell people to write down song titles. I once told someone to write down seven song titles, all seven became songs for her record, and one became a smash called "I Love Your Smile."

The main thing to a hit songwriting formula is having a strong chorus. If you have a strong chorus, then you don't have to care as much about your verses, your bridges and all that other stuff, if the chorus hook is strong. If you can imagine that you can sing this chorus in a big stadium, and everyone will sing along with you, that's the magic right there. So I write the chorus first. I always write the chorus first, because it's like a joke, you want to write the punch line, then how you get to the punch line you always change, but if your punch line's weak, why are you even messing with it? Because the chorus is where people can memorize and latch onto, so if the chorus is weak, forget it. If you can imagine radios playing it over and over and over again and not getting tired of it, as a producer, to craft it so it sounds interesting enough so there's always something a person can hear in there if they listen to it for the twentieth time, then that chorus really has all the elements it needs. Number one, it still has legs, it's going to be on the hits ten, twelve weeks because it's still interesting.

The reason I'm being hired as a producer is to bring that company a hit, that's my only role in being there, is to hopefully make an artist deliver his or her best performance, and bring that company a smash, otherwise they'll go to somebody else. Naturally, I want them to come to me, so I take it very seriously, study what hits are, and what the current trend is: is the current trend using handclaps or not handclaps? Is the current trends using a New Jack City swing hip-hop beat or more Euro? What's the UK doing? Is America onto what the UK is doing, or are they too far ahead of the curve with techno pop? What's America about right now? Well, America's more about a house sound coming out of Chicago, so you have to kind of know what the Top 10's about, where it's going, and what's happening. It's a science brother, it's a science.

Jermaine Stewart's "We Don't Have to Take Our Clothes Off" would give Walden another of his biggest radio staples, still played in regular rotation on pop radio today. Cowritten by Walden, the clever chorus preached the same type of positive message that the producer had become identified with over the course of his fountain of infectious, upbeat hits throughout the years, and "Clothes Off" was no exception. Walden recalled the radio smash as

a great song. I wrote it with Preston Glass, who I adore, and Jermaine was the right person to bring that song home. We had just opened our studio in 1985, and he was one of the first artists to come in here, along with Clarence Clemons—who was a good friend of mine—but Jermaine Stewart, Clive Davis had me do that song, and I was so honored to work with Jermaine because he was a big star. And we had so much fun, and so much vibrance and life at that session.

Preston at the time would write me four or five songs, and that was one that I heard on one of those cassette tapes and I thought, "This one we could take and blow it out," by taking the idea that Preston put down and really just giving it the full-on treatment. And I loved that he was saying, "We don't have to take our clothes off, and have a good time, we can dance and party all night, after some cherry wine." I loved the thing about cherry wine, so we had a lot of fun making that kind of record at the time, and blowing it up with a big beat and a lot of gusto. Jermaine, like Michael Jackson, was a great dancer, so I was really keen to make sure it really fit him, because he could be a great dancer and just go crazy with that kind of record, much like I would do if I was producing Michael Jackson.

Walden also found success during the height of the 1980s writing for film, including being tapped for the coveted honor of writing/producing the James Bond theme song for 1989's *Licence to Kill*. This was a specialized style of songwriting that the producer remembered he began without an idea past the concept for the film franchise of what the director wanted. Walden recalled that

people would just call and say they wanted a hit for their movie so I never got a script ahead of time, and with the James Bond *Licence to Kill* film, how are you going to make that movie title a hit? It's quite difficult, but I remember I went and sat down at the piano and smashed out something old school, like the classic old James Bond theme, so as soon as people hear it, they think "Okay, James Bond." But then you put a new part to it: "I've got a license to kill, anyone who tries to take you from me, I have a license to kill, anyone that would try to break your heart . . ." So that's how I thought I would make a hit out of it. "I have a license to kill anyone who would tear us apart," you put some of that with the original James Bond theme (starts singing melody), then you add a big old track with cool, big-ass drums, a big symphony and all that, and bam! Once again, it's about the chorus, so with almost anything I ever did, I would think about what the chorus was first, and how to make that a hit, then I go into bridges and verses and all that other stuff. But if you have a strong chorus on any one of those themes, because that's what the company want, is a vehicle to get out into the world that people can latch on to publicize the movie, making money for the movie. So I'm thinking more from a very A-B head space: how can I take this title and blow it out? Almost like a challenge, "I DARE you to make a hit out of license to kill?" (laughs)

Walden would enter the 1990s at the top of his game, receiving a call in 1992 from Whitney Houston that would wind up earning him an "Album of the Year" Grammy for his production work on the forty-five-million-selling *The Bodyguard* soundtrack album. Teaming up once again with Houston, also the film's costar, and at that point arguably the biggest female pop star in the world alongside Madonna, Walden remembered feeling relieved that the singer had selected the song they would be recording together for the film's soundtrack, the opposite of his experience working with other recording stars where

many times, I've had to go to the artist, and say, "Clive loves the song, and it's a great song," but I have to convince the artist to get inspired to sing the thing, which doesn't take too long once they start hearing themselves singing, then they can marry it. But it is nice when it goes the other way around, and they're already inspired by a song that they love and want a new tribute for it, a new version for it, a new arrangement, so I thought that was very nice. Whitney was very smart, she was very keen, she always had an idea of what she wanted to do, and on that soundtrack, Whitney asked me to cover "I'm Every Woman," and I had to first ask myself what was a hot way to do it? What was hot in the clubs, what was hot to really make that come to life again, because Chaka Khan had already had a smash with it back in the day. I wanted to make it a smash for Whitney. I remember she was nine months pregnant when she came into the studio to sing it, and she tried her very best to do homage to the way Chaka Khan had done it, because she loved Chaka Khan so much. So she did all the perfect harmonies that Chaka had done, and for me, I wanted to make it more disco/dance so it would be contemporary with everything else at the time, and God blessed us with a number one record and Album of the Year. I was very honored to be on that album, and I remember standing onstage with Whitney when we won that Grammy, and she turned to me and said, "Narada, we did it, we won Album of the Year!" I've never seen her as happy as that moment, when we were on the stage all together, and it was such a big deal, she was the one who actually asked me to cut that song. That's always an honor when the artist comes to me personally to ask me to produce them. I always like that because then I feel they're engaged, and when they're engaged, then it's beautiful.

Looking back from the ironic perspective of still hearing many of his heyday hits on modern pop radio stations in regular rotation, the timeless touch of Walden's talent begins to emerge, hitting the producer closest to his heart in the powerful fact that

I think the rewards are the success that people love it and are buying it, you're getting platinum records and all that, but absolutely hearing things on the radio, and that Whitney made such wonderful videos, her videos were extraordinary. I was actually in the video for "So Emotional" playing drums with my band, so it was nice to be in the video just kind of reenacting what we'd recorded with her. Just having fun with everything and being able to participate in the success of it, I love all of that.

I loved working with Aretha Franklin after her father had passed away, a song called "Until You Say You Love Me," and because it was the first thing I ever recorded with her, it was very precious to me, and she was very tender and very sensitive, and I massaged her back very, very tender, very soft, and she sang it so incredible. Again, I was very inspired by Prince, the sound of "Beautiful Ones" on *Purple Rain*, where I actually recorded the drums going twice the speed, and then slowed the whole track down, so it sounds very heavy and very ethereal. So that track is very dear to me.

Quite frankly, everything I do I really love, because I put my heart into it. So they're all my babies, I love them all.

CHAPTER 5

Hysteria–Mike Shipley

Most every genre with rock 'n' roll has a producer who has defined and often designed its sound in the mold of their own vision: Berry Gordy with the Motown sound that defined R&B in the late 1960s and '70s; Phil Spector's "Wall of Sound" in the 1960s; George Martin with the Beatles' British Invasion; Quincy Jones throughout the 1980s with Michael Jackson's dominant brand of pop; and in hard rock and heavy metal, Robert "Mutt" Lange has held the throne for the past thirty-five years. Beginning with the hard-rock blueprint he established over the course of producing AC/DC's two biggest-selling albums—1978's *Highway to Hell* and 1980's *Back in Black* (moving an astonishing twenty-two million copies and ranked as the sixth best-selling album of all time in the United States)—Lange continued his reign in the '80s, perhaps most seminally, via his pioneering production of Def Leppard's *Pyromania* and legendary *Hysteria* LPs. The latter album would reinvent metal's production possibilities forever and open rock and metal fans' ears to what *Guitar World* deemed "one of the more forward-thinking, over-the-top and ultimately successful albums in rock history."

The right-hand man to rock's equivalent of the Wizard of Oz behind the curtain and console, Shipley partnered in recording making and breaking in terms of sales and sonics for the better part of thirty-five years, beginning with their first fateful encounter when

I was working at Wessex Studios back in the late '70s, and Mutt had pretty much just come from South Africa, and he was somewhat new. He'd been around a little bit before I got there, doing bands like the Boomtown Rats, and he worked at Wessex a lot and holed up there, and was one of those producers who worked very intensely and very fast, and you had to be able to keep up. We were working on a 24 track, and his productions in those days were huge, so you had to be able to punch in and out and do things fast, and read the minds of people like him on "What's going to happen next?," and be out there and mic something up and wanted that kind of stuff to be done fast and furious and accurately, and I was lucky to be able to work with him.

Leading up to that first encounter, Shipley had known from the moment he'd first stepped into a recording studio control room that he'd found his calling, sharing his childhood memory that

I'm from Australia, but my family moved over to England for a few years for my dad's business, and I went to a private school in England and one of my school teachers was a musician and he invited me down to a recording studio near Wembley when I was thirteen years old, and basically, the moment I walked into the studio, I thought, "Wow, this is home!" Between the studio and the control room, the energy between the two rooms was so amazing, I was just electrified by it. It was like "That was it, this place is incredible," and I was done. From that moment on, from the age of thirteen, my whole mission was to go back to England, because I'd always been a total music fan and would wait outside the record stores for all the English magazines to come out, *Melody Maker, NME*, to find out what albums were coming out, and would always be the first person in line because I was a total music nut.

Shipley found he had an ear not only as a listener but as a musician too, a skill set that would come in handy in later years working alongside Lange and his now-legendary obsession with getting perfect drum sounds, a pursuit that began in Shipley's early teens when

I was a drummer, so I was always intrigued by drum sounds, like Keith Moon, John Bonham, Phil Brewster, and I was very much into rhythm—drums and bass—and drum sounds in a big way. Everything else is great too, but drum sounds have always been a really important and impressive thing to me. Back in the day, I was a huge Zeppelin fan, I was a huge fan of the Who, the Kinks, early King Crimson, those more progressive-type rock bands, but the mainstay back then were English rock bands. I was a huge fan of Andy and Glyn Johns, Ken Scott, all those amazing, great great English out-of-the-box record makers.

With his professional path already chosen for him based on that first studio visit, the producer remembered feeling thankful for his parents' support of his passion, clearing the path

> after my studio visit in England, to finish up my education back in Australia as quick as possible, and I high-tailed it back to Britain.

Rather than randomly knocking on studio doors around London looking for any gig he could land, Shipley had his sights already set on legendary Wessex Studios, a hit factory he recalled

> I knew very well because I was a huge, huge, huge Queen fan, and knew that they worked out of that studio, and had heard through a friend of mine just by coincidence that they needed somebody really fast. One of the assistants at the studio had gotten ill and had left, and this friend of mine just happened to know the studio manager, and also chief engineer Bill Price told me to call him.
>
> So he said, "We don't want to go through tons of interviews, if you can find our interview which is kind of out of the way, and get here in the next hour, we'll interview you," so I got over there, and met with Bill Price, who is one of the consummate producer/engineers I think of all time, and was lucky enough to get the job.
>
> In those days, it's not like it is these days where you can be a runner for X amount of years before you get into the studio, in those days, you were basically given a couple of weeks to learn the ropes and you were in the session. In England, there were lots of tea boys, but luckily at Wessex, we had Bessie the tea lady, so it was brilliant, she was an absolute character and every band loved her. So purely by coincidence, that's how Bill ran the studio, you pretty much got to learn the ropes and went straight in. Leading up to that, I'd had a very little bit of training at a smaller 8-track studio in Melbourne on the weekends, but this was the first big thing, and it was a big thing because I was thrown in the deep end.

Quickly confirming he was not only on the right path but in the right place at the right time, Shipley would run into his favorite band in the world and be thrown into the middle of the making of what would become punk rock's most notorious album/band all in his first week on the job, shaking his head in still-amazement over the fact that

> Queen was actually in the studio mixing the first week I was there, and the first record I got thrown into was the Sex Pistols' *Never Mind the Bullocks* working with Chris Thomas.

Where other kids his age were chasing girls around pubs or university campuses, Shipley was 100 percent committed to learning his craft from week one in the studio, with his education coming courtesy not of college professors but rather some of Britain's finest rock producers and a fraternity of punk rockers who, behind their rebellious and reckless public image, in the studio, Mike found to in fact be serious musicians who were also

sort of learning as they went, with the help of Chris Thomas too. Sid Vicious was in and out of the studio because he was in the hospital a couple times when he got ill, so while Glen Matlock played a lot of the bass, Sid was around too. Sid was a very simple player, but he was musical, as was the rest of the band. *Never Mind the Bullocks* was a lengthy, involved record and it stopped and started, and went on for quite some time, and was something musically that, for me, being more of a rock head, it was like "What is this??" It really was the first of that type of music, and was just staggering and an incredible experience: getting chased from the pub by Hells Angels, and all kinds of funny stuff went on.

At the same time, Bill Price was very good at showing me different kinds of techniques, different ways to mic things up. It was an incredible experience. In those days, people like Bill Price and Matt Thompson, who was a very old-school excellent, excellent engineer, and both guys were—if you were willing, and had a question—very good at sometimes stopping a session and showing you how it worked. For instance, I was working with Bill when we were doing some stuff on a Pete Townsend record, and I was asking about the overhead mics and why he miced something up a certain way, and while the band was rehearsing for a song, he'd say, "Okay guys, I'm going to come out and change something," and he'd change the overheads into a different position or use different mics and record a take, play it back, and show me the difference. So it was interesting because he would go to that length if you were that keen to show you different mic techniques and so forth. He was a fantastic person and a great mentor, and had a fantastic wealth of knowledge.

After working with the Sex Pistols, I assisted on a few records and then the Damned came in, and that's when I got to engineer for the first time, and did the bulk of that *Machine Gun Etiquette* record, and mixed a lot of it. That was pretty exciting because, again, I was going in the deep end, but it was a lot of fun, a lot of fun. It was trial by fire, because you didn't have time to stop and think, you just had to go for it.

After seriously impressing "Mutt" Lange during their first studio encounters engineering albums by lesser-known groups of the late '70s like City Boy, where Shipley recalled "we kind of took a liking to each other and he saw I was able to keep up, and I worked pretty much exclusively with him at Wessex for a while," the young engineer's seminal break came

one day when he said, "I'm going to build my own studio, and I want you to take care of it. I'm going to be off overseas for some time doing some work." He took over an old studio called Morgan Studios, and told me "You'll be the chief engineer, and you'll be in charge of revamping it," and here's me at nineteen or twenty with this opportunity. Again, I knew nothing about acoustics, I knew nothing about anything to do with that, so it was a bit experimental, and I got Pete O'Keefe, the guy who'd built A.I.R. and worked at Wessex to help redesign the studio.

At the time, there was a Cadac console in there, which was great, so we used that for a period of time, and then Mutt said, "Okay, we're redesigning, go for it," and they recommended we put in an MCI, but I kind of went around them a little bit because I'd found an advertisement for a new SSL console that they'd been building out of Aicorn Studios. I remember thinking "If Mutt knew about this, he'd want it," so I kind of went against what they had suggested and pretty much went for the SSL blind, because there was only a couple around of the E-series. Mutt was very excited when he saw what it could do, with the computer and so forth. In those days, it was very advanced and was phenomenal.

Shipley demonstrated an early example of what would prove in time to be a wildly accurate and successful instinct—technically and sonically—for knowing how to act as Mutt's most trusted ambassador toward their mutual end of achieving the sounds Lange first heard in his head. Highlighting the Cars' *Heartbeat City* as among Shipley's favorite later examples of that creative telepathy, the engineer recalled that, following his and the producer's laborious work together on Def Leppard's *Pyromania* LP,

I had actually moved back to Australia at that point for family reasons, and Mutt had started mixing the album and spent I think quite a few weeks trying to work on certain songs, and he was not well. Nigel Green, the engineer who had been working with him, was not that well either because they'd both been working so hard, and the band was getting a little frustrated. So in the end, I came over to England to work on it with Mutt, and we again spent a certain amount of time trying to mix the songs, and Mutt kept asking "Is there a console big enough in this country to mix this record on? I think the only place big enough to mix this record on is in New York, so today's Thursday, Friday can you get on a plane, fly to New York, and mix it at Electric Lady?"

So I was like, "Okay," got on a plane with these multitracks and arrived at the studio thinking they had this large console, and when I turned up at the studio, the owner was going to lunch, and I wanted to go upstairs and get a look at the console. And he says, "No, no, no, it's all good, come out to lunch with us," and I told him I wasn't hungry, I'd just gotten off the plane, and wanted to go up and see where I was going to be working, but I begrudgingly went to lunch with the owner. Well, we came back, went up to the studio, and it was not as described to Mutt on the phone by the studio owner, so I had to wait in New York for two and a half weeks while they built the control room to Mutt's specifications, so to speak.

That was a hard record to mix, because the control really wasn't set up correctly, so what I was hearing really wasn't what was happening, so I had a very funky version of a new Neve console that didn't work anywhere near as creatively as an SSL, so I was kind of painted into a corner. So we basically ended up where Rik and the band said, "Listen, you've got to slash through this stuff, we're used to working fast," and I set up the best that I could and spent a day and a half basically on what Mutt would have spent two or three weeks per song. I would get it done fast and do the best that I could. They told me to get it done as fast as I could, so I did.

Considering Lange in many ways his greatest mentor—especially in the arena of mixing, where Mike would later become as equally known as he was for his engineering prowess behind the boards—in reviewing some of the key lessons he learned from Mutt, Shipley began with the concept of "depth of field," explaining that

whenever we were mixing, regardless of the band or style of genre, we just kind of went for what seemed to be the right thing to do. So you listen to the song, and go "Okay, this is what it needed to be like," and go for that. It's always been a gut thing as well as a technical thing, and making as much space, and not really working about any rules or regulations about EQ and what backgrounds should sound like or what drums should sound like. It's about carving out the space so things could be intentionally soft but still very audible or whatever, because it's still about depth of field as well as everything being in your face. So you just need to carve out the right space for the instrument, and that's something Mutt taught me how to do and you'd end up doing by second nature. It was one of those things that was experimental, but he just would a place for it, have a sound in your head, and make it work.

The beginning of Lange's true renaissance where perfecting the latter concept was concerned had begun with the producer's long-term collaboration with Def Leppard in the early 1980s. While he'd helped AC/DC perfect their hard-rock template by making what *Rolling Stone* surmised "might be the leanest and meanest record of all time" in sonic terms, with the Leppard records, Lange had far more sophisticated ambitions for their soundscape. Knowing he was signing up for the fight of his engineering life with the ambitions driving Lange's vision for the band, Shipley signed on for his first tour of duty making 1981's *High and Dry*, which produced breakout hits like "Bringing on the Heartbreak" and "Let It Go."

Helping the band, their fans, and critics alike hear their true potential come to life on record for the first time, courtesy of production that left nothing to mediocrity, on their next studio collaboration, Lange would push that pursuit of excellence to the extreme. Refining in the process a template where *Rolling Stone* argued the producer successfully "set precedents for commercially astute songwriting and sheer studio ambition (the massive yet airy vocal harmonies, philharmonic layers of guitar) without compromising the basic thump," Shipley confirmed that heading into production on *Pyromania*, the producer had a vision so grand for the band's sound it was literally cinematic. Rooted in a groundbreaking concept for the album's drum sound that was revolutionary for metal at the time, Shipley revealed of their initial preproduction conversations that

> Mutt's whole thing was: "Kids these days don't want to hear honky little snare drums. They're all out watching *Star Wars* and having visual experiences, so let's make these records like that, rather than going the natural route, let's make something a little bit larger than life!"

Proving in many ways to be the album's most complicated terrain to navigate as they were exploring it for the first time as they created, Shipley began his recollections of the journey that followed by explaining that

> on the previous record, *High and Dry*, that was recorded with real drums and on *Pyromania*, Mutt wanted to be experimental and leave the drums to the very end because he would keep changing the arrangements, so therefore the drum parts would need to keep changing. So we had to figure out how to synch that whole thing up, and it was on the cutting edge, but somehow we managed to put it all together.

Working backwards from the traditional way records were made at the time, this unconventional philosophy would soon spread to every musical facet of *Pyromania*, with the engineer pointing to the album's biggest hit, "Photograph," as one prominent example where

> even when that song was about to be mixed, Mutt had decided to change the chorus, because songs would evolve, and he'd want that process not to be stopped and he wanted to have control over till the last minute of what the feel was going to be of the song. Rather than commit to the drums, and have to recut them and recut them and recut them, he thought that was a better way to do it, and again, it was experimental. I don't think anyone had done it before, but we decided to give it a shot—scary as it was—we just went on blind faith. So it was more about being able to change the arrangements at the last minute, which was very important to him.

Taking fans back to the beginnings of the song's lengthy evolution in the studio—with a focus on the construction of its driving drum track—to illustrate the team's experimental hybrid model of recording and importing live drum kit sounds into a cutting-edge digital sampling synthesizer for the purposes of manipulating them in any direction Lange desired, Shipley recalled that

"Photograph," like all the other songs on the record, was all samples from the Fairlight, there's no real drums. The cymbals are played, but the bass drum, snare, and toms are all machine. We had all kinds of drums in there, and I sampled them into the Fairlight, detuned them, and we'd sample them in at half-speed thinking that we'd get a better sound, because that's when Fairlight was at 8 bit, so you had to get around that part of it. So we sampled Black Beauty snares, and all kinds of bass drums and snares, and ended up with something that Mutt liked that we could detune a little bit.

When we were sampling in the sounds, we used KM-84s, we used 58s, there were so many mics. The toms were primarily Simmons toms back then, which were primarily electronic, and we experimented and EQ'ed and mangled the sound up a little bit and came up with that drum sound, which was pretty unnatural, but that was kind of the point.

The Fairlight over the course of the album would, in essence, become another member of the band, serving as an R2-D2 of sorts in helping to guide the futuristic-feeling process from start to finish, all while Mutt and Mike worked within what the engineer felt were the console-related constraints of

recording *Pyromania* on 24 track, and we spent a lot of months on that record. But by the time it came to mixing, it was peeling off in 2-inch pieces, to the point where the tape was clear by the intensity of working on a record like that, and going over and over and over, blocking out backgrounds and changing arrangements and all that kind of stuff, I'm surprised we ever got it finished, because the tape literally fell to pieces, literally fell to pieces. It was experimental because we were using a Fairlight trying to synch that whole thing up and work like that, and hadn't figured out till the end how we were going to do the drums.

Pushing technology as far as Lange was the band at the same time, Shipley remembered feeling a deep admiration for his bandmates' patience and persistence as they collectively chased their producer's vision. He confessed that at points throughout the sessions

it was hard, there were certain points where it got very hard, because Steve Clarke and those guys were used to going in and just laying it down. But Mutt's brilliant as a diplomat, which worked as a strength for him at a certain point because of the length of time, but it was hard for Joe because of how much Mutt would work on the vocals, but they understood he had a great vision and that everything was coming out great. So it was tough for them at the same time as being great for them.

One element of the album's sound that Lange and the band had gotten to work on right away was refining to perfection a guitar sound *Entertainment Weekly* would write was "powered by muscular metal riffs," an arena where Shipley felt the band was greatly aided by the fact that Lange was himself an accomplished rock guitarist. Lange's ability to relate to and communicate with the band's members on a key level often reserved only for engineers and producers who are themselves musicians would prove pivotal to the process as he quickly discovered that

> because of the nature of the way that band played and the inversions they used, it was very hard to get right what Mutt had in his head as "commercial distortion." It sounded not great with distortion, so we had hundreds of amps and cabinets in that studio, from AC/DC amps to little combos to big stacks, everything you could think of. So we spent weeks and weeks trying to get what was a commercial sound for those inversions rather than the crunchy, distorted sound, and I'm pretty sure we ended up with just a little small, Marshall combo after we'd tried everything. It's funny, because after a while, you get so fatigued, that nothing ever sounds good enough, but we had to start recording at a certain point, so we found a good combination that worked, and used condenser mics, 87s and 67s, on the amplifiers.

Turning from guitars to another of Lange's signature sound achievements, and one that would become one of the band's, that of Def Leppard's legendary harmony vocal blends, the task of creating this wall of vocal sound would prove a truly an epic one, beginning with Shipley's at times tortured memories of recording literally hundreds of backing vocal tracks. A key melodic element of the band's broader melodic musical formula and fascinating insight into Lange's perfectionist nature as a producer, his methodology began with the premise that

> in order to keep the distinction away from lead vocals, the backgrounds were usually Mutt, Rick Savage, and he would try to get everybody involved. So he would do twenty or forty tracks of one part, then dump down twenty tracks onto one track, then do twenty more tracks and dump them down onto another track to make up a stereo pair, then they'd add the backgrounds to that part and then bounce them down two tracks, and then hand-synch them back into the choruses and so forth. That kind of process, then we EQ'd them and bounced them onto a 2-track machine, and then I'd have to get the timing right, hit the play button, and keep going till we got the timing right and slide them in.

For as hard as he pushed the band's backing vocalists, Shipley remembered the producer pushing his star player in that lineup, lead vocalist Joe Elliot, even more intensely, recalling that throughout the exhausting exercise,

> Joe was an excellent sport, because Mutt was very, very hard core about the lead

vocal, very much so, and we'd spend the longest time on the vocals, and Joe would get frustrated about it at certain points but was an excellent sport. It was very hard for him, he'd have terrible headaches and stuff because Mutt was just relentless about it, and Joe was fantastic. We used a 67 pretty much for everything vocally on *Pyromania*.

Once the producer had completed the bulk of vocal recording and began the equally meticulous process of manipulating the multiple stacks of lead and backing vocal tracks more individually with effects treatments, an art form unto itself was revealed, one where not surprisingly,

Mutt always had specific ideas about delays, and we just had to figure out how to create them, so on Joe's lead vocals, I know we used all kinds of delay lengths, long delays, and they might have been created by the tape machine because there wasn't that much long-delay outboard gear out yet back then. I remember after that record came out, the AMS came out. The reverbs were usually regular EMT 140 plate reverbs, which we had four of at that studio, in a plate room.

We also used to use a lot of the old, original Lexicon delays. I remember this huge box, and the other delays we'd use would be multitrack delays, and where you'd make up the delay length by going into different channels in multitrack to get different delay amounts, and we didn't use mic-pre(s) or anything like that, we just used what was in the SSL. We used the flanger, and a couple of 2-track tape delays.

Even as attentions finally began to turn to mixing, the days only seemed to grow longer, especially for Shipley, who—sitting loyally side by side at the console with Lange—remembered the two of them running themselves ragged

working eighteen hour days, seven days a week for that whole record. This kind of commitment was necessary because Mutt wanted big, he wanted larger than life on everything, and they're all very lengthy records to mix, a lot of time was taken, more than what most people would think, especially later on in terms of records like *Hysteria*. We spent a long time, and if it wasn't working, we'd just start again, and given those machine sounds, it was really quite difficult, so we were so lost in the process. We had an end vision in sight, and I would just work and work and work, and Mutt wanted to make things as three-dimensional as possible sonically.

To everyone's collective relief, upon release in January 1983, the record would do just that, equivalent to NASA successfully launching a man onto the moon in terms of the new heights the album took the band—and rock—toward. *Billboard* would give credit to both the band for their "newly intensified focus on melody and consistent songwriting" and "to Robert John 'Mutt' Lange's buffed-to-a-sheen production—polished drum and guitar sounds, multi-tracked layers of vocal harmonies, a general sanding of any and all musical rough edges, and a perfectionistic attention to detail." Concluding that the collective accomplishment "set the style for much of the melodic hard rock that followed," acting as "the catalyst for the '80s pop-metal movement," Shipley revealed that the rocket almost didn't take flight, recalling what in hindsight he regards as

a funny story: at the time, it freaked both me and Mutt out because we'd mixed that record, and the way Mutt worked was, there was never any involvement from the labels. It was always because he didn't like involvement from people, he just wanted to do his own thing, and I remember as we finished that record, and literally, as the tape degraded, so did the sonics to certain parts. For instance, the background vocals were played earlier, and rebounced, and rebounced, and the first time we mastered *Pyromania*, we mastered it in England, and the mastering engineer sent it back saying "Mutt, this record is unmasterable." And Mutt looked at me with this look like "Oh my God, what have you done?" So then, we sent it off to Bob Ludwig after that, and he said, "This is ground-breaking, this is amazing, this is brilliant," so fortunately, we went from "This record is terrible and unmasterable" to Bob being able to master it and it is what it is.

Ultimately producing four Top 20 singles in both Britain and the United States with the seminal "Photograph" (#12), "Too Late for Love" (#9), "Foolin'" (#9), and arguably the most famous pop-culturally, "Rock of Ages" (#16), *Pyromania* would peak at #2 on the *Billboard* Top 200 albums chart, selling seven million copies and becoming "the mainstream metal sound of the Eighties," according to *Rolling Stone*.

Rather than running right back into the studio following a wildly successful, sold-out arena tour around the world, the band suffered a tragic loss when drummer Rick Allen's left arm was severed in a near-fatal car accident on December 31, 1984. Looking past this limitation toward what would ultimately become the next horizon in his and the band's reinvention of what had been the accepted rock drum norms up to that time in the mid-1980s, over the next two years, this production prototype would be perfected.

Becoming what *Rolling Stone* called "in fact, the sixth Leppard," *Hysteria* would cement producer Mutt Lange's position as "a genre master . . . (as) this LP is thick with his trademarks: the deep, meaty bass sound; the fat, relentless drums; the dazzling guitar montages; the impeccable sense of structure and separation; the preternatural clarity." The journey to that eventual height, among recording studio lore, has become the stuff of legend. While much of the album's mixing was completed during initial sessions with engineer Nigel Green in Holland, Shipley elected to take a well-deserved break from engineering to further hone his growing reputation as one of rock's hottest album mixers, showcased on a stylistically diverse spread of popular albums including the Cars' aforementioned *Heartbreak City*, Devo's *Shout*, Thomas Dolby's *The Flat Earth*, and Berlin's #1 hit "Take My Breath Away." He even found time to polish his production résumé at the helm of Joni Mitchell's 1985 *Dog Eat Dog* LP before being called back to the console by Mutt in 1986.

Once he joined back up with Mutt for "mixing," which in reality was another stage of recording for Lange with his continuous revisiting to stacks upon stacks of vocal, drum, guitar, and synthesizer tracks, if the producer by then had become the *sixth* Beatle in Def Leppard, then Mike Shipley had assumed the role of the seventh. This was based in part on the thousands of hours he sat behind the console alongside Lange slaving over every minute detail of each drum hit, guitar lick, harmony vocal among stacks of thirty and forty per part, and every other nuance that made Def Leppard's *Hysteria* among the most sonically celebrated albums of all time. This quintessential album "spearheaded a new strain of hard rock" according to legendary *Guitar World*, "one that favored lush vocal harmonies, shimmering, highly melodic guitars and intricate layers of sound over pile-driving riffs and distorted power chords. If the term pop metal was at the time being tagged onto bands as something of an insult, *Hysteria* was in a sense a reclamation of the label, and also a perfectly realized example of just what the style could offer." As he rolled up his sleeves and prepared to get down to work, Shipley confirmed that

> when I say mix it, all of the multitracks were guitars and vocals, there was no drums and bass, it was just a very, very, very basic Linn drum 16th-note hi-hat or just some very basic guide drum part. So the drums and bass were all written in the mix, all the bass, all the drums, it was all done as part of the mix process, and therefore meant *getting the sounds*. So it was quite difficult because Mutt had been listening for quite some time to just guitars, maybe a rough bass, but literally no real drums or no sonic drums or bass parts at all. He'd just been concentrating on the guitars and vocals and arrangements, so it was very difficult to put in the drums—to do that very last of all, and do the bass last of all was a very monumental task.

Thankfully already familiar with Lange's ever-fluid creative process in the studio, as mixing turned quickly into another elaborate stage of recording, Shipley shared his memory of working day in and out sitting behind a labyrinth board that resembled a spaceship's control panel, confirming that

> we had the biggest console we could get in those days, which was 64-input SSL, the first one they ever built! We've always been on the cutting edge of consoles, and so with every console SSL came up with, we'd be guinea pigs. Mutt put the studio in his house so we had no distractions, and I think it took nine or ten months to mix

Hysteria, because we'd be redoing stuff and the whole drums and bass thing we'd spend months on songs sometimes, and redo it.

Playing a key role once again in constructing what became an epic final drum sound that *Billboard* would hail as "admirably ambitious . . . (and) ahead of its time," the engineer remembered the physical process as being just that, essentially an expansion of the routine they'd pioneered during *Pyromania* three years earlier where

> again, it was one of those things where I'd have a certain starting point, and the drums were in Fairlight, so I had the ability to mess around with the tuning of the snare. We wanted something fat and different, so once I had the sample, I could detune it, and we could experiment with detuning, and I found a nice fat brace that worked for Mutt once we'd EQ'd it, and it was down quite a lot from the original snare sample. So we used that for the basic snare sound, the same with the bass drum, we'd find something we liked and detune that, and over the snare, there were different samples that we layered. A white noise sample, an ambient sample, a Simmons sample, a sample of the harmonizer with the feedback still up, that kind of thing added length to the note, so we used multiple tricks to try and get a unique drum sound.

Spotlighting the creation of the rhythm track for now-legendary hit "Pour Some Sugar on Me" as a firsthand look behind the scenes and into a world where the application of effects was again pivotal in achieving the song's maximum potential as Lange had envisioned it, Shipley—now plugged into that vision—revealed that as he and the producer built the beat,

> I was working on the new version of the Fairlight, and I just brought samples I had sampled in Los Angeles and had also sampled in Mutt's studio in England to come up with a drum sound. And the basis of the bass samples I'd used from my friend in LA, as well, I was tuning them, hard core tuning, and adding the synthesizer stuff to the bass to give it a bit of a different sound. So for "Pour Some Sugar on Me" specifically, the samples all started out dry, and then we'd get into getting pretty detailed about gated reverbs and different kind of effects, whether it was hard-gated AMS-type stuff or gated tapes or whatever, of which we'd use various amounts, having triggers for length in the harmonizer. And there'd always be a delay on the snare that would come from a unit that could put out fast reflections, there would be delays, like twenty delays to different increments, just to give an interesting perspective that would add to the width of the snare. The hi-hat and cymbals were samples as well.

Not merely Lange's engineer, Shipley became the equivalent of a coproducer during this final ten-month stage of recording, reflective of the producer's innate trust by that point in his cohort's ability to translate the sounds he was aiming for not only accurately but also artistically. Adding compositional elements to Sugar's beatscape, for instance, the engineer revealed an intensely trusting side to his collaboration with the producer during times where

> Mutt would go and leave me for four or five days and say, "I'm going off for a few days, come up with a drum sound, figure some stuff out, and come up with something unique and different," and I learned to experiment and experiment and experiment, and figure out how to add to his stuff for the drums to make it different, whether it was huge handclaps to go along with it, which you can hear going on in "Pour Some Sugar on Me" big time. Those are actually one hundred tracks of handclaps detuned and EQ'd that ended up sounding like ambience in a way, definitely had a unique sound to it. So he'd say, "Okay, have at it, I'll come back in a few days, see where you are, and we'll go from there," that kind of thing, so that's how it kind of worked out.

For the song—and majority of the broader album's guitar sounds—vs. the perceived wall-of-amplifier approach common to that era of metal record making, in what was for the time another revolution in recording conventions, the engineer pulled the curtain back on the truth that

> ALL those guitars are from a Rockman! Not amps, every sound on that record, everything's a *Rockman*.

For this pioneering leap forward in headphone-based amplifier technology at the time it was developed and patented by Boston lead guitarist Tom Scholz, *Hysteria* would become among the first successful studio test-drives of the device outside of Scholz's own. The inventor, in a conversation with Gibson.com, offered the recording of his own material as an example of the Rockman's possibilities, explaining that in the late '80s "I could plug into a regular guitar amplifier and play you the lead part to 'Peace of Mind' or the rhythm to 'More Than a Feeling,' but to play the whole song would be impossible. You'd have to make a half-dozen changes in EQ, gain, output level, and effects, and there's no way to do that with standard amps. With the Rockman stuff, we can do anything we want. It's all programmable, and you can run through every sound you need while you play each song."

Shipley and Lange would run wild in the studio with the Rockman creating Def Leppard's next wave of guitar hero hits—including "Hysteria," whose "rich sound" MTV later noted was "the result of eleven guitar parts layered and woven together into a deceptively clean wall of sound"—primarily, in the engineer's estimation,

> because that's the only way we could get that kind of distortion. There might have

been a couple passes of clean guitar through a small amp, but most all of it was recorded playing through a Rockman. That meant an awful lot of EQing and an awful lot of processing, so all the clean sounds, all the jangly stuff, all the distorted guitars were all Rockman.

So it would get a bit irritating, because we'd try everything and just keep going till we found something that worked, and again, because we did it for so long, it never was that satisfying because we'd just look at each other after weeks of working on it, and just go "I guess this is the best we could do," and that was it. We'd work for days and days on delays and effects, and it was all done kind of cutting edge.

In keeping with the signature vocal blend he had first perfected with the band's previous album, when attentions were turned to creating the dazzling and dizzyingly brilliant symphony of lead and harmony vocal parts, beginning with the application of effects in this arena, Shipley described a galaxy of them flying around the songs, shaking his head in a moment of reflective astonishment at the fact that

as far as vocal effects, I can't even begin to recall how many AMS's we used, there were hamonizers, delays, reverbs, EQs for every different section, there were so many effects going on in the background. Long delays, short delays, from ones you could barely even hear just to add to the depth of field, and backwards reverbs . . . Boy, the kitchen sink really, everything we could think of.

Sticking to maintaining a separation between singer Joe Elliot's lead vocals and the personality of the band's harmony blends as they decorated the album's broader soundscape, the engineer explained it was necessary because

Mutt wanted to keep Joe's lead vocal distinct, so as we'd done with *Pyromania*, on *Hysteria*, the harmonies would be a combination of Mutt, Rick Savage, and Phil Collins, and they would work up a blend, and Mutt would dictate somewhat how the words would be or what the parts were. But those guys were excellent singers, so the three of them together would create the sound largely, and Mutt would do some on his own as well.

As attentions turned toward the final stages of mixing, days ran into weeks and weeks into months of sleepless days and nights chasing the dream of matching live the perfect sound Lange heard in his head. Well trained to pace himself in pursuing this dream, Shipley still acknowledged that due to Mutt's perfectionism,

it was incredibly taxing and very intense actually. It would be song by song, but with that kind of process, because we'd spend so long, it was not like doing a song in a

105

day and a half, and when you work that long, you're so overfamiliar with the sound, you're so kind of done with the sound, that it was very hard, and we'd just work away and almost abandon it at a certain point. We'd spend as long as we could spend, and there had to be a point where you'd put it down, a point where we'd messed around with every permutation of what it could possibly be; every possible direction conceptually—be it delays or treatments or bounces for the guitars, or vocals—where you became so overly familiar with the sound. It's a hard thing to explain because of the process, but there just came a point where it wasn't like "Oh yeah Man, we rocked this one," but more like "I guess we've done the best we can, we better put it down," because it's like "What else can you do?," we've tried everything. We knew that the song was great, but the mixing process was really, really hard.

A double-edged sword in terms of overexposure, Shipley remembered his patience being put to the test during

certain points where we would spend weeks on a mix, weeks, and obviously, the time involved would be a whole lot longer because we were inventing drum and bass sounds at the same time. But we'd get a mix to a point where Mutt would say "Okay, let's take it," then he would hear something and go "Hmmm, you know what, I think we need to kind of zero the board, and start again and see what we can do." So sometimes, the mixes would end up being four, five, or six weeks per song because he wanted something different, and wouldn't settle for anything but the best we could get.

Still, believing implicitly in Lange's vision and ability to persevere until it was realized, the team hung in, motivated by the fact that "the songs were so exciting," and as they made progress, Shipley began to hear more and more clearly that

it was one of those albums that had such a particular sound to it, that we had to stay that course till Mutt felt it was as perfect as it could be. In comparison to the way they make records today, we were very, very lucky back then to be able to experiment a whole lot. I'm definitely proud of that record.

"Hysteria" is precisely what most producers and musicians would have been driven to with the pressure Lange put the band under throughout the making of heavy metal's best-selling album of the 1980s. Understandably, its lengthy production drove the band's label executives—who had forked out a rumored $4 to $5 million production budget by the time all was said and done—crazy, beyond the budget, because they had no idea what was being accomplished. An extension of Lange's zero-tolerance policy for label meddling in his creative process, Shipley chuckled as he confirmed that again, like *Pyromania*, there was no involvement from the label *at all* in the making of that record, they didn't listen to one note, Mutt wouldn't allow it. And I remember when A&R heard it for the first time, they said, "What the fuck is this? You can't hear the vocals, it's all weird-sounding, what have you done?," everyone was kind of surprised.

Within the industry especially, I remember some people loved it, although I remember going into A&M Studios and being pulled aside by certain engineers going "What the fuck, haven't you ever stood next to a real drum kit? Don't you know what drums sound like, what have you done? What are you doing?" So some people hated it, mostly among our peers, and Mutt's thing was always: "It doesn't matter what your peers think. It matters what the guy down at the tire store thinks, if he's banging his head, then we're winning. It doesn't matter what anyone thinks about it who's in the business, it's about what the girls think and the guy at the machine shop."

Indeed, the listening public would ultimately prove the suits wrong, validating Lange, Shipley, and the band's tireless investment in producing many of what the biggest rock hits of the 1980s, a realization that first dawned on the engineer one morning.

The first time I really heard the finished album was when I'd come to Los Angeles after that to work on a completely different project with Joni Mitchell of all people, and I was walking one morning down a boardwalk in Santa Monica in the summertime, and coming out of every frickin' boom box on the beach was "Pour Some Sugar on Me," and it was like "Holy shit! This doesn't sound too bad from a distance. I'm not sure I could listen to it through a set of speakers again," but I came over to the States and it was just *everywhere*. That part was quite exciting, because for that summer, I just remember hearing it everywhere!

A truly titanic impact would follow culturally and commercially as *Billboard*—and the rest of the world—watched it become among the "most successful and iconic albums of all time," adding at the time of its release that *Hysteria* delivered "head-banging music of a very high sonic order, executed with great élan by what remains the most exciting metal-pop band on the scene!" Hailing the record as "a huge crossover success," *GuitarWorld* would add that "its cross-format appeal was due in large part to the creative vision of producer Robert John "Mutt" Lange's . . . quest to achieve a perfectly crystalline sound."

Proud of the fact that they eventually got there, his copilot on the epic journey—reflecting back years later on the aftermath of the album's phemoenon—candidly confessed to some mixed feelings about the personal impact that success had on his own reputation within the industry, recalling that

I'm glad to be remembered for the Def Leppard stuff. I don't like to be tarred and feathered by it, and as far as being one of those records where you got labeled as being "That guy," certain people think of you as being that kind of producer, and pretty much after that when the whole cliché grunge thing kind of came in, I was painted as kind of a "rock" guy, even when that's not who you are. That's just what we created at the time. We did what we needed to do for that record, and up to that point, I'd done punk bands and all kinds of different styles of bands, but on the bigger ones like "Hysteria," you can get labeled as "that's your sound," so you do get pigeonholed because people like to do that, put you in a corner, in a box, and say "That's what Shipley does" or "That's what Mutt does." That's why after that I went off and did the record with Joni Mitchell, and other projects that were completely different and more intuitive and a totally different way of doing records, and just kind of took it out of that box.

Despite his understandable fear of being pigeonholed stylistically, Shipley's relevance as a dynamic producing and mixing talent would only rise over the next two decades, collaborating once again with Mutt Lange when he proved his own ability to produce hits in any genre by making Shania Twain the biggest female country music star of the 1990s. Collectively, that collaboration between Twain, Lange, and Shipley would produce seventy-five million albums worth of greatest hits collection of #1 classics, including "Any Man of Mine," "(If You're Not in It for Love) I'm Outta Here!," "You Win My Love," "No One Needs to Know," "Man! I Feel Like a Woman!," "Love Gets Me Every Time," "From This Moment On," "Come On Over," "You're Still the One," "Honey, I'm Home," "That Don't Impress Me Much," and "Forever and for Always," among others.

Within the mixing arena, Shipley's A-list clientele included multiplatinum rock and pop superstars such as Tom Petty, Green Day, Faith Hill, Aerosmith, Enrique Iglesias, Tim McGraw, Maroon 5, Barenaked Ladies, Josh Groban, Kelly Clarkson, Nickelback, and 30 Seconds to Mars among countless others. Dispensing some general pointers to the newer school of engineers and producers looking to sharpen their skills in this all-important phase of record making, Shipley began with the importance and the benefit of having an open mind, explaining that

when I'm making or mixing records, I like to have the ability to have everything around. That's why I've got so many different plug-ins and delays and so forth. I can experiment and there's no real go-to effects, it's all experimental.

Offering his experience mixing Aerosmith as an example of advice on treating lead vocals, Shipley added that because

Steven's just the consummate rock singer, his singing is beyond brilliant, and just has that *voice*, mixing Steven is just a matter of making it sound as good as you can, and riding every nuance of it so you hear every single bit of it.

Shipley's talents as a producer in his own right were acknowledged in 2011 when he recalled that "one of my favorite ones was one that was a complete surprise to me, when Alison Krauss asked me to do *Paper Airplane*, which we were lucky enough to get a couple of Grammys for in 2012." Following up Krauss's massively successful collaboration with Led Zeppelin front man Robert Plant a few years earlier on the multiplatinum-selling LP *Raising Sand*, this time around, the singer was back with her own band Union Station, cocreating with Shipley an album celebrating her bluegrass roots so eloquently and authentically that it would ultimately hit #1 on the US *Billboard* Top Bluegrass Albums Chart and earn the singer a Grammy for "Best Bluegrass Album."

In a nod to Shipley, *Entertainment Weekly* would compliment the album as "exactingly performed and lushly produced . . . (exuding) a bone-deep tranquility," while the *Austin Chronicle* called the albums sound "impeccable." Heading into the production, Shipley recalled feeling particularly excited because

she's an artist who I've always been a HUGE fan of, and the honor of her asking me to work on her record, and to spend the time that we did on that record with that particular band—who to me are the most awesome players in the world—was absolutely fantastic. She liked some of the vocal sounds we'd gotten before, and it was like "Where do I sign?," so we spent quite some time doing that record, and I hadn't engineered a record in TEN YEARS, literally. I'd been mixing all the time, so while it's something you never forget, I went for kind of a deliberately sloppy, wider sound vs. everything being mono, and I stereo-miced everything, and had some fun with that. It was primarily tracked live, and was a lot of fun. It was an unbelievably good-sounding record, and to win a Grammy for it was a complete surprise, and a fantastic honor. That was a wonderful experience to me, so that one is definitely a highlight for me.

Marking Krauss's first #1 album on the *Billboard* Top Country Albums chart among other commercial and critical achievements, the record would also reach the top of the US *Billboard* Folk Albums chart, and #3 on the *Billboard* Top 200 albums chart. At the 2012 Grammy Awards ceremony, Shipley's production work was also acknowledged with a Grammy win for "Best Engineered Album, Non-Classical." Sadly, this would mark one of the final awards Shipley would receive as he passed away in July 2013. In this, one of his final print interviews, Shipley's deep love and appreciation for the opportunity he'd had to live out his dream in the recording studio for the better part of forty years seemed never lost on him. In the close of our conversation, he reflected back, musing that

> I know it sounds crazy, but every day I can walk into the control room I feel like a kid. It's like "Oh my God, I can do this again? This is unbelievable." I'm glad to have done the work with Mutt, Alison for sure, some of the records I've done with Joni. Everything's been a highlight, there's always a redeeming factor in everything, because it was all so different, that's what's so great about it. There's lots of things I'm proud of, they were really good experiences. I had a lot to learn, and they were just really fantastic musical experiences, so many of them. I've been lucky enough to work with some of my favorite artists of all time, that's what's been so fantastic. I've been very fortunate. I can walk into the studio and it's exciting every day . . . It's the most exciting thing, it totally is. I'll just come sit in the control room sometimes when I'm not even working, just to be in here. I'm in my control room right now, just going "Oh my God . . ." So it's all been great!

CHAPTER 6

Rebel Yell–Keith Forsey

If they ever have jukeboxes on Mars, undoubtedly Billy Idol will be screaming out of the speakers. With his signature sci-fi brand of postpunk pop, Idol became just that to a generation of new wavers looking for a soundtrack to their Saturday night. The producer of that soundtrack would be none other than Giorgio Moroder's sideman, Keith Forsey, who—alongside his multiplatinum, decade-long collaboration with Idol—would cocreate some of the most timelessly memorable movie soundtrack theme songs of the 1980s, including "The Heat Is On" from *Beverly Hills Cop*, "Flashdance (What a Feeling)" from the hit film of the same title, and arguably the most famous among his catalog of hits, the legendary "Don't You Forget About Me," the #1 smash that serenaded John Hughes's finest film, *The Breakfast Club*.

Beginning his career as an in-demand session drummer in the 1970s, Forsey made his bones under the tutelage of Italian record producer Giorgio Moroder, who *Rolling Stone* hailed as "one of disco's greatest pioneers." Forsey recalled that their fateful introduction came after

I had moved from England to Germany in the mid-'70s to join a band called Elenbort

Spy, a German psychedelic kind of music, and there weren't a lot of English musicians in Germany at the time, especially not on the session scene. I kind of broke into that scene with Carl Stoliner, who still is a famous jazz musician in Germany, and I guess my name got around being an English rock and roller, they didn't have that in Germany. So whether I was good or not, because of the fact that I was English and I was a rocker kind of opened the door and got me into the studio, and that's where I met Moroder, and that's where we established a lifelong friendship and relationship.

Prior to that, growing up in Britain, my initial instrument was drums, so I play drums, that was my first love, and then just working my way up through the different bands, being a session musician, and that took me to the studio, and that's where I started to see the art of production and just how fantastic it could be. It just presented way more possibilities than playing drums. Playing drums was fantastic, I loved it, but once I started doing sessions and moving into that arena, I just realized how much more fun it was to be able to play with all the instruments, and not actually be a musician anymore, but to help paint the picture with artists.

Highlighting some of the greatest lessons in the latter craft he learned in working under Moroder's wing, Forsey began by proudly noting that

I was always around the studio with him, so I guess what I really learned from him was "BIG PICTURE." Musicians, we tend to be focused on our instrument: "My hi-hat should be this, and the kick drum should be this," and we put all of these different little inflections into our art and our music, whereas Moroder would say "Strip it down, no I don't need that, don't worry about that, no one's going to notice that." He was big-picture song oriented, and although I don't think that's totally correct, I think it's a big part of making records. This big picture, of where the guitarist wants to noodle a solo, sometimes it's important to say, "Dude, you know, there's probably a lot of guitar players out there that would love that, but it's probably not necessary. Let's let the air breathe, let the space be there, let the song speak," those kind of things.

Forsey would also gain a unique perspective on the art of developing talent from the ground up when Moroder picked disco-starlet-to-be Donna Summer out of the choir, so to speak, just as the genre itself was beginning to trend as an underground style on the rise in the mid-1970s. In addition to playing drums on some of Summer's signature singles, Forsey would here showcase for the first time his talent as a hit songwriter, cowriting "Hot Stuff" among other radio and dance-floor favorites. Taking fans back to the beginning of his introduction to Summer, Forsey remembered that

we met her through the studio. Donna was a backup singer in Munich, a session singer, and she worked for the Englishman Pete Bellotte, who was a coproducer with

Giorgio at the early stages of Donna's career. He actually recorded her first song, "Lady of the Night," which was a hit in Holland, and that's where I met Donna. Pete had actually brought Giorgio into the picture, and Giorgio being the heavyweight that he was, he took the reins and production into his hand as it were. So knowing Giorgio was enough for me to play on all her records, up until Quincy Jones took over, and even Quincy asked me if I would play on the records, but my loyalty was really with Giorgio, as totally flattered as I was at the chance to play with Quincy. Quincy understood that, but it was an interesting moment, to turn Quincy down. When I was cowriting with Donna, my role was a combination, with people like Pete Bellotte and myself. Pete would come up with the lyric, and I would sit in the studio and play drums and Hal would play piano, we'd both have mics, and we would all sing, and between the three of us, we would collect different parts and put the songs together.

Forsey's discovery of Billy Idol would put him on the back of albums—and on the map—as a producer in his own right for the first time, serving as testament to another of any great producer's requisite instincts, to spot talent and develop it from the ground up. In Forsey's case, with Idol, he had found a unique stylistic fusion that *Rolling Stone* in 1982 would size up as "equal parts hard rocker, glam rocker and punk rocker, Billy Idol has managed an estimable synthesis of the music of three decades," adding of the specific characters his voice embodied that they suggested "a hybrid of Bruce Springsteen, Lou Reed and Dave Clark." Of this rock star in the rough, when the producer first laid eyes and ears on Idol's demo tape, he remembered instantly hearing opportunity rocking and knocking, feeling it was indeed

a magical moment for me. I used to live in the same house with Giorgio Moroder, and would listen to a lot of material that would get sent to Giorgio. So I'd go through it, and sift through a lot of the garbage, and at times think, "Oh, this is really good," and present him with the good stuff, and say, "Hey Giorgio, what do you think of that?" So one day, we got a cassette from Billy, and I didn't even know what Billy looked like, I was in America, Billy was in England, and he was on that punk-rock trip, and I'd been in Germany and now I'm wrapped up in the disco-techno world, so we're looking at Moogs and moving into that whole drum-triggering and all of that stuff, which was all very fascinating for me. And Billy was over there with the punk-rock thing still going on, but I think he was beginning to get ready to step out of it.

So I popped in the cassette and listened to his voice, and those early Gen X songs, and remember thinking "WOW, that's really cool." When I played it to Giorgio, and he said "Naaaa, I'm not interested," and off the top of my head, I asked him, "Maybe I could produce it for your company? Because I'd love to work with this guy, he sounds fantastic," and he said, "I don't think you need to produce him for my company, I'll just put a good word in for you, and tell them you've been working with me for years." So he called Bill Aucoin, who was Billy and Generation X's manager at the time, and Bill came to LA, and I had a meeting with Bill, and got along incredibly well with Billy, because Billy has a great sense of time and he really understands pocket, and he understands groove, and understands simplicity as well. I think he really was into disco, and felt the whole disco groove, elements that we loved, so I think it was a match made in heaven at the time. Bill, Billy's manager, felt the combination of the disco and punk-rock thing with Billy would be fantastic and said, "Yeah, let's do it." So we went to AIR Studios in London, and we cut "Dancing with Myself" and another couple of songs during that first session working together.

Knowing this was not only Idol's shot at the proverbial brass ring but also his own as a producer, Forsey hopped a plane to England shortly thereafter to produce a "trial session" of sorts with Idol. Among the demos he'd heard back in LA, the producer saw "Dancing with Myself"—which *Billboard* would hail as "one of the best power pop numbers ever"—as the silver bullet single to launch the singer into stardom. Building the recording from the ground up in the studio, Forsey—who throughout his collaboration with Idol would take a consistently hands-on musical role in the production of all of his albums—began by calling on his instincts as a drummer, intent on crafting a rhythm track where

I was trying to combine the groove and the pocket that we used to have in disco, because back then, it was all played, we played it, and there's guys like Ed Grooms who played drums, he was my competition: a straight-ahead groove guy. To me, that was as good as Billy Cobham, and I mean Cobham's got the chops and all that, but Ed had chops as well, and the guy from Jazz Crusaders, Stix Hooper, straight ahead, straight ahead. There's that one song, "Put a Wiggle on It," original disco song, there's no drum fill on that record at all, if you listen to that, he plays 4-on-the-floor all the way through, even the stops, it's fantastic. So I was trying to bring that element of groove that was hypnotic and fantastic to me, and try and bring in the rock elements of Billy and what we were doing in that disco world. I could see there was a confluence of ideas there somehow, because Billy had such a big voice, a great voice, and energy, and it just seemed like a great combination.

Rolling his sleeves up to contribute what would wind up being one of the stand-out signatures of the frenetic energy alive within the drum track, Forsey revealed that while

that's Terry Chimes playing drums, I did play a rolling snare, which you can't really hear, but once again, we concentrated on pocket and groove, and I got them to play with a click track. Although it's not tight with click, it sits pretty good in there, and in those days, I didn't give drummers clicks, I used to use rhythm boxes, that made rhythm tracks that had almost like percussion tracks. So they weren't playing just with a click, they were playing with upbeats and accents and things like that that would help the drummer hang onto the pocket, hang onto the groove, but also, it would be more fun. That's the way I used to do it, used to play with rhythm machines, because there's more stuff to hang on to, instead of aiming for that quarter-note click all the time, which is horrible and no fun. So I wanted him to play with something that was a little bit more musical, and got Tim to play along with that, then I put a rolling snare drum, which kind of grooves along all the way through the track, and think I actually called a session musician in at London at the time.

And of course, the band—all the guys in Gen X at the time—looked at me like I was absolutely crazy, because they were all punk rockers, and were like "Oh no, he's going to get a session guy in," and of course the drummer turns up with sandals on, and these guys are all in black leather! So Billy looks at me, and says, "Jesus, you've got to be kidding?!" But anyway, there's a rhythm guitar that plays midway through that song, really tight with the drums and that rolling snare, and that's what holds the beat down. I think that's what gives it that infectious quality, I hope anyway. On the snare, I also used an EMT reverb, and the drums were recorded live at AIR Studios, which is quite a big room, the Beatles room upstairs, which was exciting, because the engineers would say, "Oh wow, that's the compressor that John Lennon used on . . . ," all of that history!

"Dancing with Myself" would serve precisely the purpose Forsey had predicted it would in launching Billy Idol and Generation X up the pop charts in Britain and landing the punk star-in-the-making his first major label deal in the United States with Chrysalis. Remarkably, even after their smash debut, the producer discovered resistance from Idol's label as the freshman solo artist prepared to enter the studio to record his first EP when the suits tried the classic trick of attempting to place Idol with a more known producer, a move the singer roundly rejected to the relief of Forsey, who recalled that

> after we made the Gen X record, Chrysalis wanted to bring Billy to the States, but didn't want me to produce the record, they wanted to pair him with one of the great American producers, and he said, "Nope, I want to do it with Keith." So this was fantastic, off we went, and did the first EP.

The *Don't Stop* EP, along with "Dancing with Myself," would also feature a radio rendition of the Tommy James and the Shondells classic "Mony, Mony," one that would also score for Idol, staying a radio and fan favorite over decades to follow, identified by All Music Guide as "Billy Idol's biggest hit." Crediting the idea behind the cover to the singer himself, Forsey remembered that as he and Idol were putting the track listing,

> "Mony, Mony" was Billy's idea. Billy loves pop songs, he loved Elvis, and used to love

the classic pop songs, anywhere from Presley to Johnny Cash to Bowie, he liked guys that were very unique in a way.

With its distinctively driving groove, the single also showcased what would become a signature effects treatment on the singer's lead vocal track that stuck for years of hits to come, a blend that the producer recalled

> back then was a 414, believe it or not, it was very bright, and we would use the AMS Harmonizer a little bit, a little bit of that would have been in there, and a little bit of delay, we always used a little bit of slap delay on him. Maybe that came from my early impressions of Presley, that always fascinated me in the early, early days, it was a really hip sound. Once Billy heard that slap delay on there, he looked at me and said, "Yeah, that's it." In terms of vocal sound, I think he pretty much loved whatever we did. Usually if I'm doing things right, he's happy as hell, you can see it. If I put a foot wrong, Billy wasn't terribly good at explaining himself, he'd get a little aggressive, and I'd know I was doing the wrong thing and would have to figure out what it was, but he liked that right from the first time we used it on.

That same Elvis-style slap echo would help electrify "Hot in the City," among the next Idol hits to follow off the full-length LP he and Forsey headed into the studio to make together in his self-titled debut. Featuring the rising new wave punk star's next two Top 40 hits, "White Wedding" and "Hot in the City," Forsey not only produced both smashes, but brought his considerable songwriting to the forefront as well. Writing the song in real time with Idol in the studio, Forsey remembered getting an extra-special thrill from the fact that

> the song was made in Giorgio's room where I'd first heard Billy's demo, and I played drums on that track. I played drums first, I just played the whole drum track, and we built on it. That song was written minutes before we actually put it down, Billy was up at the house, and we needed a song, and he had a part that went "Hot in the City, Hot in the City tonight!" And I went "Yeah, that's cool!," and we kind of jammed it together very quick, and I just laid the drum groove down. In those days, especially with "Hot in the City," that was close mics I was using on the kit.

Applying a unique production method for fleshing out songs written in the moment of recording reminiscent of his 1970s disco session days, Forsey shared from his bag of magic tracking tricks that he utilized in recording the album's other smash single, "White Wedding," that

> what I did as well in those days was usually make songs that were fifteen, twenty minutes long and then we'd edit. I came from the disco world, so we used to play

fifteen, twenty minutes, and I didn't know where I was going, and a great example of that was an instant twenty-minute piece. The original goes from live music, and then after about ten minutes, it transitions, I pick up the kick drum with a Linn kick, and pick up the snare with a snare from the Linn, and it transitions everything from live band into all programmed. You probably don't hear that on the radio and on the single, probably just on a couple of the early 12-inchers, and what wound up on the album was more live.

We recorded that one at Westlake Audio, and the story behind that one was we were short on songs again, we were always short on songs, and always took a while to get these songs together. I remember saying to Billy, "Well, just go in the studio, we'll set you up with the mic and a remote to run the machine backwards and forwards. Go in there, and put something down, see what you got." So we left him in the studio by himself, no techs, no anybody, and after about ten minutes, he came out and said, "Okay, I think I've got something," and started singing "Hey little sister, what have you done . . ." And it was like "YES!," and off we went. So we spent two days going crazy, instantly went with the twenty-minute version, laid the groove down, and Sylvester Leroy was playing keyboards, he came from Germany and the techno world. He jumped in and helped with some of the splashes and sounds, that was exciting.

The breakout success of Idol's eponymous debut LP in the States set up great expectations for his 1984 follow-up, appropriately titled *Rebel Yell*, as the true breadth and brilliance of Idol's hybrid sound was revealed fully for the first time. Fusing multiple subgenres and generations of rock 'n' roll styles into one masterpiece that *Rolling Stone* recognized as including derivative influences "from the Sixties . . . he's brought a fair measure of pop economy and a kaleidoscopic palette of sound effects; from the Seventies, he's taken the larger-than-life sound of big guitars, thunderous drumming and industrial-strength singing; and from the Eighties, he's adapted the sonic Bauhaus architecture of new music, with its straight, streamlined edges. In short, *Rebel Yell* is a ferocious record, sharp as a saber, hard as diamond, as beautiful and seductive as the darker side of life with which it flirts . . . *Rebel Yell* is an intelligent assault upon the senses, and a rallying cry to the reckless enthusiasm of youth."

To rally his new and growing generation of teenage followers, Idol brought an almost combustible energy to bear in the studio as he tracked his lead vocals for the song. Forsey joked that he resembled

a caged lion, because Billy's got all that energy. So, for instance, with "Rebel Yell" in that middle section where Billy sings "I walk the walk for you babe," that section we didn't have, and we were looking and looking and looking, and I like to give him room to free him up, rather than just to stand him in front of a microphone sometimes. So I gave him a handheld 57 so he could wander around the studio, and I had 16 bars of drum groove punched in there, and I was just waiting for him to unload on it, and after two or three weeks, suddenly we're at a studio somewhere in New York, and boom, it hit him right there. He was walking around in the studio, and that's where that part comes from. "I walk the walk for you babe . . ." We had those 16 bars, and I knew we could do something great in there, I was just waiting for him to do it, and he did. With "Rebel Yell," every time you put that song on in the studio, it would be like "WOW, that's cool, that's really cool," and you could play it again, and so with that song, we really knew we had something.

When I was recording vocals with Billy, in general, he would be two or three takes max. After three takes, I'd make a comp of what we had, and even if there was stuff that was out of tune but had the right feel for what we were going for, I'd make that comp, and he'd go home, listen to it, and catch what we were looking for, then come in the next day and do another two, maybe three takes, and that's all we would end up doing. Usually, it was me and him, not too many people around. Billy was living in New York, and usually what I would do is go look at three or four studios, see which were available, and Electric Lady was available and is a fantastic studio. It was state of the art there at the time,

Though he and Idol were working against the aforementioned cutting-edge studio backdrop, Forsey revealed that for all the ground they broke on the new LP, he was proud of the innovations they accomplished making

Rebel Yell, that whole album, on just twenty-four tracks! In that respect, I personally think that the digital age has been great in some respects, but it kind of destroyed a lot, because when you had sixteen tracks, if every track was valuable, then every performance was valuable. *Rebel Yell*, again, was made on just twenty-four tracks, so you bounced stuff over: if you had tambourine over on this track, then you would march it across and work it around in the mix, and you had to make decisions, where—in the digital age—you don't make decisions.

It's easy just to say, "Well, okay, that's good, that's great, no, just do another one," and you end up with twenty-three tracks of guitars, and it takes the decision-making process in the opposite direction of the days when it was: "You've only got two tracks to do this, so let's make it count." So I think the digital age just makes it more complicated, there's no doubt about it, because it gives you so many options, so I'm definitely not fond of the digital world where recording is concerned. With songwriting, however, I am, because you can sit at home and do what we do today and throw a quick rough demo together, whereas before, you're working with 4-tracks and had to play the thing from start to finish, you take your time writing the song in digital.

A few of those tracks were used to serve the 6-string king Steve Stevens, who'd boarded Idol's flight to stardom back on his EP and first solo LP, a selection for sideman that the producer credited to Idol's manager

> Bill Aucoin, who had stepped into the picture and seen Steve Stevens for what he was, and thought, "That combination was great," because Steve was the classic American rock guy, and Billy was this English punk. And as a matter of fact, at first it was a little rough there, because Steve was the noodley guy and Billy didn't like that, but somehow or another, with a little bit of racket and me stuck in the middle, we made it work. So there's that little bit of edge and that little bit of rock between those guys, and somehow or another, we made everybody happy.

Acknowledging Stevens's musical contribution to the sessions, Forsey highlighted him as a key player throughout the recording of *Rebel Yell* and the other Idol LPs/hits, confirming that

> Steve was a mainstay in the studio. We wouldn't labor on the solos, and back then, we only had twenty-four tracks. Maybe we might have had a slave or two, but on *Rebel Yell*, we didn't have the tracks to do it, so we might record two or three takes and make a comp of the solo. Steve always had his sound together, Steve was always ahead of the game, and very hip as well in terms of the delays and gear and pedals and all of that stuff that was coming out, he was so on it, which worked for Billy and worked for me.
>
> Sometimes the speed and the heavy stuff might have been a little bit too much for Billy, and I would always defer to Billy when it came to doing that kind of work, because I could very get off on Steve's guitar playing, it was fantastic. So Billy would be there when we were doing guitars, and I'd look at him, and he would give me the nod or he'd let me know the other way. Or I'd have something from Steve that I thought was really good, and would suggest to Billy, "You know what, it might be a good idea to live with it for a little bit, it might be cool," and I think we all kind of gave in a little bit and made it work.

Forsey turned next to the recording of another of the album's massive radio hits, the haunting "Eyes Without a Face," which became *Rebel Yell*'s biggest hit—peaking at #4 on the *Billboard* Hot 100 singles chart—and perfectly summed up Billy Idol's ability, in the opinion of *Billboard*, to combine the "catchiest, most consistent fusion of synth-driven new wave pop and hard rock guitar pyrotechnics (courtesy of Steve Stevens)" that the decade had seen yet. Beginning with the hypnotic drum machine pattern, the producer shared of the sound's creation that

that is a drum machine, I programmed that. I know Sal Cuevas played bass on it, very groovy bass player, and that was done at Electric Ladyland downstairs. He sang with a little bit of that slap delay in the headphones. I'd give him the sound that he would hear in the room, a little bit of that so he could work it. For the bass sound on Billy's albums, we would have always had a D.I. and a cabinet, and it was usually the D.I. that got used.

As a drummer, generally, I tend to play with D.I., just because it was fat and clean and manageable, and probably once again, because in the disco world, we didn't use pedals that much. Those were direct D.I. guys, that's what we did, was try to isolate everything, so if you break the track down, there was nothing, there was no spill: no guitar leakage, no hats coming into the snare drum, there's nothing coming from the room into the kick drum mic.

In those days, you'd always have guitar and bass probably in the same room, and there might have been isolation, but not quite as good as now, so we tried to isolate everything. Everything we could, we tried to do, so each instrument—especially the kick as well—that's what you got and nothing else.

The producer found a great thrill in recording another of the album's massively popular singles, "Flesh for Fantasy," which he thought was a perfect sonic serenade to Idol's punk roots. He recalled it as

a punk-rock song that was up-tempo, really really punk-rock, and one evening the guys went home, and I was trying to make sense of it, and thought, "Maybe if we cut it in half, and maybe go a little bit more blue-eyed soul on it," so once again I programmed the Linn, and just demoed a little bit of the thing. Then Steve Stevens came in, and once he started playing that riff, it just built from there. We knew it was a single, once we finished it, just like "Rebel Yell."

Rebel Yell's success would make Idol a superstar, courtesy of the perfect storm of stages on three fronts that he would dominate from 1983 on, including MTV, radio, and live concerts, where Idol became an arena star in the wake of the album's success. Selling two million copies at the time of release, peaking at #6 on the *Billboard* Top 200 albums chart, and giving Idol his first Grammy nomination for "Best Male Rock Performance," producer Keith Forsey was also at the top of his own game. Based on the success of Billy Idol's growing catalog of hits, alongside his reputation working with soundtrack hitmaker Giorgio Moroder, Forsey began to witness his own breakout as one of the film industry's most in-demand headline songwriters.

Considering the fact that between 1981 and 1988, Forsey was responsible for cowriting/coproducing many of what became the 1980s' signature film-radio hits in real time, his compositions not only fit the feel of the films he was composing for, but also created a frenzy on radio that made the listener feel as energized as if they'd themselves been up on the silver screen. Beginning with his hit in 1981 cowriting the title track and #1 hit for Irene Cara, "Flashdance (What a Feeling)," Keith Forsey was actually living the popular millennium saying "You wrote the soundtrack to a generation," as suddenly his songwriting could be heard everywhere, on film screens, music videos, HBO, and VHS TV screens as films made their way to video release just as the advent of home video viewership was taking shape, and on radio all around the country. Taking fans inside the story of the song's creation, Forsey—who was responsible for writing the song's lyrics as well as performing the driving drum track—recalled that

> we wrote that down at Giorgio's house in Beverly Hills, and the melodies were there, and obviously the movie was called *Flashdance*. And there was a studio in the back room at Giorgio's house, which had a video monitor and a big screen, and I could see the studio and the studio could see me, and we had drums back there. So I would go back into the drum room and sit with the dailies from the movie, and just collect bits and pieces of dialogue and write down pages of ideas and thoughts, and then Irene Cara became the singer, and she joined in and helped us define it. I wrote the line "Take your passion and make it happen" because it just seemed to sum it all up, you know.
>
> I did have a big hand in the drum sound, but we did do it on marble floor with glass walls in a big-ass room, it was actually the living room of Giorgio's house, very live, and I don't know why we chose that room, because we were used to using the drum room in the back, which was more of a tight Westlake Audio R&B kind of sound. Westlake had a really tight drum room with drum booths in the back, very dry and very controllable. That's the room that we used to have at the house, but for "Flashdance," I don't know whose call that was, but they said, "Let's go for the marble and glass," so I didn't have much of a hand in that call, but I did play the drums.
>
> As a drummer, I used to go in and pretty much knock it out, that's what we used to do, and from working with Giorgio as well, like I said, he was a big-picture guy, and you knew you didn't have to sell chops, you don't have to be flash, you don't have to prove anything to him, you've just got to put down good time, and that's probably the essence of any great drummer. A lot of kids I don't think realize that, that drums are about time and understanding the song.
>
> I find that's a problem I run into a lot when I'm working with bands, the approach. There's certain stances a drummer can have: you can lean forward, you can lean back, there's certain ways you can put a pocket down which represents the song you're working with. Not all band drummers get that. I think session guys do because they play on so many different kinds of records that they learn to be adaptive. So with

some of the younger bands that I've worked with, if you throw out the word "pocket," they look at you and say "pocket?"

A perfect illustration of this pocket would come courtesy of another of Forsey's greatest hits—and a monster indeed in defining a generation—when the producer-songwriter sat down behind the same drum set that had helped inspire the latter hit. Tuning his creative antennae this time toward the title track to the upcoming John Hughes' classic *The Breakfast Club*, Forsey offered a fascinating look inside his knack for reflecting in lyric what a character is feeling on-screen, sharing that as he began working with cowriter Steve Schiff on what would become the '80s anthem "Don't You (Forget About Me)," the inspiration for the song came from a biographical root based on

a scene in the movie where you have the nerd talking to Molly Ringwald and Judd Nelson, and it reminded me of when I was in school when I was a bit of a back-of-the-class kind of guy and not particularly scholarly, and hung out of with my friends and be a little bit obnoxious, but if I was by myself at the bus stop and the nerdy guy was there, you'd talk to him. Because you didn't have your boys around you, and you could talk to him and be friends with him, and so in that scene where Anthony Michael Hall says to Molly Ringwald, "Are you going to remember me tomorrow morning when I come down the hall?," and that's kind of a statement in itself. I remember that myself, because when you were with your friends in the school halls, you weren't talking to the nerdy guy, but you would befriend him when nobody was around, and I thought that was a great moment in the movie, and the line "Don't You (Forget About Me)" came to me. The rest of the song's lyrics are probably a little bit more nebulous, but that scene's where the idea came from.

When I am writing lyrics, as was the case with that song, I kind of just mumble and try to get the soul of the song, and sometimes words will just pop out and something will make sense, and then you strip it all back from where the melody feels really good with those words that you said, and it's all one package, then strip it back and try to put the lyric to it. When a melody and words fit together, whether they mean anything or not, when the melody actually connects, it can mean so much somehow.

Steve and I started writing that song at Oasis Studio in Studio C, and Shipp had a guitar strung around his neck and we're just in the room with a microphone just going at it. I had the pocket, and the drummer from Simple Minds, he picked up the same kick drum pattern and everything, and got the meaning of the pocket right there, it was beautiful. That's one of those songs where, when you put it down in the studio and go "WOW!," where it's working really, really good, and that was one of those songs I think I knew it had that X factor. You can never really tell, because there were other songs in the past I felt that way about that nobody ever heard, but that one had it.

Once they knew they had a hit on their hands, in picking the perfect band to record the song, Forsey would get practice working an at times vital function of any producer's job description: talking a reluctant band into recording a song he knows will be a hit record. The band was in fact reluctant at first to record the song, in spite of the promise of stardom, with the tiebreaker coming after the *LA Times* reported that "a factor that finally helped sway Simple Minds was Forsey's enthusiasm about the band's previous work." Knowing his instinct was right that the band would knock the hit song out of the park, he remembered having a gut feeling that

> Simple Minds would be fantastic with that song, and that is definitely my favorite song of those I wrote over the years, no doubt about it, that's the only song I could really sit down and listen to over and over again that I had anything to do with writing. It's my favorite song.

With "Don't You (Forget About Me)," critics credited both the band and its producer for the #1 hit's massive success, including *Billboard*'s taking notice of the fact that "Keith Forsey's production gives the song . . . kick," added of the momentum that followed "the song's prominent and perfect placement within *The Breakfast Club* movie did wonders, and, for the first time, Simple Minds not only entered the top half of the American pop chart, but amazingly shot to its very top. Back home, the single also took the band to new heights." Underscoring the validity of the industry catch-phrase that "when you're hot you're hot," Forsey was hired in 1985 to write what would become the headlining track to Eddie Murphy's upcoming "*Beverly Hills Cop*" soundtrack.

Boasting a saxophone lead that flew wildly around the high-octane track, with "The Heat Is On," Forsey and cowriter Harold Faltermeyer would outdo themselves and expectations, delivering one of the most popular and seminal jukebox, radio, video, and motion picture soundtrack hits of the 1980s. Revealing that the team felt on fire at the pace they burned through the song's writing, Forsey recalled,

> with "The Heat Is On," I believe I came up with the melody for that sax lead, but Harold Faltermeyer—my cowriter—and I were banging around ideas back and forth so much. Harold was definitely the chords guy, he would put the chords down, and I would be singing, and there's a version of me somewhere demoing that "The Heat Is On" chorus melody, and we built the song from there. The actual vibe and the melody for that was probably put together in an afternoon, then we would work on it lyrically and build the lyric up, but the essence of the song would usually be done within a day.
>
> We did have that opening scene, but with a temp song underneath it. When you're working on movie soundtrack songs, the director usually has a temp song underneath the scene and they fall in love with those songs. But then if they can't get the rights

to use that song, and you've got to write something to replace it, we would usually try to get exactly the same kind of tempo and then try and write in a similar feel that the music supervisor has put underneath that scene.

Returning from the big screen to the studio with Billy Idol in 1989 to record what would represent a reboot for the singer, who'd struggled with both drug addiction in the intervening years and a near-fatal motorcycle accident about which the *LA Times* reported on February 7, 1990 that "British rock star Billy Idol suffered a broken leg and wrist when his motorcycle collided with a car Tuesday in Hollywood, police and hospital officials said. Idol was not wearing a helmet when his Harley-Davidson cycle allegedly ran a stop sign and hit the car about 8:30 a.m., officers said. The 31-year-old woman driving the car was not hurt, Officer Don Lawrence said. Idol . . . was taken to Cedars-Sinai Medical Center, where he was in serious but stable condition after seven hours of surgery for a break in his right leg between the knee and ankle and a fractured left forearm." Seeking to reinvent Idol's sound for the 1990s, while the singer recovered, Forsey set his mind to putting a new band together, beginning with the all-important position of a new lead guitarist who could hold up Stevens's musical pillar within the band. Forsey recalled that

I put the band together for that album, which was our first without Steve Stevens, and picked Mark Younger-Smith because he'd worked with Charlie Sexton, that's where I met Mark, and he has a very soulful and free way of playing. And I remember before I called him I had been auditioning guitar players, and thought "You know what, I think he might get along really well with Billy," and I think Mark had to go to the pawn shop and get his amps out, pick up his stuff. He got himself to LA, came and played an afternoon session with Billy at Leeds rehearsal studio, and got the job. I think it worked well between them because Billy's kind of a Goth guy, he's doesn't like the techno kind of thing too much, and Mark's got this kind of feel that worked really well.

A *Charmed Life* is precisely what Idol had led surviving the punk-rock roller coaster ride up the pop charts that had been the 1980s, and the phrase seemed an apt fit for the title of the LP as Forsey and Idol set foot inside the studio for the first time in three years. Seeking to announce with authority that Idol was back, the producer sonically pursued essentially the same blueprint as he had on their previous collaborations, sans programmed drum tracks of course, wherein Idol's new band

recorded that album at Conway in Studio A, and they don't have a lot of isolation there, so I think we had basically the bass, drums, and rhythm guitar as a live take. Mike Baird played drums on most of the tracks on *Charmed Life*, and we had Tommy Vicari engineering on that album, and I remember making that choice because Tommy's a real engineer's engineer, he's really good at tom sounds and is a really organic kind of guy. I thought Tommy would be a good change for that album, vs. on past albums, where I'd tended to usually go with more techno kind of engineers.

The team would tackle Billy Idol's first Top 5 single in years with "Cradle of Love" (#2), a lightning bolt of a song from beyond that came to Forsey as

a demo that was originally a bit like that T-Rex "Bang a Gong (Get It On)." It sounded a bit like Marc Bolan, and we kind of vibed on that a little bit, but we took it out of the Marc Bolan sound as it were to record it. I had a slap delay on his voice same-old, same-old as I had done with his past records, that was a signature to his vocal sound on record by then. I was always fond of bands like David Bowie, who's my hero, because it's not just rock, or whatever you call it. It can be funk, it can be groove, it can be anything, but there's always nice twists and turns in Bowie's music, it always used to blow me away, and I guess Billy and I tried to do a little bit of that with all his records.

With another of the album's hits, an explosive modernization of the Doors' classic "L.A. Woman," even mainstream critics like *People* magazine welcomed Idol back to Hitsville, ruling that among the "tracks with the sting one associates with the maker of 'Rebel Yell' are 'Trouble with the Sweet Stuff,' parts of 'The Right Way,' and a bang-up cover of the Doors' "L.A. Woman." MTV would add that with their decision to update the latter classic in Idol's '90s mold, "this made his channeling of Jim Morrison on a rowdy cover of 'LA Woman' even more apt. He had done so before, of course, most memorably on 1986's *Whiplash Smile*. But where Idol's clever amalgam of dance beats and punky guitar breaks had done its part to define the 1980s, his update of the classic Doors song was the new sound of the same old seedy, City of Angels underbelly, remixed for the cusp of a new decade. Its mirthful screams and bizarro beat speak ("She drinks my wine spo-dee-o-dee") also marked one of *Charmed Life*'s . . . memorable moments."

Knowing from the first take that they were onto something with the dice rolled on such a ballsy endeavor to pull off credibly, Forsey was confident based first and foremost on the fact that, sitting behind the board producing the track,

I thought it was a fantastic vibe! That was two takes, old school, 2-inch tape cut together, so I cut the 2-inch tape of the front end of the song from one, and the back end from the other, great vibe! For the bass, Arthur Burrow played bass on that record. Arthur used to play with Frank Zappa, and was a really, really talented, talented musician, he plays keyboards and bass really good, and I think he was playing with the Doors as well at the time, and he was an old friend of mine, so it was a good choice to put on "L.A. Woman."

Charmed Life would peak as a Top 10 hit for Billy Idol, completing a comeback from the brink that could have only been navigated in the hands of a producer as capable as Forsey in knowing both Idol's safe bases and those plays where he needed to take a new risk sonically to shake things up. No matter how the team had rolled the dice, the outcome had usually paid off, working against all odds at the start of his career gamble on Idol at the start of the decade, and sticking with him throughout the roaring '80s. Reflecting back on his collaboration with Idol, the producer proudly declares that "*Rebel Yell* has to be my favorite record out of all his stuff."

Speaking more broadly on a lifetime making hits, though he quipped at the beginning of our conversation that "It's very seldom I actually do interviews or any of this kind of thing, but I looked at all of those names, and thought 'Wow, it's pretty nice company,' I should open up a little bit (laughs) . . . ," in crediting those he felt helped him most pivotally on the way—along with Giorgio Moroder—Forsey turned affectionately back to his childhood—and his brother.

> My older brother was six years older than me, and loved Elvis Presley, he used to pose in front of the wardrobe mirror with a guitar strung around his neck, and to be quite honest, the relationship between my father and my brothers and I was never too strong, so I kind of looked to my older brother as a father figure, and I guess he just turned me onto music in a big way, and I followed in his footsteps.

In setting an example for a new generation of soundmen-in-the-making that grew up on his sound, Keith Forsey advises that any such journeymen make the most of their moments of the Wild West that is the studio when they're first sitting in front of the frontier that is the modern-day SSL or MCI board. Seizing the reins of the moment is a must, with the producer recommending that

> I would say: Try to get it right, right now, don't say "Oh, we can this on there later, we can throw that on there later." So I would say get a performance, get a really good performance, and I think it will speak volumes. That all comes down to pocket too, because you can put a band out there, and all of a sudden, they catch a groove and it might start in one tempo and end at another tempo, but because it's so groovy and feels so good, you won't even notice. And if you did, you wouldn't want to even fix it, so if you can get those moments, I think that will step over all of the digital records. That human moment will probably step on all those guys, or at least I hope so.

Reflecting back on his remarkable legacy—from helping to write and produce many of the biggest film soundtrack hits ever to discovering and guiding Billy Idol to a decade of #1s—and how all of those hits continue to hold up on radio after so many years, Forsey confesses in closing that, at times, it blows you away, especially at my age. I'm semi-retired, I don't do that much, and to tell you the truth, the music that's out right now, there's so much of it and it's so homogenized, and when I was a kid, to grow up and be a rock musician was something special, now everybody does it. So if I'm out when any of those songs come in, people don't know I've produced any of that stuff, and I kind of look around and watch people still moving to it, I think, "That's pretty cool!'

CHAPTER 7

Tuesday Night Music Club–Bill Bottrell

In the 1980s, 1990s, and the millennium, it would have been any young record producer's dream come true to be sitting in the same studio working side by side with Michael Jackson. This kind of highlight shined brighter than most gold or platinum moments ever could in sales for the mere experience itself. But what if you got the platinum album award too? What if you found yourself spending two years working day in and out with the King of Pop as his right-hand man in developing from the ground up his next number one record coming off the heels of the thirty-million-selling *BAD* LP?

That's precisely where Bill Bottrell found himself in 1988, as *Sound on Sound* reported that "having worked as an engineer on the Jacksons' 1984 *Victory* album and then on Michael's *BAD* three years later as part of the second-tier team working at his Encino home, Bottrell received a call in 1988 to commence work on the follow-up. The fact that he was already a producer by then was quite timely, as the Gloved One was parting company with Quincy Jones and looking to create a more hard-edged, streetwise image with the help of some new writing/production/arrangement collaborators."

Jumping at the opportunity, the producer recalled personally the phone call that would act as the catalyst for his graduation from engineer to producer at a time maybe two years after the *BAD* LP, when I'd been working with the other Jackson brothers a lot in the meantime, and Michael called me up and basically booked me straight through working at his house, where I spent like the next year and four months working with him, with a "just messing around/do it yourself" approach with him and John Barnes, who was this brilliant keyboard player. So Michael would bring a song in, hum it to us, and we'd flesh the demo out, get a rhythm going, etc. He'd have written the melody himself, and the title and words, and would beat-box me rhythms and bass lines. He was really good at writing and getting out of musicians what he heard in his head.

Because he wasn't an instrumentalist, that's how he did it, and on all those songs, I got to hear the song emerge, and wouldn't know what the vocal melody sounded like until he came in to sing it, till there was already this whole track laid out with groove and everything, and then he'd come in and sing it, and it would turn into a pop song, and a brilliant one.

Already familiar with Jackson's process of composing and producing based on a catalog that included time logged in the studio engineering the Jacksons' *Victory* LP in 1985 and then the aforementioned *BAD*, Bottrell from project one has taken pride in one of his signature production ambitions to encourage an organic, D.I.Y. approach to record making, precisely the freedom Jackson was seeking with his follow-up to *Thriller* when he first met the producer. Feeling kindred from the start, Bottrell remembered his first audition with Jackson's solo material coming

while I was working on the Jacksons' *Victory* LP, and he brought in a home demo from his house with him and Freddie Mercury singing "State of Shock!" And I just did what I wanted to do to it in about twenty minutes while he stood there and watched, and I rocked it up really good. All it was was Michael on a snare drum, David Williams on guitar, and Michael and Freddie singing, very do-it-yourself, and I responded to that.

So I think Michael picked up on my openness to experimenting, and that wide-open/*what can this be* approach. You don't bring a lot of techniques or set goals, and that's what was fortuitous, and I don't know if maybe his brother said something about me, but once he brought this raw tape in, I mixed it really quick, and hyped it up and whatnot, and it was really rocking and sounded great. So he took that cassette home, then sent one over to my house with five stars on it, and said, "Billy, remember exactly what you did on this tape," and so I think he responded to that sort of attitude of freedom.

The roots of the producer's fundamental belief in this approach to record making was molded during a decade-long tenure as E.L.O.'s brain trust Jeff Lynne's right-hand man in the studio. Bottrell affectionately recalled that as a producer, I always liked the do-it-yourself ethic, and I ended up as a producer making a lot of records with the artists where I was willing to play most of the instruments, if not all sometimes, and I learned that from Jeff. It's a matter of arrangement: if you're hearing something in your head, an arrangement in songs, sometimes it's easier to do it yourself than to bring an accomplished musician in and be harping on the poor guy, saying "No, go (sings out three notes), that's all we need." It's not efficient, and you can just pick up the instrument and do it yourself. With that element of discovery, if you bring in an accomplished musician or let's say a band who has their ways and means of doing things, then you kind of lose that element of wide-open discovery of what could happen. I learned MASSIVE, huge things from working with Jeff. I was twenty-eight when he first came into the studio, and was the $10 an hour head of maintenance and staff engineer. It was me and the owner, and Jeff came in to do a demo for *Xanadu*, and he chose the studio that had a Harrison console and Zuri speakers.

Touching on some of the *huge* later '80s smash hits he helped Lynne record—Bottrell's collaborations include such multiplatinum hits as Harrison's #1 smash "I Got My Mind Set on You," the Traveling Wilburys' (starring Harrison, Lynne, Roy Orbison, Tom Petty, and Bob Dylan) *Vol. 1* LP, which sold three million copies and featured hits including "Handle with Care," "Congratulations," and "End of the Line"—the producer began with Harrison's comeback album *Cloud 9*,

which Jeff did without me engineering, brought it back to LA and asked me to help out in the postproduction, and so we made a little 12-inch out of "I Got My Mind Set on You," once again with the *do-it-yourself* where we all just showed up. We made the 12-inch off the 2-track and just had to slice it and dice it and have George play a longer solo, but the point is: Jeff had been hanging out with George making records, and during the making of that 12-inch version, George turned to me and said, "We'll have a group, called the Traveling Wilburys," and later on, Jeff started calling and said, "Okay, we're gonna do this, we've got everybody going." Eventually we all went down to Bob Dylan's house, went into his garage, and recorded the first song, "Handle with Care." It was brilliant, in ONE DAY, and working on really cheesy equipment that had never been unwrapped! I had to plug the stuff together and get it working, and I watched them laughing and writing the song line by line, and then they'd leave in groups of two or three, and write a few more lines and come back in. George had come in with the chords and the hook line, and everybody with that D.I.Y. attitude, just having fun, and of course that impressed me. It's what I'd learned from Jeff and what he did on his own records, and now I believe he had influenced George, and they in turn had influenced Bob and Tom and Roy to get together and the song came out really good.

I was Jeff's engineer, from '78 to '88 pretty much, and I was doing plenty of other things too, and then I eventually graduated to producing. I think my first real production was on Tom Dolby's *Aliens Ate My Buick*, and at that point, I thought, "If I'm a producer, then I'd better be a producer, I should go back and engineer for Jeff," so we were still really good friends, and would have dinner, etc. It's impossible to put into details everything I picked up from working with Jeff: it's an attitude, it's a creative process, or creative lack of process, it's an openness to a thing being started and taking its own direction that you hadn't planned on. He comes from Birmingham, and I don't really see where he would have got a Zen education, but Zen is the word I would use to describe the way he allowed a song to form and define itself. Also, the idea of do-it-yourself, he wanted to do everything himself, or at least with the two or three people who were in the room.

By the time he was reinventing that concept in his own artistic application for *BAD*, Jackson's equal appetite for experimenting with and expanding pop's boundaries would result in the singer's taking advantage right off of Bottrell's cutting-edge beat-making talent, such that

I did a lot of drum programming on that record. I really liked samplers, and was quite into that from the beginning, because it's a powerful tool for a guy sitting in the engineer's spot, to help create the sound of the song. They were crude devices, and then there were keyboards that came out and people were using the stock samples out of the boxes, and I didn't like that approach, I liked making sounds myself. So we'd use an AMS sampler and put sounds in there, but it was mono, and I had a real problem because I wanted to create Moogs and samples myself. So I started using a Publison, where you could trick it into a good stereo image of a sample on a Moog, but it was very convoluted and very hard to use, but that's what I was using during the *BAD* era, that and a Linn 9000 drum machine, just banging on things. Part of the technique—that I had first learned from Jeff—was to look around the room and see what's there, but we certainly labored over those grooves.

During that time, I never took cassettes home from the sessions at his house because Michael had this whole security thing and I wanted to honor that, but when the record came out, it was hard for me to tell a lot of it from what we had done in the demos. I did believe Michael wanted to get some creative control, and that was the point of that year that me and John Barnes spent there, where Michael could experiment with the album's grooves and sounds in this freer environment and then ask Quincy and Bruce to replicate it, so seven or eight of the songs on the *BAD* album came out of our demos.

The finished product would move Jackson's sound forward with the times, pushing them with a daring collection of songs that *VIBE* magazine observed that "Jackson ran the show, leaving all-world producer Quincy Jones to settle on backseat driver duties." The King of Pop would take the reins even more tightly when he began work on his follow-up to *BAD*. Calling on Bottrell in an even more essential role with the *Dangerous* LP, Jackson had established enough confidence in Bottrell to promote him to the coveted status of coproducer, a gamble that would show immediate creative dividends when, within the *first two* days of recording, Bottrell had already fleshed out the bulk of what would become the singer's first #1 hit of the 1990s, "Black & White."

The song's potential to be a hit was crystal clear when Bottrell had first heard Jackson bop nonchalantly into the room humming the song idea for the first time, unguarded and arguably in his purest and most open state as a songwriter—that is, the best place for a producer to come across new song ideas to build on, especially if you were a composer as well. Vibing off Jackson's knack for pulling infectious melodies out of thin air, once that one began bouncing around in his own mind, he knew they were on to something as he began producing what would become his first #1 hit as a credited producer. Bottrell talked about the creative chemistry between him and Jackson at work, saying that

the idea for "Black and White" came at the very beginning of the *Dangerous* sessions. Before we even knew he was going to go record a new album, we were going to record two songs and put them on a greatest hits of some sorts. So the day we started working at Westlake, Michael came in the studio and hummed out the lead riff of "Black and White," and he wasn't referring to guitar or anything, but there was a guitar sitting right there, so I picked it up, played it, he liked it, and I thought it was a great guitar riff. He'd come in that day just to scratch out some vocals, and the way we hear the song today, I encouraged him to leave it the way it was, and he was not one to listen to me if he had another idea. He normally would say in those moments, "No Bill, I want to do it again, because I want to do this, this, and this . . ." But this time he didn't. I think he appreciated the rawness of the vocal, and I don't think some of the words were even finished, but we both agreed on leaving it, and there it sits. So that was a rare case where I got to hear the whole melody and lyric pretty much by day two.

Each song was different in how we wrote, but on that one, we got a real crude track together based around the guitar riff, which was there from day one, and almost the only thing that stayed, because that song got worked on a lot and evolved quite a bit. I programmed the drum track for that eventually, and at first it was a very crude Linn 9000 drum machine beat on there up until the very end. Because it was such a little ditty with very little to it, we both knew it needed a bridge, and the bridge was done for like a year, I think, where we had this long 16-bar middle section with just a click. That song finally came together in the final days of making *Dangerous*, because at the time, while everybody loved the song, it wasn't sounding that great until I used my own samples and reprogrammed the drums.

A catalyst for Bottrell to spread his wings fully for the first time as a songwriter in the studio, his ideas were so electric they would cause longtime fan *Sound on Sound* to later note that the sum of his compositional contributions, "in all . . . (on) the *Dangerous* project accounted for about 18 months of Bill Bottrell's life, and working on it brought him into direct contact with the overblown megastar ethic at its most extreme. This, in turn, was an education for him, both in terms of conforming to this type of sensibility and in concluding that in future he'd rather work on rootsier, more understated, less commercially obsessed projects—ones that would connect with his own Appalachian and country leanings." Beyond the personal, professionally, the album would mark Jackson's first #1, crossing over into an age where many '80s R&B pop stars were suffering in sales. Bottrell and Jackson—based on the radio strength of "Black and White," a song they'd written and coproduced from the ground up—showed that Bottrell had plenty of inspiration to spread around.

Bottrell's next collaboration after his wild success with Michael Jackson would launch the career of one of the '90s' biggest female pop stars, Sheryl Crow, earning her a Grammy for "Best New Artist" and a shared Grammy for her and Bottrell for "Record of the Year." The *Tuesday Night Music Club* may have become the title of the album they made together, but it started very much as a living, breathing musical experiment that, for the producer, began

toward the end of *Dangerous* when I built my dream studio, and had all my favorite mics, and a Neve 8058 console that was modified from 48 bits, and I had a large concrete room with fabric over the concrete, and fifteen-foot ceilings. I did a lot of mixing in the early '80s, different mixes for people, so I worked out of a lot of studios, and I got the chance to work on lots of different boards, and liked the Neve 8078 at A&M and Motown, just the way it sounded, it made everything sound better. I'd also once worked on an 8058 in a mobile truck up in Woodstock, and dug that too, so I was happy with the Neve.

Then we had a drum booth that was also concrete with really heavy fabric over it, which I'd learned from famous studios and seen how to construct it. I really applied a lot of what I'd seen traveling the world in the previous ten years, and I really liked that studio, particularly the drum room, which I think I really got right. There was a lot of wood and carpet ceiling, and my brother was a builder so he built this room for me. It had a low eight-foot ceiling, a lot of fabric and wood panels, and then some glass doors, and a big A-top at the back, and it worked so well, the drums were just busting in there. The bass drum, on one wall was a cavity that went back six feet or so filled with absorptive material, so the room was actually bigger than you could see, and so all you saw was a bookshelf.

I kind of got into books and bookshelves in studios, and that album was the first time I did that and have done it ever since, because I found over the years that records sound better when they're played in houses as opposed to studios. Specifically big manor houses that are dramatic and dark and have book shelves from floor to ceiling and interesting things in them, things just come out better that way or maybe it's just more fun to do it in a space like that. It was a Disneyland touch, you know, and by the way, every book was chosen by me too, but it was a sonic thing as well. So this bookshelf in the drum room looked like a fireplace or mantle, and behind that, was black fabric and behind that was this gigantic, 6 x 8 x 10 cavity.

Describing Toad Hall Studios as "an unconventional environment," *Sound on Sound*—elaborating in 1994 on its layout—depicted a recording refuge "with its high, long, faux-stone room, neo-Gothic lighting, tapestry-draped walls and opulent array of classic recording equipment . . . (located) in Pasadena, a few miles north-east of Los Angeles." The magazine added of Bottrell's vision for the music he planned to produce within its walls that, by that point, "he had chosen to turn his back on contemporary recording methods and on what he perceived as overblown superstar projects in favour of employing old techniques with new artists—working live, working more immediately, leaving things raw, never doing demos." Indeed a dream come full circle for the producer, the studio's opening coincided with a truly liberating time in Bottrell's career he fondly remembered feeling

was quite a moment for me, because "Black or White" came out and stayed #1 for six weeks, so I was very happy with my Michael experience, but by the time that happened, I'd just finished building the studio, and had done a couple records, one of them being with David Baerwald, a really brilliant songwriter-lyricist-thinker who had inspired me about songwriting, and through recording that album, started to develop this crew of players. So when David's record was done, neither of us wanted to stop playing together, so he called me up and said, "Well, let's just get together every Tuesday night and do something for no reason," and we started doing that, and it was freer than I'd ever dreamed we could be.

Started well ahead of Crow's joining the gang, Bottrell was eager to expand his songwriting collaboration with David Baerwald to include other like-minded musicians whose organic organization featured some of LA's most talented players, including Kevin Gilbert, a multi-instrumentalist (guitar, bass, drums, keyboards); Brian MacLeod (Madonna, Seal, Pink, Melissa Etheridge, Jewel, Stevie Nicks); and Dan Schwartz on bass. Bottrell felt this progression was a natural fit after

I had written some pop songs for Michael, and did consider the next step in my evolution would be writing, so I started letting go of engineering. At that time, I was wearing a lot of hats, and decided to take a couple of them off, and so I still engineered, but didn't obsess, and in fact, kind of became obsessed with the concept of crude engi-neering, and that first became apparent on *Tuesday Night Music Club*. It became an aesthetic for me not to do that, I wanted the songs to come through in the lyric and the story. David was very inspirational in that, but always with a priority of the story or the meaning of the song, and initially we weren't going to make an album out of it, but eventually decided to with Sheryl's album, though that wasn't the first idea.

I had done this album *Toy Matinee* a couple years prior in 1990 and had really engineered the crap out of it and made it sound awesome and everything, and had already become intrigued by songwriting through making that record. But then, after it was released, I got all these comments about "Aw man, how'd you get that snare sound?," and I really rebelled against that, and never looked back. I later on in my career went back to trying to get "good sounds" again, but really went for ten years being the engineer that never got in the way of anything. Luckily, that worked to the benefit of the concept we were trying with what became *Tuesday Night Music Club*.

The conduit that would ultimately channel all of these talents into one electric, eclectic sound on tape arrived the night Crow first did, with the producer recalling that

Sheryl first joined our little club through being Kevin Gilbert of Toy Matinee's girlfriend. She had a deal at the time on A&M, and they hadn't really liked the album she'd made, so Kevin was coming to me and saying, "Help us out, see what you think," and I just said to him after one of these calls, "Well, bring her down on Tuesday night."

The invitation would help bring a creative order of sorts to the proceedings with Crow turning out to be the missing musical member the club had been unknowingly searching for to round out their sound. Highlighting the #1 single "Leaving Las Vegas" as electric evidence of the latter, Bottrell confirmed that

the first night she came down, the chemistry was there immediately because we made "Leaving Las Vegas" that first night! She sang her ASS off, I had never heard a rock vocal that good, and I was convinced that I wanted to make her album, and the four or five of us should stick together and make it in this way, make it up as we go, write the songs and record them.

A brilliant showcase for what *Electronic Musician* magazine felt was the producer's un-common "knack for creating records that combine the refinement of a modern studio-re-corded CD with a profound sense of rock 'n' roll vibrancy," Bottrell revealed that "Vegas" was in fact an extension of the rhythmic ground he'd first broke working with Michael Jackson, sharing that the song's rhythm track was a loop made of recorded elements that I had saved up over previous years. For instance, there's a conga and distant mic kit, and there's one mic on the conga, which is Lenny Castro on conga, because previously, I'd hired Lenny Castro and Jim Caravela to play a loop for a Michael Jackson song that never got beyond the groove. So I had that in my Akai, and I took it and turned the drums off, so you can still hear them, but the main element of those drums is the conga loop from Lenny Castro. I had Brian MacLeod play snare fills later on, but that's about it, and the handclaps, they came from the Dynacord.

An instant fan of Crow's voice, the producer opted to team her range up with a multipattern tube condenser microphone that had long been his favorite vocal microphone, explaining that

I had two U-47s, they are my favorite. I bought the first and second ones I heard, and I used them ever since for vocals. I like that mic because it's kind of dirty, good for rock, and you can use it carefully and make it kind of pristine too, it's got a rich midrange, and is not that bright. I don't like brightness on vocals, probably on that record because I used a lot of compression on Sheryl's vocal, and the compression makes that microphone sound ugly. Sheryl's vocals were recorded half live off the floor, it was different on every song. But for instance, her lead vocal on "Leaving Las Vegas" was tracked live with the band, and the loop. Then the other half of the time, she would have recorded a scratch vocal and then we would overdub the vocal. I didn't have booths and things except for the drum room, so on some songs, there would be leakage and that could have complicated matters.

Once the magic of "Leaving Las Vegas" was down on tape, what followed would become a weekly Tuesday evening recording session that embodied a stylistic kaleidoscope of musical influences at play synchronously. It was the decade's first record of its kind to be an avant-garde, pop mishmash of every possible style the ear wants to hear mixed up in one album that would dazzle critics upon release, with the *New York Times* praising *Tuesday Night Music Club*'s "informal, homegrown arrangements," while the *LA Times* liked the compilation of "oddball gems" that *Billboard* would conclude "has a loose, ramshackle charm."

Turning to another of those jewels in that collection—one that *Rolling Stone* felt was a brilliant musical melange of "L.A. folk funk, piano-bar blues"—to elaborate on the evolution of the hybrid drum sound he'd perfected by the recording of "All I Wanna Do," Bottrell explained that its development dated back to

the late '80s, when I was growing kind of tired of the drum kit as a sound in records. I remember working with Madonna, and she came from drum machines and club

137

music. We were doing "Like a Prayer." I was engineering and that was more of a rock record, so we didn't have a lot of the drum machines or electronics, we were trying to make a rock record for Madonna, and she was reasonably into that, early on (laughs). So I miced up the kit, and we start running through the songs, and she gets a look on her face and asks, "What's that clicky thing?" And Pat looks at her and says, "That's the hi-hat," and she replied, "I don't like it," and I remembered that, and kind of agreed. It's like, there's certain things about a drum set that I felt by 1990, or even during the *BAD* album, had run its course, and I had sat there for so long with Michael and others inventing sounds to make a groove, as opposed to having a musician come in and play on this standardized kit thing, which is so limiting.

So by *Tuesday Night Music Club*, I was really applying that theory, so there were click tracks and loops and grooves that I put together ahead of time, and then I'd have the drummer—Brian McCloud, who was totally into what I was trying to do—just play part of a kit, or some fills, or play along with the loop. By that time, I'd found my dream stereo sampler, which was an Akai and was the first stereo sampler that actually worked, and once I got ahold of that, I just loaded it up, I spent days and days during work on the *Dangerous* album just loading it up with all these stereo files. I used those to make these loops, and along with that, there was this Dynacord 8-bit cool-sounding little drum machine. I got used to the settings and would run those.

Where there were live drums throughout the record, I suppose I would have started with a U-47 Phet on the bass drum, an SM 57 on the snare, and depending on the arrangement for the rest of the kit. Quite often we weren't recording the whole drum kit, but for toms and things when we did, I liked KM-54s, and then I had these Shoeps mics that I would sometimes change with the KM-54s and put in front of the kit about a foot and a half above the ground pointing up, left and right.

Another of the record's Top 40 hit singles, "I Can't Cry Anymore," would demonstrate the true boldness of the fly-by-the-seat-of-their-pants approach the gang took with both creating and capturing performances to tape throughout recording. Bottrell pointed to the song's central riff as evidence of that bravery, confessing that

I regret it to this day because it's a great guitar riff, because I just took the first idea from the first time I ever played it, and didn't really play what I was hearing, and I've heard other people play it from the record since, and I'm like "It doesn't go like that," but it does actually! I went back and listened to the record, and realized I was just barely writing this thing when I laid it down on tape, and kept that first take. I was playing an old Telecaster, and this little 5-watt Marshall amp I used to like a lot, and it would have miced it up with whatever was closest to the amp. By then, again, it was anti-engineering, and the focus was to get the song written and get the thing on tape, so we had a bunch of microphones on booms and stands, and they were swinging

around the room constantly while people changed instruments, and so besides vocals and acoustic guitars and drums, I didn't really get picky about it.

Touching on the album's softer side with the creation of "Strong Enough," a fem-power ballad that *Guitar* magazine felt helped Crow become "one of the leaders of the Lilith Fair generation," Bottrell remembered his go-to microphone for capturing the song's gentle acoustic sound as

a KM-54. Sometimes near the soundhole, and sometimes if the player could sit still, I'd place it a quarter-inch from the back of the guitar behind the bridge, just micing the wood for a midrangy sound. The main acoustic on that song also had this Roland delay on it. I used to have these Roland delays, and I'd set them for very short delays with a Wobbler on them, that's how Jeff Lynne used to work, "Put a Wobbler on it." And I'd put them left and right, and just crack it open a little bit on something I wanted to come forward in the mix efficiently, and be a little important. It's a cheap trick, it's a chorus effect, but it didn't come out of a box. I had to set it up myself the way I did at the time. With another of the record's slower numbers, "I Shall Believe," I tended to love the B3 and used it all the time, including on that song.

A massive success creatively in the studio and commercially upon release in August 1993, *Tuesday Night Music Club* would peak at #3 on the *Billboard* Top 200 albums chart and launched Sheryl Crow into global stardom. While he found the album's success an artistically satisfying validation of the experiment he'd begun two years earlier with Toad Hall Studios, its popularity proved to be a double-edged sword that cut the other way in the fallout with Crow that followed, leading to a deep disillusionment for Bottrell that

started with *Tuesday Night Music Club*. And if you go into the late '90s and into the 2000s from there, the industry was really changing, and I would say up until '95 or so, I wanted to stick with people, I wanted them to be friends. I wanted to work with them repeatedly, and me and Michael couldn't help but develop a bond over pretty much being either alone or with one other person out at his house for a year, and that certainly informed much of our relationship on the next album, *Dangerous*, and I understood that. Me and Jeff were friends, and going forward, I just really liked work- ing with my friends, that's how projects came to me. There were no managers that called me, or record company people. I didn't even know a record company person until Sheryl's album went big and I got on their radar, it was all artists to craftsmen.

Elaborating on Bottrell's disenchantment, *Sound on Sound* shed further light on the circumstances surrounding his and Crow's falling-out, reporting that "Sheryl Crow's rela- tionship with Bottrell and the *Tuesday Night Music Club* had been productive, but it would not last. By the time that she and Bottrell commenced work on her follow-up album towards the tail end of 1994, they found it hard to conceal their mutual antipathy, and before long there was the inevitable explosion. Crow and the record company were now reluctant to allow Bottrell to do what he wanted, and demanded more rock-oriented material. In a purported attempt to diffuse the tension, in the Summer of 1995 the recording locale was switched from Toad Hall to Daniel Lanois' Kingsway Studio in New Orleans, but on the second day there was a heated argument and Bottrell walked."

The producer would find redemption a few years later with another of his treasured studio experiments when he returned to the studio to make Shelby Lynne's 1998 *I Am Shelby Lynne* LP, earning the rising star a Grammy for "Best New Artist." A continuation of Bottrell's independent streak with defying major label conventions in favor of an approach that the *Austin Chronicle* in its review of the album would conclude proves "beyond a reasonable doubt there are second acts in American lives. After a stint as a CMT ingénue gone awry, she dropped off the radar before re-emerging with this out-of-time gem." For the producer, the experience of having a comeback hit with his

> do-it-yourself approach was a very pure process for me. Danny Goldberg was the head of Mercury Records at the time, and he suggested I get with Shelby and see what happens. This was five years after *Tuesday Night Music Club* came out, and it was a great process because she brought so much that I learned from and gave in to my wisdom when it was appropriate, and put that album together. I still love that album and am quite proud of it, because it was like the further adventures of *Tuesday Night Music Club*. It felt like the next step, even though there was five years in between, of that concept. I would say *Tuesday Night Music Club* and *I Am Shelby Lynne* defined an aesthetic that did catch on that I never stuck around to take advantage of, which I sometimes regret, only from a financial perspective.

Reflecting in more depth on a career he had walked out on and then back into more times than most producers would dare based on principle, for Bottrell, his successes were never about security, but rather a chance to further free himself from the kind of corporate confinement that commercialism tried to impose on him.

> From a spiritual level, I always move on a little prematurely, because I like to stay really engaged and challenged, and now I don't even make records, and still try to stay engaged and challenged in things because I just sort of evolved out of that because of a lot of factors: everything that goes in the record business that made it not very fun for me. So I moved on, and have always done that, and sometimes I say, "Man, I wouldn't have to live month-to-month today if I hadn't left," but the rest the time, I'm happy.

That bliss, when it has come, hasn't come easily to Bottrell in spite of the good times his music has given a generation. For a producer who has gambled—more successfully, it could be argued, than not—on principles over commercial output for the better part of thirty years, he confessed that even when success ran integrity out the studio door once a record he created was a hit, from the purest perch of music fandom,

> I could put any of those songs I made on, and I don't, but if it ever happened, I have the greatest nostalgia and the greatest love for each moment that I can remember, and I'll hear any song I recorded or engineered or mixed over all those years, and I loved every minute of it. My ears are kind of gone, but I just salute them and say, "Well done, lads, you served me well!'

Ultimately, whether Bottrell chooses to hear them or not, a generation of music fans did, in ways that shaped the best times of their lives, nursed them through the worst, and in the end, gave the producer hopefully the greatest reciprocal gift any record man could ask for in the long run, of passing his influence through those records on to the next generation. Bill Bottrell has returned to the studio in the past few years, arguably out of artistic necessity, perhaps sometimes financially, but at the end of any day, his talent hasn't gone away, even if his passion has at times. He acknowledges that once he's sitting behind the console, he finds a sort of peace with the whole process.

> When I do go back into the studio occasionally to make a record, it's old hat, and is very comforting, and I can't deny that I've used it for that in the recent decade a little bit. I'm getting older, and just to be in the studio just feels good in a world that is kind of scary, because it's what I did my whole life. I endeavored to move on from that, to stay vital and stay alive, and the work I was doing was not fair to anybody. The system wasn't really working for me or the artist or for the businessmen that were paying for it.

Baring his soul in every track he every touched, he advises breathing the same spirit of trying anything out of the box or entirely in the box—speaking in a digital context—that might help a young, up-and-coming engineer or producer to

> keep challenging yourself with each piece of music, keep challenging the artists. I do feel we're in an age where the wheel of refreshing pop music and music itself doesn't turn as well as it used to, and for anybody out there making music now, they should keep trying to move that wheel forward.

CHAPTER 8

Magic Man–Mike Flicker

Female-fronted hard-rock acts are a rare thing period, but especially one that has hung around for as many decades as Heart. In the opinion of the Rock and Roll Hall of Fame, which inducted Ann and Nancy Wilson into their little club in 2013, "With a mix of hard rock riffs and lush, driving harmonies, Heart emerged from the Pacific Northwest with one of the most original sounds of the 1970s . . . Heart recorded a series of albums that stand as the best mix of hard rock and folk rock of their era: *Dreamboat Annie*, *Little Queen*, *Dog & Butterfly* and *Bebe Le Strange*. Those records included hit singles that remain standards of rock radio: "Magic Man, Crazy on You," "Barracuda," Straight On," "Little Queen, "Dreamboat Annie," "Dog & Butterfly," and a greatest hits' worth of others that helped "break the mold and rock as hard as their male counterparts," the *New York Times* would argue, "(paving) the way for women in rock."

Mike Flicker, who produced the entirety of the band's classic 1970s catalog, including albums like *Dreamboat Annie* (1976), *Little Queen* (1977), and *Dog & Butterfly*, reflecting back on his own rise with the band, began by offering that

it was probably an unusual situation with the starting of Heart and my career as a producer was based in Vancouver. It was a different situation because my early successes were strictly in Canada, so what happened was I had basically started off in production. I had gone from being a musician in a band called the Zoo—and the significance that has with respect to Heart was my band mate and the person I grew up with since the age of fourteen was Howard Leese. I was actually the person that put Howard into the band. Howard and I went to the same junior high and high school, and were in bands together growing up, and had put a band together when we were in high school called the Zoo, and was probably one of the youngest bands at that time—in the early '60s—to have a recording career. Howard played lead guitar and I was our drummer. We had our first album out when he was fifteen and I was sixteen—back in 1966—and so we worked together there, and the band had pretty good local success in the West of Canada. We toured with Spirit and the Paul Butterfield Blues Band and Blue Cheer. These were big bands back in the 1960s, and for myself, I never enjoyed the live and touring part, so I got involved in the recording side.

We were lucky at that point in time by somebody who wasn't a good match for us—we were kind of a progressive band, and he produced a pop band called the Standells. So I found him very frustrating, and turned my ear toward production, asking "What's wrong with this picture?" I think there's a certain organizational, structural concept in the rhythm players—between the drummer and the bass player—you're sort of the foundation and the structure, and you really get into looking at the structure of songs, and the production. And that translates naturally to the studio, and then from an actually silly point of view, in the production, what happens is usually you put down your basic rhythm track first. Then you're done. So then it's like "Oh, what do I do? Go home?" But in my case, I stood around and watched, and so because you're concentrating on that beginning, structural thing, then my interest perked, and I didn't have any overdubs to do later or vocals to sing, so I was just in watching the process. And some of the people I had the opportunity to watch were good craftsmen of the time. The engineer that did our stuff and that I got to watch was a guy named Ritchie Podler, who did Steppenwolf and Three Dog Night, a lot of the more successful bands of that time.

And just like any other artist of any nature, if you're talking about architectural or graphic or someone who paints, you're influenced by who you were a student of—and when I began to get interested in production, I would say my two biggest mentors who I just really watched everything they did, listened and dissected everything—were Gus Dudgeon, Elton John's engineer, and George Martin, who of course produced the Beatles. So if you dissect the Heart records I made, you'll find all those influences. At the time we started working together in 1975, a big influence of mine was the Elton John *Yellow Brick Road* LP and probably *Abbey Road* and *Sgt. Pepper*.

So once I discovered my interest in producing, still years before Heart, I started out as a runner at American Recordings in Studio City, Los Angeles. I was either at a band practice or at the studio rolling cables. That was Richie Popplar's studio, where all those early Three Dog Night and Steppenwolf albums had been recorded. Through situations and opportunities, I eventually got a job as a demo producer for United Artists Publishing Company, which today is EMI. That's where I really got my first experience producing, because especially back then, doing demo production for songwriters was a mill. On Monday you'd have three different songwriters with six different songs, and you had to produce their demos in a little 3- or 4-track recording studio. So that's where I got my chops, and that led to my doing a demo for one particular songwriter who the head of the publishing company really liked, and sent over to the record company, and they liked the production of the demo and the artist, and gave me my first opportunity to produce a proper record, which turned out to be an R&B duet between Vella and Jimmy Cameron. And it was a great experience, and was the first time I got to work with studio musicians, so I had guys like Billy Preston playing electric piano, and had a budget, and was able to use Gene Page, who was a very popular arranger at the time. He actually became very famous for the Love Unlimited Formula, so that was an influence in my early life as a producer, and that has to do with the time and growing up in LA when R&B was very popular. R&B has its influence in all rock music rhythm-wise.

So at the age of nineteen, whatever opportunity you get, you go for it. So my next thing was, in doing demos, I came across a singer that I really liked, and introduced him to Howard Leese, and Howard helped put together a little band for him, and I had an idea for doing kind of Joe Cocker version of "When Tears Go By," and so we went in and did the master recording of it, and I went about trying to get it placed myself, which ended up with it being released in Canada. So what happened from there was this upstart label in Vancouver picked up the master and wanted to do more recordings, and brought me there to do so. So the head of A&R for that label brought me up there, we did one record, and he got financing to start his own label. He then gave me the opportunity to build a studio and be the in-house producer, and that ended up becoming Mushroom Studios, where we recorded *Dreamboat Annie*.

Owning your own studio is any veteran producer's dream come true, let alone a young up-and-comer like Flicker when he was handed the opportunity. As he began hunting around town for the ideal building to house Mushroom, Flicker knew he wanted a spatial setting for his live room, but kept running into the reality that

back then, what they didn't have in Vancouver at that time was a large room, so I ended up finding the studio that somebody had built, and I just fell in love with the room because they hadn't done it out of necessity, but I felt acoustically it was wonderful because it was built on the side of a hill. So about three-quarters of the room was underground, just in the shape of the way they had dug out from the hill. And had built it out of a cinder block construction, which I just think is wonderful for sound. It was a large room with twenty-nine-foot ceilings, and what had happened was the guy who had built the studio was an older guy in the recording business in Vancouver, who had just had a heart attack and wanted to retire. He had just built this place, and the building was brand new. All he had in there was this beautiful room that had a 4-track tape recorder and a four-bus board, it was basically a POS. So I went to look for my favorite sound, and I was just always a fanatic of tubes, and one of my favorite experiences was recording at Western Studios (now Ocean Way Studios) in LA because they had a completely tube board. This was the time when everyone was going solid-state and getting rid of their tubes, and of course, everyone needed larger consoles now because things were moving from 8-16 and 24 tracks at that time. And this particular console at Western was originally built as a 2-channel stereo console, and then had been modified by Western, which was a division of United Audio, so by the time I saw it, it had been upgraded to a 4-bus board. And I just loved the sound of it, I think it was the warmth and the punch of tubes, and just the whole kind of transparent sound.

I was in the middle of watching the transition, and when I started out, every console was a tube console, and as the solid-state consoles were coming in, I wasn't liking what I was hearing. So what happened was basically I bought the tube console from Western because they were upgrading to a solid-state one, and had it shipped up to Vancouver and retrofitted by adding some line amps to it to a 16-bus console. It was a cumbersome console to work on, because every kind of EQ and everything was all outboard gear. I was very fond at the time of outboard gear like LA2As and LA3As, and I had a lot of old tube gear. So it was a lot of tube compressors, but I also had 1176s, and some of the better solid-state compression and things of that nature, but used a lot of passive EQ, which maintained the integrity of the tube. When I purchased the console, I purchased just a shitload of UA-mated passive graphic equalizers, where we had 8-ban and 12-ban graphic equalizers. The biggest issue with a tube console was heat, because you have to have a huge air conditioner because it really heats up a room, really hot. So we got a big air conditioner. The studio had one really good built-in vocal ISO booth, rather large, and right off the control room. In terms of the mics, it kept changing, but I found my favorite bass drum mics, and would go between the RE 20 and the D 12, and I liked AKG dynamic mics, and my favorite snare-drum mic was using a C 61, which was an old condenser mic.

Aside from being just an exceptional microphone, it had all these wonderful capsules that you could screw on, and had one that was this really tight cardio pattern that was really good for the snare. And these million-screw on pads that allowed you to really pad the microphone prior to its own internal amplifier, and would allow you to use a good condenser microphone without overloading on the snare. And I'd go from using that sometimes on the top, and sometimes would use it on the bottom with a Shure 56 or 57 on top, it just depended on the situation and the sound. And I'd simultaneously mic the bottom and the top of the snare that way. For overheads, I used a C12A, and what I always liked to do was use an unmatched pair set of mics. I know everyone always liked to use matched sets at the time, but I would use an unmatched pair set, because one of the other things I liked was the midrange crack that I would get out of an old U-87 Neumann, so I would put that above the snare on the left side, and the C12A just always has this extraordinary top and bottom that would pick up from the floor toms and the cymbals on the right-hand side. Also, I pretty much had my drum kit set up with that mic set-up, and had a band's drummer play my kit—which was basically a mutt, in that I had an old Rogers Bass Drum that I really liked, and a couple Ludwig snares, and the toms were a combination of Camco and Pearl toms. The range of the mics to the drum set would often depend on the drummer and the size of the drummer, and the throw and how he played.

For *Dreamboat Annie*, I only had one side of the kick drum miced, and pretty much the traditional sound of that time. Basically, what happened was the drummer who ended up on about three cuts on *Dreamboat Annie* —Michael Derochier, ended up being their drummer. And he came from the John Bonham school of drumming, and strictly was a double-headed kind of guy. For guitar and bass, I used to use a combination—with the bass, again because I loved the sound of the tubes, I used a direct sound that went through tube preamps, then had this little Ampeg 15-inch single speaker that I loved the sound of, and had that as the mic sound, and it would kind of combine the two of them to get the sound I wanted. Mostly for that, I loved the RA 20 on that, and it was the bass sound you heard on *Dreamboat Annie* and most of the Heart records I produced. For guitars, I was really a Marshall guy, and had my own 100-watt stack that I really liked, and had tweaked out. I always liked a close and a far mic with a condenser close—a Buyer M69—that had this really nice 3K and 300 cycle hum to it. And I would then use a condenser mic from a distance, which was a 414. For acoustic guitar recording, I typically would use condenser mics—my C61 console mic, an AKG, and a C12 A. I had some guitars that I liked including a D 12, as well as—for Heart—Nancy had this wonderful custom-made acoustic guitar that was made for her by somebody. I loved the sound of that guitar.

Once he had the studio set up, Flicker found himself pulling double-duty in the best possible training ground for any up-and-coming producer, gaining a hands-on education in the art of sound recording due to the fact that

locally at the time I was the only record producer in Vancouver who had hit records, and when I got to town, I discovered there wasn't a good engineer, so by default, I became an engineer as well as a record producer. So through working with local bands I developed that craft, but I had brought with me more knowledge of what I had seen happen rather than done as an engineer. So being that I ran the studio, and was a partner, what we were used to was doing our own production, we could spend all the time we needed because we didn't have the budgetary constraints, so everything was an experiment. So I would hear something on the radio, go out buy the record, put it on and listen, then go into the studio and try to get that. I'd sit around with people who wanted to do demos and would play for free, and I'd play, and tweak, and try to figure out how they had gotten that sound. That approach worked perfectly for producing Heart, where things were kind of backwards as far as what usually happens. In a certain sense, the first album was their studio days—where if you take the Beatles or someone like that, their first five or six albums were rushed out there, and they didn't really get a chance to take their time and work in the studio till their latter days after Sgt. Pepper's, where Heart got that opportunity right out of the gate.

Introduced to the band when they were still local unknowns playing small rock clubs around the Pacific Northwest, originally with Ann Wilson as the sole sister in the fold, Flicker revealed that he initially passed on the chance to work with the band, explaining that

when I first became aware of Heart, there was a band called Heart, and Nancy Wilson wasn't in it, it was only Ann at that time. And they were playing locally in Vancouver and didn't have a record deal yet. When I went to see them live, I LOVED Ann, I thought she was excellent. Her attitude, and tone, and power, but the rest of the band didn't impress me at all. And they had a couple of original tunes which also didn't impress me. So I basically on first listen passed, and told Ralph "If anything happens with the band, keep me abreast." So then months later, he came back to me and said "Ann's sister Nancy was coming up to join the band." And that intrigued me, because it would be two girls in the band. So I basically authorized them to do a demo based of just hearing that news, without even hearing Nancy, who had been down in Oregon going to school. When Nancy joined the group, they became a different band, and went from being just a stock, rock 'n' roll cover band to Nancy's addition of the acoustic guitar and harmonizing vocals with Ann, it just added a different flavor that made them original enough for me to think they had something special. I thought they were definitely stars.

It was only after sister Nancy joined her older sibling onstage as the band's guitarist in a history-making move that the *New York Times* would argue "in its original literal sense . . ." describes "women who rock," " with *Goldmine* magazine adding that the duo "paved the way for female rockers to stand shoulder-to-shoulder with any male musician on the scene." While for critics their greatest accolades may have come from the *way* the Wilson sisters rocked their hits, producer Flicker back at the top of his collaboration was primarily concerned with getting the girls' songs to the point where they were recordable. He offered a fascinating look inside their song development process that began with their

approach to writing back then, which was to treat it as a collaboration, such that the first album—every time Ann and Nancy would write a song—in the rawest sense where sometimes it was just a verse and a chorus, they'd call me up, and we'd sit down and they'd play it usually on an acoustic guitar with vocals. Nancy usually came with the music, and Ann not only with lyrics but also with melodic ideas. Sometimes they had pre-worked out their harmonies. So what we used to do when we were arranging for the album, most of the times, I would play drums and we sat in the studio with the two girls, Howard Leese, and I, and the bass player they had at the time. He had a really great attitude, and ended up staying in the live version of the band, but the problem I had was I didn't feel his playing was up to par at the time for studio recording. But he sat in on the demos.

Our process for developing songs always was Ann and Nancy would come with a song and have something worked out—basic theory. They usually had in mind what they were going to write about before they wrote about it. The two of them would sit down, talk about it, and I'd say "Well, how about if we double a chorus here, and how about let's repeat this bridge here." It would always be taking the pieces they had and restructuring them. Ann was a pretty quick lyricist, so if we were in the studio, and I suggested a new lyrical part was needed, she could whip something out pretty quickly. A lot of times, at the very beginning, they'd play me songs that weren't even finished yet where they were just looking for input. They were just really quick on that, and what I even noticed throughout their career is: whenever I would talk to them about structure, or work on a song in the aspect of structure, that the next time they would write, they were such quick learners that those concepts were now incorporated and adapted to everything.

For instance, they played me "Crazy on You," and the first time we put it together with the band, when we got to the out section, Roger Fisher played the riff, and that was the first time I'd heard that. They'd written the song, and the first time I heard it with the band with that riff, I just loved it. And we sat down in rehearsal and restructured the entire song around the riff. Nancy had written that riff and played it for Roger on the electric guitar, and we created the beat for the song in the studio. Ann and Nancy had come up with the rhythm, and then just sort of knowing Kat's style as a drummer, that's why I chose him for that song. And he picked up on that rhythm and threw it into the shuffle on his hi-hat, and put that into the groove.

On "Magic Man," it was more like we took one part and expanded on it, and got different grooves into it. We did various takes that we all liked, and then I'd comp together different parts. We didn't have a real length in time, and I think each time it was a different length. I think they jammed it out a little more live, and we had a three-minute radio edit of "Magic Man," and I would go in and work on those things, and then Ann and Nancy would approve it. The album-length version ended up being 5 minutes and 35 seconds. When I edited for radio, I was cutting out repetition, trying to keep attention going all the time, and keeping new stuff happening and progressing, and not allowing the song to stagnate. And you're also focusing on radio at the time—I would do something different in 1977 than I would in 1980. The girls understood that game as well. For the recording of that song, and all of the songs on *Dreamboat Annie*, they always tracked live in the studio as a band. Most of the songs on the album were all done in the studio first, and then live, so they were really morphing as a band during the studio process.

Recording as they wrote what would become their debut LP, *Dreamboat Annie*, the producer found that the Wilson sisters were fearless from take one, recalling that

in recording Heart, the girls were totally easy in transitioning from the stage to the recording booth. There was no mic-shy, they transitioned into the studio without any problem, which can often be a problem with artists who are totally green to recording, which is very different in nature from performing live. They were a pretty good collaboration in part for that reason, I think because we were arranging the songs together, it always was that way.

Diving headlong by this point in their collaborative relationship into the making of *Dreamboat Annie*, little did the producer nor his diamonds rocking their way steadily out of the rough know that they were creating in the process an album that would forever alter the female rocker paradigm. Injecting the kind of credibility with their sound that would inspire *Billboard* to later note that "in the 1980s and '90s, numerous women recorded blistering rock, but things were quite different in 1976—when female singers tended to be pigeonholed as soft rockers and singer/songwriters and were encouraged to take after Carly Simon, Melissa Manchester, or Joni Mitchell rather than Led Zeppelin or Black Sabbath. Greatly influenced by Zep, Heart did its part to help open doors for ladies of loudness with the excellent *Dreamboat Annie*," making it clear that "Nancy and Ann Wilson had their own identity and vision early on." Communicating that vision through performances made recording a debut LP much easier for the producer, Flicker reasoned, because

first of all, Ann was an excellent performer, so once she got warmed up, you just started taping and keeping. *Dreamboat Annie* was recorded over a little more than a year, and back in those days, we were working on sixteen tracks, so there wasn't a lot of many, many takes. I always recorded warm-ups from the get-go, and sometimes the first, second, third take there's stuff there. With Ann, it didn't take long, and at that point in time, we never had the luxury of keeping one or two takes at a time because of track availability. So once I'd got what I called my master take, then I would just start punching in, fixing any little flaws. Ann usually got a performance in one take, and it was usually 60–90 percent of the song, and then it was a matter of fixing this or that. Then there were the exceptions, like "Crazy on You," where conceptually I had something different in mind. We approached it differently, to where conceptually I always had in mind that the verse and chorus were coming from a totally different place—so I had Ann sing all the verses first, so I always felt the verses and the chorus were two different songs in a certain way. And I always wanted to feel like it was coming from two different places, and they actually overlap.

Ann's still finishing the choruses when she comes into the verses. The way the recording on that album went, first we went in and recorded some songs. And back then, we were making a record for Canada, and had our own label, Mushroom Records, so we recorded the song "How Deep It Goes," released it as a single, and it had moderate success. Then we recorded "Magic Man," and that had big success, so after that we said, "It's time to do a follow-up single and an album." That was pretty much proper marketing in Canada at that time. You couldn't really market an album without a couple successful singles. So they were playing me songs, and one day played me "Dreamboat Annie," and I said, "I don't only love this song, I love it as a concept for an album." And so threw that back at them, and then we talked about the way it would work in an album. So they said, "Conceptually, we hear it this way," and played it. And also, I said, "I think it would sound great as kind of a perky, country-ish song, with the banjo and whatnot. Then to wrap up the album, let's reprise it with an orchestral version." So with that in mind, we basically recorded all three at the same time. We recorded them as three separate songs, but that album title and theme came out of a collaboration of ideas.

When I recorded Nancy, it was usually after I'd get a master track of Ann's lead, then Nancy would come in and do her harmonies, or at the same time. A lot of times, Ann would harmonize to her own vocal with Nancy, and sometimes they'd be together. This was a sisters/partners team who'd been singing together since they were five years old. If you look at further credits on *Dreamboat Annie*, you'll see I brought in their sister Lynn because the three of them together was crazy, in terms of how much that sibling tonality was right there. When I mixed *Dreamboat Annie*, I liked working with the end in mind, and because of the limitations of the gear we had at the time available, and sixteen tracks, I was always doing final steps as we'd go. I'd always take great lengths at making my monitor mix something that was a representation of where I was going with the mix, to the extent of 90 percent of all the delay, reverbs, etc. that were on vocals and lead guitars. Most of those decisions were made when we were recording. I used to record Ann's voice, all treated with effects, totally with repeats and everything on it. A vocal microphone that I found and kept through my entire career recording with Ann, to where every vocal I recorded was recorded on one mic, a very early U87. When I was recording Ann for the first time, I was actually in the market to buy a new microphone, so I had a rep in Vancouver who repped both AKG, Buyer, and Neumann, and he came and brought every vocal mic they had. So we lined them up in the studio, and I had Ann come and sing one day, just playing with sound, and she sang into every microphone they had, and one microphone just grabbed me over the others, and I bought that microphone personally and kept it with me for a long time.

Attached at the hip onstage and in the studio, personally and musically, the kindred kinetics of Ann and Nancy's dynamic translated to a united front of support for one another artistically that was loyal to such an extreme that

throughout the first album, *Dreamboat Annie*, I never remember doing a vocal with Ann without Nancy by my side at the console. Ann would usually ask for Nancy's opinion when she finished a vocal take. I think Ann felt better knowing Nancy approved. The thing about working with them was, right off the bat, they were—just as people—reasonable people. There were never big egos—if Ann would do something, and I said, "I think you can do that better," there was never a problem. And I think it was a mutual respect thing, because if she got a take that I really liked, and she came back in and listened, and said "I think I can do this part better," I'd then say, "Well, go back and do it." So I think it comes down to if you have that mutual understanding and respect, it just works that way.

As far as effects I put on Ann, I had this disc delay system—it would kind of be like an Echoplex, but it was made in Germany, and instead of being tape, it was a magnetic disc with movable heads. And so you could get the exact delay that you'd want, and then it had its own regeneration feedback loop, so you could get as many repeats as you want. I used that till it broke, around the end of "Dreamboat Annie." What I liked about it was the degradation of the high end, you'd be lucky by the time you got to the slap if there was anything above 5K, and the further out you got, the worse it got. So it was kind of like the old 7 ½ IPS slowed down tape-delay kind of thing. Then MXR came out with this thing called MXR DDL, and it was a horrible effects box that I loved, that did the same thing.

Again, this was in the '70s, and technically when you got to five hundred milliseconds, there was no frequency response, so to me it sounded like when you'd be in a stadium, and hearing things coming off of a wall. But it worked relative to Ann's voice. The first time I used that second effect was on "Barracuda," and throughout the recording of *Magazine* and *Little Queen*. As far as the mixing on *Dreamboat Annie*, and most of the Heart records I made, Ann and Nancy would come around for some of the mixing sessions, but their concept of mixing, at first, but in general, mixing was like watching the paint dry. Later on they got a little bit more interested, but usually they'd like to hear something that was more of a finished product and then comment on it. I think my production style, where there was never a surprise when the mix came—for myself, I always took great lengths of making monitor mixes that were representative of where I was going.

Mixing to me wasn't a big production, where all of a sudden you'd hear things that weren't there before, or that there'd be some crazy things. Even when we were recording *Dreamboat Annie*, I'd bring in the ocean effects while we were recording it. It wasn't like we did that at the end of the process, all those things were developing as the production was developing. The guitar blends were created as we'd go, and one of the things that I used to like to do a lot—and was one of the things that got Howard and Nancy at an early stage working together—was to record acoustic guitars at the same time. A lot of their stuff was two-part acoustic guitar things, so Howard would play one and Nancy would play the other. They fed off of each other's instincts. Howard was more structured, and Nancy was more unstructured and free, a little more raw and I think that helped a lot. Either one—Howard could get technically where he could get cold, Nancy sometimes left alone could get too wild in abandon. They had kind of a yin and a yang that worked well together. In the early days, anything that was dual guitars, Howard wrote and taught to Roger Fisher. Nancy was more there for rhythm and groove.

Upon release, *Dreamboat Annie* took the mid-'70s hard-rock world by storm, producing Top 10 singles with seminal hits including "Magic Man" (#9) and "Crazy on You" (which even reached #1 on the French singles chart). *Rolling Stone* would summarize the success the Wilson Sisters had achieved as "shrewdly pulling off a Led Zep role reversal. Lead singer Ann Wilson can shift from pop-thrush blandness to piercing shrieks with a stroke of a power chord, as she does on 'Crazy on You' and 'Magic Man,'" adding that the group's sophomore LP, *Little Queen*, would up "the heavy quotient on hits like 'Barracuda.'"

"Barracuda" overnight became an anthem for the ages, political campaigns (including Sarah Palin's 2008 vice-presidential rallying cry, to the great ire of the band, who demanded she cease using the song at events), sports events big and small, and a radio staple that still rotates regularly around the country on classic rock radio. Heading into the smash hit's recording, producer Mike Flicker remembered recognizing right off the bat that

we knew from the outset that the big hit single off of *Little Queen* was going to be "Barracuda." The interesting thing about that song is it wasn't recorded at Mushroom Studios, which was different for me. It was a different console and different studio. After they'd gone on tour for a while and after I'd recorded some of the stuff for *Magazine*, they wanted to move back home to Seattle. And I knew this, so I had an opportunity at the time to make a deal with a studio down in Seattle which allowed me to go in and make some adjustments to their room, which mainly involved making it live. It had been one of those '70s Westlake rooms that basically was like walking inside of a marshmallow. The studio at the time was called "K Smith Studios," and so they allowed me to go in and start from scratch, so I gutted the room, and did as much as we could in the space to make it live. We ended up having to record "Barracuda" in their other studio because the one I was working on wasn't ready yet. I ended up using the same mic setup for "Barracuda" that I had on *Dreamboat Annie*, but the kit was different because by then we were using a hybrid.

Michael Derosier was still letting me use some of my drums, and he was using some of his drums. So what we did was I built a kind-of almost like a room for his bass drum, because he wanted to use the double-headed, and to get a little bit more concussion, he allowed me to cut a little hole in his bass drum. And so I did a thing where I was able to isolate the bass drum in what looked like a little tunnel in front of the bass drum. For that setup, I used an RA 20 mic right directly on the bass drum, then I had a 57 mic on his beater with a gate to get the attack, and finally had a 414 A as a distant mic. For the guitars on that song, there was a particular flanger which was an experimental thing that a friend of Roger's had built. It never actually saw the light of day outside of "Barracuda," it was in this aluminum box with knobs and whatever, and just had an extreme flanger that really helped that crunchy guitar sound. We've never gotten that guitar mic since.

What was kind of experimental about it was it sat between the preamp and the power amp, so Roger actually had a jack built into his Marshall where you could take the preamp out and do direct sounds. So it came out of that, into this flanger, out of the flanger, and back into the power amp. Then Howard had his own flanger that he used for his rig, and they flanged up a storm together. There were three guitar tracks on that song including Nancy, who played an Ovation, which was miced and direct. As with *Dreamboat*, my electric guitar mic of choice is an M 69. My theory with mixing guitars, with that song and all the other Heart songs, was if you had one guitar part that does the trick, you can turn it up louder, and it will do more. So less is more kind of theory, which I always felt was the Beatles' success. George Martin would have twelve guitars doing one part, so that you never really heard any of them over another. So that's how I mixed the guitars on "Barracuda." Whenever we'd do rhythm, power acoustic guitar—and I think this is something I developed that became a trademark—most of the time it was three guitars at once, and I would record Nancy, Howard, and Roger playing acoustic guitar, mic it all live, and put it on one stereo track. That kind of positioned them the way I wanted to hear it so they'd get the balance. That was stationary throughout the early stuff on *Dreamboat Annie, Little Queen,* and *Magazine.*

If "Barracuda" reflected a fighting spirit, it's because that's what the band and their producer were in fact in the midst of, a battle against a mountain of odds and obstacles that would have driven most artists crazy, but the pressure driving Ann and Nancy would write a different story entirely. Racing against a lawsuit deadline to finish up work on "Barracuda" in order to retain rights to the master, the song's subject matter reflecting just such a battle against corporate control over the band's image and creative destiny, Flicker confirmed that

what happened was, for the album *Magazine*, we had recorded four or five studio tracks before *Little Queen* when the lawsuit happened between Heart and their label Mushroom, and the band left and signed to CBS Records. There had been certain promises made regarding the marketing of the group, which had to do with the conceptual subject of *Magazine*, that the girls would not be marketed as a piece of meat. Luckily, "Barracuda" had not been recorded yet, so we still had rights to it, so after getting past the lawsuit, we started creating the next album that became *Little Queen*. When we went in to record *Little Queen*, the lawyer had sat us down and said, "There's a hearing in three weeks, and at that hearing, we don't know if you're going to be stopped from completing *Little Queen* until the lawsuit is settled, or not. It's going to be up to a panel of nine Federal judges." Mushroom was going after a temporary restraining order to stop Heart from doing any more recording at all till the lawsuit was settled. So the lawyer said, "But, if you actually get the album on the streets before then, the chances are way, way in your favor that the judge is not going to stop it." So they gave us our choice, and the group decided they were going to finish the album. So for three weeks, I had the group recording in two studios at one time for three weeks, where I was running from doing a vocal in one room to listening to a guitar solo in the other room. Then when some songs were finished, I would be mixing in one room, then running in and listening to overdubs in the other. And literally had to make the deadline, so they had chartered a jet for me that flew me directly from Seattle to Santa Maria, California, where the album was being pressed.

So I went from Seattle to Los Angeles, had it mastered, and then out to the plant in Santa Maria in less than twenty-four hours to meet our deadline, and we just made it. And a lot of the energy you hear in that album's tracks reflects the frenzy of that recording schedule. It was a natural reflection of the pace we were working at, plus there was a certain intent by the group of saying, "Hey Mike, we want this to be more of a group album, and we want it to be less of a polished album." That album was a specific reaction, so you didn't have to talk about what was going on to motivate the energy in the performances, because it was in the air 24-7. It was a war. The girls' performance on that album was different because everything was done with a sense of urgency, and there was no time for reflection. *Little Queen* was a conscious effort on the band's part to be a straight-up rock record, their intent was to make a *come-see* album. I saw it more as they wanted a less-produced, as far as polished, more raw and more of a group sound, which was not what I was going after on the first album because there wasn't yet a group. So it was a different approach, because with our deadline it was also literally like working in a war zone.

Stripping down to bare rock 'n' roll essentials on the album—vs. out of their clothes as the powers that be would have preferred—Ann and Nancy Wilson with *Little Queen* sought sonically to announce their rebellion with authority, inspiring their producer to proceed throughout recording

> with a less-is-more theory in the studio, and more towards a live vibe. Having that opportunity to spend a year and a half ahead of this through the whole evolution of recording the first album, and they respond intellectually to things, and by then, they got it, and the thing that struck a chord with them was—before we even sang—I talked to them conceptually about the fact that, to me, every song is like a script and a mini-movie. And that the vocalist is the lead performer, I believe a singer has to put themselves into character when it's time to go in and record the vocal, and so that's why we've always spent time talking about songs, and making sure at the beginning that we all understood. And as things progressed, and they would take the lead in that, so that when trying to get the performance, I knew conceptually where the song was coming from. I always felt like the role of a producer, generally, and specifically with them, was more like the director of a movie, who's trying to direct a performance.

When things were back on track business-wise, the band were already well on their way to striking a brilliant balance between harder electric fare like "Barracuda," the melodic rock middle ground of "Crazy on You" where they show hints of their acoustic sensibilities, and their outright softer side as was the case with the band's third studio LP, *Dog & Butterfly.* Praised by iTunes for producing an album that, "as its title indicates . . . is both earthy and ethereal, balancing crunchy rock tracks with billowing, mystically tinged acoustic ballads, Ann Wilson comes on strong in hard-pumping tunes like 'Straight On,' 'Cook with Fire' and 'Hijinx,' unleashing her trademark shivery high notes as the band swelters behind her. 'High Time' stands out for its swaggering groove and optimistic lyric. Following these up-beat tracks are a series of atmospheric numbers that show off Heart's more contemplative side . . . Filled with rich instrumental colors and fiery vocal flights, *Dog & Butterfly* may be Heart's most unified artistic statement." Tasked with maintaining that balance sonically from behind the console as the Wilson sisters pursued their latest musical ambition, Mike Flicker shared his memory that

> when we got to the point where we were ready to record *Dog & Butterfly*, I think it conceptually was a little bit of a reflection of the fact that there are two sides, that it's all about yin and yang, and it was an attempt to even go further in both directions. I think there's the dog and butterfly in everybody was our theory, so the record was supposed to reflect both the acoustic side of them and the live side as a band. That's why we went even further to where I was still occasionally going on the road, listening to songs, doing things with them. And they would break in new songs live sometimes

without even telling people, they'd just play them in their shows, songs they had just written. Sometimes they would retool those songs based off the reaction of the crowd.

They came up with a song called "Cook with Fire," which I heard them do live, and we went in the studio, and it just wasn't happening. It just didn't have the energy. So I said "This is crazy, let's go do the basic track live," and that's what we did, because it required the energy of the band live working the crowd. When we recorded that, I brought in a lot of the same studio mics, but leaned—especially on the drums—more towards dynamics. I brought in different overheads.

A lot of the band's live sound grew out of the way we recorded in the studio, so it wasn't that far away. The people who did their live mixing were the same—Ann's boyfriend, Mike Fisher, was their live mixer, and their assistant live mixer was a guy named Brian Foraker, who, when he wasn't on the road, used to come into the studio and apprentice with me. "Mistral Wind" was another one I heard live first, and usually I'm thinking in terms of both the band's playing and the audience reaction, because you can tell what the audience is vibing on from the group. To me, it's always been more about the song, so I would make mental notes when they were playing live. At that point, everyone in the band was pretty collaborative too—a guitar lead would be more Nancy, in terms of the arrangement. Ann and Nancy did as much prearranging as they could, and they used to get together and jam the songs out.

Recording by that point was a lighthearted thing in terms of the band's attitude, they had a sense of humor about it, and that made sense as it was their fourth studio record in three years and the lawsuit had been settled, but because they'd had some success, was a less pressured affair. In a certain respect, after working on the early stuff—which to me is *Dreamboat Annie* through the first half of *Magazine*—things were at a certain creative level, in a good way, but the next creative phase was different. After the lawsuit, and the release of *Little Queen* and then *Magazine*, that to me was a whole phase of that whole aggressive/anger/intense making records out of a wartime environment. Then *Dog & Butterfly* became a reaction to that, where it was like "Okay, now we can take some time."

We spent about a year making that record, so *Dog & Butterfly* was the first album that they had a chance to really spread their creative wings. And upon completion, everybody—but the group, meaning myself, the record company, the management— felt in a certain respect that when they said *Dog & Butterfly* was finished, that it lacked a single. It had a lot of good esoteric and musical qualities, but lacked a commercial hit. At that point, both myself and the manager knew their emotional investment into the album, and so we made a conscious decision not to say anything. Because, first, we felt it wasn't good for them, that they needed to deal with this themselves.

So we went to the record company, and voiced our concerns, but told them we felt it wasn't our place to bring it to the girls, and turned them into the bad guys. But contractually, the record company could not do anything, they had to accept the record as is. But they could say something, so we got the head of Portrait, which was a division of CBS, to attend a listening party, then we all sat down and had dinner, and he said, "We love what you got there, but think you're missing one song. That's our professional opinion." And the girls took it the way I thought they would—which was not very well—but that then allowed the band to sit down and talk to us in a different way, and asked, "Well, do you guys agree?" And in a sort of cowering way, we agreed, and basically from there, the band was given ten days to produce another single. So it went from the girls—who then had a new writing partner in Sue Ennis—going away for a weekend, and coming back with "Straight On," and finishing the album.

"Straight On" became a Top 20 hit for Heart amid the *Dog & Butterfly*'s release in the fall of 1978, keeping the album on the charts for a record thirty-six weeks, moving two million copies in the process and solidifying Heart's status as a major-label arena rock act, one they'd proudly reached on their own terms musically. Not without significant struggle along the way, Mike Flicker seems most proud of the fact the team had produced an against-all-odds catalog of hits that have endured through modern day, offering his assessment that

to me, the place in musical history and the significance for those albums and that band was part of our whole struggle—I produced *Dreamboat Annie*, the whole album, and they didn't have a record deal in the U.S., and when we first tried to get them signed to a label, we got almost the same thing from every label, from every A&R man: "Well, are they a rock band, a pop band, or are they an acoustic band?" That album was all these things. "We can't sell that." A girl rock 'n' roll band is a great idea, but that's not what they were, and I think what happened was Heart was at the forefront of opening up the gate to: you don't have to be pigeon-holed. Especially being females, they got it worse, but you don't just have to be one genre, which was the norm at the time. And I think Heart opened up a lot of opportunities for a lot of females in rock by doing a multiplatform crossover at radio with that album. I think there's a lot of gems in the first five albums, that when people go back to rediscover them, don't just go to the hits, that's always been my hope.

What I enjoyed about the years that I did it was it was more about the performance. To me, I grew up under the guidance—and I think it still holds today if I were going to give anyone advice—that there are three elements to producing a record: the song, the performance, and the production, and it has to come in that order. The number one emphasis should be on the song, and then getting the best performance of that song, and then however the production can help those—then that's great. *Dreamboat Annie* is consistently my favorite Heart record, first because of the songs, second because of the performance, and finally, the production. And I would say that's the only album where I felt all three of them were at the same level.

CHAPTER 9

Eye of the Tiger—Frankie Sullivan

Artist-producers are as rare in rock 'n' roll as the talent would seem. There have been famous examples like Jimmy Page with Led Zeppelin, Brian Wilson with the Beach Boys, Prince, and in the case of one of the top-selling rock anthems of all time, "Eye of the Tiger," Frankie Sullivan of Survivor. From *Big Bang Theory* to countless television commercials, gyms, live sports events across the professional spectrum (NFL, NBA, NHL, etc.), and most famously, the Rocky movie franchise, *Tiger* has broken every record known to hits. As Sullivan mused,

> it's kind of become an iconic part of pop culture. We got nominated for the Oscar, won "Best Pop Rock Performance by a Duo or Group with Vocal" Grammy, the People's Choice Award, and it was a learning experience for me and just a big step. They did some Nielsen rating on the top 10 most downloaded songs off the Internet since they started tracking it, and "Eye of the Tiger" was #1 for over a decade. I still get plaques that people send me, it's amazing . . .

Taking fans back to the beginning of it all—Sullivan's sensibilities as both a player and producer began as a child of the late 1960s and early 1970s—he recalled that my childhood was great. I grew up in the best time, in my opinion, to be a guitar player, because I have four sisters, and I lost my favorite one to breast cancer, she was hip and had the FM radio I used to borrow. It actually had a turntable on it too, and I would find radio stations that were playing Jimi Hendrix and Cream, and I remember the first time I heard "Strange Brew," saying, "What's that sound? That's awesome!" Cream actually played at a club in Illinois when I was fifteen, and I couldn't get in, but I stood outside and could hear them, and remember thinking to myself, "I would love to do that." Who wouldn't at that age? But I used to take my sister's radio and sit under this tree and listen to AOR radio when it first started out, so in Chicago, XRT was playing Hendrix and Cream and Zappa and you can go on and on, they were playing the Jeff Beck Group and the Faces, and I was thinking, "What is this stuff, this is unbelievable!" So every day when I would get home from school, between thirteen and fifteen, I would go snatch my sister's radio because she worked, and I would listen to the most amazing music. Everyone has their own version of amazing, but here I'm turning on the radio and hearing this unknown guy named Jimi Hendrix doing "Crosstown Traffic" and "Wait Till Tomorrow," they used to play all that stuff on the radio. So I grew up in the era where you got Beck, you got Hendrix, Zappa, Clapton, the Stones, when he was really, really cutting edge, and Ritchie Blackmore from Deep Purple, the guy was amazing, and I think that was great for someone who was aspiring to be a guitar player.

I didn't start really playing guitar until I was fifteen. Up until then, I was more intrigued by the music, so I would sit in my room all day and play guitar, and my parents at first would say, "What's wrong with this kid? He just sits in his room with his guitar . . ." But that's what you do, and my friend had a super-reverb that his dad had bought him, a 335, and this was old, like a '64, it was a really cool guitar, so he lent it to me, and it had that little Boss distortion box that you plugged into your guitar, everybody had it, that's kind of what Clapton was using at the time. So I started out playing guitar and trying to imitate guitar sounds you heard on the radio, and again, this was the greatest time to be a guitar player in history, because those guys were all nineteen, twenty, running around in the Yardbirds, and they were kids, but they were making records, and we were listening to them.

Sullivan's first big break came just out of high school when, instead of shipping off to a liberal arts college somewhere

between junior and senior year, I was in a band called Mariah, and we got signed to United Artists' label, but then at first, my dad wouldn't let me make a record till I graduated high school. But eventually he came around, so between my junior and senior year, I made my first record. I remember going in the studio, looking at the gear, thinking "Wow," but was still wrapped up in guitar at the time. After Mariah, I joined

Survivor, and when I first joined the band, those guys were all older than I was, and were listening to lighter stuff, like Blood, Sweat and Tears, and that kind of thing, and I was like "That's not for me, man," and it wasn't. Some of the stuff, like the Byrds, I dug, but at the time, so when I got in the band, I really started focusing on my playing and had just gotten my first Marshall Amp.

His—and the band's—second big break would come when they were assigned one of the business's hottest and most visionary A&R men in record industry history, John Kalodner, who *Billboard* reported "was legendary for discovering, signing and working with a wide array of artists," including Survivor.

We went into the studio to make that first Survivor record in '79, and this was another lucky thing, this unknown A&R guy at the time, John Kalodner, was our A&R man, and he went on to be iconic. He went on to sign Aerosmith, Foreigner, and Guns N Roses, and so when we went in to make our first record, one of the things he did was have us come out to California for about a month. We all lived in this beautiful four-story home on the beach in Marina Del Rey, and we rehearsed and wrote songs, did a lot of practicing every day, and I'm young, nineteen at the time, and was like "This is unbelievable!" So John tells us one day while we're out there, "I want you guys to come play for producers," and I can remember looking at a Cream record, and would say "Produced by Felix Pappalardi," and that was the first record where I'd actually looked at the credits. Well, he was the bass player in Mountain, so I remember wondering out loud to myself, "What's he doing producing Cream?" So thanks to Kalodner, we auditioned for the best producers in the business at the time, every day, for two weeks straight. Every afternoon he would send in another producer, and it started with Roy Thomas Baker, then Tom Weman, all those guys, he had them all come in.

The band's third big break would come with the final producer they met with, one who by that point had racked up multiplatinum records, many of which had been among the most popular in Frankie's record collection growing up. The producer made quite an impression on him from the moment he pulled up to the rehearsal studio. According to Sullivan,

the last producer we met with that day was a guy named Ron Nevison. By this point, we were near the end of the two weeks and had played for everybody, and when Ron came in it was a whole different thing to me: the way he carried himself. First off, he pulled up in a Rolls Royce, and when you're nineteen that's pretty impressive, and when he got out, he dressed impeccably and had a really great vibe and demeanor about him. So when he walked in the room, I sensed there was a difference, so I did a little bit of thinking, and I was a huge Zeppelin fan growing up and had seen every one of their tours. And Ron had worked with Zeppelin, and I was also a huge Stones fan, and I knew Ron had done some work with the Stones too, and then to top it off, I was a huge Who fan, and knew from reading the credits on the backs of all these albums as a teenager that he had helped make *Quadrophenia,* and even as I found out later on after I'd gotten to know him, Ron was even the front of house mixer for Derek and the Dominos! So he had an unbelievable history, and was so rooted with these guys I'd grown up on, but nobody in the band could really decide at first on which producer we wanted to work with! Well, at first, I didn't really feel like I had a say-so, the other guys in the band were all older, and I was the new kid in town. But I was thinking to myself, "I really hope they pick Ron," and they did. So John Kalodner agreed, and we went with Ron.

Sullivan considered Nevison a mentor of sorts, beginning as someone he remembered watching closely in the studio from the first day of recording on, an interest the guitarist remembered the producer took note of quickly.

From the first day I worked with him until the last time I worked with him when I was older, he was unbelievable as far as engineering, being creative, what to do/what not to do. You could pick those things up from him because he made it look so easy, and to me, I think producing a record is the hardest job. I think it's a really, really difficult job, and Ron made it look easy. So one day, about a month into the project, I'll never forget, it was just him and I in the studio, and he says to me, "You kind of like all this, don't you?" And I said, "Yeah, I like it," and he said, "No, I don't mean the playing, I know you like the music, but you like the gear, you kind of like what it does, or what somebody can make it do," and Ron always had a way with words. So I said, "Yeah, I never thought about it, but I suppose I do," and I'll never forget, next he said, "Well, you know what, whatever comes out of here has very little to do with the equipment. All this stuff does is capture it, all you're looking at are gadgets and gear, but they don't really matter without the song and performance." And you can't go to school and learn what Ron can teach you . . . Ron had a vision for that record. So to take his tracks and rerecord intros . . . Ron was a guy who was into that whole "live" vibe, he was into "When the Levee Breaks," and you can't take a record that's recorded like that and try to dry it up and put sterile and newly recorded intros that he would have never liked, and that's what we did, and when the record came out, it didn't do anything, and I felt that had a lot to do with it.

Following disappointing sales, the band found itself working with a far more limited budget heading into the making of their sophomore studio LP, 1981's *Premonition.* Because they couldn't afford a producer of Nevison's stature, Survivor made the fateful decision to self-produce the record, tapping the songwriting team of Frankie Sullivan and Jim Peterik to coproduce the effort.

We went in the studio, Jim Peterik and I, and were producing that record because we had a budget that did not allow us an all-star producer, *or so they thought*. I'll tell you what the drill was: from the day we started even with the song selection, I always said, "Well, you know, if we're gonna write a lot of songs," and Jim and I wrote a lot of songs together, "We gotta have a third ear. Who's gonna listen to them? Are we gonna know enough to put our best work on vinyl?" I really never was sold on that, so every day—as we would record stuff—I was running over the Hill every night with a cassette of the day's work, and through Mike Clink, who would get me into the studio with Ron Nevison, who was doing a Starship record at the time, and I'd play the songs for him. And I'd say, "What do you think?," and with some songs he'd say, "Well, you know, I told you, you can't polish a turd, what else?," and I'd play him the next song. "That's pretty good, but you really should have a section before the chorus that's different from the verse, different from the chorus, you need something a little more," and I did that through that whole project. I felt that it was kind of imperative that, if you really want to be objective about your work, sometimes you have to jump the fence and break a few rules. And I don't know how popular it would have been with the guys at that time, because nobody knew I was really doing it except Mike Clink, who I would call up and say, "Mike, is it a good time?," and I'd run over. But I didn't really think we were qualified to self-produce. Did I think we could write a good record? Yes, and with Phil around, I thought we could get a good sound, but could we be objective enough or did we even know enough to pick the right tracks? Considering that Jim and I could probably write thirty-five to forty songs for a project, that's a lot, and there were that many on the first album, but we had Ron around to help us pick the best ten or twelve.

On the *Premonition* record, I was learning a lot about engineering and recording and what I wanted to do with the guitars, and if I'm gonna double a track, I don't want to double it with the same guitar. Maybe I want to double it with an acoustic guitar, because back then, doubling and quadrupling, that was happening back then, people were really starting to discover that, and if you go back to listen to some of Ron's records, like Led Zeppelin or the first Bad Company record, there's not that much doubling. So I was kind of doing *Premonition* working a lot with Phil and really hands-on with the console, and I don't know if that was good, because I was supposed to be writing songs and that's what I'm supposed to be focusing on. But I wanted to engineer too, and I learned a lot watching Ron and listening to Ron and observing Ron and really taking note about what he would do, but all the while, I knew and he told me, "If you think watching me is going to get you the same sound, you're sadly mistaken." That was a pretty big statement too, I learned from all those things. So by the time Jim and I were producing *Premonition*, we were doing what we had to do with the budget we had, and I don't think we made that bad of a record: "Poor Man's Son" and "Summer Nights" were on that record. Sometimes the beauty's in the youth, and at that time in my life, I thought we needed a producer, but now when I look back on it, I say to myself, "Yeah, but that youth is why *Premonition* sounds the way it sounds." It really is, because there's beauty in not knowing certain things, and actually having to experiment to find out, because in that journey, sometimes you find magic in between those points, and we found that. So is it the best record we ever made, I don't necessarily think so, but is it good, yeah, and there's a lot of really, really special moments to it.

Scoring a hit with "Poor Man's Son" at AOR radio, the band found themselves by 1982 in the position of journeyman rock band with a story that autobiographically mirrored much of what would become their true shot at the brass ring on album number three, *Eye of the Tiger*. Opportunity would knock courtesy of a phone call from the president of the band's label, Tony Scotti, who the guitarist recalled

changed everything for us. We got a lot of radio play from "Poor Man's Son" and started to get noticed back then, and it's when we were rehearsing to do what later became the *Eye of the Tiger* record that Tony Scotti called. We were on Scotti Bros. records, and the reason we were there is because John Kalodner put us there because Tony Scotti was the best promotions guy in the business. Everybody hired him, you name it, he worked their records: Olivia Newton-John, from Donna Summer to Genesis, he was the guy to get your records on the radio. And Tony, who was the president of Scotti Bros., he knew a lot of people, so one of his friends socially was Sylvester Stallone. So they were out to dinner one night, and Stallone had finished the *Rocky III* movie, including the scene where "Eye of the Tiger" was, but he was unhappy with the music enough that it was holding up the release of the film. He kept saying, "No, I want something new in here," and while he's explaining this to Tony out at dinner, Tony said to him, "Well, you know, I got that band Survivor, and you kind of dig them, they got that song 'Poor Man's Son,' why don't you give those guys a chance, see what they can come up with." It was that simple. So then Tony put Stallone in touch with us, and he gave us a little bit of direction, but Sly's kind of a cool guy because he's been there before, he did it his way, and knows that if you're gonna give somebody a chance, you give them direction, but they gotta do it on their own. It was like him doing the first Rocky film, getting chased all over Philadelphia because he didn't even have the permits to shoot, and then winning the Oscar for Best Picture after doing it for less than a million dollars. So that was the hookup with Stallone.

Stallone's well-established film franchise based on the success of *Rocky I* and *II* had a fan base that shared much of Survivor's own sales demographic and biographical narrative as a journeyman rock band fighting their way onto the charts, looking to stay a contender with hits that—very much in the spirit of the boxing metaphor—would keep them climbing the ranks until they reached the moment of a title shot. That proverbial shot would come with Stallone's phone call, and as Sullivan began preparing mentally and musically for the challenge of his career, in the course of conceptualizing the song compositionally in his head, the guitarist was grateful for a visual aid that arrived.

> After talking to Stallone on the phone, he sent us a VHS of the film. The funny thing was: the very first time I put it in, the opening segment goes by, and then it stops! So I say, "What's wrong with this machine?," but I had another one in the bedroom, so I put the VHS in there, and am watching it, and it stops again. So I'm thinking, "What's wrong with this thing?!," I look at the tape and said, "Well, there's nothing on it . . ." And you could kind of see, you got the montage where "Eye of the Tiger" is, some of the beginning, and then it stops, and you don't get anything else. Well, I thought this was weird, because you want to get the whole vibe of the film, and so did Jim, we wanted to know what this whole movie was about. So then I call Stallone back and said, "Listen, is there a problem, because I thought it was my machine, but I only have the first eight or ten minutes . . ." So he starts to say, "Well, you know . . ." And I'm like "Dude, I'm not going to go in the garage and pirate Rocky," and this is before the Internet, so he didn't have that much to be nervous about, but I assured him he didn't have to worry about it, and the next day he sent the whole film.
>
> Mark Droubay, our drummer, was staying with me at the time, so we watched the whole film, and we watched it a couple of times, and Mark really liked it, and said "Look at the way he lost!" And then I started to notice, "Gee, Stallone is chiseled," people are going to be talking about his build, because the guy transformed himself. So I went by Jim's, we watched it, then watched it again, and remembered that Stallone had told us on the phone, "Whatever the song is, I want it to have some kind of a pulse, I want it to move, I want it to pulse." So on the way to Jim's house, I was driving over there thinking in my head, "Well, it has to be dramatic intro," and I'm not a drama guy, so it was kind of a weird thing to say, but it did, and then I said, "Well, okay, let me think of dramatic in a different way . . . There's something we can do with the guitars, and something we can do when Jim plays the piano," because Jim would play piano and I would play guitar a lot of times in our writing sessions.

Arriving at his cowriter's house with the song's pulse beginning to march to a specific beat in his head that was already rocking as hard as Rocky hit and got hit on-screen throughout the film, Sullivan remembered feeling tempted at first to experiment with rhythmic ideas outside the band's traditional rock drum sound, a concept that on the surface looked appealing after

> I said, "Maybe we just don't leave that and visit another genre," because if somebody like Stallone puts an idea in your head, "Well, I need a pulse," you can go berserk

and end up on a Mini-Moog back then. But we decided to just stay true to what we do, and both of us played piano, and I wasn't great at it, but just about anybody can play in middle C and sound decent. So Jim holds the sustain pedal and played a few notes, and hit the C on the bass end, and just started just kind of chugging in C (sings opening rhythm of "Eye of the Tiger"), and I started playing that riff that opens the song on the guitar while he's going "bom, bom, bom" with his left hand on the piano, and I said, "Oh, that's kind of pulsy, that's cool."

With a groove going, the writing team next turned their creative energies toward the lyrical side of a song that *Time* magazine would celebrate as "the 1982 smash hit (that) . . . channeled Rocky Balboa," Sullivan felt that he and his cowriter did just that as they began sketching out the anthem's lyrical landscape. Basing the song's lyrical character around the visual aids of Stallone's print of the latest Rocky film (its implied dialogue, characters, plot, etc.) as the movie's first few opening minutes unfolded,

driving over there, I remember I'd already had lyrics in my head, and Jim did too, and with the lyrics, Jim and I were really prolific, man, and at that time, every day, one of us always had something, and we'd put our ideas on a cassette tape, and it was embarrassing at times, because back then, singing into a handheld cassette, say at the airport, people kind of looked at you like "Man, that's a weird guy over there." One time I can remember Jim ducking down behind a trash can to put something down on tape, and now you wouldn't think twice about it. So that day, once we arrived at that session and got that groove going, we really wrote the song in about a half hour, with most of the lyrics except for the song title. We did tweak them for about two or three days, but as lyrical ideas kept coming to us, by now we knew the story, where Rocky's character had become what he'd never wanted to become.

He'd become very wealthy, and become very civilized, and was doing those commercials. I loved that montage where he was doing commercials for American Express and Core Watches, and then he's on the cover of *Lamborghini* magazine, and I started thinking as I was watching that, "Okay, he's become what he didn't want to become, and lost his edge as a fighter," because leading up to that point, Rocky was a street guy, and now here he is down about seventy pounds, and he's fighting and winning all these easy fights. So in my mind, now I said, "Did Rocky sell out? Is that really what Stallone's trying to say at the beginning?" So as I was driving over to Jim's house that day, I don't know why but I had the radio on, and I heard a Sammy Hagar song, maybe a Montrose tune, and after a minute or so, I turned it off, and a fuller picture started coming together in my head, and I thought to myself, "You know what, I think what Stallone wanted to get across in that beginning and the rest of the movie is: it's really about getting back to your roots, man, and finding your edge." And that made sense to me conceptually because now he's wearing $3,000 suits and driving

$350,000 cars, and before he was jogging with Converse on through the streets of Philly and trying to pick up a chicken, if you go back to the first Rocky movie.

Pinnacles of success that often blur the lines of rockers and boxers in how "trading passion for glory" can swallow up any star on the rise, *Time Out* magazine would later hail the song/film's success in "pacing the boxing scenes with an increasing fury that makes them less like a sport than the epic symbolic struggle . . . (of) the fighter's struggle to come to terms with success." Internalizing the character as a songwriter, Sullivan strove to keep those thematic boundaries clear in his own songwriting mind and didn't have to reach very far to relate to the film on a personal level. He explained that

> *Rocky III*, to me, not because of "Tiger," is my favorite, and I do like all of them, and obviously I do owe Stallone for the opportunity, because you can say what you want, luck has a lot to do with everything in larger life, and especially in the entertainment business. So when you're lucky enough, and the stars align, and you get the opportunity like we did with that song, yeah, we were lucky, but we still had to deliver with the tune, and these were the things that I was thinking about when the lines started coming to me. Because I'm a real street guy, and I grew up in the city, I'm from a family of eleven, and a three bedroom home with all the boys in one, and all the girls in the other, and then Mom and Dad and one bathroom. So this was pretty easy for me to wrap my head around, I think I know what he meant: that as the movie opened, Rocky had lost his edge but hadn't realized it yet. So from that, I started thinking about lyrics about that and the streets, and with me—as I'm writing lyrics—I get like buzzwords or phrases, like "Rising up," those two words can spring on others.

Hitting a right cross squarely on the chin of the point they were trying to put across in the song's opening lines, as he felt the music and lyrics begin to synergize with the visual fabric of Stallone's film reel, Sullivan remembered feeling a rush as the song started to come together.

> As Jim and I started going back and forth from there with the song's opening verse, as we'd write lyrics, we'd sit together, and I remember I told him, "I got this idea," and started playing that opening guitar riff, and sang "Rising up," and he said "Oh, that's pretty cool," and then we'd stop and one of us said, "Back on the street," and we'd go at it, we go back and forth, almost like sparring, if that's not too cliché. We like it, and like the idea of going and forth, it's competitive, and keeps us on our toes, and writing that song is a great example of that back and forth in action.
>
> As we started writing the lyrics, I remember feeling like we were writing about ourselves, writing about what we'd been through in the band, all the guys in the band—our experiences—because they hadn't all been pleasant, but they hadn't all been bad.

They'd been what they'd been, and we had realized and learned by now that "Hey, the music business was not for the faint of heart. This is a fucking battle here, man, you gotta fight," so then the gloves come off and we get down to writing and it was "Rising up . . ." "Okay, *Rising Up* and something with *Streets* would sound really good." Like "Rising up, back on the streets. YEAH, that's it! Rising up, back on the streets, took my time, took my chances," and if you think about it, once you start—when you're onto a good idea—when Jim and I were onto a good idea, it rolls.

I mean, there's times it rolls really quick, and that was one of those examples where it started rolling really, really quick. "Did my time, took my chances, went the distance, now I'm back on my feet," so we're talking about—in retrospect, but only maybe as Rocky sees it, or Stallone when he wrote the script—that wasn't in our mind, but obviously that's kind of the target area and we used it. Any songwriter, man, that's telling you the truth, will tell you most of what they write about comes from their personal experience. It's the guys who have to kind of fake it, who haven't grown up on the street, they can't write about the street because they don't know it. You gotta live it, man, you gotta live it to know it, and then you gotta know that you lived it to put it to pen, and if you can do that, then you're on a good track, and that's kind of where we were when we started it and when we finished it. So the lyrics started coming really, really quick, till the only thing we were really hung up on was the tagline, unfortunately. Jim and I didn't get hung up that much, but for THREE DAYS we couldn't come up with a tagline for the chorus!

The lyrical montage would come together thanks to the driving pulse of the beat, motivating Sullivan and Peterik as it would Rocky and his fans in the theatre seats around the world in time to focus on the opening scenes of the movie, where the writing team felt listeners would be drawn in by

that guitar bom, which I wanted to hit first, and Jim had said, "Let's get that vocal right in," but I said, "Yeah, let's get that guitar in too," so it became "It's the . . ." then the guitar stab, "Eye of the tiger, it's the thrill of the fight, risin' up to the challenge of another . . ." And we had "And the last known survivor stalks his prey in the night, and he's . . ." That's all we had, for three days, and we got the whole thing done, the song, from beginning to end, no tagline, and what good is any song without a tagline in the chorus, especially the end of the "Tiger" chorus, because it was open, "It's the eye . . .', and that's like a writer's nightmare, "Uh Oh, I gotta fill a void, and it's gotta be good, it's gotta go way high and the end of it is going to be alone with no other music playing."

So after three days, we went to the health club and were working out, then took showers and were getting dressed in the locking room, and I said, "This is really bugging me man," and Jim says, "I was up half the night last night, this is gonna drive me crazy, we gotta get the song done." Because Jim and I wanna finish a song the day we write it, we don't wanna go three days because generally speaking, as time went on to prove itself, whenever we went three days, we went bad. And when Jim and I are bad, we're really bad, so we're finally thinking: "We're really making a lot out of this thing . . . Think about it: The Eye of the Tiger . . ." And we started thinking about the lyrics to that chorus, what were we really trying to say? "And he's watching us all . . . ," because he really was, if you look at the film, "With the eye . . ." So then Jim says, "Yeah, well what is it?" And I said, "I don't know, you tell me, we really have no clue," and finally together—and it's moments like this where we do our best work—where we didn't say that tagline at the same time, but both had the same thought pattern of what we wanted to do with it as far as the melody, and finally decided on just three words to fill that void at the end of the chorus, "Of the tiger . . ." That just turned out to be three words, but to get to those three words, man, we went through a whole trip, and don't forget, we were feeling pressure by then, and all that stuff plays a role in your life.

The finishing touches on the song's compositional side came with the addition of what *Time* magazine highlighted as Tiger's "iconic opening notes," a creative moment that arrived

after we had the basic song fleshed out. I watched the movie again with our drummer Marc, and I can remember watching him throw punches and saying, "Boy, it would be good to accent those, Marc," and he goes, "Yeah, it would be! But what am I going to accent?," which kind of sprung the idea of . . . because I was thinking to myself, "It's a cool thing, we are a rock and roll band." And at that point in time, I think we were kind of struggling to prove that to people, and were kind of in the same boat with the character in the movie. So I was thinking about who are we as a band? We're really a band that's based around a guitar, a grand piano, bass and drums, and then we got the singer, but we're basically a four-piece. So I was thinking to myself, "I'm not trying to rewrite history, we just have to be ourselves," and I suddenly heard that opening riff in my head and asked Mark, "What if the guitars went 'Bom, Bom Bom Bom?,'" only I was going really fast, so every time Rocky threw a punch in the movie, I was going: "Bom, Bom . . ." And if you watch the film, the first three punches go "Bom, Bom Bom Bom," but I kept going "Bom, Bom Bom Bom, Bom Bom Bom . . ." I had a bunch of them going on, and I got over to Jim's house and said, "Let's fucking nail this today!" And he said, "I'm ready to go," and had this smile on his face.

So I told him, "I have this idea, but I can't figure out how many to put. I think what we need to do is a pattern. I hate to use that word, because then it's like I'm selling out and turning corporate, but it can still have a vibe to it," so we had to figure out what would the pattern of those stabs be? Because they really, besides the opening chugging strum, that's when people know *"Eye of the Tiger*'s coming . . ." Now, that is a backwards piano and a cymbal crash, and remember we're in the analog days now, so digital was not even a concept to any of us, so what can we do to build it up to a crescendo so when that first "Bom," people listen and go "Wow, what is that?" Also, that enhances what's going on in the film, which is the whole jig right there, so we were thinking as we were writing this, "What can we do to enhance this part of the film? We need something . . ." So then we said, "What if we did something backwards, like a backwards guitar and piano . . . ," and Jim and I were just talking with ideas, and then it still wasn't right." And I think Phil was sitting there with us while we were brainstorming, and Phil said, "Maybe a cymbal crash!" And I said, "Let's try that," and I hit a cymbal crash, and that worked because if you listen to that opening crescendo building, you hear more of the cymbal crash than you hear the piano, although you do hear the piano. But without the cymbal crash, man, you don't have the impact.

As the band rushed into the studio to record what would become the final production heard in the film's opening moments and coming out of rock radio antennas for decades to come, rather than stay in California working out of a fancy studio, the band took the very approach Rocky's character had in III, heading back to their urban roots, setting up shop in downtown Chicago. Feeling the backdrop was right sonically for the sound he and Peterik as producers—and by extension Stallone—were going for, Sullivan recalled that

once we had the song written, I called up Phil Bonanno, who was working as engineer at Chicago Recording Company, and asked if he could call up the studio manager and give us a deal, because back then studio time was like $,3000 a day. So we went to CRC Studios on Grand Avenue, in their old location, which was just off of East Ohio Street, and this was a place where we'd done all our demos, and it was kind of cool because that's where Survivor started in late 1978. We set up in the room that we knew, and we knew which part of the room was live and which part was dead, and where to put the amps so the guitars will sound good, and we knew where the bass was going to sound good, and then we had Phil engineering.

Phil had an amazing talent for capturing humongous low end, and if anything could use low end, it's "Eye of the Tiger," especially the beginning, and it's hard to get that amount of bass, and on analog. On digital, it may be a little bit easier, and if you go too loud it just stops, it doesn't make noise, it drops out, but on analog tape, it's really hard to get that kind of low end. But that song needs that, the kick drum, and that's why we decided "Let's not put it on 2 and 4, let's put it on the 1 and 3, and put the snare on 2 and 4 because that drives it more." So when we were setting up, I told Phil, "This has got to be balls to the wall," because I had a clue that's what Stallone was expecting.

To achieve the legendary wall of crunch that accompanies the song's opening series of electric guitar stabs, Sullivan—playing and producing—remembered feeling strongly that he needed to take a layered approach to tracking his rhythm tracks as stacks, an approach that he revealed ran contrary to his previous recording norms, explaining that while

> I don't like to double myself, I did double those opening guitars stabs because I felt that why shouldn't they be in stereo? If you heard it without 'em you would say, "Okay, you'd have to be an idiot not to double them," but I did think about not doubling them, and when I decided to, I was playing a Les Paul, and thought maybe I should double them with a Telecaster or something? Then I said, "No, at least if it's the same guitar . . . ," because one of the things that Ron had taught me and also told the band was that I was really good at doubling. And it's not an egotistical thing, he did say that, so I said, "If I double if with the same guitar, and play exact and we don't spend forever on it, and get so analytical we never get it done, it will have more impact." Well, once I doubled it, then it was easy because a pattern started to develop, and then it started to make more sense with the punches and what we were doing.
>
> With my amplifier setup, I used to use a 50 Watt Marshall, and a 4x12 bottom, and we used an SM 57 to mic it, and used an 1176 on compression, and for EQ, Phil likes to do real little EQing on me, very little, and I like to give him a sound where he doesn't have to do any if I can. So it was just a real simple chain: a 50-watt Marshall, 412 Cabinet with greenbacks in it, an SM 57, and we didn't even put two mics on there, the 1176 into one of the greatest preamps of all time, a Neve preamp, and that was the kind of console they had at the studio. Those are really good for guitar, because they keep it fat, give it a little bit of the edge, so maybe when we mixed it we put a couple db of 10K on it and I think I put a little bit of 1K, and it's pretty raw if you listen to it, it's not a lot of EQ on that whole track. It's pretty raw. We recorded that whole record without an ounce of EQ, we did not let Phil touch the console, and I remember telling him, "Let's just record everything flat, and then we'll fix it later," so that's what we did.

Thinking outside the box in the tradition of how some of rock's greatest drum sounds were captured—a popular instance being when John Bonham's "When the Levee Breaks" was famously recorded in a stairwell at Hedley Grange—Sullivan and Peterik followed a similar strategy. To that end, when they set up the drums for tracking on "Tiger," Sullivan revealed that

> where we put the drums wasn't even a studio! It was an open room upstairs and we just ran a big snake to it. We wanted a live drum sound, and back then it was hard to find that, especially in Chicago, and I think drums like anything else, if you get really good sounds from the drums in the room, then you gotta record them right. It's gotta sound really good to your ear in the room, and if it doesn't, then don't go back in the control room until it does. Mark had a great sound going back then, he had a Ludwig drum kit and was one of the few drummers out there who actually used a 26-inch

kick drum, and not because John Bonham used them—partially because of that—but mainly because he knows how to tune them and how to make them so they're not only functional, but where they sound unbelievable.

So I think the challenge was: how do we capture this on tape, and we tried several things, from "Let's take the head off the front of the kick drum," or put sandbags in it, and then put the mic right up maybe a couple inches from the head where the beater is, and that never worked with Marc. The best thing we ever did to get the drum sound we got on that song was to leave the front head on, cut about a 6- to 8-inch little round hole—not in the middle—but off to the side so it was facing the drums, and you look at the middle right directly to the side, almost all the way to the side, and put the mic maybe about four inches outside of that whole. Then we stuck a Phet 47 in there, and put that up against the drum Mark was hitting the kick against, so then you'd get the attack, but you'd also get the massive sound from the little hole in front.

It was a cool thing to do that, and playing a 26-inch kick drum is not easy, you gotta know what you're doing, and you gotta know how to tune them. Then we had an AKG D-12 mic on the outside of the kick drum, and we put a 57 on the snare, and we always top and bottom miced the snare, but in the end, I remember saying, "Oh, this bottom sounds terrible," and just push the fader down. I never liked it from the bottom with Mark because he hits the drum so hard, you don't really get much from rattle on the bottom. Then we used Sennheiser 441s on the tom toms, and we had a matched stereo pair of Scheps as the overheads, and they were amazing! They were so open, and picked up the room so nicely, because micing ambiently is a whole different trip, man, so we had the Scheps on the room as overheads, then we had a C-24 as our ambient room, then we had the Sennheisers on the toms, an SM57 on the snare, and a 57 on the hat, and that's pretty much it. We always put, on every snare drum hit, we always put tambourine, right on the snare drum, and in fact, one of us would actually do it, hold it and hit it just to hit the wood and get the ring of the tambourine. It was fun.

The only effect we put on that drum was a little bit of the plate reverb on the snare, and then the ambience you hear is the actual room, and I believe we used a C-24 about six to eight feet up in the front of the drums, and then the balance now is more up to Mark. Because when you're recording those ambient sounds, it's inherent that the drummer has to be in touch with the fact that he's in charge of the balancing of the drums. He's gotta realize that if you're in a really loud room, you gotta play that way, and Mark kinda had that niche of doing that. So we combined it all and it all worked.

Sullivan felt that balancing the challenges of recording live off the floor to capture the power fans hear in the performance that went down on tape while keeping track of all the song's important sonic aspects was essential. It was an approach that, he explained, the band never deviated from, such that as a band, when we made records, we focus first and foremost on getting a great performance, and then built it from there. So we cut the track, we redid some of the overdubs, and redid the opening chugging rhythm part from the basic, and we doubled those, so those are doubled, and the opening stabs are doubled. And then we did the bass, and there's a couple cool bass lines in there, but the bass is basically following the piano opening, and was basically pulsing through the whole song. We played it through an SVT amp and we miced the amp, and we'd also have him play direct, and ended up combining his amp with the D.I., and always favored the direct by maybe twice as much, so if you're at + 3 DB on your fader on the direct, then his amp would probably be down around −3 DB, maybe a little less or more. The piano you hear throughout the song was a Bossendorfer that CRC had, they've had it forever, and that's one of my favorite pianos in the world. Jim beats the crap out of it, which I like. The guys in the band used to joke with him, "You're playing with your elbows!" As far as mics, I used to like to put a Scheps on that.

Laying down the song's lead vocal last just as the clock was running out on their deadline to submit it to Stallone for review, Sullivan and his bandmates decided to hedge their bets, submitting a second song—a ballad titled "Ever Since the World Began" —bringing lead singer Dave Bickler to add the final touch that tied the song together as a grand gamble for a band who had everything to lose if Sly passed. Admitting that while he felt understandably nervous throughout the final hours of recording, Sullivan at the same time was confident because

when Dave came in to do the vocal, I can remember sitting there at the console listening, and Dave was having a really good night. The song sounded really good, it was fat, it was big, and on "Tiger," I love plate reverbs, and that's what we used on Dave's lead, just a plate, and we just put a little bit of echo and EQ, and the mic I believe was a Phet 47. The funny thing was Dave sang two songs that night we were submitting for the Rocky film, one was "Eye of the Tiger" and the other was a ballad called "Ever Since the World Began," and we said, "This is the song he's gonna use," I can actually remember hearing that and participating in saying that! But then Jim and I played "Tiger" again, and we both thought it was pretty good, sent the tape in to Stallone, and didn't hear anything for a few days. So then I started to think to myself, "Okay, so now what's going on? Is he not using anything? Did he not like either one?," and you're biting your nails by then because you *want that gig*, and we knew we did our best work, but were starting to ask ourselves, "Did we not give him what he needed?," and the wait was killing us!

Biting their nails down to the point their fingers were next, Sullivan recalled the moment of truth finally coming courtesy of a call from label boss Tony Scotti, who spilled the welcome news that

"Sly loves that first song, he's going crazy over it! He also loves 'Ever Since the World Began' as well, and wants to put a hold on it," and I remember asking him how you put a hold on a song, which Scotti explained to me that he wanted to put it in another movie. But once he'd heard "Tiger," he wanted to get his movie out, he'd finally said, "I got the music," so he said, "You guys have to come out because Sly wants to put the song in the film." So now all of a sudden Jim's getting pneumonia so he couldn't fly out there with me, so I had to go myself. Well, I get out there, and find out that the reality of Stallone's reaction to the song was the OPPOSITE of everything I'd been thinking. I had made such a big deal out of it that it was almost insurmountable for both of us, and when I landed in LA and saw Stallone's brother Frank, I asked him "How's your brother?," and he says, "Man, the last time I saw him he had that song SO LOUD on his stereo, he was jamming to it and he was SWEATIN'!"

Turning the pressure back up just when he'd begun to feel it fall, Sullivan flew solo out to LA with engineer Phil Bonanno to begin round two of work on a song he knew would soon make the band world famous. Still, the first day Frankie walked into the film studio, he found himself momentarily startled by his greeting

as I got down to the soundstage, because when I walked in, playing on the screen is the movie, and right where our music wound up in the film is playing Queen's "Another One Bites the Dust." At this point, all the editing was done, and Sly says, "Okay, now we're going to work on the opening montage," and he requested that the engineer Phil Bonanno come along, and we had to do nothing to this song, no change in tempo, and he puts "Tiger" in there and for that movie, this thing was just meant to be, and in that spot, I finally saw it. So we worked on it all day, come back the next day, and Stallone says, "I want it louder," and he goes, "Frank, sit down over there and do whatever you do when you guys do what you do in the studio. Not what movie people do, do what you do." So I said, "Well, I don't know how it translates. They have to stay sonically within a certain decibel, DB, otherwise, I don't know what happens. I know with the music, we like to be up there, like +2 every once in a while peaking," but the movie people, they were very conservative about the amount of decibel that you put music to film, and wanted it right about at 0.

We got around it by Stallone saying "Hey man, this is my show." He did say that, "This is my movie, I'll do what I want, push the faders up," and it's kind of a cool thing to be in his position back then, and it was good for us because we get to make it sound like Survivor. And these guys have won twenty-two Oscars, and are sitting there going "This is never going to work," and when we pushed the faders up, I remember the meters were kind of lighting up, and Sly just closed his eyes, and was digging it, and I'm thinking to myself, "Well, everybody else here hates me. They want to know: who's this kid sitting here, he's nineteen," and I think what Stallone wanted was

174

to really get that low end that you could get out of analog tape back then, and that compression you get. When you hit that tape right, you get that compression back.

Inspired and vibing creative in and off the moment, Stallone began collaborating even more closely with Sullivan, who recalled that

when we were done, Stallone was sweating, I can tell ya when I looked at him, he had a lot of sweat, and he says, "You guys did a great job!" Then he said "Don't go anywhere, you wanna hang around," so for the next ten or eleven days, we got to spend down there till the movie was done. During that time, he also had us put "Tiger" in other spots of the movie, so I took bits of the music, and Sly would say, "Can you speed the song up here?," and I sped the song up and it sounded like Alvin and the Chipmunks, so then Sly says, "How about if we do an instrumental?" This was during the part of the movie when he's training, when he goes to LA with Apollo, and Phil and I would synch and speed it up so it matched with him jumping rope and they used it in three or four different places. Then the final thing was, Stallone said "Can you guys give me a version for the ending where it starts, "It's the . . . *Eye of the Tiger*," and that was really easy, because normally you would have to cut the tape with a razor blade, it wasn't copy and paste like it is nowadays with Protools, so it was easy because there's a lot of space there, so we did that edit, and Sly said "Perfect." So the whole thing was kind of always developing until the whole process was finished.

As excited as he was to see how well Stallone felt the song fit the film's theme, Sullivan was eager to gauge fan reaction by going right to the source, the movie theater, catching a seat in the back on the movie's opening night. Remembering a sense of nervous anticipation as the previews ended and the movie's opening moments started to roll, as "Tiger's" opening notes began,

I remember when I went to the theater to see it with other people on opening weekend on a Friday night, and it was packed because everybody was a Rocky fan, and I sat in my seat, and I can remember watching that opening montage, and it worked so well that the people clapped. The people clapped, so that kind of flipped me out, and I remember saying to myself, "Maybe we've got something here."

A monumental understatement given the overnight stardom the song would shoot the band into, the song would touch every corner of pop culture, from the corner bar with Drinksmixer.com reporting in 2013 that the iconic song had been given its own mixed drink, "a delicious recipe for *Eye of the Tiger*, with gold rum, coconut rum, cranberry juice, lemon juice, sugar syrup, orange juice and dark rum." On the political corner, the song made national news in 2012 when Sullivan filed a lawsuit against Republican presidential candidate

Newt Gingrich, with *Time* magazine reporting that "Sullivan sued Gingrich in federal court, citing the GOP candidate's use of the song at several campaign events without permission, the *Chicago Sun-Times* reported. According to the lawsuit, filed on behalf of Sullivan's publishing company Rude Music Inc., Gingrich's transgressions began as early as 2009. Sullivan cited political events such as the Southern Republic Leadership Conference and public appearances in Iowa and Pennsylvania as instances of Gingrich's unlawful use of the copyrighted work. The suit also claims a video on the Newt 2012 Inc. website features Gingrich entering a crowded Pennsylvania venue as 'Eye of the Tiger' blares in the background."

In the digital age alone, coupled with physical sales of six million copies, the song by 2013 had already moved an additional 3,492,000 downloads and 500,000 ringtones. Clearly a song on the prowl without nostalgic borders, looking back on its initial success, Frankie Sullivan is proudest in a way of "Tiger" becoming the band's first #1 hit on the *Billboard* Hot 100 singles chart and #5 on *Billboard*'s End of Decade chart, and for the band winning a Grammy for "Best Rock Performance by a Duo or Group with Vocals," and in the context of mainstream esteem, receiving an Oscar nomination along with cowriter/coproducer Jim Peterik for "Best Original Song."

As a touchstone moment for a career that he still shakes his head at, quipping that "my life is kind of humorous to me honestly, which is how I like to live it," in offering closing advice to the generations of up-and-coming rock fans considering a career in the studio or on the stage, Sullivan begins by reminding this crowd that

> my advice goes back to: you gotta start with the song. It really starts with the song, because that's what's gonna resonate with the fans. It's only rock and roll man, it's not rocket science. It really isn't. It's about everybody doing the best they can do and contributions, and in this case, the contributions. Inevitably, you want to write a song that everybody can relate to in their own ways, and when people ask me "What's this song about?," while "Tiger" was movie music, it turned out it was about a lot of other things: it was like about my life, about Jim's life, the band's life, what bands go through, and for other people, how the song relates to them and their own life. One of the things I think we all relate to with that song is how sometimes we all kind of lose grip and take our eye off the ball, and find ourselves questioning where we're at in life and are we doing the right thing? Everybody does that, it's part of being a human being, and that's what "Tiger" was all about, so I tell younger artists, to make it, it's going to take a lot of perseverance and you better be persistent, and it's going to take the hardest work—and I mean the hardest work—you've ever done, but when opportunity knocks, and you never know when it's going to knock, just make sure you're ready. Make sure you're ready!

CHAPTER 10

Start Me Up—Chris Kimsey

With the "triumphant release of *Tattoo You*," *Rolling Stone*—the legendary rock publication whose name the band inspired—announced in 1980 that "the Rolling Stones are back!" The smash single that would announce that fact loud and clear at the dawn of the 1980s was "Start Me Up," which *RS* would celebrate as "the catchiest Stones single in ages!" "Start Me Up" is the sort of quintessential radio anthem that the band had invented the template for in popular rock 'n' roll. Producer Chris Kimsey begins our conversation on the inside story of its creation with the revelation that

> "Start Me Up" started out as a reggae song! It was recorded during the *Some Girls* sessions and was hanging around for quite some time. It really morphed into what it became quite quickly. I was quite surprised actually. In fact, I'm almost sure that after we recorded "Miss You," which maybe took about a week, we went straight into "Start Me Up," and it just happened really quick, where we recorded the final version the same day or the next day.

Even after the band had committed to the final version of what ultimately became their biggest hit of the 1980s, though Kimsey knew instantly that it was a smash, the song's composer still wasn't sure, so much so that while that one stood out to me completely, because after we kind of nailed it and cut it, as much as it went down really quick, Keith really wasn't quite sure about it because it wasn't the song he was thinking of for the arrangement, so it was kind of binned at the time, it was trashed. I seem to remember Keith saying to me, "Oh no, it sounds like somebody else, wipe it, erase it." But of course, I didn't, so that's pretty much how that one came about.

Kimsey amplified this legendary hit with an ambient guitar sound that he had spent the better part of a decade recording, dating back to 1970 working as an assistant engineer on his first record with the band, the legendary *Sticky Fingers*. Working under the wing of the perfect tutor to learn the ins and outs of the band's sound, Kimsey recalled that

> my relationship working with Glyn Johns and the band, the way that all happened, was I was doing the orchestral sessions and daytime sessions for quite some time, maybe a couple of years, and then there was an opportunity where they asked me if I wanted to do an evening session, and I said yes of course, because an evening session was good because overtime is more money. But it was going to wreck my social life, but that didn't matter, because I was all about the sound of the music, so my first evening session was being put on a Glyn Johns session! I don't remember but believe it might have been a Rolling Stones session, and Glyn just became my mentor. I just loved Glyn's strength and again, kind of no-bullshit approach to record making.

An extension of a happy accident that had first given the producer-to-be his foot in the door landing a job working at his first recording studio while still a teenager, Kimsey's journey began when

> after leaving school, I bummed around doing different summer jobs—a month here, a month there—nothing doing music or recording, and was dating a girl who lived in Barnes, where Olympic Studios was located. So I would just stick my head in there when I was going over for a date and ask, "Do you have any jobs?," because I knew there was some type of recording music going on in there, and they'd always say "No, no go away, we don't need anyone," but I kept going back.

Not a bug Kimsey had suddenly caught, his fascination with sound recording in fact dated back to much earlier in his childhood where a young Chris had first become fascinated with the concept of sound recording

> from playing with tape recorders, but it was more that I was absolutely fascinated with sound as well. Not so much popular sound, at school in the age of I think about fourteen, I got very much into the theater aspect of sound, because I was asked to

augment the theatrical productions with either music or sound effects. So I was doing that at a very early age, and that led me onto music, but my discovery of music was more into the sonic thing. Everybody else was into Hendrix, and I was more into big band sound, and even Frank Sinatra as well, early Frank Sinatra and Nat King Cole, and film soundtracks as well.

That's really where my sonic background began, and it was arrangement-and-orchestral-based for sure. Then my school did a (Son et Lumiere), the school building had quite a big history, and I was asked to go interview a very notable actress, Sybil Thorndike, at the time, who was in her eighties, and I believe I was fourteen at the time, and then there was a very small recording studio that was set up by the inner-London educational authority, which was in Soho actually, and I lived out in the suburbs. So I would trek pretty much every other Saturday morning to this studio, which consisted of a Vortexion 4-channel mixer, a phonograph stereo tape recorder, and I think a couple of regular ribbon mics, where we would record speech and drama. At the same time, the guy who was teaching drama courses—Ray Cooper—was a bit of a musician, and in later years, it turned out he would play with Elton John. So Ray was one of my first teachers almost, and then I didn't see him for twenty years afterward till he was playing with Elton and I was producing, so it was quite a small world in that respect, quite fascinating. Then I went on when I was a bit older, and was very fortunate because I had a Revox tape machine by the age of fifteen, and I would make up my own pseudo-radio programs, just for my own enjoyment.

By the time he was lobbying Olympic Studios for a more serious shot at pursuing what the producer already knew was his professional calling, after demonstrating a knack for persistence,

eventually, they finally put me on a list and over a space of a couple months, I got a phone call for an interview, and went and had that interview with Keith Grant, who was the studio manager. He built the studio as well, and within three or four weeks after that, I got a phone call back from Keith, which was quite lucky because I think three or four days before that phone call from Olympic, I was just about to start a job as a supermarket fitter, fitting out supermarkets at nighttime because the brother of my girlfriend had a company who did that and it was very good overtime. So Olympic called and said, "Can you start next week at eleven pounds a week?," which was fifteen dollars a week, so I said "Yes!"

I started at Olympic in 1968 or 69, and that studio was just booked 24-7 really, so it was like commercials/jingles from 7 AM to 9:30, then you stripped out of the studio, and then had possibly Shirley Bassey—the popular music of the day—or film scores until 5, and then the rock 'n' roll would come in from 7 in the evening till about 1 or 2 AM. That helped give me a vast overview because every style of music and every artist, every kind of format that you could record, was different how you would handle the artist or orchestra or arranger or the producer, it was a little different for everything. So it gave me a wealth of knowledge of how to deal with people with artistic values, and to help them get the best out of what they were looking for.

Some of the early sessions I assisted on as a young kid, one was Cat Stevens's *Mona Bone Jakon*, which was a brilliant record. I love that album, that was really quite special. (Another was) *Jesus Christ Superstar*. And because I worked with Keith Grant a lot to start off with, it was mainly film scores and things like Shirley Bassey, who was a Welsh singer, and that's how it all kicked off.

Reviewing some of the basics he picked up that would stick with him through present day, under the tutelage of his first teacher in the studio, Kimsey shared that

from those early sessions and working under Frank Sinatra, I learned the Boy Scout value of being prepared for everything, that was vital in recording, and I soon kind of figured out that the best performances were coming from artists when they almost didn't know they were being recorded, or when there was that thing of "This is the one, this is the take," rather than what's kind of happened with recording now where it can get endless versions . . . There was a spontaneity that was really quite special, and I kind of strived to keep that alive in music, mainly because then everybody was playing together.

So, for instance, with jingles, obviously it was the rhythm section and backing singers and orchestral, so everything was going down live and quick. Keith had built a recording studio with a sonic quality that could handle an eighty-piece setup to a four-piece, and all of it would sound fantastic. So the room was definitely part of the magic, and the engineer was part of the magic, facilitating it all to go really smoothly and effortlessly, and also in a good spirit as well, no hang-ups with technical stuff, to where if something broke down, it was quickly remedied and fixed without the artist or producer knowing, really.

That skill was one Kimsey discovered he had a knack for as quickly as he put that talent into action for the day's top record producers, impressing a key member of that club who would soon recruit him as his go-to assistant engineer, the producer observed, because

Glyn really fell in love with the fact that he could walk in and I'd have everything set up, so he'd literally just have to push the faders and it was ready to go. That was my teaching from Keith, and I just applied it to the rock side, and Glyn loved that, he thought it was fantastic. In having things ready for him, so we had a really good relationship from the off, and because of that, I suddenly got put on almost every Glyn session. We became and remain very good friends to this day, and he became my mentor in the current rock world, and I really kind of, I suppose, built myself on his style and what he was doing.

Though he would mold himself after Johns's recording preferences as a producer, those tastes ironically didn't extend completely to the music Johns was recording. Kimsey confessed that

> when I was first brought on the Stones session, the Stones didn't interest me at all, I wasn't into that type of thing, musically I was more into film scores and other things. So the fact that there was this rock 'n' roll band who were very big at the time, they didn't impress me at all, as they didn't really impress Glyn—they only impressed Glyn when they played really good. I really learned that from Glyn, and felt the same. But the early sessions with the Stones were quite different to other sessions, because Glyn would put up with a lot more . . . I think because his relationship with them started in the very early days, when they were demoing at IBC, he goes way back with him, and it was the beginning of his and their career, so there was that relationship.
>
> Then when Jimmy Miller came along working with Glyn, it was a formidable team, it was fantastic. Jimmy's focus was really quite special, and his comments to the band, to the musicians, were purposeful and meaningful. He could really feel when something wasn't happening, and he would have pretty much an answer for it, which didn't kind of humiliate anyone in the room, it was a team effort. I fondly remember him sitting at the console next to Glyn Johns, and just his whole body moving in beat with the music, and if he wasn't, then there was something wrong.

Involved firsthand in the recording of one of the Stones' greatest riff-rockers, "Can't You Hear Me Knocking," a key Kimsey remembered to the sound Glyn Johns, Jimmy Miller, and later Chris himself captured on tape came not from any fancy studio tricks, but first and foremost from the fact that, as a matter of course,

> the band would track together live off the floor, and I continued that when I started with them years later on *Some Girls*. I would always have a live vocal going down, even if the lyrics weren't finished. I can't imagine recording anything with the Stones without a vocal going on. At Olympic, we cut "Bitch" and "Can't You Hear Me Knocking," that was all put down live. It was pretty much three or four takes, and one of them would be the one, I don't remember much editing between takes with the Stones on those sessions with Glyn. It was pretty much the take happened and that was the one for sure, as it did with "Can't You Hear Me Knocking."
>
> Our drum setup for those sessions would have been an AKG D-30 on the bass drum, a 57 on the snare, a U-67 Neumann valve mic overhead, overtop of the kick, and another U-67 valve at the left-hand side kind of looking at the floor tom and the snare,

and that was it. Sometimes, Glyn would add a hi-hat mic, which was an AKG D-224E, but that was pretty much it. For the guitar amplifiers, it would have been one mic, a U-67 through, 67s were in abundance then, 67 on acoustic guitar, on electric guitar, so it was mainly 67s. There were no pedals at all, it was just guitar pedals and amps, which might have been Ampegs and Fenders for those sessions. We even did vocals with Mick on the D-224E, I remember doing that a lot. That was used a lot when Mick was on the floor with the band. It didn't pick up as much as a 67 would, although we did use it for some overdubs, so maybe Glyn was trying to match the sound.

Graduating from his apprenticeship working with the Rolling Stones under Glyn Johns's direction, Kimsey soon stepped out and into the spotlight as a producer in his own right throughout the early 1970s courtesy of his collaboration with former Humble Pie guitarist Peter Frampton, with the producer recalling that his work with Frampton

started kind of in tandem with when I started working with the Stones. I first worked with Peter as an assistant on some Humble Pie albums Glyn produced, and that's where I met Peter for the first time, and we actually became good friends because we both had a love of Motown records. So we became really good buddies, and would hang out either at his place or mine listening to Motown a lot and Stevie Wonder as well, it was great inspiration. So that kind of relationship happened while he was in Pie, and then when he left Humble Pie, he asked me to record his first solo album, *Wind of Change*. I remember that album distinctly because he had this wonderful Ampeg Reverber Rocket Amplifier, and I came up with this idea of putting a microphone in the back of the speaker to sort of capture the push-pull of the speaker, and record it in stereo, which was pretty wild then. It created quite a special sound and he loved that, and he was really into using a Leslie for his guitar as well. So that combination of the Ampeg and the Leslie definitely was his sound.

Frampton and Kimsey's stars would both shine brightly for the first time on 1975's now-legendary *Frampton Comes Alive*, the best-selling live album of the 1970s at a time when the trend was just beginning to take off. "The biggest selling live album of all time," according to *Billboard*, the album's success "made Peter Frampton a household word." For the producer, heading into the live album's recording, he remembered Frampton was badly in need of a hit

because his career after two solo albums was not really taking off, and was not going well. Then, fortunately, he was out on the road forever, which was normal back then: you go out on the road and create your fan base, and it really started to kick off. So recording the shows for *Frampton Comes Alive* was almost like "If this doesn't happen, I'm not sure what's going to happen for Peter after that." So the live album was recorded, and then mixed at Electric Ladyland in New York with Peter and Bobby Mayo, and it was just fantastic.

Kimsey's task with *Frampton Comes Alive* was to mix a live album that would make the audience feel they were part of the live show they were listening to on record or radio. Underscoring the importance of emphasizing the live audience as a driving force in the sonic balance of the mix, Kimsey said

> the greatest thing about mixing that album was, you just put the audience mics up, and already you were so elevated, the audience made that really happen, it was wonderful to hear that. And a lot of people have said: "Oh, I'm sure this was added and that was added," but nothing was added. There were no fixes or overdubs, it's what it was. When you get the balance and it's all glued together, and nothing sort of sticking out, it just feels like you're back at the gig listening to it and experiencing it. I do remember the actual audience mics, a part at the end of the songs when they were cheering. We did use a lot of the ambience of the audience, because that was something quite special.
>
> Rather than it being taken out and it being very close and sterile, we made it purposefully quite an ambient-sounding record, so that even though the audience weren't applauding during the song, they were still there. As far as effects, the only thing I remember is using the MXR flanger on Bobby Mayo's electric piano, and we might have used an EMT digital delay on the vocal on some tracks, or even the guitar, because it was a period when Eventide was a very young company, and I remember their delay line had just come out, so I'm sure we used that. Apart from possibly an Echo plate reverb, that was about it.
>
> I think because I knew all the material so well, it was fortunate, because this was done in a time when we didn't have a big budget, and had to get it done quick. We were advised at first by Peter's manager that it was only going to be a single album, that no one wanted a double album. So we finished it as a single album, and then Jerry Moss came down, listened to it, and asked, "Where's the rest of the songs?" And we said, "Oh, you want a double album?," and when he said "Yeah," we went back into the studio and mixed the rest of the shows.
>
> We just became really good soul brothers, and he was just a wonderful player and a great bloody songwriter, and we just got on really well. Two years ago, in 2011, I got together with him and made his last solo album, *Thank You Mr. Churchill*.

Boasting two of the biggest radio hits of 1976, the seminal "Baby I Love Your Way" and "Show Me the Way," Peter Frampton's career would not only come alive in the wake of the album's success, but Kimsey's did as well as a producer, as his next proper studio collaboration would prove when the Rolling Stones came calling seeking a new coproducer for their

Some Girls LP. An understandably big break for any producer on the come, in Kimsey's case, the opportunity came knocking when

> after working with Glyn so much, I think it had gotten to the point where Glyn had almost had enough of working with the Stones, and having a conversation between the band and Glyn about who should do the next Stones record, I think my name came up because of my working relationship with Glyn and Ian Stewart. In fact, it happened after I'd been in New York for four or five months working with Peter, and I remember getting back and the next day got a call and it was Ian and he asked me what I was doing, and when I said, "I'm just unpacking my bags, I just got back from the States," he told me, "Well, don't unpack, you go to Paris tomorrow." And when I asked, "What?," he said, "Yeah, you're going to record the new Stones record," and that was it, that's how that all happened.

The album, produced at Pathé Marconi Studios in Paris, in many ways would prove to be the Stones' comeback record and one *The Guardian* would argue was "widely considered their last great album," the BBC adding that its release came at a time when "the Sex Pistols et al. began deriding the Rolling Stones as Establishment and old, (to which) they, stung, responded by going back into the studio and knuckling down to an album that they knew had to be better than their recent underwhelming output . . . *Some Girls*, their first full album with Ronnie Wood, was the best Stones album in (years)." Coproducing with the Glimmer Twins, aka Mick Jagger and Keith Richards, Kimsey remembered that as he and Jagger descended on Pathé Marconi to get the lay of the land,

> there were two main recording rooms at Pathé Marconi, and a mixing room, and one recording room had this very small 16-track Dolby EMI desk, a tiny control room with maybe only enough room for two or three people. But a big recording space, and Mick had negotiated a very cheap deal to use that room, so it was almost like Mick thought, "Well, this is the demo studio." Then next door, there was a similar-sized space with a brand-new Neve desk, I mean *massive*. It almost took two people to work it, it was so big. Then this mixing room with a Neve desk. So we started out in Studio 1 with the little desk, and we set everything up and the band started playing through songs, and I was getting very excited with the sound I was getting with this desk! I also had a small P.A. set up as well, so that the band would play with headphones while Mick's voice was going through the P.A. and Charlie's bass drum and snare were going through it.

In the first real production decision he made on the project, Kimsey would have to stand up to Jagger's suggestion that the band move live rooms after the producer had set up the band with a sound that he felt was fantastic. A necessity at times for any producer, objecting to the legendary front man was luckily a situation in which the coproducer had an ally in Richards, who preferred the sound the band already had going. Kimsey explained that

> after a week in there, Mick kind of said, "Well, okay, we should think about moving to the real studio," and I said, "Well, I think this is the real studio, I love the sound in here," and Keith agreed so we just stayed in there for that album, and then came back again for *Emotional Rescue*, and that sort of became our home.

With tape running, an amazing adventure began that would re-energize the Stones' sound for fans while still maintaining their classically fluid formula of recording live off the floor as they tracked, a trick only true instrumental magicians could have pulled off given the traditional rules they were breaking in the process. Underscoring the importance of a young producer's knowing when to throw out the rule book he was taught as an engineer, Kimsey was luckily already well versed in the Stones' way of working thanks to his previous experience working under Glyn Johns. He recalled that with the Stones jamming song ideas live as tape rolled,

> the songs were born in the studio, so it was a long process, maybe four or five days per song. I possibly wouldn't see anyone for two days. If anyone came in it would be Mick and Keith, but Bill or Charlie would never come in, Ronnie would occasionally come in, but nobody would ever come in to check the sound, they just left me to get on with it. And when they did come in, it would be because there was a possibility we were getting somewhere and there was something happening with a take, a song, and they would come in and listen and say, "Yeah, it's nearly there, let's do one more.'
>
> I was never really nervous. I remember that Chuck Levall had just been called in to play with the band, and Chuck and I became very close mates because we were the new kids on the block, and I couldn't figure out why no one was coming in to tell me about the sound. I just said, "Well, they must have liked it," and that was it. I think it became a situation where I was very, very observant about, if something started to sound good, I would make note of it so if after two or three days, somebody said, "Well, you know, there was something on that tape a few days ago," I would know what it was. So I kind of made intense logbooks and observations about what I felt or what was maybe commented at the time by a band member about the takes. In that sense, it was long, and a slow evolution of recording, but it was really interesting because you knew when it sounded right, because it just sounded good. It really sounded like there was something magic happening, and sometimes it took a while to get there, but when you got there, it was great!

Singling out the album's title track as one such by-product of this spontaneous exploration in action, Kimsey remembered calling heavily on his editing skills after the Glimmer Twins gave him autonomy over picking and choosing the highlights from the jam that would ultimately make up the final, keeper take fans heard on record.

> "Some Girls," the title track, is actually about 17 minutes long, we had so many verses, and I actually did the 17 minutes, and Mick just came in and said, "Okay, well, chop it down to like 4 ½ minutes," and I said, "Which verses?," and he said, "You choose." So after about 45 minutes, an hour of editing, he came back in and said, "You done now?" And I laughed and said, "No, bloody hell, it's going to take me at least three or four hours to get 17 minutes down to 4 ½ minutes," because remember this is all 16-track analog tape, with bits of tape hanging everywhere! So there was editing on all the records I made with the Stones, there's multitrack editing between the takes to get the best out of the two or three takes, for sure.

While guitar royal Keith Richards was usually the brain trust for pulling the band's instant hits out of the air during the Stones' jam sessions, Kimsey revealed that the true gasoline for getting the band's creative engine motoring in these moments was

> really all up to Charlie. If he gets the right take, it sounds great. I do remember in a lot of recording with the Stones, the groove's the most important thing, to get the groove right, so for them to get the groove right, which was basically jamming and grooving a verse, then you've got to change gear to a chorus, everybody did that well. But when it came to the middle 8, you'd hold your breath, because with the middle 8, nobody really knew when it was going to appear or how it was going to be happen. And Charlie would be the last one to get to the middle 8 pretty much, so when it did happen in a good way, it was like "Yeah, fantastic!"
>
> That's just Charlie following Mick really, with the arrangement certainly, because things weren't really mapped out in the "Okay, we're going to do a verse and a chorus, verse and a chorus, middle 8." If it was feeling good, the band would keep going on the verse, or keep going on the chorus, and then "Okay, change," and change to what? So it was one of those situations where there were *no set rules*, nothing down except what you're feeling like at the time, and that benefited the band absolutely.
>
> The amazing thing about that is Charlie's playing is so tight and on the money that, for instance, through seventeen minutes on "Some Girls," the tempo never changes, so you could do that. A lot of bands don't understand that today, "Oh no, we've gotta have a click," and I say, "No, no, no, if the drummer's good and the rhythm section's good, you'll be tight together all the way through, and will be amazed at what you can edit together."

Kimsey took equal advantage of Watts's natural sound behind the kit as he bottled the band's live lightning on tape. The producer credited the sonic storm that was Watts's electric drum sound throughout the record as coming courtesy of

> a combination of all of it, it's the room, and the fact that I had the drums going through a little P.A. as well. It's the fact that leakage is your kind of friend in that situation, and I set the band up in a semicircle—with screens in between them—but it was just like watching the band pretty much on band actually. So people could wear headphones—Charlie had to because he couldn't really hear the guitars and the vocals, being set back as it were. But sometimes, Bill or Keith or Ronnie wouldn't really wear headphones, because it was like a club atmosphere, and there was definitely something special about the fact that the snare and bass drum were being gently pumped into the room in the P.A., and that would have picked up a little bit on Charlie's mics as well.

As Richards and Ronnie Wood batted riffs back and forth amid the thunder of their drummer and Jagger's vocal dancing on top of it all, the producer took particular pleasure as a listener from behind the console in appreciating

> what Ronnie brought to it. It was wonderful, because he and Keith's two styles are quite different, and with Keith's quite rhythmical playing and very basic playing, the strength and Ronnie, it was almost like one guitar. There was never any kind of interference between the two sounds or their playing, they just managed to gel really well. But, also the fact that I had the vocal going at the same time meant a lot, so there wasn't overplaying, there was a focus around the vocal because they were hearing a vocal performance as well while they were recording, so it wasn't just like a rhythm section.

As the band got going in moments like these, the BBC among a globe of fans and critics alike had their hair blown back by the way the band "raised energy levels of tracks like *When the Whip Comes Down, Lies and Respectable,* forcefully make the point that this ensemble were practicing breakneck tempos when the punks were in short trousers." When the band's attention turned to laying down one of the album's—and the Stones'—biggest radio hits of the '70s and beyond with the recording of "Shattered," focusing specifically on Keith Richards's guitar sound, the producer remembered that

> on that album actually, there were two pedals that Keith had started to use. One was the MXR *phaser* and the MXR analog delay pedal, which was a green pedal that kind of gave you like a slap delay. So, for instance, I know "Shattered" had that MXR Fazer on it, and I would have recorded his and Ronnie's guitar amplifiers with 47s all around.

Once attention turned to mixing, Kimsey made the same requisite exodus to Electric Lady Studios in New York that every Stones production teammate had throughout the 1970s, finding that as he listened to final mixes, another of the record's biggest hits—arguably the biggest—leaped out immediately, a song that he remembered being

> actually one of my favorite mixes. I loved that track. I just loved the sound of everything about it, and it was just such a joy to work with. It was also during the time when Bobby Clearmountain was also starting his career as a remixer, and Bob had been given "Beast of Burden" to mix as well, and I think he spent the day on it and just said, "No, Chris's mix is just great, use it." That was a wonderful chap.

Sessions so magic in sum that they would produce not one but two of what critics and record buyers agreed were the Stones' best albums of the 1970s, much of *Tattoo You*'s material would in fact come from the now-legendary jams the band laid down at Pathé Marconi Studios during one of their most prolific periods in years. The Stones were inspired in part by the desire to show the younger generation how it was done, and *Billboard* would conclude the band had succeeded in doing precisely that in an era when, "by 1978, both punk and disco had swept the group off the front pages, and *Some Girls* was their fiery response to the younger generation. Opening with the disco-blues thump of 'Miss You,' *Some Girls* is a tough, focused, and exciting record, full of more hooks and energy than any Stones record since *Exile on Main St.*" MTV added their opinion that with the album, the band had definitely reclaimed their "brand of glitzy, decadent hard rock," making *Some Girls* "a definitive Stones album."

The band would return to the studio with Kimsey one final time in the '70s to record 1979's *Emotional Rescue* LP, which contained the hit "She's So Cold," and perhaps more importantly adding additional jam sessions that would help make up the balance of *Tattoo You*, still considered by fans to be the Stones' last great studio LP before they disbanded in the early '80s. The chief catalyst for the album's existence at all was unequivocally Chris Kimsey, who shook his head in amazement years later at the fact that

> there were quite a few songs that were put on the cutting-room floor. That's how "Tattoo You" came up, because I knew of all this material that was hanging about that I'd recorded. And I figured, "Well, if I've done six that haven't been used, there must be more on other albums," and I started to dig back and found more and more material.

Validating Kimsey's instincts, *Sound on Sound* added of the amazing backstory that "*Tattoo You* is widely regarded as the Rolling Stones' last great album; an ingenious division of rock tracks on one side and ballads on the other captures 'the world's greatest rock 'n' roll band' close to their best. Nevertheless, despite the confident musicianship and apparent consistency of material, the record was actually . . . a compilation of tracks that had been discarded from previous albums, with virtually no new input from the musicians themselves. And it was Chris Kimsey who devised this idea out of necessity. Mick Jagger and Keith Richards, you see, were no longer on the best of terms. While the guitarist wanted the band to remain true to its rock and R&B roots, the front man was more interested in movie acting and following contemporary trends, and the result was that neither fancied spending their nights together in the studio. So when the band's financial adviser, Prince Rupert Loewenstein, decreed that it was time to deliver a new album, Kimsey came up with the solution."

Taking fans back into the studio for the recording of the ultimate rock 'n' roll anthem that "Start Me Up" became, opening stadium shows for the shows upon reuniting in the late '80s through the next twenty-five years, starting with Richards's gloriously ambient rhythm chords that kick off the party, Kimsey recalled that

> a lot of that guitar sound is the room. I can hear the ambience of the room in there for sure, and some reverb was added during mixing. Everyone just had one Boogie amp, and the Boogies are really loud, they can be really horrible, and were a pretty new amp at the time, and it was actually quite difficult to get a decent sound out of because they had graphics on them. They were quite a different amp to work with, so it would pretty much end up that everything was turned up to 10!
>
> For Mick's vocal on "Start Me Up," I was using a U-47. It just sounded very full for him, and also, the great thing about Mick is when he's performing a vocal, he's actually dancing as well, he's not just standing in front of the microphone. He's performing in other ways, so then he'll suddenly leap up to the microphone, so it was a good present microphone for him to aim for, and it sounds full and rich.
>
> Recording the Stones on those last three studio albums, it was all done on an EMI TG1234, it was a 16-track machine, and there was one track allotted for each guitar, drums were on four tracks—bass drum, snare and then everything else mixed on the other two—and Bill Wyman's bass would be on one track, a combination of bass/D.I. and the bass amp.

With Kimsey shepherding the project to the finish line, *Sound on Sound* reported that even as he was mixing the final tracklisting for what would become *Tattoo You*, "none of (the band) showed up—Keith, who lived in Paris, would only show his face during the New York mix sessions. Instead, Kimsey was pretty much left to his own devices, and, fortunately for his blasé employers, he turned out an album that would top the US charts for nine weeks on the strength of an extensive stadium tour and the smash hit singles "Start Me Up" and "Waiting On a Friend."

Throughout the 1980s, Kimsey's starring role as one of rock's hottest producers would continue via platinum collaborations with Bad Company, the Escape Club on the seminal '80s hit "Wild, Wild West," the Cult's debut LP *Dreamtime*, Joan Jett and the Blackhearts' *Glorious Results of a Misspent Youth,* the Psychedelic Furs' *All of This and Nothing*, INXS's *Big Moon, Dirty Heart,* Duran, Duran's comeback hit "Ordinary World," along with hooking back up with the Stones when all of the band's members decided to get together in one room again for the recording of a new studio LP, 1988's *Steel Wheels.*

Ahead of recording, *Rolling Stone* chronicled the tension surrounding their return to the studio that Kimsey as producer was navigating, with their report in 1990 that "most of the songs on *Steel Wheels* were written by Mick Jagger and Keith Richards during a three-week session in Barbados. That get-together was the make-or-break point for the Rolling Stones' 1989 reunion—a reunion that had been imperiled by Jagger's and Richards's solo records and by a year of public backbiting between the two . . . Their attitudes in approaching the Barbados session say a great deal about the differences between them . . . Musically, Jagger was concerned that the songs on *Steel Wheels* not repeat the sort of problems that had made him feel constrained in the Stones."

Jagger would add that he had "no such doubts about his ability to work with Richards: "I never worry about things . . . I just get on and do it. Keith is very supersensitive about all that sort of thing and worries that maybe it can't happen. I said, 'Well, we'll just try. If we don't do it, we don't do it.'" Each man brought material to the session. Jagger had a rocker, "Hold On to Your Hat," while Richards had a ballad, "Almost Hear You Sigh." But they began writing together immediately. "We got two or three songs in the first hour, and once you get a roll going, there's no problem," Richards says. "What's good for the music will be good for us personally." Those songs written in the moment included the album's biggest hits, proof the Glimmer Twins hadn't lost their touch on collaboratively creating some of the greatest rockers of all time. In this case, those #1 smashes included the album's lead singles, "Rock and a Hard Place" and "Mixed Emotions," which picked right up where the band had left off stylistically, based in part on a foundation the band rocked out on in the studio where Kimsey recalled, even with a decade passed,

> there was a trust there absolutely, like an unspoken word, where we all knew what we were doing, and we got on with it. Again, it was just teamwork really, making that album.

Singling out the recording of the album's lead single, "Mixed Emotions," as a highlight of the magic still flying back and forth between him and Jagger in the studio during production of his lead vocal performance, the producer points to the experience as a closing example of what about the recording process still gets him up out of bed every day after almost fifty years in the studio. Still getting the biggest kick out of creating and capturing great performances in the studio, Kimsey recalled of this mastercraft in action one more glorious time that

with "Mixed Emotions," when Mick was doing that vocal, it was not just about the sound coming out of his mouth, it's very physical. I tell a lot of singers that now, because a lot of them get kind of frozen in front of the microphone, and I'll say, "Come on, dance, move around for God sake, that's not what you would do live, free yourself . . ." Because you've got to put your body into it as well, not just the sound coming out of your vocal chords, it will help everything, and it does. It's a physical thing, singing. So that was part of Mick's sound, absolutely.

CHAPTER 11

Bloodletting–Chris Tsangarides

Concrete Blonde emerged in a time the *LA Times* declared "an era when rock music could be both primal and experimental, flamboyant and expressive, beautiful and emotional," one that with "Johnette Napolitano's voice—captivating in range and depth," *Goldmine* magazine argued "Concrete Blonde were real musicians in an age where the commercial and catchy and hooky was ruling the '80s and they were marching to their own beat." That independence led the band to head back in the studio in late 1989 to produce what the *LA Times* would hail as "an excellent new cycle of dark, haunting songs," adding that "in a just world (which the pop sweepstakes most assuredly is not), *Bloodletting* would be a career-making piece of work . . . (and) is indeed dripping, and gripping, stuff."

Indeed, it was career making for a group who with the album, in the opinion of Popmatters.com, succeeded in providing listeners with "a gothic alternative for anyone who might have found the Cure's *Disintegration* too mannered or stately. As part of a three-album run that included 1992's *Walking in London* and 1993's *Mexican Moon*, *Bloodletting* began a creatively fruitful period for the band, one in which they explored issues such as failed relationships, addiction, and a blend of Catholic and Hispanic imagery with often inspired results." Their copilot on this flight would be Chris Tsangarides, a metal producer from

Britain who remembered his inspired journey with the band had begun in a truly serendipitous fashion after

> they literally turned up in the U.K., and I got a call from the Immigration Department
> saying that this band is here to have a meeting with you, is that correct? And so I said
> yes, but I didn't know they were there. We'd made contact before through a phone
> call when Johnette was in England, several months prior to that, and she says to me,
> "We've got a band, and would love you to work with us," because they liked a Thin
> Lizzy album I'd made. So I said, "Great, send me your stuff." So they sent me their first
> album, and I heard it and said, "Cool, okay," and that was it.
>
> Then next thing I know, a few months later, I have this phone call and they turn up
> in the studio. And I think it might have been Black Sabbath I was working with, and
> had a week between that and the next project I was doing, and we managed to slot
> them in to do the mixing of *Free* at Britennial Row Studios, Pink Floyd's place. And
> there were some vocals we had to do, and they came over with their 2-inch tapes, and
> I thought it was pretty cool and off we went. When we were doing those vocal tracks, I
> couldn't believe Johnette's range, it's just amazing. Her voice is just so resonant and
> wonderful and in tune, and she could deliver at any time, really great.
>
> So I remember putting the tracks up and listening to what they were doing, and
> there was a song called "God Was a Bullet" that I thought, "Wow, this is great." And
> normally, the way it works with me is sort of on a personal level, if I like the individ-
> uals and it's reciprocated, we get on with it. Obviously, the music first, but we hit it
> off pretty quickly, and after hearing her sing, I said "Yeah, we've got to do an album."
> And so when *Free* came out and did pretty good, that led to our doing the *Bloodletting*
> album together.

A gorgeous experiment in everything alternative that was allowed stylistically to blend
into a gallery of works of musical art, *Bloodletting* would inspire *Entertainment Weekly* to
report that "you don't run across albums with a range this wide every week. Nor do you
find albums so consistent—there's not a single routine song—or so often beautiful." Tsangarides recounted a less attractive start to sessions for the album when, the day before the
band was set to begin recording,

> Harry, the drummer, left the band! So we were suddenly scrambling to find a replace-
> ment, and I remember their guitarist, Jim Mankey, saying to me, "Chris, do you know
> any drum pros?" So I went home, and was talking with my wife, and she said, "Well,
> why don't you get Paul Thompson from Roxy Music to play on it?" And I thought that
> was a good idea, because Concrete Blonde had played a few nights before at the
> Borderline Club, and Paul and his wife had come along with my wife and I to see them.
> So he liked what he heard, and I called him and said, "You on board for it?" And he

said, "Yeah, absolutely." And they were completely over the moon, Johnette couldn't believe Paul was going to play on their stuff. But he came in, we set up, and that's exactly what happened. We didn't have much time for preproduction, only a couple of days.

In setting the album's sonic mood, the producer was seeking a live room—ultimately choosing Battery Studios in London—that suited his and the band's desire to

make a very warm, fat-sounding record. I'm a big fan of Phil Spector's, and the old Tamla stuff as well, because those records were recorded with a couple of mics, stuck in some old office, because there weren't any studios, so it was wherever they could do it—especially the Tamla people. It was like "Wow, why does this thing sound so nice, so pleasing?" Look back at *Physical Graffiti*, which was recorded in castles and all manner of funny places, and it was really bloody good because they wanted a natural thing as opposed to studios, which really are the most ridiculous places to make music. Everything is deadened down, it's not . . . where did music come from, the live hall? Were studios there first? Chicken and the egg, and all that bit, and I've always had this thing in my head that if you're a band when you play, you need to sound like you do live. If the drum's got a resonance to it, then let's hear it, because that's what it is. So it was a very general sort of picture for Concrete Blonde of how I wanted the record to sound. So we recorded in Battery Studio 3, not a particularly large room, but a very modern room that had just been completed basically.

Believing the band's rhythm section would deliver their best performances laying basic tracks live off the floor together, Tsangarides reasoned this approach was essential because

with the way I do basic tracking is everyone plays together, and all that gets kept is the drums and the bass. Because you're limited in studios with separation, rooms, and what have you, there just isn't enough space in most of the places you go to set out to get something that is a usable sound, especially if I'm using room mic and stuff like that. It's pretty hard to find a studio that has the sound of the room—the two or three great big rooms you're going to need for each individual player to be in. The point is, I like to record everything in the same room, so once I've done my drums, they get broken down, and then I can put the amps in, and have the echoes and reflections of the room. So the whole thing ends up sounding like they're playing live.

Johnette and Jim would come in with a song, play it to Paul, and off he went. There would be a loose description for the kind of groove he should be doing, and that was it. The songs were pretty well sorted. We had enough time to do what we needed to do, and it was two or three takes, four takes maybe at the most, it wasn't laborious as I remember. Jim came and did the bass, but Johnette laid it down on the guide track.

Between Jim or Johnette, there was an argument or two between them if I remember, but musically they were on the same planet. I was their creative referee, but what won out in any musical argument was what was good for the song. I think their songwriting was their strength, because they came up with these tunes.

When he miced up Paul Thompson's drum kit, seeking to take advantage of a player who had by that point been labeled "The Great Paul Thompson" by fans, according to London's *Evening Chronicle*, for his dazzling "skill behind the kit," the producer recalled that

I used a Neumann U-47 mic on the kick drum, and a Neumann KM 84 on the snare, and Sennheiser 41s on the tom, and 87s in the funky overhead micing technique I used. It's basically that the left and right mics that I use—I do it as you look at the drums from the audience perspective—and the right-hand overhead is directly above the snare drum—three feet, four feet high. Where the floor tom is, about a few feet higher than that, pointing at the snare is the other one, the left-hand mic. But the trick to this is they're both exactly equidistant from the snare drum where they're placed. I do every one of my drum kits like that, unless it's a double-bass kit, which kind of makes it a bit hard to do. But generally that's how I do it, and the majority of the sound comes from those two mics, in combination of course with the drums being tuned properly. So we got the nice drum sound that we got on it, and everything was added to it.

That *everything* was the sum of a band the *LA Times* would compliment for striking "a comfortable level at which nothing is forced, giving even the grandest moments an intimacy, and lending quieter ones the easy empathy and spontaneity of a jazz combo." Led musically by guitarist James Mankey, who explained exclusively that "mostly, my sound comes from the touch in my playing, but also a blend of hi-watt 100-watt heads into 4 x 12 cabinets. I was also a big fan of Mullard output tubes, and so when we recorded, Chris would put Johnette in an ISO booth for a scratch vocal, which could have occasionally turned out to be the final, Paul on drums in another room for isolation, and I would play whatever, because then later on I would redo everything." Excited to be working with Mankey, the producer added of his approach that

I was very aware of Jim's style—his finger-playing and all that—we ended up using my old Aiwa amp for him to play through, and it was bloody marvelous. We used the old famous vortex system, that I sort of developed, which is basically a micing technique where I use a series of close mics and distant mics, and the guitars are recorded in stereo with the distant microphones on one side and the close mics on the other. With Jim, I think it was an 87 close up and a 47 in the room, which gets all these banding waves that come from the guitar. And in certain places and certain notes and certain frequencies that the guitar player hits, they faze themselves out, which gives the illusion of sort of like an autopan. And that's kind of what the vortex is, but also, depending on the scenario, if I've got some baffles, I'll put a baffle on either side of the speaker cabinet in a V formation to blast the sound out, direct it more toward the microphone. And it works really well. I used that on pretty much everything I did—especially on lead guitars. You'll hear a lot of it on Yngwie Malmsteen records.

I thought Jim was absolutely unique as a guitar player, a complete one-off. There wasn't many people I'd worked with who didn't use a plectrum, and he was playing me some Chet Atkins stuff, and I was thinking, "Okay, this is excellent." Watching someone that was playing in a completely different style that I haven't seen too many people do was very, very impressive because there's so many facets to the instrument, like anything. As a music fan and music lover, this was something really special, and to see this guy coming up with these sounds, pulling them out of his fingers were wonderful. I coached performances in as much as encouragement, "Ahh, I know you can do better than that Jim," and he was not impatient.

As the group went about weaving the mysterious soundscape that was *Bloodletting*, *Entertainment Weekly* noted that "knitting everything together is the smoky sound of Napolitano's voice, sometimes intimate, sometimes sardonic, sometimes torn by passion, always unguarded." Blessed with among rock's most stirring voices, *Rolling Stone* would argue that "her singing throughout *Bloodletting* is passionate and catchy, with a deep throaty ache on many cuts." Delivering performances that required absolute freedom from distractions, Tsangarides remembered that, not surprisingly,

whenever we were doing vocals, the atmosphere was lights were low, and there wasn't anyone in the studio except maybe Jim, but mainly just me and her, a bottle of wine maybe. She would do a few takes, not many, and then I would compile if I needed to, or keep the first, and drop in the odd word here or there, but it was about getting her vocals right. She was a very technically versed vocalist, so there were no problems where I'd have to say "Breathe now," or anything like that. She knew what she was doing. I always used a Neumann U 87 microphone for her vocals.

As the group progressed toward the wrap of tracking, for as smoothly as things had gone in the studio between the band's members and producer, the reason why Tsangarides preferred the presence of only principal members during tracking was revealed when

I remember Miles Copeland coming in to have a listen, and asking me while Johnette was standing in the room, what did I think the first single was, and Johnette stormed out. And he's going, "What did I say, what did I do, what happened?" And I said, "Well, you put a commercial slant to her music." Which was a perfectly legitimate question as far as the record company was concerned, but to a real artist, it's not good. Artistic integrity was always important to her, and with the type of records I produce, you cannot pick a single ahead of time, because it's all organic, real music, and if there's something that lends itself to a single, then it is, but the point is: people don't know what a hit single is, as far as real people who play. If we did, we'd be making them every bloody day.

The band's biggest-selling and charting single off the record, "Joey," was a song guitarist James Mankey recalled came in at the last minute, after "we had recorded the entire album with Chris at Battery Studios in London, we had one song that still didn't have a vocal, and that was Joey. So Chris called Johnette up at the hotel and said, 'Come on over, it's our last day, you better come in and sing this.' And she wrote the words in a cab on the way over to the studio. She came in and sang it to the preexisting track, and that was it. I don't know if anybody thought it was a single, but it was obvious it belonged on the record." Tsangarides remembered being particularly pleased with the vocal performance Napolitano delivered at the last-minute session, confirming that

I loved that song very much, I loved the way she sang it. There's the big Phil Spector bit with the big echo on the snare, because I liked Phil Spector, that's why that's there.

Once Tsangarides had his creative attention turned from tracking to mixing the performances the team had laid down, he revealed of the somewhat intuitive process that

as I was mixing *Bloodletting*, I managed to interpret them I think in the way they wished them in their heads, and add whatever else it was that I put into it. That's I guess the X factor. I spent a lot of time with percussion—triangles, and tambourines, and shakers, and God knows what, and if you listen to it, you'll hear these funny little things that keep coming in and out in maybe not quite the obvious places. In terms of making decisions on where those sounds show up in the mix, it's done pretty much as I record it. I'll record a shaker, and then decide it should go over on right, and there's a triangle that answers it later on, and that's all in my head.

Whenever you make a record, it's a team effort anyway, and you're really dumb if you don't listen to what they say. You don't have to agree with it and do it, but you have to be able to deal with that scenario and say, "Your suggestion isn't quite as good as I'm doing because . . ." and here's the proof, and what do you think of that? And because you know the people and have worked with them, they'll accept it, and vice versa. And they were really responsive, and we had occasional storming-out-of-the-studio sessions, but it never had anything to do with the music.

Feeling with the final product that the band had "recognized the strength of its material and . . . (delivered) it with maximum effect," the *LA Times* would quickly join a chorus of critical acclaim for the record that also included *Entertainment Weekly*, who said that "*Bloodletting* is a strange, strong album from a group that deserves a shot at mainstream success." That shot would come courtesy of "Joey," which *Goldmine* reported "(jumped) onto the charts at #19 on the Hot 100 Rock in the US." Of this unusually deep song for the Top 20 and the group that created it, *Goldmine* added that "they stood out from the pack with (a) . . . tune that was almost eerie while at the same time being thought-provoking and mysterious. With Concrete Blonde you were dragged along willingly with the words guiding you and the musicianship enticing you." Recalling smiles all around from the band, Tsangarides remembered feeling proud of the fact that

> the band was considerably happy with the sales they got, it significantly outsold the first record, and suddenly they were on the climb, as it were. People were moved by that band, and responded to their sound and songs. I've met people who say, "I met my girlfriend because of that record, and got married, and had a kid." That's not a goal, but a great thing to think that maybe some of your work means something to somebody on a more different level. I think Concrete Blonde touched a lot of people that way.

The producer would strike success in a different genre entirely the next year in 1991 when his collaboration on Judas Priest's *Painkiller* LP earned them a Grammy nomination for "Best Metal Performance," which marked the band's final studio collaboration with famed front man Rob Halford for a decade to come. Returning fifteen years after engineering the band's *Sad Wings of Destiny* LP, as Tsangarides entered the studio to begin working with the legendarily controversial British heavy-metal band, as he'd sought to do with Concrete Blonde,

> when we got around to *Painkiller*, the first thing that was decided was that I wanted them to play the album live, because the one before was drum machines and God knows what. And I'd heard the demos, which were basically a little drum box and a voice and guitar, and was incredibly fast, and they had just gotten Scott Travis, so we went in, set them up, and tracked it with everyone playing together in the same room. With Priest, I was trying to get them to groove a bit more, and by the time we get to *Pain Killer*, they had an American drummer, ironically, who sounded absolutely phenomenal, that combination. After the drumming was done, they wanted this particular bass sound I'd gotten with a lot of bands, which was a Moog synth bass, and Don Eerie came down to play the Moog, which we double-tracked with the live bass track.
> I'd first done that with a band I'd produced out in Minneapolis called Blade Rader, and the result was hearing this really fat bass with an attack that you'd never get on a

bass guitar alone. It's not a keyboard, it's a bass effect, and it changes the character of the bass a lot, so that's what we did, and then added guitars, which was a whole load of fun, because they used these four-way JBL studio monitors, and when they showed up at the studio with these, I thought, "Where the hell am I going to put a mic on this?" What it was, their rig was Rockmans and DI guitars, and they took that sound out on the road with a little mixer each with a Rockman preamp, driving a couple of Crown big old power amps, driving JBL studio monitors, that was the back-line. So when they turned up with this, it was funny because you couldn't record anywhere near it, because do you mic the tweeker up, or the bass driver, what do you do? And luckily we brought over a (Seldano head), and that's what I used all the way through it. The guitar was close-miced in a different room with the Seldano and a 4 x 12 cabinet, and then the guitar was split into their big JBL studio monitor rig, and I put a room mic about one hundred feet away and got my echo off that.

Vocally, Rob was all overdubbed, and we double-tracked his vocals and added harmonies, all sorts of wonderful things. He's an absolutely terrific, terrific vocalist, because he doesn't sing falsetto, it's full-voiced, and he has such a high, high voice range, and a really good tenor range as well. He's easy to record, he doesn't mind whoever's around, and is very relaxed, and chews gum all the time. I recorded him on a Neumann 87 mic. Recording metal vocals, I've tried all manner of things, but it's always a Neumann 87 or a Neumann U-47 depending on if you want it a little brighter. I have found those mics work best for male voices, especially one that's going to be giving it from low to high. When I did the second Priest record, they put "Co-produced" by me and them, and the same with Thin Lizzy, and I think it's kind of a courtesy thing on my part, because they're not there 100 percent of the time. They're not there having to record it, having to make that kind of decision. They'll come in later and say they like something or not.

Touching on his coproduction collaboration with Thin Lizzy, another rock legend, on the group's final studio LP, 1983's *Thunder and Lightning*, which *Billboard* would praise as "their most consistent album since 1979's *Black Rose*; 1981's *Renegade* album; and the band's farewell live LP, 1984's *Life Live*;" the producer recalled that with

their last recordings, which I produced from *Renegade* onward, that collaboration first started when I was already working with Phil on Gary Moore's solo album, and while we were making that record, we were doing some work on Phil's solo record, *Solo in Soho*, and we also did the next one, *Fatalistic Attitude*. So through that, we had worked together, and Thin Lizzy had started the *Renegade* record and were sort of in trouble, because Phil couldn't differentiate between what was a solo project and what was Thin Lizzy, so he asked me to come in and take over. So I tried to focus it more on the rock side of things, and so we did *Angel of Death* and *Pressure Will Blow* and *Renegade*, and I sorted out the other tunes they had done before, and it was an S.O.S. of sorts.

We didn't recut the album, but we rerecorded a whole load with stuff, and did a bunch of editing and rearranging a bit. Phil's incredibly easy to record, but the trouble with the band at that stage was they would just throw everything on tape. And of course, being a 24-track, we'd run out of tape pretty damn quick, so you'd have three different instruments on the same track. So it was a constant of jumping up and down and turning things on while the song was playing to actually get it into the order that it should be.

So when it came to the band's next album, *Thunder and Lightning*, I insisted that we go first into a rehearsal room and rehearse the songs, figure them out, and that was the first time they'd actually done preproduction. And it helped big time, and helped with the budget, of course. There's an example of why I always prefer to have songs written prior to going into the studio, especially nowadays where the budgets are so much smaller. But with them, it was literally "I've got a riff, let's go." With John, he used Marshall stacks, and we miced the same way I always had with close and distant mics.

Equally proud of his work with the Tragically Hip on their 1993 platinum-selling *Fully Completely* LP, about which MTV said the band had "finally come to the apex of their talent," the producer agreed, hailing the band throughout their collaboration in the studio as

absolutely brilliant. It was a lighter affair than a lot of the metal stuff I'd done, and was because of Concrete Blonde that they were interested in working with me. I flew over to Canada to see them play at a gig they had set up especially for me to check them out in a smaller club, and I didn't realize at that point that they were pretty successful over there. I was really taken in by the way they could build up a crowd and an intensity in the music just by themselves playing, with just two guitars and a bass, and thought, "If we can get that on a piece of vinyl, we're laughing." And basically that's how we set them up in the studio, they all played together, then we redid the guitars, BUT the guitars were done like they would be live.

Whatever they played live would be like that, and I think it's a credit to them that they managed to do that again in the studio, because their songs built up in intensity without me pushing faders up to try and make it louder. Because it's different from an intensity to a volume, it's a completely different thing. And you get this tension they can create, and I think it's the way they played between them. They had terrific songs, and we were fortunate the songs were real good. When we were recording the guitars, they used half of my guitars and amps, one of the guys would use my Tele Deluxe with the 100-watt head that I used with Jim on Concrete Blonde. It had four number one singles, and is coming up to a Diamond award now. They were so easygoing and their songs were fantastic, they were incredibly receptive, and we turned the album around very, very quickly—in five weeks, I think.

Tying his closing thoughts together after looking back over thirty-plus years in the business where he's succeeded in producing platinum albums for a stylistically diverse universe of stars, Tsangarides seems most proud of his catalog's variety in that respect, musing that

I have done a lot of metal acts, and also I've managed to carve myself a career within alternative music, if you will, but always the darker or heavier side of each type of band I do, because I've never done a poodle band, if you will, a corporate rock band. It's always been some kind of either extreme metal or something that had something to say for itself. Music first.

CHAPTER 12

Times Like These—Nick Raskulinecz

Over the past two decades, the Foo Fighters have become one of those rare bands known for consistently churning out the kind of anthemic rock singles that never seem to get old to the ear or airwaves. Just consider the *Hollywood Reporter*'s declaration that "in 2011, today, (Dave) Grohl is practically a guitar god and the undeniable star of his own show, and it's hard to imagine a time when that wasn't so." This has been the case from their debut hit, "I'll Stick Around," and "Everlong" to "There Goes My Hero" and "Learning to Fly" to perhaps their finest musical moment, one where the BBC felt that with "the Byrds meets Husker Du rush of 'Times Like These,' things are set up for a knockout victory." While the rock star or band often receive the lion's share of the credit as the hit comes from their lips and licks, the sound that comes roaring out of the speakers is another matter altogether, and behind a board in Dave Grohl's Virginia basement capturing that sound was producer Nick Raskulinecz, whose time had come by 2003, following an almost decade-long apprenticeship as one of the lead engineers at legendary Sound City Studios (the subject, ironically, of a 2013 documentary directed by Dave Grohl).

I moved to California in 1995 and started working at Sound City Studios, and came to realize that a ton of my all-time favorite records had been recorded there, and I started as a runner and worked up to assistant engineer, and started getting to assist for some of the best rock engineers there are, guys like Garth Richardson, and Silvia Massey, and Jim Barisi, and Matt Hyde, and Jim Scott, Dave Shipman, people like that. So I was working for all different kinds of engineers and bands from all over the world, just learning how to make records sound like records. It was the first time I'd ever seen a Neve, or an LA2A, or an 1176, or a tape machine, and really just started to absorb it all.

I think it's important for any up-and-coming engineer to record on as many different consoles and as many different rooms as you can, because to me, the best engineers are the ones who are able to make something sound great in less-than-satisfactory conditions. You end up being a good utility person taking advantage of spaces. I used to make records in houses all the time, which I don't really like, but if you can record a record in a house and make it sound good, then you understand how sound works, because there's a lot of modifying and tricks you have to learn how to do in order to make things sound good.

Applying that logic to his own situation tracking Grohl and musical twin Taylor Hawkins in what can only be described as an out-of-the-box backdrop from traditional recording studios like the latter Sound City, Raskulinecz recalled that

we tracked everything with just Dave and Taylor playing, they made the basics together, and then Dave laid down a scratch bass and we did all the vocal overdubs, then we went out to LA and did the bass and lead guitar overdubs. But it was just me and Dave and Taylor in Dave's house for about two weeks. With a band like the Foo Fighters, we would go for twelve to fifteen hours a day during sessions for *One by One*, and Dave was there the whole time, that's pretty much the case with most of the records I make. Dave and Taylor are both musically total spazzes, and I'm all about energy, man. If you listen to the records I make, there's kind of a common thread through all of them, and that's an energy.

With Taylor's drums, his energy and his technique, he's just awesome, not only with Foos, but he played drums on a Coheed and Cambria record that I made, *No World for Tomorrow,* and I think it's some of his best work ever. He's one, two, three takes and he's done. I miced his drum kit with a 57 on the snare, 421s on the toms, two 51s for the overheads, and a Sennheiser 602 on the inside and D112 on the outside of the kick drum.

Winner of the 2004 Grammy for "Best Rock Album," in delving into how he approached capturing the fiery arpeggios that blazed through "Times Like These" opening moments, Raskulinecz said we recorded *One by One* in Dave's basement, so it was close-miced for the amps, and we used some Hi-Watts, some Marshalls, and Mesa Boogies. As far as mics, I like 57s and 47 Phets, SM7s. A 47 Phet is a large capsule, a super high-end condenser mic that is very full range, I like it for that. The SM7 is just a bigger version of a 57, and it's got a wider dynamic.

Dave works really fast, and I have to say, I was blown away at how good of a guitar player he was when we first started recording together, because he's known for his drumming, and I was like "Holy shit! This guy's a fucking awesome guitar player too!" He's a great bass player too.

That song's got a cool thing on it, the console Dave had at his house was an API board, and I think on accident, we were recording that song and plugged one of the guitar mics into a channel that was broken, and it was totally super fuzzed out. I actually heard that song on the radio the other day and you could totally hear that guitar on that song, so that's kind of what gives that song its sound in a way, that guitar track. It's a great song.

Raving that "*One by One* is the most accomplished album Foo Fighters have made," *Billboard* magazine would add of the next album Raskulinecz made with the band, the double CD half-electric/half-acoustic *In Your Honor*, that "splitting music along such a clear dividing line is dangerous." The producer couldn't have agreed more heading into the collaboration, sharing his memory of feeling that

as a producer, when you're passionate about something, you want to fight for it, but Dave's one of those artists that's usually really great. There might be just a little thing here or there, and we'll listen, and take it if he wants, and if he thinks it's the right move, we'll do it. That pretty much goes for any songwriter/musician/kind of visionary of the whole project, and he's got the talent to play every instrument himself and do everything and it's awesome. I think it was easier at first in that we became really good friends, and then got harder, which is usually the case with most bands: it can be tough to work with the same band multiple times, because during this two-three month process of meeting these people for the very first time through finishing a record, it's like "Okay, the record's done, well it was nice to meet you, we just spent three really intense months together, I don't know when I'll see you again." So you become friends, and when you go through that experience again, you're already friends, so it can be harder to take critiquing, and it goes both ways.

Going from making *One By One* to *In Your Honor*, that reality made it easier and made it more difficult, because it was easier on a hanging-out level, because you're more comfortable: you know what each other likes to eat, you know what you like to watch on TV, your kids' names and wives are hanging out, and this happens with multiple bands. But then when you're talking about music, it can be more complicated, because it's like "Oh, really, you think so? You're just my bud, you don't know," and that happens with most bands. That's where being a producer, there's a tremendous amount of psychology involved, because you really have to understand how people work and how they deal under pressure in certain situations, because making a record isn't like playing a gig, it's not like rehearsing in a rehearsal room. You just don't play it one time, you play it a lot of times, and listen to it over and over and over again, and then hear it back in ways that you've never heard it before, when you're actually tracking.

Working with Dave by that point, things had gotten pretty intuitive, but we were both pushing each other. He was pushing me to get different sounds, more variety of sounds, so we used a lot of different guitars and a lot of different amps, it's a heavy guitar album with lots of different layers and overdubs and parts. I think I really pushed him vocally, because the vocals are fucking awesome on that album. He wanted to make an anthemic record with the song "In Your Honor," that cool intro, it's like the gnarliest scream he'd ever done in his life, and he couldn't talk for like three days after. I know for a fact he blew his voice out playing that song live, and has never played it again since.

As the team set out on their sophomore sonic sojourn, Raskulinecz remembered an ambitious spirit whipping around the studio, one that had begun with preproduction discussions where

Dave talked about making a double album from the very beginning. Preproduction to me is very important, essential. I'm always a fan of coming into the studio with songs written, so preproduction is the next stage after I get the band's demos and we talk and decide we're going to work together. That's where the dialogue starts of "Okay, if we're going to work together, this song needs that, and this song needs that, and this part could be better, and that's a great chorus but you need to rewrite the whole rest of the song, we have to work on all the drum parts . . ."

I kind of think of it as when I join the band, and consider myself a fifth member essentially. The band and I talk about that at the outset, and it's kind of like I join the band with a completely fresh and objective perspective that the guys in the band don't have anymore because you wrote it, and you're in it so deep, you think it's amazing, and nine times out of ten it is. But let's just say there's that 1 percent of every song that might need a little arrangement shift or a little bit of help here or there. Other times there's none, where it's like, "Well, that's great, we just need to record it." Then it becomes more of a sonic element of "What are we going to do with the sounds?'

My main focus when we began that album was just keeping the proper focus on everything and allotting for the proper amount of time, because we spent three or four months working on that record, it took a while. We built a studio, and we started the record before it was finished, so as the studio continued to be built around us, the sound of the record changed. So all of a sudden, the drum room wasn't as live after the first three or four drum tracks, and we didn't try to adjust that. I think it's what makes that record interesting, is that it sounds different, it's got a sound to it. I like to record in big rooms.

For Grohl and Raskulinecz, the album's plugged/unplugged medium provided an opportunity—in the opinion of *USA Today*—to pull "back the vocal roar and (sing) . . . with restraint on the second, unplugged set, his pleasant croon nicely fitting." For the producer, that meant first and foremost taking advantage of Grohl's gift for being

really quick, he's fucking really quick at all of it. He hears it in his head, and it's his ability to be very clean and then all of a sudden get really dirty and really hairy. He's just a really great performer too, a great singer, a great guitar, and one of the best drummers there is in rock music. For vocals, on *One by One* we used a U-47 tube mic, but for *In Your Honor,* we used a Sound Deluxe 251, which is just a great-sounding tube mic. It's the closest thing I've heard to a real old Telefunken 251, it's just a fantastic mic. I bought one back in 2004, and it's been the vocal sound on 99 percent of the records I've made. I used it on Evanescence as well.

With vocals, usually I prefer just me and the singer, and I kick everybody else out. No band members are allowed, and I usually lay that one on them right as we're about to do them, because I don't want to hear anyone talk or make noise, and I don't want anybody's opinion. When I'm working with a singer—especially someone like Amy from Evanescence or Dave Grohl—pretty much everybody, because vocals is guitar player and the drummer hanging out, and there's a friend in the room, and a very different part of making a record. I like to really get that bond and that relationship and get in each other's heads, and there's too many fucking distractions when you've got everybody fucking talking, so "Get the fuck out, everybody, when it's done you get to hear it."

With vocal effects, it just depends. I mix it up on every song. Some might be different kinds of slap delays, longer delays, usually there's a couple different delays and a couple different reverbs. I'm a fan of the Eventide 910. Dave likes to have effects going while he's singing, most people do.

In Your Honor was widely hailed, receiving five Grammy nominations including "Best Rock Album," "Best Surround Sound Album," both "Best Rock Song" and "Best Rock Performance by a Duo or Group with Vocal" for "Best of You," a *Billboard* Hot 100 Singles hit (#18), and #1 hit on the U.S. Hot Modern Rock Tracks and US Hot Mainstream Rock Tracks. Raskulinecz revealed that, for all its eventual success,

"Best of You"—that was not the song we picked as the first single. John Silver picked that song. That was definitely not one of our favorite songs. We loved the song, but weren't like "This is the first single!" I think we'd picked "Free Me," and his manager was like "Are you crazy? 'Best of You's' the song, that's a hit," and he was right, because it went #1 for like seven weeks.

It's hard for me to know what the single's going to be, that's not really my role, and I try to make every song great. Then somebody else, an A&R guy or a manager, that's why they have their jobs.

As the team transitioned into work on the acoustic side of the album, the producer recalled an inspired session that began after

we'd started the electric side first, and then kind of got burnt out on the electric side of it and switched gears into the acoustic side of the album, and did the whole record in like a week, eleven days! On a couple of the songs, Dave tracked his acoustic guitar while he sang. "Laser" is a live vocal, and we used a Sound Deluxe mic for the majority of the sound on that acoustic record. My favorite is "Another Round" from the acoustic side.

Raskulinecz's wild success with the Foo Fighters allowed him the freedom of the litter's pick with the rock world's new and reunion LPs, the latter of which would become a specialty niche for him. Starting with legendary Alice in Chains' comeback in 2008, as Blabbermouth.net reported that same year, because of "Nick Raskulinecz (FOO FIGHTERS, RUSH, STONE SOUR, TRIVIUM, SHADOWS FALL, DEATH ANGEL), the album promises to be a sonic journey guided by eerily psychedelic solos, and unforgettable riffs." Rather than seeking to reinvent the band's sound, the producer preferred to celebrate its signatures, recalling that

Our discussions going into that album were: I wanted it to be the record after *Dirt*. I spent a lot of preparation driving around and listening to the old albums, because I used to LOVE Alice in Chains in the '90s, and Jerry's guitar tone and Sean's drumming. So sonically, I drove around really listening to the guitar and the hi-hat and the gated reverb on the snare and toms, and sonically I wanted to make it so before those guys even opened up their mouths to sing, people knew "That's fucking Alice in Chains." Then, vocally, it was really about creating the atmosphere of the feeling of what it used to be like with Layne. It's not Layne, but when those guys sing together, it's about as fucking close as you're going to get.

Channeling his inner rock-child, Raskulinecz tapped into his own influences going back to teenage metal days when in our house growing up, there was always a piano around, and both of my uncles played guitar, and my parents listened to a lot of music. My mother was totally into music, so she was listening to the Beatles, Jimi Hendrix, the Who, Yes, Rush, so I was exposed to that music at a young age, and I got my first guitar when I was ten, eleven years old, which is now '81, so I was absorbing Iron Maiden, Van Halen, Judas Priest, the Scorpions. In fact, "Rock You Like a Hurricane" was the first song I ever learned how to play on guitar.

Seeking to return lead guitarist Jerry Cantrell to his proper place among the most timelessly relevant players of his generation, Raskulinecz paid particular respect and attention during his own preproduction preparations to the reality that

they'd spent YEARS preparing for that record, writing and rewriting, and arranging and rearranging, and then I came in during preproduction and put in my two cents, which was mostly arranging where song structure was concerned. So when I say arrangement, I'm talking in general about the verse and the chorus, and the prechorus, and the bridge, and "Is there a guitar solo?" and "Why is the guitar solo that long?," because I'm bored, and if the solo's going to be that long, it's gotta be more exciting. Otherwise it's too fucking long and people are going to be switching over to the next song. That's probably the biggest things—song arrangement and structure and drum parts—those are the biggest elements I bring to preproduction, and then, it's every little detail after that.

I remember even back as a kid, my ear had an attention to detail at that age, even listening to music I didn't necessarily like, or songs that I really don't like. I listen to them for the sonic value, and did back then, especially electric guitar, I was always fascinated by that. I remember I would take my mom's big-ass Technique stereo speakers and pull them away from the wall, turn them in to each other, and just lay down in between them, and just sit there and close my eyes and listen to all the different instruments, and reverbs and effects and shit that was going on. Albums like Yes's Going for the One and the Beatles' Abbey Road. So the Rush and Yes albums always grabbed me, those kind of sonic not-just really dry recorded '70s records, like records that had lots of effects. In my own productions, I try to create different spaces in my own productions, which totally comes from that.

Those details would collect to create what the LA Times would celebrate as "the heavy guitars, submerged vocals and thunderous rhythm section quickly assured fans that the band has lost none of its menace." As the producer got down to capturing the energy of that rhythm section live in the studio, he recalled that

I wanted it to be modern and fresh but also feel like the '80s, so the gated reverb and the big toms and all that shit. As far as effects, we used the AMS and a preset in the Eventide for gated snare, and put all that stuff down to tape.

Upon its release in September 2009, fan reaction to the band's new material blew "highly anticipated" sky-high as the group's first new studio album in thirteen years—with an unknown singer, the biggest gamble of all for any band in AIC's position—debuted at #5 on the *Billboard* Top 200 albums chart! A huge success that was further validated by the *New York Times'* declaration that "the reactivated band has scrupulously maintained its 1990s sound, with its down-tuned guitars and bass, its minor keys, its booming drums that land just behind the beat and its mostly dirgelike tempos, broken every so often by a faster hard-rock riff." As a guitar player himself, Raskulinecz viewed the opportunity to work with Jerry Cantrell as a chance to celebrate

just his sound and the way he plays, because it's so unlike everybody else. He's got an identifiable signature that I wanted to make sure not to change that in any way, just bring it out. I made him use all his old guitars and amps, the same guitars he used on *Facelift* and *Dirt* are the guitars we used on both that album and *The Devil Put Dinosaurs Here.*

As a producer who plays guitar, it's easier to communicate. I have a band I'm working with right now. If I can see the guitar player's struggling with something, I can pick up the guitar and say, "Try this version of that," or "How were you playing that, is there a better way to play it?" So I think it helps, but it's not a deal-breaker. Being a producer I think is more about the songs than the sound. It's more about the song than having an overall vision for the sound.

Turning to the in some ways greater risk of attempting to authentically blend William DuVall and Cantrell's trademark harmony vocal sound, *Billboard* would argue that the payoff came for fans after Raskulinecz succeeded in producing a "vocal blend with guitarist Jerry Cantrell (that) ensures that that integral harmonic trademark remains intact." *Mix* magazine added that "Cantrell and DuVall break out those unique underneath harmonies in the goosebump-inducing refrain," with the producer sharing his memory that,

we did some songs at the same time, but most were done separately. I didn't realize how much Jerry sang on those old albums, and when I started working with him one-on-one vocally, I started to realize that he is responsible for A LOT of the vocals on those albums with Layne. A lot of the harmonies and the way they're written and the lyrics, and kind of like realizing how great of a guitar player Dave Grohl was—who's of course known for his drumming.

That was similar to realizing how great a singer Jerry Cantrell was, who's known for his guitar playing. It was a parallel kind of thing. It's like "WOW, this guy's multitalented," and he's a great songwriter. Jerry comes in with all his harmonies worked out, and he's a master at that, and really gives the band its sound with the way he does his harmonies. I used a 251 mic on Jerry, and he usually does between nine and ten takes for each song's harmonies, and he has really good pitch, he's a really good singer.

Tapped again to make the band's sophomore LP with new singer William DuVall four years later in 2013, Raskulinecz and AIC took an if-it-ain't-broke-don't-fix-it approach to the album's production, recalling that

with *The Devil Put Dinosaurs Here,* we were seeking to do kind of a continuation of where we left off, to be honest, and we started with the same bass tone as the previous record, the same four amps, and then we added a fifth amp this time. So it wasn't exactly a duplicate of the record before, there's a new element that we added that kind of brings a freshness to the guitar tone. But it's still very much relatable to Jerry Cantrell's signature tone. I think the new record has more great songs on it.

Even before he would be back on the charts with Alice in Chains' sophomore post-Staley LP, which NPR would note "created an unexpectedly vibrant update of the band's sound," Raskulinecz would find himself in the studio for the second time with legendary prog-rock pioneers Rush, and the experience was just that for the producer, who remembered that

my goal was just to get them to play with the unbridled energy and character and intensity and not caring about getting songs on the radio, just playing like that. Not ten three-and-a-half-minute-long songs with everything but the kitchen sink jammed in, but let them grow and expand and repeat, because that's what I loved about Rush.

Addressing the challenge producers at times face when sitting behind the board recording their idols, Raskulinecz reasoned that while

I never feel intimidated, that's part of the job, I do get excited, "Wow, I'm working with Rush!" But when it comes to sitting down and listening to a song and being asked "What do you think?" by the band, it's like, "All right, well, this is what I think: I think you need to change the drums in the chorus, I think the guitar solo sucks, I think you need a better lyric in the chorus, I think you might need to put some harmonies on there, I think the intro's too long . . ." That is for anybody, specifically with Rush, being there from the beginning, I was able to be a part of all those decisions and choices from the start. So it was half and half: half making the record they wanted to make, and the other half was the record that I wanted to hear, and I felt like all the Rush fans had been wanting to hear and waiting to hear.

Those guys are in their sixties, so it was about my just being energetic as a producer, and reminding them of that feeling. Shit, I'm forty-three, so I'm not in my twenties
anymore, but I still get so excited about the music and working with them individually,
tracking the drums with Neil and standing five feet away from him and guiding him
and helping him remember the arrangements, and creating a trust relationship with
a player like him.

Working with Neil Peart, the shadow the drummer cast was never lost on Raskulinecz, a shadow that—in the opinion of *Drummerworld* magazine—made him "the most popular drummer today. When it comes to voting in *Modern Drummer* or *Drummerworld*—Neil
Peart is always the No. 1," adding of the skinsmith's legendary skill that "Peart is known for
his creative and intricate drum parts and extensive drum solos that delight both drummers
and non-drummers alike." On the band's latest studio LP, according to Raskulinecz,

I pushed him to do all kinds of new things. It's hard to find territory that he hasn't
done, but it's not hard to push him to do the kind of territory that he does the best,
which are the odd, complicated things that he would never allow himself to do because he feels like it would be too much. Geddy would always joke that I keep trying
to make him famous, because I want to hear him do the incredible. I want to hear him
do the things where we all like to hear him play drums, and go "Man, I could never do
that, he's almost superhuman!" So to get him to really take the handcuffs off, so to
speak, and try to not lose himself. When I was micing his kit, I think I used a Beta 57
mic on the snare, and a KM-84 on the side of the snare, and a 441 on the bottom.
His drums are such finely tuned instruments, it really pertains to his drum sound,
because he tunes them a different way, the sizes are the way they are for a particular
reason, so getting his drum sound is not hard at all.

Raskulinecz encouraged lead singer Geddy Lee in the same spirit he did Peart to pur-
sue new vocal paths that took the front man full circle to his roots. This was a challenge, the
producer said, because

pushing him vocally to get back up high, to sing like a soprano, was a lot more work
because he's older and has been singing for forty years and his vocal chords are
stretched out, that's just how it is. He exercises, eats right, sleeps right, avoids all
smoke of any kind, doesn't talk when he doesn't need to be talking. To get the kind
of performances that I need to get out of him in the register that he's best at singing
at requires a lot of effort.

Upon release, in addition to its #2 debut on the *Billboard* Hot 200 albums chart, critics
fell quickly in love with the project, with one notable example coming from the *Hollywood*

Reporter's praise for the "terrific new *Clockwork Angels* album . . . *Clockwork Angels* is a 'concept album,' there could be a knee-jerk tendency to say Rush is reverting to its prog roots. Not so; the disc features some of the band's hardest-rocking songs in decades, several of which hew more closely to Led Zeppelin than King Crimson . . . Several new songs recall the hard bite of early Rush. 'Headlong Flight' copped the feel of "Bastille Day," and the suite-like title track channeled the band's late-'70s records. 'Seven Cities of Gold' flowed like a Watergate-era riff rocker, its string-bending finale recalling the last few notes of '2112.'" *Rolling Stone* was impressed by the fact that "the first Rush album in five years isn't just one of the band's Rushiest; it's also very good—frenetic and heavy, low on prog thought puzzles, high on power-trio interplay that could put guys half their age in the burn ward . . . Modern-rock production actually adds power to these ancient masters' gnomic turgidity." For producer Raskulinecz,

> I think this record is one of the best things I've ever done. I would probably rank it up there as being most proud of it, for a lot of reasons: sonic reasons, and song reasons. For them to make a record of this caliber and magnitude twenty-plus records later, I just think is fucking awesome.

Another comeback collaboration of sorts for the producer came in 2010 when he found himself in the studio working with multiplatinum rockers Evanescence, who—like Rush—hadn't released a studio album in five years. Working with lead singer Amy Lee, Raskulinecz was brought in after an initial attempt with Steve Lillywhite wasn't working. In hooking up with a hard-rock producer like Raskulinecz, Yahoo Music News would note that on "this current album, (it) . . . appears that the band is actually having fun. The songs are campier and fit more along the line of a rock or metal album, and not the gothic label they were slapped with on past albums." Yahoo concluded that "Evanescence . . . is (the) band's best effort," which was precisely the producer's goal:

> With that album, Amy had tried to make a record, and it wasn't necessarily the record that she needed to make. It wasn't the record the label wanted her to make. It was very electronic driven, and still great songs, but it was very much a departure from anything she had done. She's the group leader, it's her band, and she's got the vision. She was kind of out of the spotlight for four or five years, and it might not have been a good move for her to go that direction coming back from being away for so long. So we started out to make more of a rock album, and kind of reworked some of the songs she had already done in less of an electronic form. Then we did preproduction, which was the FIRST time she had ever done preproduction with four other dudes—a drummer, a guitar player, a bass player, and her up on the stage.

While they worked as a team to breathe new life into Lee's songs during this crucial preproduction phase of production, *USA Today* offered their opinion that "producer Nick Raskulinecz . . . dials back the leaden melodrama, lightens the gloom and sweeps away some of the thick gothic fog to better sharpen melodies." Working with the singer to establish the necessary trust to help guide her vision to fruition, the producer remembered observing that

> she was scared to death going in, but after the first couple days, she realized that it was fucking awesome, and we reworked five or six songs, and she and the guys wrote five or six more songs over the course of about five weeks. She's super smart, a great player, and was very open to my ideas and suggestions, because she had never really done what we did the way we did it. She was very much a get-in-the-studio by herself and play all the instruments and program the drum machines, and get somebody to play guitar or use synth guitar. So all of a sudden, she was in a rehearsal room with a live P.A. and a guy like me in there going "No, try this, try that, stop this, start." Sometimes bands are shocked when I do that, but I can't be intimidated. That's not why they want me there, because a lot of these rock stars I work with *crave* honesty, they crave objectivity from someone like myself, or the other people that do what we do.

When attention turned in the studio to working one-on-one with Lee on her lead vocal tracks, where *Billboard* would note in their review of the record that "Lee's default mode is to sing to the rafters, her operatic bluster sometimes overbearing when her settings are gloomy," they found with the performances the producer coached from the singer, "Raskulinecz pulls off a nifty trick of brightening the murk, retaining all of the churning drama but lessening the oppression by brightening the colors and pushing the melody." Speaking from his own memories and methods for helping Lee reach such heights, artistically and literally with her soaring voice, the producer recalled that

> when we were tracking, she likes tons of vibe, turn the lights down, burn some incense, get candles going, I think that bands feel more comfortable when they feel like they're in their bedroom or rehearsal room, so I put up posters, tapestries, all kinds of shit. I usually do a song a day. Sometimes it takes two days to do all the lead vocals and do all the harmonies. Her vocals are very involved, lots of layers, lots of doubling and tripling, lots of vocal tracks, and her voice is very powerful, she's a hell of a singer. She's a total perfectionist when she's doing her vocals, she likes to overcook it sometimes. But if the artist tells me they can do it better, I'm not going to say no, I'm going to let them keep going till I feel like they've got it, or until they trust me enough to feel like I know they've got it, spread out across multiple takes. Because I take tons of notes, and I'm sitting there staring at the lyrics, making notes every single time

they're singing. I get to know every word and every syllable in intimate detail. That's what making a record's about, intimate detail.

Amy Lee would pay equal attention in that respect to her piano compositions throughout the album, an arena where she spread her talent around in both variety of styles and sounds, resulting in a record where

there's all kinds of shit on there: Moogs, and her Roland keyboard, and piano on almost every single song. She was playing a Steinway, and we put probably fifteen mics on that piano. I remember with "My Heart Is Broken," I think we spent three days on piano, because she's a perfectionist, and she can feel it when she's playing, whether she has it or not. That's one of those things she needs to stick with, no really matter what I say. We did all of her piano to tape.

When their attention turned to the creation of the album's lead single, "What You Want," a song whose musical elements *Entertainment Weekly* would celebrate for its "grinding guitars, massive drums, goth-princess piano frills, and warrior-grrrl vocal rage," focusing specifically on the driving drum track, Raskulinecz mused

that was us making up an anthemic drumbeat live, that was Will Hunt, me and Will Hunt came up with that beat. He's a fucking monster man, he's one of the best drummers I've ever worked with. We tracked that at Studio B here, and we used twenty-five or twenty-six mics on a drum set—three or four different pairs of stereo room mics and mono mics, etc. On that song, we used compression and even more reverb on the snare drum.

That whole album just turned out fucking great, again, because the way we made it. I'm really proud of her for letting me in and letting the guys in the band in, because I think it's the record she needed to make, and it's really fucking good. The songs are really strong, and she put her heart into that record, and she's very emotional and very talented, and she worked really hard on that record.

Coupled with his most commercial successes with rock's superstars, the producer takes equal pride and pleasure in working with unknown up and comers he feels have the potential to rise to that level. Feeling the balance is an important one for him personally and as a professional, Raskulinecz explained that

I also work with a lot of new bands that aren't even on the radar yet, groups like Red Line Chemistry and Year Long Disaster, and it's awesome working with the big, famous rock star bands, but I also like working with up-and-coming bands that a lot of people don't know about. A lot of the bands I work with already have established careers, but it keeps me energized and hungry and focused to work with bands that don't have that yet.

Something I say to a lot of bands at this level is: "I want to make the record that gets you to make another record." I want these bands to succeed. It makes me feel good to know that they're out there on tour playing songs we just recorded and loving it, and people are reacting to that and buying the record. So that's what I get off on . . . because you only get to make your first album *once*. Sometimes it's hard for bands to better their first album, because you have your whole career to write that first album. When you make that first album and put it out there, that's going to decide whether you get to make another one or not.

If you're a new producer coming up out there, it's important to just work on everything you can, look for bands with great songs, and look for bands with crappy songs and try to make them better. Retain the band's sound, it's not a factory. I always say, "This isn't a factory and it's not a race." You don't need to try to make every record sound the same, and make them all really fast. Great songs take time sometimes, and I don't want an album to be one kickass song and nine fillers. If I don't like every song, I can't sit and record it for twelve, fifteen hours a day, and I turn bands down all the time because I don't like their songs, huge famous bands, that some people would think I was crazy for not doing. But it's like, "You know what, I didn't like it. I can't bring anything to it if I don't like it." Because as much as I want to succeed, I want the bands I work with to succeed. It becomes a really intense relationship, because you get to know these people, and I put my heart into these fucking albums. I'm away from my wife and children twelve to fifteen hours a day, five, six days a week. So I sacrifice a lot, and put my heart and soul into these records.

Reflecting in closing on his favorite moments, platinum, multiplatinum, or otherwise (although most have fallen into the first two categories), Raskulinecz—along with his Grammy for "Best Rock Album"—seems happy to take the nod of approval from the bands he's produced, beginning with Rush, whose front man Geddy Lee told *Revolver* magazine in 2011: "there's no point in hiring a producer who's not going to speak his mind, but it's a tall order to find someone who can hear Neil's playing, amazing as it is, and still say, 'Maybe you should try going in this direction . . .' It was a pleasure to be challenged [by Nick]. That's really what a band like us needs," while Dave Grohl has hailed him as "the greatest rock producer around!" For his own part, Raskulinecz considers

the highlight of my career, as far as I'm concerned, to be working with Rush. I also got a thrill out of being the first person to record Velvet Revolver. Duff was the guy who brought me into that project actually, because we'd worked together back in the '90s, and when it came time to put Velvet Revolver together, he just called me up out of the blue and said, "Hey, I've got this new band, I want you to come down and check us out." So I showed up without knowing who was in the band yet, and there were those other guys! They had no singer then, it was still just the four of them, and they were still auditioning singers when I got involved. I was in the room with them when Scott came in for the very first time, when he got up on that stage and they started playing "Set Me Free." That was the first song they recorded, and he came in, sang it, took off, and that's when they decided he was the lead singer, and we were in the studio a couple weeks later recording that song for the *Incredible Hulk* soundtrack.

It was totally new, a different sound, it was just fun because, shit, those guys were in Guns N fuckin' Roses man! It was very surreal. Slash was amazing, Slash and Duff and Matt and Dave were just a fucking joy to record, and I wanted to capture just the energy of those four guys playing together. We were working together when I had my first child, and they came down to the hospital, and I'm sitting in the hospital with my baby hanging out with Slash and Duff. It was one of those awesome moments that I've been privy to and privileged to have since I've been doing this.

CHAPTER 13

Building the Perfect Beast–Danny Kortchmar

The late 1960s was a glorious time for rock 'n' roll, indeed its magical mystery tour, with new styles exploding on the streets and radio waves everywhere. New York City was a hotbed for this commotion, and for a young musician just discovering the organic side of being both a live music listener and player, there was no greater a place to be on a Friday night, as producer Danny Kortchmar discovered

when I was growing up, which was in the '60s, when I started listening to music, all hell was breaking loose, from a number of different genres, and I grew up right outside of New York City, so I was able to get into the city and participate a little bit. There was a huge folk movement going on, tons of folk music, people like Dave Van Ronk, and then there was jug bands, I was interested in them. Then, of course, what was called folk blues, artists like Muddy Waters, and so my first taste of the blues was guys playing acoustic guitars. Then I got real interested in like Chicago electric blues, real interested, when I was still a teenager, so like Howlin' Wolf and John Lee Hooker records, that was it for me. That stuff, also jazz, labels like Riverside, Impulse, Prestige, Blue Note, of course, every record that they put out was great, Blue Note couldn't go wrong.

So I was very into jazz, not so much desiring to be a jazz musician, but I loved listening to it, especially growing up with what they called "hard bop" or "soul jazz," that kind of stuff. At the same time, R&B was huge, obviously including Motown, and Chicago R&B as done by Curtis Mayfield, and R&B from New Orleans, like the Meters, I was heavy into that stuff. Then when the Beatles hit in 1963, that's when I realized how you could translate rhythm and blues, which is basically piano, horns, organ, to guitar, because the Beatles was basically an R&B cover band that translated all those songs to a guitar combo. So when they came out, and after them the Stones, I realized, "This is how you can translate R&B into something I can participate in," and that was an epiphany certainly for me.

As he began exploring this feeling in tangible terms, Kortchmar's first experimentations with sound recording began with the good old Wollensak tape recorder, a bulky box of wonder that captured young Danny's attention after discovering one his parents had lying around the house. Utilizing a portal through which many a multiplatinum producer first climbed into the world of recording music onto tape, Kortchmar started out

recording tunes onto that when I was fourteen, fifteen, so I was always interested in recording, and playing. My immediate family wasn't always particularly musical, although on my mother's side, my grandfather and his brothers were very musical and actually played in the NBC Philharmonic under Toscanini. But it skipped a generation, and then I guess I'm musical, although certainly not on the level that they were.

He discovered he had not only a fascination with recording music but also playing it, picking up the 6-string in his early teen years where the previous generation had left off. Displaying the kind of natural talent that would inspire *Billboard* to note that "through his extensive work with artists including Carole King and James Taylor, ace session guitarist Danny Kortchmar helped create the signature sound of the singer/songwriter era." Leading up to that breakout period professionally, Kortchmar began like any other aspiring adolescent 6-string slinger

taking guitar lessons when I was ten years old, struggled through the scales and learned a few chords, and all through my high school years I studied guitar with a really terrific teacher named Allan Schwartz on 48th street in New York. His studio was right across the street from Mannie's, and Allan also taught me basic theory, and then I used to go to his house and he'd teach me applied theory, and relative pitch and tonal centers, and stuff that would turn out to be extremely important later on. To start off as a player in bands and then doing sessions, for instance, the first thing you've gotta know is what key you're in, so if the tune's in E, but the first chord you hear's in A, you gotta know what key you're in. So if you're in E, then you can figure everything out from there, everything relates off of that. You have to be able to figure out what the relationship from one chord is to the next, so there's some logic to it, and that's how you can learn songs.

That became extremely important later on, especially when I started playing with Carole King, because her songs were all over the place, they changed keys, they moved around a lot, and there were a lot of interesting chord progressions and movement in them. And without some basis and understanding, like I said, what the tonal center is, you wouldn't have a chance to be able to learn and make any sense out of them. So what Allan taught me became very, very important as I started playing pop songs and singer/songwriter stuff, and also learning R&B, just being able to play basic rhythm and blues: What key am I in? How do I solo on this? What's my basic solo that I can solo in? And if you can't figure out what key you're in, or how the chords relate to each other, you have no idea how to make a solo.

Honing his skill on the live stage around his local music scene before breaking into the "big time" a few years later, Kortchmar had a charmed artistic association as a child that would help hand him his first big gig a few years later. Regarding his entire professional life in a charmed light, he mused of his serendipitous beginnings in the business that

I'm a perfect Clive-wellian kind of guy in that I was born in exactly the right time, and fell in at exactly the right time and place to participate, especially in the singer/songwriter situation. I knew James Taylor as kids, we grew up together as young boys when I was thirteen and he was fourteen at Martha's Vineyard, and we used to hang out all the time and play music and listen to music.

I had little bands when I was in high school, and we used to play bar mitzvahs and whatever we could, covering Elvis Presley, Little Richard, Chuck Berry, and I was playing guitar. Guitar then wasn't divided up so much between lead and rhythm as it became in the '80s, you could either play guitar or you couldn't, and guys like James Burton and Eddie Cochran weren't about lead and rhythm, they were about playing the guitar, and so I was interested in being able to play songs on the guitar.

Then when I graduated high school, I started a band in New York called the King Bees, and we were kind of an R&B band and played all the Manhattan clubs that featured that kind of music. That lasted a couple years, and after that, I started another band with James called the Flying Machine, and that was more of a Lovin' Spoonful type band. In other words, we used to get the kind of gigs that Lovin' Spoonful perhaps would have gotten before they made it. So we played the Night Out Café in Greenwich Village, played there for a long time, and that's where James developed his performing and started writing songs, and we used to do a bunch of his songs in our band.

Then one night another band called Middle Class was playing on the same bill who were being handled by Carole King and Gerry Goffin, and that night, Carole came down to hear us play, and I struck up a friendship with her and she started calling me to play on her demos, which she recorded in New York. So you talk about going to college, that was going to college: in other words, working with her and playing on her demos and learning how to play on records from her was like going to Harvard or Yale without any question. That was an incredible influence on me, and enabled me to learn how to play on records.

The breakthrough would start him down the path to becoming one of the hottest rock session guitarists of the decade to come, as well as allow him to pick up where he'd left off with his childhood fascination of recording sound, albeit this time around in the far more professional environment of the studio. Working almost overnight under the direction of the top producers with the top rising stars of the day, Kortchmar's wheel of fortune kept turning in his favor after

playing in a band with James, I introduced him to Peter Asher, and one of the gigs my band, the King Bees, had was backing up Peter and Gordon on a short tour. So when the Flying Machine broke up, James went to England and I gave him Peter's address and phone number, and he showed up at Peter's house one day. Peter got him signed to Apple Records, they made a record there which didn't turn out that well, then moved back to LA. Peter started producing in Los Angeles, and he started calling me to play on James's records. So I played on "Sweet Baby Jane" a little bit, and at the same time, Carole was there and starting to make her albums, which I would play on as well. So that was really my introduction, and what I learned about record production from that time I would say I mostly learned from Peter Asher and Lou Adler, and of course Carole.

That first step for me was, as a guitar player, learning how to play on records, learning how to perform important functions on records. I found out that the simplest parts you played, those were the parts that got turned up loudest in the mix. In other words, because they were simple, they helped the singer. And I realized very early that the way to play on records, you have to play something that's going to help the rhythm section and help the song and help the singer, and that it isn't about you, it's about how much you can provide to the overall picture. So that's why I was able to play on records, because I had that kind of sensibility, and aesthetic, that I was interested in playing something that was going to help the overall record, so I was able to get gigs because I was able to do that.

Every record I got to play on I took very seriously, and I learned from every record I played on, every musical experience I've ever had I learned something from, and that is how you learn: you learn by doing, and learn by what is going to fit in and help the record. What's going to make the song sound better? What's going to make the singer smile? What's going to make the drummer smile, and of course, what's going to make the producer smile when you're working for someone? You've got to make people happy, make them glad to be there, and if they add something to the record that wouldn't have happened had you not been there. So I learned how to bring stuff to records based on every experience I had in the studio.

As Kortchmar found his playing weaving continually into the fabric of a genre whose fan base continued to grow in both hits up the charts and crowds at live sold-out concerts around the country, whether sitting in a session or on the stage, by 1973, Kortchmar's influence as a player was already making its way into the mainstream. *Goldmine* magazine would remark on this friendship-come-full-circle that by then, the guitarist was already "a long way from the coffee bar hootenannies of Martha's Vineyard, where the teenaged Kootch and his best friend, James Taylor, cut their performing teeth back in the early 1960s . . . (By 1973), the work of the under-sung guitarist whose name was paradoxically emblazoned across some of the best-selling, and best-loved LPs of the previous year, Danny Kortchmar, aka Kootch, established himself among the elite of American sidemen with three successive James Taylor chart-busters (*Sweet Baby James*, *Mudslide Slim*, and *One Man Dog*)." With an endless list of hits to pick from, reflecting back on the experience of being in the studio with Taylor creating much of what would become the folk icon's signature singles, Kortchmar surprisingly revealed that they did not include the singer's legendary "Fire and Rain," a struggle the guitarist remembered began with

a version of us playing it full band, and it's not very good, that we had done maybe six months before they recorded the famed version, and then Peter realized he had to tone it all down, so I didn't play on the finished track. I love those James Taylor records, especially "Gorilla" and "In the Pocket," those were a lot of fun to make. That's when things opened up a bit in terms of how we all could play, because remember, playing with James was like walking on eggshells, because he's playing an acoustic guitar and playing quietly. So we all had to find a way of interacting with this. At the time, there were no acoustic guitars you could plug into an acoustic guitar amplifier and make loud, it was all dependent on leaning forward and really listening to James and his delicate style and finding a way to play to it. So those two albums, when things got louder and a little more open in terms of the way the rhythm section played, were fun.

Following his collaboration with Taylor, Kortchmar and his band, Russ Kunkel on drums and Leland Sklar on bass, comprised the instrumental core of Jackson Browne's live band for what would become his biggest-selling album, *Running on Empty*, an out-of-the-box concept from the traditional studio album, where Kortchmar recalled that

he wanted to make an album about the road and he wanted to record it on the road, and he'd written a bunch of songs based on his road-type experiences. At first, he was going to call it *The Road and the Star*, which was based on his previous experience and used to always do in the show, so it never was going to be a studio project, it was always going to be on the road. And he got us—at the time I was playing in a band called the Section with Russ Kunkel and Leland Sklar and we were kind of an instrumental band—and we had fun and were a good band and played well together, Russ, Lee, and myself were an excellent rhythm section. We had a lot of experience playing with James, Jackson, and various other people, so Jackson hired us as the core of his backup band, and out there we went, and we just made it up as we went along. Jackson is a very adventurous fellow, and once he gets something in his head, he pursues it with dogged determination, and this was his concept, and we were there to help.

Kortchmar turned next to the cutting-edge aid of the mobile recording studio as Browne's tour rolled down the very roads he was serenading with songs like *Running on Empty*'s title track. *American Songwriter* celebrated this classic-rock staple as "an album dedicated to detailing life on the road in all its glory and squalor," adding that "to emphasize this notion even further, Browne literally recorded the album on the road, in hotel rooms, on buses." Blogcritics.org continued the praise of the record's "fantastic . . . engineering, seamlessly transitioning from recording in room 301 at the Cross Keys Inn, Columbia, Maryland to the Garden State Arts Center stage eleven days later in Holmdel, New Jersey." Giving fans of the classic an all-access look inside the experience of recording against a backdrop that also helped enhance his knowledge of the art of recording/producing, Kortchmar remembered that as the 2-inch tape turned,

> we had a 24-track machine, and Greg Ladanyi was out there with his gear, and he had made it all roadworthy so that it could travel from place to place. Nowadays, all you need is a laptop, but back then, you had to carry a Studer 24-track with you, plus all the outboard gear you could fit, you had to take tons of stuff with you. So a lot of *Running on Empty* is just from live gigs, recorded live, and he would set up the mics, split them out, run them into his board and machine, Greg would, and then it would also go out to the P.A. But some of it was also recorded in hotel rooms. I remember one time we were at a Holiday Inn, and one of the rooms they'd rented, they just cleared all the furniture out and we put a set of drums, some amps, and recording gear in there, and started recording. A guy like Greg was a brilliant, brilliant engineer, he could not be daunted, nothing stopped him, no problem even fazed him a little bit. It didn't matter what you asked him to do, he would just find a way to do it.

Finding his ear was most impressed and inspired by the emphasis Browne was placing with the band on performance, a focus long-lost to many modern bands in the digital age of overdubbing each instrument individually, Kortchmar felt it was essential to achieving the sound the singer/songwriter had in his head on record. Beginning with his recollection that "back then, the idea was to capture a terrific performance, which is very different from the way records are made now," Kortchmar explained that

> the idea of capturing a performance meant the band had to play great, all in the room together, and that's how you made records then: you would make a sound together. Now everything's done piecemeal, where pretty much most of the instruments are recorded one at a time, and it's remarkable when a record is made where you get four or five guys in a room anymore, that practically never happens. Most of the musicians I know get files sent to them where they overdub, so it's a very different recording process from what it was. Back then, the first goal was to capture a performance, so for instance, those records we did with Peter Asher, those James Taylor records, the take was the one where James sang the best, and the band was expected to play great all the time. If there was any fixes, we'd go in and fix, but the complete opposite philosophy than now. It was the same thing with recording a song like "Running on Empty." Also, there's a sound that gets created by four or five guys in a room together that cannot possibly be duplicated by overdubbing one step at a time digitally. With that song, it was a live take, and we rehearsed for two or three weeks, and then we just went out there and started playing gigs, and they recorded all the gigs, and we used to record at sound check too. But "Running on Empty," that's live, that's us playing live!

Coming on the heels of "Running on Empty," as the '70s approached its close, Danny Kortchmar stood at a crossroads of sorts, one where he could have continued stepping onto stages across the world with the biggest acts in rock as one of the industry's most in-demand players-for-hire. Or he could take a different path not unfamiliar to him from the live room of the studio, but one where he desired to switch views to one behind the console in the control room as a producer in his own right. It was an opportunity he would finally get after the stars lined him up for a fateful meeting with a member of the biggest rock band of the 1970s looking to go solo.

With *Rolling Stone*'s report that "in the wake of their unannounced breakup around the turn of the decade, the individual members faced the Eighties with a much less certain hold on their audience," in 1981, Eagles drummer/vocalist/songwriter Don Henley—the lead vocalist for such #1 classics as the band's biggest hit, "Hotel California," "The Long Run," "Desperado," "Life in the Fast Lane," "Victim of Love," "One of These Nights," and "Witchy Woman" —was eager to keep the creative wheels moving forward on his debut solo LP, *I Can't Stand Still*. Once word got out that Henley was looking for a coproducer, Kortchmar—like all of his competition, both established and newcomers—was itching to get a shot at the hottest gig in town, knowing the stakes were high for Henley because he knew at that time he pretty much had to do something because the Eagles were nonfunctional, and Glenn had made a solo album, so Don felt compelled to go out and create something right away. Everyone knew everyone in LA at that time, so I knew Don. I didn't know him that well, but knew him, and the Eagles had broken up, and Glenn Frey had made a solo album that actually I played on, and I had produced a couple of records for Louise Goffin, Carole King's daughter. She had a deal on Asylum, and Peter Asher had recommended me to produce, and that was the first production stuff I'd ever done. Don heard it and thought it was good, and was looking around for people to collaborate with to do a solo album. So he had people coming up to his house to jam with him a little bit, just trying to find a way to do things, and after a couple weeks, I got a call, and went up there, played him some ideas. We fooled around for about three hours, and right then, he said, "Listen, you interested in working on this album with me?" To which I said, "Absolutely," because everybody knew Don was a super-talent, so that was a huge thrill to be asked, and that was it for me.

Longtime Henley fan *Rolling Stone* would note that in crafting his first LP as a solo artist, "while his band mates—especially his erstwhile writing partner, Glenn Frey—have steered a safe, commercial course, Don Henley (chose to write) . . . and recorded songs with a sociopolitical conscience." This was a brave step that Kortchmar remembered the pair first truly captured on his breakout solo single, "Dirty Laundry." Of this anti–tabloid media anthem that lashed out with lyrical precision at the shallow end of the press pool, Kortchmar—as the song's cowriter—remembered feeling he needed to answer with an equally driving instrumental track. Recalling that, as he began composing based on a broader conceptual canvas that Henley began painting for the coproducer the first day he walked into the collaboration,

almost as soon as I started working with Don, he was talking about "Dirty Laundry," and wanted to write a song about the media and how all they're interested in is people's hard-luck stories. He had been raked over the coals by the local media in Los Angeles and was pissed off at them, and really wanted to write this song taking the happy news entrotainment media to task. It's a very sarcastic, very caustic, criticism of popular media. So we talked about it a lot, how it was going to go, and because I was working with Don, all I would do is sit in my little crummy home studio, which consisted of a very cheap Fostex 8-track, and I had a Farfisa Organ and an Echoplex tape delay effect unit, just all cheap stuff, but it was 1981. So I ran the Farfisa through the Echoplex, and started coming up with what you hear. That riff that starts the song is my Farfisa organ through an Echoplex and a Fender Deluxe amplifier. The Farfisa had that bass, and I could only play in the key of C, so I would play this thing over and over again in the key of C and basically came up with the whole structure, which is very simple, it's the same thing over and over again largely. But I realized it was the perfect template for him to tell his story, because it had this kind of static, repetitive quality!

Ironic in the context of his former role as a side-man, as Kortchmar slaved away through the night recording much of what would become the song's instrumental side, he got a surprise visitor at his door who would wind up being the first set of ears to ever hear the song as it came to life on tape, with the producer revealing of the mystery guest that

while I was writing it that night, around 2 in the morning, suddenly Jackson Browne shows up at my house. We all lived near each other and always used to go to each other's houses all the time, him and me and Russ and JD Salen and Jim Keltner, everybody used to hang all the time. That's the way LA was at that time, it was a great, great city. So when Jackson shows up, I said, "Dig this!," and play what I was playing, and he goes, "That's the same thing over and over again! Aren't you going to put more changes in it?," and I said, "Nope, it's just this over and over," and of course, Jackson was kind of shocked, but he thought it was the perfect beat for Henley to tell his story about the media. The very fact of its repetitiveness gives him a palette so that immediately you're drawn into the song. So on the one hand it has a great beat and is kind of an ass-shaker in terms of its groove, and on the other hand, it's a perfect template for Don to talk about "Dirty Laundry" over.

So the next day, I brought it into the studio and we had at that point gotten our hands on one of the first Linn drum machines, and I was freaking out because I loved it. I'd always had little rhythm boxes to play with, starting back in the early '60s, and once that LM-1 came out, I just never left my house after that. I'd get a drum beat going and jam along with it, it was so much fun, it was great. So on that particular track, we used a Linn drum and then Jeff Porcaro also played over the top of it. Don played drums sometimes, but he was more interested in writing and singing on his solo albums.

The song was a unique hybrid given Henley's classic rock influences and a brave one considering programmed drum tracks were primarily reserved for new wave and dance hits, as new electronic beat-driven subgenres began to pop up all over the dawn of the '80s star chart, thanks to what MTV later argued was "his stalwart partnership with producer and songwriter Danny Kortchmar." Kortchmar triumphantly highlighted the fact that

"Dirty Laundry" is one of the very first techno records ever made, keep in mind. At the time, I couldn't play the Farfisa in any other key, and I remember Don wanted it in the key of E-flat and modulated to F, and I couldn't do it. So he brought in various keyboard players to try and get the same thing going, and no one could get it going the way it sounded in the key of C the way I played it. So Steve Porcaro brought in this huge bank of processors and sequencers and it took forever, and we finally got the exact groove that I was playing through my Echoplex. And it's all on the clock, and you can hear these teletype machines that come in, and that's all cued and sequenced and in time, and back then, it was very difficult to do it because there was no Protools, no digital recording, and no Midi. For that gang chorus, Don got a bunch of us together to sing "Kick 'em when they're up, kick 'em when they're down," and on Don's lead vocals, back then, we used the EMT plate reverb.

Following the breakout solo success of "I Can't Stand Still" with his sophomore LP, Henley set his sights on *Building the Perfect Beast*, once again enlisting Danny as coproducer with sights on crafting what *People* magazine would celebrate as a "swift, slick album with catchy background riffs and clever tunes, written mostly by Henley and Kortchmar." Seeking with those songs and the album's broader sound to expand on the sonic template he'd established with his previous studio effort, first and foremost, this ambition began with

Don wanting to do something, even from the first album on through to the second, that didn't sound at all like the Eagles, and there's certain things we didn't do at all, like there's no acoustic guitar on either of those albums, and he didn't want those typical Eagles harmonies. He wanted as a solo artist to continue to build away from that in his production sound, so we also, for instance, took the tape off the drums, and at the time it was popular to tape up and deaden the drums, and we said "No Way" to that. We wanted to do everything that hadn't been done in the '70s, which involved back then a lot of isolation, where the drums would go in a booth with shag carpet and the guitars were baffled off, and the idea there was to give the engineer more stuff that he could do. And we said, "The hell with that, we're more interested in what happens when everyone plays together," and Don was adamant about wanting to go in a totally different direction. On that record, I remember we worked out of a few different studios, Record One, Sound Factory, and Bill Schnee's studio in Studio City.

Embracing the new wave of programming technology becoming available in the early '80s as a key ally in this endeavor, and working with a budget where cost was thankfully no object in the course of acquiring the cutting-edge equipment he and Kortchmar would use in building *Beast* in the studio, Henley's coproducer fondly recalled that

one of the great things about working with Don was that any new piece of gear that came out, he would turn to his assistant Tony and say, "Tony, get it." So, for instance, when the DX-7 synthesizer came on the market, we had one of the first ones in LA, and whenever new shit came out, we got one. So when we started working in principle on *Building the Perfect Beast*, Don had also gone out and gotten a set of Simmons drums, which now of course are horrible, but back in '84, people were using them and we wanted to see what we could do with them. So we get them set up, and I started playing that beat, and the riff in 7-4 time, and Don was on the phone in my living room, and I started playing this groove, and he yells back "Yeah, that's it!," and went back to talking on the phone.

One key piece of gear that would play a pivotal role in creating the sound that defined one of the album's biggest radio singles, "All She Wants to Do Is Dance," was the Yamaha DX-7, which Kortchmar remembered feeling excited and inspired by because

it was probably the first DX-7 in Los Angeles, and I took it home, and there was one stop on there, which was the "sample and roll" stop, so I slowed it way down, and started playing bass notes through it. Then ran that into my guitar amp, and turned that up, cranked up the distortion on the guitar amp, and that's the sound you hear. When we were in the studio, that's how we did it: ran the DX-7 into a Marshall stack cranked, and that's what you hear: a "sample and roll" preset slowed down, and me playing that line you hear.

Don doesn't sit with a guitar when we're writing together. He knows a few chords, but he just sits there with whoever's collaborating with him—and for about ten years it was me—and I'll play some changes, and he'll go "Yeah, that! Yeah, yeah, that!" Or "No, no, not that, play what you played before, just keep playing it over and over again," stuff like that, and whatever he'd shout out, that's what I would do, and then he would start singing or writing along, and before you know it, there was a song.

So with "All She Wants to Do Is Dance," I'd written the track one night, and looked at it the next day, and wrote the words very quickly. I just wrote them as they occurred to me. I had the idea "All She Wants to Do Is Dance" that sang well with it, and then I just started filling in, and it came out the way it came out. I had no particular agenda or political statement, although as I was writing it, I realized I was writing about this really spoiled American couple that went to some third world country and started throwing money around, and don't realize what's going on around them. But the song came very quickly, and I started figuring out what it was about after I wrote it.

Kortchmar flipped next to the album's biggest single, and for that matter, among the biggest radio hits of 1984, "Boys of Summer," which won the Grammy for "Best Male Rock Performance" and ranked #146 on *Rolling Stone*'s Top 500 Songs of All Time. The producer revealed that the team had outside help on the track's compositional side from Tom Petty and the Heartbreakers' guitarist Mike Campbell, recalling that

most of that song comes from Mike. He wrote the track, and made a demo of it on a 4-track, and it had the Linn drum part that you hear, so most of that record's a re-creation of his primitive demo. He brought that into the studio and we did the best we could to duplicate it, which drove Mike crazy, because Mike is not the kind of guy who repeats stuff over and over again. Don was crazy about the demo, though, and wanted exactly the guitar sound that Mike had gotten for those opening licks that you hear, and then we started adding stuff to it and filling it out. I played a guitar synth on that track, the original Roland guitar synth, you see them in rock videos from that period.

For Don's vocals, on that song and the broader album, we recorded his leads using a U-47, and as far as effects, the EMT was always there and was omnipresent, and there's a tuned delay on the vocal, down low in the mix. Don as a vocalist was very meticulous, and he would go over and over the tracks and had very high standards about his own vocals that I thought was great, and I would listen to it and go "Oh, that's great," and sometimes he would go "No, it's out of tune, and needs fixing here and here," and would do a lot of takes and then comp them together into a vocal that was satisfactory for him.

Looking back over the experience of working with such freedom against a dream backdrop with an "anything goes" attitude, Kortchmar felt the experience was one that only comes along once in a lifetime for any producer/songwriter, holding Henley in the highest of regard twenty-five-plus years later as

an absolute genius. Writing with Don, does it get any better? No it doesn't. He was a great, great lyricist, and an unbelievably soulful, badass singer. I used to wake up every day trying to think of more ideas for Don, because if he liked it, a day or week later, we'd be in studio recording it. Then you have Don singing a song you collaborated on, what possibly could be better than that? That experience was a total thrill, and I mean, Henley can be difficult, but he also is a great artist and just a great guy, so we had a terrific time together, absolutely terrific time together. "Sunset Grill" was a fantastic track, and "All She Wants to Do Is Dance," "Not Enough Love in the World . . ." Those records really were one of the highlights, if not THE highlight of my musical career.

An in-demand producer by the second half of the 1980s, after dipping his toe back into the film soundtrack world with production on the soundtracks to *About Last Night* and *The Color of Money* among others, Kortchmar returned to his home base alongside Henley to coproduce "The End of the Innocence," garnering the singer another Grammy for "Best Male Rock Performance" in an acknowledgment of the production formula he and Danny had mastered in their almost decade-long working relationship. Steering Henley into a less dance-friendly stylistic space than their previous efforts, Kortchmar blamed this deviation in direction on pressure from the singer's record label, who

thought that he was a balladeer, and wanted him to do more ballads. At the time, everybody listened to the record company, and also, he's great at that, so there are a lot of ballads on that record. There's some rockers on there too, but they kind of took second place to the ballads because the label wanted to market him more as a balladeer, and of course he had that great song, "End of the Innocence," which he wrote with Bruce Hornsby, and is just a fantastic song. Another of the big slower hits off the record, "New York Minute," Henley had that idea, and said, "I want to write this song "New York Minute," that's all we had. So I remember I sat down and just started playing those chords you hear on the piano, and built it up from there, and next thing you know we're in the studio cutting it. And then he came up with that awesome lyric, it's a fantastic lyric. Henley's a genius, man, lyrically, he's just as brilliant as can be. So is Jackson Browne, so is James Taylor . . . I got to work with a lot of really brilliant people at that time.

There's also some heavy-duty rockers on there, and one of my favorite tunes I ever did was "I Will Not Go Quietly." We had gone to see Robert Plant play at the Forum in LA, and the next day, I wrote all that music, and that whole track is me: it's all drum machine and guitars through the whole thing, and I played all the instruments. By then, I had the latest MPC and the latest Linn drum machine. By then you could program your own sounds into it, and that's what I did. By that time, you also had Midi, which I used in order to get that bass groove going. I played the guitars live and bashed away, I wanted to be really hard but also wanted to have it be interesting musically and have some changes in it, and that's what we came up with.

Coming off the end of his latest collaboration with Henley, Kortchmar found himself back in a similar setting and circumstance—ironically, given the way he'd started out with Henley—working this time alongside the biggest rock star of the decade on his first solo album. In recalling how he wound up sitting side by side with Jon Bon Jovi coproducing the *Blaze of Glory* LP, the producer began with his recollection that

the funny thing about that is I got a call from Jon, and I guess he'd been recommended to me by Jimmy Iovine or someone because I'd done the Henley records, and he loved the Henley records and was a fan, so that's where it started. So I got a call from him, and we started putting together ideas about who should be in the band. He sent me a demo of "Blaze of Glory," and I picked the guys who I thought would be best, and we just had a ball! I don't think Jon had ever had that much fun in the studio, and realized that when you're playing with the cats, everybody knows each other, and not only is the music going to be good, but it's also going to be fun and there's not going to be any tense confrontations, it's just fun.

Receiving Oscar and Grammy nominations and winning a Golden Globe Award for "Best Original Song," the title track would take off up the charts, earning Bon Jovi a #1 smash on the *Billboard* Hot 100 singles chart that defined the summer of 1990 with the same radio and video rotation domination that "Boys of Summer" had back in the mid-'80s. An acoustic rock 'n' roll anthem that *Rolling Stone* celebrated as a "bubble with so many tight harmonies, rhinestone chord changes and buddy vibes . . . 'Blaze of Glory' sounds even better than *New Jersey.*" As the team began working in the studio on crafting the massive hit, beginning with its signature acoustic sound, Kortchmar remembered a breezy pace and vibe where

> we just tried different stuff. That album happened very quickly, and we just tried whatever worked. There's a lot of acoustic guitars on because it was music for the *Young Guns II* movie soundtrack, so we wanted to add that kind of flavor to a lot of it. There's a lot of guitar overdubs on that. Ronnie played on the basic tracks, and I overdubbed a ton of stuff on it, and then Jeff Beck came in and played the leads. I spent four or five days with him in the studio while he overdubbed his lead guitar parts for the album. With Jon's vocals, he did them pretty quickly, he knows what he wants. Jon was—and still is—a consummate professional who knows what he wants.
>
> We were at Studio D at A&M, which is now Hensen, and that record was recorded using a lot of old analog gear, and each piece had different characteristics. Any producer or engineer you talk to's going to tell you the same thing: that old analog gear all had personality. We were tracking on an SSL console, and we'd go through the Neve preamps to record and then bring it back through the SSL.

Driven by a thunderous rhythm track laid by none other than the hardest-hitting skinsmith in the business, Kenny Aronoff—who'd risen to fame playing on a greatest hits collection of smash singles by John Mellencamp throughout the 1980s and was named "Drummer of the Year" by *Rolling Stone*—as opposed to highlighting mic placements or room ambience, in reviewing how he'd achieved the sonic brilliance of the song's drum sound, Kortchmar mused matter-of-factly that

> the main thing we used was Kenny Aronoff. Let's face it, man, the drummer's gotta walk in with a good drum sound, you know, the engineer doesn't make the drum sound, the drummer makes a good drum sound. And my philosophy is not to mic everything, but to use as few mics as possible. You put one under the snare, you put one over the snare, two overheads, a D-112 on the kick. That ambience you hear on that famous breakdown in the song is because of the live room far-miced, and the reason you can hear it is there's nothing interfering with it. There isn't a big guitar chord or something else happening that takes away from it. Even if you go back to that famous big, massive John Bonham drum sound, that's made largely by getting stuff out of the way, so in other words, if you have three or four guitars pounding away in the midrange, then it's going to cover up the snare drum, no matter how loud you turn it up.
>
> It's going to get covered up, so you gotta move guitars out of the way, or it's gonna eat up your drum sound. You can't have both, and this is one of the things I've

learned, the reason John Bonham's drum kit is so huge sounding is because of those great Jimmy Page and John Paul Jones arrangements. They were playing parts, and everyone thinks those guitars are recorded with like four Marshall stacks, and weren't at all. Jimmy Page used the Princeton amps, small amps, and that's the other thing, that big sound is not created by massive output from the amps. Power and volume are not the same thing, that's a lesson you learn in the studio. What always killed me about '80s heavy metal/hard rock was they all thought they'd go in there and stack up those Marshall amps, and that's not the way you get a big sound. You get a big sound by getting out of the way of other stuff, arrangement always wins, and I applied that concept to the production of the LP.

Riding high indeed on a blaze of glory into the 1990s, Danny Kortchmar was among the hottest rock producers in the business, coming off a decade of Top 10 hits in a trend that would continue with his next superstar studio assignment, one that would call on his expertise at blending programmed and live percussive elements and with bringing a rock energy to a pop record. The artist, piano pop-rock icon Billy Joel, fresh off a twenty-plus-year collaboration with longtime producer Phil Ramone, was seeking a fresh set of ears to help complete what would become his final studio album of original material, an assignment Kortchmar was keen to take on after

my manager told me that Billy was looking for an East Coast–based producer to work with on this album. He'd already recorded a bunch of stuff with his band out at a homemade studio on Shelter Island. He'd rented this place and brought a bunch of gear in, and when I heard the stuff he'd recorded, I thought I could do better, and pleaded with him to please go to the Hit Factory in New York City and record there.

Demonstrating a skill he'd learned over the years of wearing the hat of psychologist as he appealed to Joel to give his approach a try in what became a make-or-break audition for Kortchmar's involvement in the project, the producer explained that

this is toward the end of his career as a songwriter, and some of the last kind of pop songs he wrote back then, so I asked him to try a couple tunes my way at the Hit Factory in New York, and if I'm not right, then we'll go our separate ways. I also asked to bring in a sideman I thought would give him a boost, so I asked T. M. Stevens on bass and Zachary Alford on drums to come in, and they kicked serious ass on those tunes, and that made a lot of difference in terms of the feel of them. So we recorded them, he liked the way they came out, and we kept recording the rest of the record there.

Along with the adjustments he'd made in Joel's recording backdrop and lineup, the artist's sound was updated to reflect what the *New York Times* felt was a "driving and exuberant" pace with a "stylistic bottom line (that is) is a well-oiled all-purpose rock that slides his keyboards neatly into chunky guitar-driven arrangements." Focusing on the production of the album's title track, a Top 5 hit for Joel on the *Billboard* Hot 100 singles chart, the producer first fell in love with the song after

> he'd made a demo of it with the drum machine that's playing on there, and then had drums playing along with that, and it was pretty obvious what the groove was, and I remember we sat Zach up and he started hitting the groove, and it came together very quickly. With the drum sound for that album, if we felt it was too big, we'd start moving gobos closer to the drum kit, because it's a huge room we were recording in. So to make the drums tighter, we moved gobos and make a box for the drums. I put a little guitar part on it which gave a drive to it, and Billy sang and played live with the band in the studio. We'd do twenty takes, and every take was great from him, unbelievable singer, fantastic singer. I used a great tube mic on Billy for vocals, and when we were micing his piano, we'd lift the top up, and mic it ten feet high but also mic it close, and mix them together, blend them together, and decide which we liked.

Nominated upon release for four Grammy Awards including coveted categories that prove the producer did his job, including "Song of the Year," "Record of the Year," and "Album of the Year," the album sold seven million copies and sent Joel out on top as he delivered what *Entertainment Weekly* hailed as "a popmeister's epiphany, a pensive record that also manages to be irresistible!" Ranking his experience working with Joel in the studio as a pleasant one throughout, Kortchmar—looking back years later—affirmed that "it was a real pleasure to work with Billy, he's hilarious, a very funny guy, and we had a good time."

Another project from Kortchmar's catalog he had a blast making when he was just beginning to make the transition from session player to producer called on his former talent, as he'd been hired by Lou Adler to score the soundtrack to the Cheech and Chong *Up in Smoke* film. A massive hit that would give Kortchmar a different level of exposure for his compositional skills, the gig came in 1978 after

> Lou Adler called me up, either me or Waddy Wachtel, but I immediately got together with Wad and we sat down in my living room and came up with a few tunes, a few ideas for some jams we could put to the film, and they'd shown us some footage without music, so we came up with two or three ideas, put together a band, went in and cut it with Lou producing. Lou had told us, "Just a basic rock thing," because *Up in Smoke* is not *Avatar* or some Hans Zimmer soundtrack. It simply required some basic rock and roll with a big beat, and so Wad and I got together with the guys we knew and started slapping some stuff together.
>
> When we saw the finished movie with the score, it was funny, it was hilarious, and

when we finally got to see it all done, it made sense to us, but before that, the only person who knew what was going on was Lou, because we were doing it piecemeal, being shipped scenes and coming up with stuff for those scenes. But again, rocket science it wasn't, pretty basic stuff.

To quote from one of the most famous—and most favorite—songs Danny Kortchmar was involved in, "Looking back at the years gone by," the player-producer highlights *Running on Empty*, alongside others on his greatest hits collection of collaborations that includes

those James Taylor records I mentioned, and all the stuff I did with Peter Asher was revelatory, and I learned a tremendous amount from the stuff Peter was producing. Another great album was James's first album for Columbia, *JT*, which Peter produced, was a great album, we had a great time doing that. I loved playing with Linda Ronstadt, and working on those records with Peter Asher. I loved playing on James Taylor's records, who I learned a tremendous amount from.

On the Henley records, I was more involved because I was producer and cowriter, and the stuff we collaborated on closely is very close to me, the stuff where we really broke some rules. "Dirty Laundry" was 1981, and there were no records like that at the time, and it was a huge hit, and that was very gratifying, to be able to come up with something as cool as that and other stuff on his first album, was just spectacular. So the standout stuff was the stuff I did with Don from that period, because as I said, I was heavily involved as a writer, as a musician, and as a producer, so it was a wonderful collaborative effort, and that's what I'm all about: collaboration. That's what Don's all about too, he's a team player, so those records were the height of creativity. "Sunset Grill," "New York Minute," "I Will Not Go Quietly," "Dirty Laundry," and "All She Wants to Do Is Dance," those tunes stand out to me as songs I'd like to be remembered for. There really is nothing in my career that is as intense or satisfying as working on those three albums with Don.

Feeling his collaboration with Henley best sums up the substance of any advice he'd dispense to the Protools generation of record makers, with all the ease of the digital age on the technical side of the recording process, Kortchmar in closing points to the timeless importance of old-school fundamentals still as relevant as ever to great record making, beginning always with

writing great songs, having a sound, and a great vocalist—that's the hard part. Recording is not as hard as writing songs, and creating a band sound, which you do in your garage, your rehearsal studio. Since all records are made on Protools and are all done piecemeal one part at a time, I would say try going in the studio with everyone in the same room together, and let there be some leakage, let there be mistakes, let there be accidents, let stuff happen. Instead of making stuff happen, let it happen, let the music breathe a little bit. Everything doesn't have to be perfect, and resist the temptation to time-correct and pitch-correct everything, that's what I would say. Why does everything have to be edited together to where there's no humanity in it anymore? Give it a try and see how that works, and if you don't like the result, then go back to doing it one part at a time. But try and use the new methods and combine them with the old methods.

CHAPTER 14

Bay 7–Howard Benson

Howard Benson is arguably the most successful rock producer of the millennium, if you follow the sales charts anyway. He has racked up a staggering thirty-plus-million albums sold in an era where few bands go gold anymore, let alone platinum. This position was authenticated by *Mix* magazine in 2007 when they wrote of "this year's Grammy-nominated Producer of the Year Howard Benson, this acknowledgment has been a long time coming. Since 1989, Benson has been acquiring a long list of impressive production credits, including My Chemical Romance, All American Rejects, Hoobastank, Papa Roach, Flyleaf, Three Days Grace, last year's *American Idol* finalist Chris Daughtry, Blindside, Cold, P.O.D., TSOL and Motorhead, to name just a few. For the Grammy, he is nominated for his work on Hoobastank's *Every Man for Himself*, Flyleaf's self-titled, Less Than Jake's *In with the Out Crowd*, Three Days Grace's *One-X*, Papa Roach's *The Paramour Sessions*, Head Automatica's *Propaganda* and Saosin's self-titled."

Looking back to his childhood as a rock fan when he first discovered his potential as a record producer, it began like so many other kids playing behind an instrument in a garage band. Raised in a musical home, Benson remembered being exposed to music early because my father was a music teacher, used to listen to a lot of music and had a great record collection that was very esoteric and had a lot of jazz and that kind of thing, and I'd hear the music downstairs, and took a bit of piano lessons, not very much, but when I was in seventh grade, a friend of mine decided they wanted to start a band. This was in the '70s, and I seriously had no idea about that, that wasn't in the wheelhouse and I wasn't thinking about that. I remember downstairs in my basement of our house, we had a little pump organ, an old Estes, and one day I told this kid, "Hey, I've got this organ downstairs, let's do it at my house," not realizing really what I was getting myself into. So that Friday night, they show up with drums and guitars and from there on, it was sort of like the minute I remember sitting down and playing, it was something I realized I wanted to do. Right away, I realized, "Wow, I'm actually pretty good at this, I can pick up songs by ear," and granted we weren't playing very complicated songs, but they were the songs of those eras: the Doors, and a lot of stuff like that. So I learned how to play, first just by ear, and then I went and also bought sheet music, and now I realize of course years later that all the bands I played in as a kid were actually things that led me to be a record producer, because I could draw on all the chord changes, the melodies, etc.

Fast-forwarding into college, I joined a disco band, and made a lot of money doing that, which was great because you finally see income from this like hobby of yours, and looking back, I used to take meticulous notes at like every gig I played. I show my kids this stuff, and I'd write down who played, what songs, what instruments, who drove, obsessiveness almost with the whole thing, and I think that around me, my friends knew that producing was something I was going to do, but I don't think my parents knew that, so they insisted I get a degree in something else. So I went to Drexel University and got a degree in material engineering, and when I first came out to California, I worked in aerospace for four years, and worked at Garrett on a lot of aeroplanes, like the C-5, the F-18, the 767, stuff that has nothing to do with music, but at night I was moonlighting playing in a band in Hollywood, and we were just awful. We were a terrible band, and the only good thing about us was: every time we made demos, people would say, "Oh, your demos sound really good!"

Using his ear for recognizing good sounds to pick up on directionally, Benson—already equipped with an innate technical understanding of engineering principles as a result of his degree—decided to read the writing on the wall and retire from his dream of becoming a rock star. In its place, he set his sights on the studio, landing a foot in the door at Sunset Sound, a fateful transition that came

after four years of getting absolutely nowhere in the music business but continually hearing people say "Your demos are good," I was finally able to hook up with an engineer at Sunset Sound who was just starting out as well, and was able to use one of their rooms in the evenings. Because back then, that's what you had to do: make friends with a studio, and force your way in, and let you use their room when there weren't clients in there. And of course, in return, they expected you to bring in paying clients eventually. So a lot of my early producing stuff came from being at Sunset Sound and watching guys like David Foster, and there was this whole '80s rock/pop thing going on there. That's one of the studios I've always remembered and never forgotten that, and still bring them business.

That's even something I insist on with the guys who work with me and have been with me a long time, that they bring in paying gigs, and it's not only the money, it's really not the money actually, but the respect that you give back. I own my own studio now, where I bought a house that had a studio in it, we put a Neve 8058 in it, but I was at Bay 7 Studios a long time. So even with the guys who are the runners and interns and all, I always say to them, "Look, eventually you have to bring work in here," and again, it's not the money, but it's a goal for them, to realize this is something you're doing to make a living, that it's a living. And looking back, I always credit Paul Camarada over at Sunset Sound, because there was a time after I'd been working there two or three years and hadn't really brought in anything, and was getting a lot of free studio time, and Paul called me in his office.

I'll never forget it, I was really mad when I left, because he says to me, "Look, we can't let you work here forever, you have to start bringing in paying gigs," and I was shocked by it at first. I was like, "Wait a minute, what do you mean, I'm trying to do that . . . ," but it accelerated my development actually, and was sort of something that was like "Okay, he's right, this is something I have to start getting serious about." Those are people you meet along the way that really have a lot to do with your career, and I hope that I can do that for some guys as well, give them good advice and guidance.

Benson's first great mentor in the art of sound recording would be none other than legendary record producer Keith Olsen, who *Billboard* celebrated as "one of the more prolific and successful music producers of the second half of the 20th century, with over 200 productions to his credit, yielding sales of 110 million copies on single, LP, or CD, 45 Gold (or Platinum) Record Awards, and six Grammy Awards." Back at the dawn of the 1990s, however, Benson thought he was looking at the fast sunset of his prospects at taking off as a record producer. In a fateful turn of events that he regards as the first of several career-defining moments,

probably the biggest turning point in my career was meeting Keith Olsen, who is probably the guy I give most of the credit to, because I was doing a band called SouthGang, which Butch Walker was in at the time. I'd coproduced the record with Desmond Child, and though the record didn't really sell, meeting Desmond was awesome, because back when you're just a starting producer, it's like meeting the Mount Rushmore of the writing business. I met Diane Warren then too, and learned a lot from her. But when I got to do the second SouthGang record, three weeks into it, their manager got fired, and a new manager came on, and the first thing he did was fire me. He'd looked around and said, "Okay, what can I do to be the manager? The first thing I'll do is fire this amateur producer guy who's only done four records, and bring in the big guns."

I also think that, at the time, I was being much more band friendly than I really needed to be, so I was listening to everything the band wanted, where it was a collaborative effort. And while I think that's important, what I didn't realize was, after this event happened, I talked to Keith Olsen once he'd been brought in, and said, "Listen, I know you're going to produce this record. I will, for free, stay here and help you produce, I'll do whatever it takes, get coffee for you . . ." And I was, at that point, throwing myself at his mercy in a way, and he looked at me, and I remember he said to me, "You know what: I think you're pretty good, it's pretty amazing what you just said to me, that you're willing to do that. I'll let you hang around, as long as you don't question anything I say. I'm the producer, you're not the producer," that kind of thing, and I was like, "Fine, no problem."

So the band shows up Monday, and guess what, I'm still there, and immediately, their new manager asks Keith, "What's Howard still doing here?" And Keith said, "I want him there," and about two weeks into it after Keith has taken over the production, I realize: he is in complete control of this process. He's the man, and I loved the fact that he was not taking any shit from this band, and all of a sudden, it was his project, and at that point, the band comes up to me, and says, "Hey, we really liked it better when you were producing, at least you listened to us . . ." See, Keith was so famous, he didn't have to listen to a bunch of kids, he was making his record the way he wanted to make it. Keith was a classic guy, he was a producer of those times, and I remember at one point he took the singer into his room in the back and the room had platinum and gold records literally from wall to wall, there wasn't a space of wall left in that room. And he looked around the room, and said to the singer Jessie, "What do I know?"

He called it the "Intimidation Room," and I remember thinking "Wow, I just don't have that. I don't have that gravitas as a producer, I'm acting like one of the band, and this guy, he's the guy." Plus the fact that his vocal production was so detailed, he'd put these vocal charts and went through every single line, and that's the kind of stuff I wasn't doing, I was just setting up tape and putting up the amps and drums and hitting record, stuff that you don't see happen anymore now (laughs). The best records are still made with the right amount of organization. I was kidding around a second ago, but if you dig deep into a lot of records, there is a serious amount of organization going on in most of them, and that's when I really learned how to be organized. I learned from Keith that you still have to work with the band, but that they look to you as the producer for guidance and control.

Benson's production prospects began to improve after his experience working under Olsen's direction, honing his skill-set at being assertive—at one point with a true test of all tests producing three Motorhead albums in the mid-1990s, which brought him face to face with the legendary Lemmy Kilmister. Kilmister was an adversary in his attempts to antagonize and intimidate the producer from the first session they had together. Benson underscored the extremity of the effort after

I met Lemmy. That was the next record I produced after my Keith Olsen experience in 1993, and I was prepared, not completely, but to a certain extent to let out my inner "producer" the way I'd watched Keith do it. People always give me a lot of shit sometimes for being very serious, very organized, and kind of like: I don't take shit from people in the studio, and people know that. It's not because I'm a dick or anything, but that keeps the project going, it just makes it move forward. So when I started working with Lemmy, the first record I did with him was a test of wills! He would try to intimidate me every day, like he came in dressed in WWII memorabilia to try and distract me, and it was very interesting, and when I got with him, I had to really hold on to myself, because I almost left the project a couple of times. It got so bad that I ended up in the hospital one day after we worked so many hours in a row that I was freakin' exhausted.

I actually learned a lot from watching Lemmy perform, he really is like a guy that plays all the way. Like when he sings, his harmonies are actually a secondary melody line, that's just how he comes up with them. He'll just literally sing another part, and then you just have to put together and make it into a harmony, and if it matches, it's a harmony, if it doesn't, it doesn't get in there. So, for instance, there's a song called "On Your Feet or On Your Knees" from the first record, and I never did get the harmony, it's like a diminished 4th or something, and I remember thinking, "How the hell did he come up with that?," you know, it's just so radical, because when he records his harmony parts, he basically says, "Turn off the lead vocal," and he sings the other vocal, and then you just put it in there. He's an original, and his bass is super loud in the studio, so we actually had to wear airplane earmuffs, and he's got two amps, one's called Killer and one's called Murder, so it was pretty loud. And it's all midrange, because he wants it distorted, I think he secretly wants to be the guitar player, so the bass is all midrangy and distorted, and in fact, from that sound, we have actually recorded distorted bass on every record I've done since. For every track, we actually feed a bass signal out to an amp and distort it, and always print that along with a lot of the other bass tones we print, just because I loved what I got out of Motorhead, and I never really forgot how much that adds to certain parts of the song. I loved working with Lemmy, and the whole band, I don't know where else you find guys like that.

But we ended up making some great records together, and then Lemmy's somebody who really likes consistency, strangely enough. You wouldn't think that, but he just, every other year, would call me to do a record. Todd Singer, his manager, would call, and I would do them, and after four of them, it just got a little stale for both of us, and I actually decided that I didn't want to do anymore, and he really got angry. I saw him after that at the Grammys and I expected him to be very warm because I'd done four records with him, and he walked by my wife and I, and he's got the belt on and the open jacket, and I haven't seen him in a while, and he goes "Fuck you Howard." That was it, and my wife starts laughing, and says, "Wow, that was a badge of honor, Lemmy calls you out at the Grammys!'

Unlike many producers who resisted Protools and the notion of recording in digital as their mainstream platform in the mid-1990s, as soon as the technology became available, Benson said he "actually recorded some of that stuff in an old program called Turtle Beach, believe it or not, on a PC, literally flying tracks back and forth to the computer to try and edit them and all that." A huge fan from its very first editions, citing both the convenience and cutting-edge benefits of a technology that would revolutionize the recording industry, the producer viewed this as an advance for his career as well, sharing that

the second turning point, after Keith, was when I discovered Protools. I have an engineering background, and was always really good with computers anyway, so even before Protools went mainstream, I was making records in the computer NOT using Protools. I was using these really unwieldy programs like Turtle Beach and Saw, and this stuff never worked, it always crashed, because it was all in the PC. And at the time, Sound Designer was out, but it still just wasn't good enough to really work with, it was still clunky and everything, and when I went to São Paulo to work with Sepultura on *Against* at ION Studios, the engineer actually had version 4.2, which was way better than 4.0. You could actually run it and it wouldn't crash. You couldn't do any graphical stuff, but it worked for twenty-four tracks, and you could deal with it. And the hard drives at that time were literally 8 gigabytes, that was the biggest you could buy, so we were constantly deleting stuff all the time just to make sure you had room, and there were no undos.

I remember sitting in the studio, putting my hand on the mouse, and all of a sudden, it hit me that I don't have to discuss a lot of these things that are in my head. Because in my head, I had production ideas going around in my head, and I knew what they wanted to sound like, but I wasn't Bob Rock with five assistants and a big studio and two years to make albums. I didn't have that kind of budget, I had smaller budgets where I had to do it all myself, a lot of it, so with smaller budgets, especially back then, for what I wanted to do, you were hamstrung a little bit. But here, all of a sudden, here's this computer and you could edit, you can change things, and whatever's in your head you can get out. And people at the time would say to me, "Oh, that's cheating, it's a computer," and my reply would be, "That's not actually true: If you think about Mozart, when he wrote his stuff, he could erase everything with an eraser. He could go through his score, and rewrite all the stuff all the time," and this is actually more true recording in digital, because this is what you kind of want to be able to do.

You want to be able to actually get the music the way you want it, as opposed to being limited by the technology. Not only that, but you can be enhanced by it because now if you wanted to, you could get a flanger, or a chorus, or a limiter faster, and when they put that Sound Designer program out, there were millions of plug-ins and they were all online for free, and everyone was cracking them, and my engineer at the time was just throwing things at me. In truth, I was one of the first guys who really felt uncomfortable about that, I always said to my guy, "We gotta buy these plug-ins." And he would say, "Yeah, but we can just take them," and my reply was always, "Yeah, that would be great, but these people won't be in business a year from now if we do that." If you think about it logically, people like me who can afford to buy the plug-ins *should* be buying them, because we're the ones who can afford it, so why should we even try to do something like that.

Looking to the future at a time when many of his production peers were still fighting it, to Benson, embracing the technological shift early was a win-win for him in both technical and professional terms.

Of course, at the time, using that technology made you cutting edge as a producer because a lot of the established guys weren't doing it, they wouldn't change, they would say "I'm not doing it," and eventually the bands started seeing what the advantage was to that. Of course, now the bands are in there using their computers and replacing the producer (laughs), but it was still a HUGE breakthrough. I think a lot of the new bands, especially some of the great work that guys like Jeff Basker's doing, and the Lumineers, where stuff sounds a lot more played by humans and live, and that is an important element of record production because—like with my records—people who listen will say, "Oh, that sounds unbelievably live." And the truth is, it's not unbelievably live, it's really edited, it just depends on how you do that and how much you leave. For instance, I tend with the bands I produce not to edit our guitars very much, and I always say this: a lot of it has to do with who is in the room playing.

A great example of that is when we did Daughtry, where we had Josh Freeze playing drums, we had Paul Bushnell on bass, we had Phil X on guitars. Come on, that's like a super group! So how much editing do you really have to do? You don't, it just sounds amazing. Now, go to another record, without naming any bands, where you don't have that musicianship, and of course you have to edit, because strangely enough, what happens is—and I find this all the time—if you don't edit it, what people say is "You did edit it." They say to you, "Oh my God, your record sounds too stiff," and that's actually not the case. The case is: it's not good enough, if it's so played poorly that you can't really do anything with it. So the other producers are correct, that it is about the performance. If you get guys who can perform, if you bring Taylor Hawkins in there vs. the drummer from an average band from the 2000s—and I did A LOT of those bands—it's not even a comparison!

Discussing some of the highlights of his millennium catalog of massive successes that emerged over the decade that followed, as he rose through the ranks and up the charts to the position of one of the industry's most in-demand hit-makers, Benson came to consider the digital recording medium another band member in his record-making process, highlighting early successes as coming when

I did a Sepultura record, and a Less Than Jake record I recorded digitally which did pretty well, and then P.O.D. came into my life, and that was really the game-changer for me because that was my first gold record. And let me tell you, man, I could *never have made that record* without the computer. You couldn't do it, it was a fundamental element of that one. Just because the competition at the time was like, Limp Bizkit, Korn, and I wanted to beat them all. I thought we could get pop radio, and I'll admit my ego was way out there at that point, and I just thought, "If I can take my pop sensibilities, and apply it to this band . . . ," because they already had everything else. And on the first album, we didn't quite do it, but on the second album, *The Fundamental Elements of Southtown*, we succeeded with songs like "Southtown" and "Youth of the Nation."

At that time, I started to produce a lot of big records, because I was really inside a pop guy, so I just surrounded my pop sensibilities with rock production, and with the computer—especially when Autotune came out—that was one of those moments that you just go, "Oh my God!" I remember when I got the disc in the mail, somebody sent it to me from Atari, it was a program for the military that they turned into something to tune vocals. And I remember putting it in the computer the first time, and it was a revelation to me, when I put the vocal through and it came out tuned!

That was one of those moments where you could see the future twenty years out, like I remember seeing it all, and thinking, "Oh, now anybody can sing," within reason. But there are people who can sing now who are gonna become famous that just could never do that before, because prior to that, vocal tuning was the kind of thing that producers and engineers took hours and days and months sometimes to do. Those are things that had to go through the Harmonizer, and Publison, and samplers, all just to tune these vocals, and now, all of a sudden, you can put it through one side and it comes out the other side tuned, it was just like a crazy thing! And all that stuff happened at once, so you can imagine someone like me, who was used to tape, all of a sudden, at your fingertips are all these things that, instead of taking three months to do, you're now doing in three minutes. So it was amazing, an amazing moment.

Still, no matter how much Protools could help him improve song structure, arrangement, and performance, the producer felt there was no replacement for an artist's ability to bring in solid material to work with at the outset of a collaboration, even if the producer had to contribute compositionally to making them commercially viable singles. One of his purest projects in this respect was his collaboration with the debut LP of *American Idol* finalist Chris Daughtry, a songwriter who, though Benson would eventually come to respect him enough to make three albums together, initially remembered feeling hesitant about the prospect, reluctantly agreeing to produce at the urging of his wife:

I almost didn't do it, and think I was very adverse to doing it at first. I used to watch *American Idol* with my wife, and I would fall asleep before they even got to the credits. So I remember during this particular year, she was very upset when this guy got let go. "Oh my God, they let Chris Daughtry go!," and I was like, "Who is Chris Daughtry, what are you talking about?" So I watched the show and thought, "Yeah, he's very good, he can sing," but I don't really know the realities of the whole thing, and I hadn't been involved with it yet, and hadn't done anything with the *Idol* franchise at all.

So six months goes by and I get a call from my manager saying, "Oh, by the way, they're looking for you to talk to Chris Daughtry about producing his record," and I'm thinking, "That's the guy my wife got all weird about when he got let go." So I said, "Monica, what do you think? Should I do this?," and she said, "Oh my God, you have to work with him, just so we can have him at our house," and I brought it up to my guys, and their wives all said the same thing, and my risk was: I'm going from My Chemical Romance to Chris Daughtry, that's my risk. I knew I could do it, but it's also that I was a little worried about working with guys like Pete Gambarg, Ashley Newton, and Clive Davis, because I'd never worked in that kind of environment with songs, and four A&R guys, it's nerve-racking a little bit. But I'd had a lot of hits when I came in, but Clive actually didn't even know who I was at that point, but Pete actually gave him my résumé, and he was like, "Oh, I didn't know he produced all that stuff."

With everybody now on the same page, on the first day he walked into the studio to begin working with Chris Daughtry, Benson recalled feeling extremely and immediately relieved at the fact that

when Chris and I had a meeting, luckily for us, Chris shows up with this song called "Home." He'd written that song, and when I'd first met him, I was still not into doing it yet. But when he sat down and played "Home" for me, oh my God, I just couldn't believe how good it was! I kept saying to myself, "Am I really hearing this song? This is so good," and I pretty much know going into a record what I think the hits are. Frankly, for a record like Daughtry, there's certain records where you have the right combination of people, and you think every song's a hit, so it's a little harder. But on the band records, you kinda know, because you're not just blowing songs out left and right for new songs, and in fact, most band records are cowritten. Like the Skillet record I did in 2013, I thought all the songs were awesome, but there were a few songs that stuck out to me that were like, "Okay, that song's definitely sitting heads and tails above the other songs," and by the way, that's good when that happens because it makes decision making a lot easier.

Billboard praised the album on this point, giving both producer and artist equal props for making a record that "sounds like the work of a bunch of professionals, which is true to a certain extent: it was produced by Howard Benson . . . but Benson and Daughtry didn't draft in a bunch of pros to write the songs—each tune bears a writing credit by Daughtry, and most of them are solo credits. Listening to these songs, it would be easy to mistake them for the work of seasoned pros: they not only follow the template of post-grunge well, they do it with better hooks and a commercial flair lacking from bands like Fuel and Shinedown, bands that have inspired Daughtry but who he betters here. To put it mildly, that's a surprise—not just that Daughtry pulled off the tricky move of being pop enough for his *Idol* fans and rock enough for post-grungers, but that he pulled it off on the strength of his own work." Agreeing that the collective strength of the album's songs helped sell Daughtry as one of those rare *Idol* winners who actually becomes a household name post-season, the producer recalled that

for Daughtry's first record, along with "Home" and others he'd written for the album, we went to get some cowriters to write songs, and Pete and Clive and all these guys do what they do best. Clive is just great at finding songs, and Pete is one of the best—he's the Senior V.P. at Atlantic, and is now a good friend of mine. He does Hailstorm with me, and Skillet, and we went on to have a great relationship beyond that, but I first met him doing that project, and he was really from the Clive Davis school of songs. Even though I knew at that point how important songs were, I'd never gone outside the project for songs, because we always were self-contained, so this was a situation where we didn't have fifteen songs for the project, we had five thousand songs. So there was song after song coming in, and finally we got in the studio and started the album. So that record just had great songs, and great musicians, you can hear it, phenomenal guys. We recorded that album at Bay 7 Studios using a Neve console and all analog stuff, because the front end in our records has to be extremely analog. When it gets to the computer, we're in the computer for the rest of the time pretty much.

Turning to the recording of "Home"—which would, in addition to becoming a #1 smash, gain a massive amount of exposure as the exit song for Season 6 of *American Idol* whenever a finalist contestant was voted off the show—to discuss what strengths he felt Daughtry brought to the table as an A-list vocalist to help keep their collaboration a largely organic one (in the context of other bands where Benson relied heavily on aids like Auto-tune to create a keeper vocal performance), in Daughtry's case, the producer remembered feeling impressed from take one with the fact that

> Chris is amazing in the studio, he loves working with these session musicians, and the record blew up! Even when we finished the record, I wasn't sure about it, I didn't really know, but when we listened to "Home," we knew we did something special on that song. It is a perfect song to me because it's minimal, so Phil X came in and put just the minimal amount of guitar parts on it, all those cool little hooks and little guitar things that coo in and out of the song just to create a vibe, and Josh is playing minimal drums, the bass is minimal. Debbie Lurry, who did all my string arrangements back then, did a fantastic string arrangement, so it's sort of like, if you look at an old track sheet that Atlantic used, for instance, there's a track sheet for a Roberta Flack song I remember looking at back in the day, and it had minimal stuff on it. It was just like four instruments, and yet it sounds like forty instruments, so I just wanted to keep that particular song very simple, and Chris to deliver it in a very almost nostalgic feeling.
>
> I felt the song had to be delivered with a feeling of nostalgia about being home, and to me the best line in the song is the one in the bridge where he says, "Be careful what you wish for, because you just might get it all . . . and then some you don't want . . ." I think that's what makes the song have legs, because it was like: you really want to get home, but when you get home, it's not exactly what you thought it was going to be either. You get there, and there's still those problems that you have, even though you can't wait to get there. So I think that gave the song a certain amount of gravitas as well, and it just says intelligence on his part.

Delving into some of the recording choices he made in selecting which microphone would best suit Daughtry's range as he produced vocal performances, as well as how the impressive sonics of the album's drum sound were set up in that respect, Benson observed that

> I think he'd never really worked with a producer up to that point, but frankly, it's not that much to harness a guy like that. He's a great singer and he just has to get a great mic and make sure he doesn't over-sing. We used a Sony C800, which was my mic, and we tried a lot of things with him, but a lot of it was just getting the right microphone and the right compressor and the right Neve preamp. We don't really EQ anything, everything is flat, so we just used the preamp and the Tube-Tech CL2A Dual Opto Compressor. So not a lot of compression.

It's funny, on his next album, record #4, I'm probably going to produce some of it, probably not all of it. I think we've done three records together, and both of us have kind of run out of things to say to each other (laughs). So he said to me, "You know what, Howard, everything I learned in the studio, I learned from you: how to sing, how to enunciate, how many takes to do, all that stuff." And when somebody says that to you, it just means a lot. It means they're going to take your stuff and pass it forward, and I think what Chris has picked up more than anything would be enunciation, and how to not worry so much about the actual singing in tune and in time, but more the feeling and getting the words to mean something. That's what I focus on more, I don't worry about the other stuff.

With the drum sound for Chris's first album, we used a Gretsch kit, and still use the same Gretsch kit, and did very traditional micing on the kit. Where we did change a lot was where we put the room mics at Bay 7, where we took out the glass ceilings and made the ceiling bigger. We repositioned the drums a few times, and the great thing about my engineer Mike is he's a fundamentals guy: he was at Little Mountain, so he learned from Bob Rock, he learned from Bruce Fairbairn, he learned how to mic stuff the right way. So, for instance, even with guitar amps, he still does that whole thing where he'll move the microphone around to find out where the white noise has the most frequencies through the mic, and that's where he positions the mic. So it's not a lot of trial and error, he knows how to do it the right way.

While Daughtry could carry his own water in the songwriting department, another mid-millennium collaboration would showcase Benson's talent as a composer after he signed on to produce Hoobastank's *The Reason*, whose title track would go on to be a #1 smash single, garnering a coveted nomination for "Song of the Year" at the 2004 Grammy Awards. The song was a brilliant example of Benson's creative craft in action in the studio, specifically his talent for polishing what many critics felt was a turd of a song that never would have had a chance at the success it eventually had on radio without him.

Benson didn't disagree in discussing the lengths of his involvement in crafting the hit for a band that, in 2004, *Entertainment Weekly* poked a bit of spot-on fun at, opining that "most groundbreaking bands that sell well create a market for dumbed-down versions of themselves. We've had Alice in Chains paving the way for Stained, Radiohead leaving a wake for Coldplay, and, most recently, Incubus setting the stage for California's Hoobastank . . . On Hoobastank's second album, they've once again come up with decent enough radio fodder. But ultimately, they're still just a crummy Hydrox answer to Incubus' creamy Oreo." Benson began by clarifying the record on what he feels have been

a lot of interesting stories behind that song, because—and the band actually says this in a lot of interviews—I actually wrote the bridge to that song, and I never asked for writing credit back then, which I'm starting to do more and more now, because I do so much of the writing. But in that song, when it goes to the big bridge part, they didn't have that, and I kind of stole it from Lennon/McCartney when they did that stuff on "Little Help from my Friends." But those are the things as a producer that you have to do, and it's the same with "Move Along." If you look at the lyrics in "Move Along," in the inside liner notes, you'll see my handwriting. They kind of fucked up and put my handwriting in there instead of his, that's probably why I never worked with them again. But I think that you have to do that, and then if you start taking publishing, back then I thought there was a divide, but nowadays because it's so driven by songs, I don't feel it's there as much. But back then, my artists all wrote their own songs, everybody wrote their own songs, so we never went outside for songwriters. The first time I did that was Chris Daughtry, when I worked with Pete Gamhart, and Pete introduced me to that way of making records, because he'd made a lot of records with Clive like that.

But "The Reason" was one of those songs that everybody who heard it, loved it right away, even just in the demo form. The opening line is amazing. I put that little quarter-note piano part in the beginning, and somebody said to me, "It's so genius, why did you put in in there." And I said, "Because I loved the song so much, I wanted to make sure that every time I heard it, that I heard me." Also I thought, "What would Count Basie do? He'd play one note, so that'll work," and it actually ended up working, so a lot people think there's this big reason behind it, no pun intended. But the fact is—a lot of the ideas, even on My Chemical Romance, which I think is one of my best records I've made—a lot of the Queen influences were really a result of the fact that we didn't really have any idea of what to do with some of those parts. And I think my engineer said, "Hey, how about a guitar solo with a harmony in it?," and then all of a sudden it sounds like Queen, but it wasn't intentional that it sounded like that.

Highlighting one of his magical moments as a producer during the record-making process, when "happy accidents" happen that wind up improving a song's compositional structure, Benson confirmed that indeed

those are absolutely some of my favorite moments in the studio, and in fact, I'm trying to get back to that a little bit more on a personal level, and the guys in the studio are seeing it a lot more from me now, where we're really just letting a lot of stuff go through that we haven't let go through in the past. Because we've turned from being those guys into hit-making guys that have to make hits, so you tend to normally try to make things really work on a perfection level, and I think what's great about music right now is it's changed to being a bit more of the chaotic thing.

So we're doing a lot of tempo changes and things like that, and we're not trying to follow a trend, but are trying to get it back to where we were back in those days where we were a little bit looser about the production. So it's something where I think you consciously have to edit yourself as a creative person, and you can't just say, "I'm great, I'm not changing." I think you have to go, "What can I do better?" A lot of times I'll go, "Okay, I think a C chord will work here. Well, I'm not going to use a C chord because that's just what I thought, I'm going to do the opposite." I almost do that a lot now, where I'll just think the opposite, just because I'm so used to thinking one way, like "Let's put 8th notes in here." So, in fact, yesterday in the studio, my engineer goes "No 8th notes," and I said, "Exactly, no 8th notes."

Benson turned next to his collaboration with a far more naturally talented and musically-and-compositionally-competent band, the amazing Hailstorm, who *Metal Hammer* magazine hailed for bringing "polished, emotionally-driven pop rock erupts into a mosh-pit friendly stomp while . . . (proving) there's more to them than just radio-friendly melodies, ballads and gratuitous drum solos, Hailstorm have worked hard to reach headline status and the only way for them now is up." Benson produced the band's self-titled 2009 debut LP and 2012's *The Strange Case of . . .*, the latter album earning a Grammy for "Best Rock Performance" for "Here's to Us." Working with a singer of Lizzy Hale's range and power was a new adventure for the producer, who revealed that

with Lizzy, before her, I actually hadn't worked with any female singers before, and then all of a sudden, I got her, and then Kelly Clarkson, and Allison Iraheta, and a whole lot of singers. The one thing about Lizzy is that she comes from a touring background. She's toured since she was twelve, and when I got her, she was twenty-two or twenty-three, she could really sing, but she was just singing almost like a guy a little bit, because she's so powerful. So I wanted to make sure there was a feminine vibe on the first record. I wasn't as concerned with that as much, but on the second record, I asked her to let her emotion and vulnerability out more. So on *The Strange Case Of . . .* , you can hear a lot of songs, like on "In My Room" and "Beautiful" and "Here's to Us," that there's a certain quality to her voice that she hadn't really demonstrated before that shows up on those songs.

Then on others, like "Love Bites (So Do I)," she can go back to screaming like crazy, so she's just done that ten thousand hours of work, and she's great at it. When you do that much singing, and you're talented, you're going to be great, so she's put the time in, and when they won the Grammy, I said to the whole band, "You know, of all the bands I've worked with, it's not like you came out of nowhere, you deserve this," because they've criss-crossed this country so many times to get to where they are, that they absolutely deserved it, to me.

It's different working with Lizzy in the studio because we do some real cool shit vocally that nobody knows we're doing, where it's just literally going down on the fly. It really has to do with just, as the singer is singing, making sure the levels are the best levels you can get, so you're not just depending on the compressor to do the work. So it means learning the songs, going through the lyrics, knowing where the high points and low points are, things like that. That's kind of the way they used to do things, and why those vocal sounds are so good back in the day, because you have these super-clear vocals that don't sound processed. So you want to get a lot of emotion out of those guys.

Benson spotlighted another important ally any good producer needs to have in his corner at all times, especially when he isn't mixing the project himself, as some producers insist upon. The next best thing, in his opinion, is to have a mix engineer he trusts implicitly with sonic decisions that would mirror his own preferences, such that an almost intuitive creative relationship is established, as was the case in the mixing of both Hailstorm records by the man many consider to be the greatest mix engineer in the business, Chris Lord-Alge. Benson recalled that

I kind of knew what he liked, because we'd done so many records together between me and my engineer Mike, Hatch my second engineer, Paul, my Protools guy, Ted Gensen, my mastering guy. What happens is: you develop a sense of process. And because of my engineering background, I sort of know what my vocals are going to sound like at the end, so I kind of go, "Okay, this matters, this doesn't matter." Or Chris would call me up and go, "Hey man, you know what, there's a little bit too much compression on this, next time do that," so we always had an open exchange of ideas, and I always told Chris, "Tell us what you don't like. When you're mixing, make it easy for us to give you something you can mix really well," so I think that's what made our records better and better and better. It's good to have the same team together a lot. There's good and bad things about that, but it's good when it gets like Pixar where you're banging hit after hit out. But it's bad when you start to get into the redundancy, so you have to sort of be aware of what you're doing.

Coming full circle in a way in his own journey as a record producer by the time he was sitting behind the boards preparing to produce Creed's reunion studio LP of the same title, Benson regarded the opportunity as among his proudest moments in a career that had begun with Bang Tango at the end of the hair-metal movement almost twenty years before. From the production side, Benson remembered his first focus being squarely on the fact that

I was a little bit thinking about it, it's hard not to, especially when the band's worked with really one other producer before me, and didn't really have any idea of how to work with another producer. They kind of did, I think more Mark Tremonti did because he'd done the Alter Bridge records with another producer, but with Scott, he hadn't

BEHIND THE BOARDS II

really worked with anybody since then, even when he made another solo LP. But as a band, I think John Kurzweg did all their other records. So I had to learn a lot about them and how they made records, and there's always, with every band, stuff that nobody talks about, but once you're the producer, you go, "Oh, I see, I see why that sounds that way."

Every band has secrets, that only their producer knows, and so for instance, I've actually had bands—not Creed, of course, because they all can play—who actually don't play on their records! And nobody knows it, and then you go to produce it, and find that out, and ask, "Well, who played on these records?" And the band is like, "Well, the producer did," and you're going, "Okay . . ." Meanwhile, they're set up and ready to play when you realize they can't play, and that happens more than you think.

For instance, I have a band I've done three records with, and the first album I used Josh Freeze on, and the last two albums I didn't, and it's just so obvious, it's so obvious, that the playing deteriorates. It's not even what they're playing, it's what they're *not* playing, because if you get a guy like Josh or Taylor, when they come in, they barely play that much, but it's so fulfilling and the groove is there, that you say, "Well, I don't need anything else, no overdub." Then you get a drummer that kind of blows, and it's all overdub, I had a band like that in the mid-2000s, and they had a lot of hits, one of them called "Move Along," and I remember listening to this record when it was done, and at the end of the record, saying to myself, "There's no groove on this record at all." I didn't know what to do about it, the drummer was average, and we brought in Lenny Castro to play percussion, and it was like the record took off! And when you listen to the record, it's mostly the percussion that makes that record go, because it's got such a feel to it, but we had to edit the drums so much that there just wasn't a feel to it without that percussion.

And the bands don't know that stuff, they don't know what you're doing as a producer because they've never played with a good drummer, so they don't even know what a good drummer feels like. So they have to trust you, which again, goes back to what I took away from working under Keith Olsen, which is, in the studio, you really have to be "the man." You have to make hard calls like that, and even right now, I have to make a hard call on a record I'm currently working on, and I told the A&R guy yesterday that the drummer just has to go, or I can't use him on the project. "If you want to know why this project's not happening, it's 'cause of that," and his response was like, "Well, just use a drum machine and editing, blah, blah, blah," and I said, "Okay, let's get a great programmer in and we'll do it that way, but just don't be surprised when the drummer calls you up on a Saturday night at 2 in the morning and goes: Where's my fucking drums?" So, all the performances, one way or the other, have to be notched up a lot, and guys like the Black Keys are doing a great job of that, or Mumford and Sons, guys like that who are bringing real playing to the table. When you watch the Grammys and watch them play the Levon Helm tribute, that was awesome, and brought tears to my eyes, first because I love Levon Helm, but secondly, hey, it's not Katy Perry, it's actually real people playing real music. It was pretty awesome.

Benson would experience a similar thrill with Creed, whose collaboration with the producer would be hailed by MTV as "the most sonically palatable (the band) has been on record . . . (sounding) heavier yet more open than they did in the past." In outlining his ambitions for the group's first studio album in eight years, heading into the collaboration, Benson's first concern wasn't with the band's musical abilities, but rather with managing the very public

> tension between the members of the band that I had to mitigate, which was probably a lot of it. It was obviously great because they could play and sing, but just getting through that process, and I'd heard that—by the way—from the label ahead of time, that that was going to be part of the job, just getting the project done. I always look at the word producer literally, your job is to produce, to finish it and get it done. So all of the individuals in Creed, individually, were great guys, they really were, you could go out to dinner and hang out with them and they were awesome. But there was so much water under the bridge, and Motorhead was like that by the way. Lemmy would bring stuff up that happened twenty years before with him and Wurzel and Phil, things that I had no idea what they were talking about. But that's just part of the deal.

Though the Creed frontman was known as an at-times volatile presence, Benson experienced no such difficulty in the studio. Stapp proved to be a consummate professional who—the more one-on-one time he spent working with him—led Benson to conclude that

> Scott is one of the most misunderstood guys I've ever been around. He is, first of all, a great guy, he's a sweetheart, and I think he went through a pretty bad phase with his life that unfortunately played itself out in public, but yet on a personal level, I don't think you could meet a guy who is cooler or nicer, and the guy works his tail off. So, for instance, he'd never cowritten with anybody before outside of Mark, and for this record, we sent him out on cowrites, and he did maybe thirteen, fifteen, twenty of them, and he showed up on time, did the right things, let the writers do their thing. So that's the kind of stuff that happens when you walk into a project, sometimes what you hear is not necessarily what's going on. And a lot of that can have to do with the agenda of the other band members or the manager or label, but with Scott, even on the Creed record—where I think it was a lot harder to do than the solo project because the band was involved—he was still just a gentleman. And I don't see what happens with the band outside the studio, and I don't care frankly. All I care about is what happens when they walk through the studio door, and Scott's voice is phenomenal

right now, I have to say. He's doing things in one or two takes, so the thing with him is harnessing him, because he can sing the phone book and it sounds great. The same problem I had with Bon Jovi, when I did his song, I remember thinking, "God, he can sing anything right now, and he sounds amazing." So in some ways, you really do have to focus on the songs with guys like that, because you can get fooled easily if the songs aren't good, because the vocals are so good.

Scott is never happy with his vocals. It's not even that he's never happy, he just loves the process. So we'll do a vocal, and I think the vocal's done in like an hour and a half, and he'll keep singing until he can't sing anymore, just because he loves to sing. I have my ways of getting around that, and success there again depends on who you are and just where you are in the process. I mean, a lot of times, I will sit there for the entire time, but for Scott's project, there was a guy named Lenny Skolnik who worked at Wind-Up, but who was also a Drexel student, and I actually found this guy when he was a senior. He's a programmer and actually did a lot of the programming on the last Hailstorm record, and doing really well in his career, and Scott likes Lenny a lot, as a friend and a person. So when Scott gets in his mode when he says, "You know what, I want to sing for the next fifteen hours," I go, "Lenny, you wanna just punch here for a while, get a bunch of tracks, I'll go through it later, star the ones you like." Because what I know Scott's kind of doing is experimenting, and sometimes me being there is actually the wrong thing, because he just wants to do his thing and doesn't want Dad around. So I can tell you, there are a lot of producers who don't know how to do that, because their egos are just too big, they have to be there for every single note. In fact, I think a lot of producers are like that, and I think I'm one of the few guys who knows how to delegate, because I know what's important. What's important is the song, and the main vocal that I end up using, and the arrangement, things like that, the big macro stuff, like Quincy Jones said: "Anyone in Hollywood can cut tracks," it's not that hard. Any good engineer, good studio, but the hard part is finding great songs and assembling a great vocal and great arrangement, that's where you get paid, is that kind of stuff. So if Scott wants to sit around and sing for the next fifteen hours, I'll have someone else I trust to sit there and do it with him, and if something comes up, I'll look at it and maybe say, "Okay, let's do this again." He's not the only singer to do that, by the way.

Reflecting back after twenty-plus years in the business, Howard Benson is a producer whose catalog of platinum rock hits shows no signs of slowing, even moving across stylistic borders into country with his production in 2013 of country music superstars Rascal Flatts' new studio LP, as well as Christian rockers Skillet, who have racked up an impressive 150 million YouTube views in the past few years. As current as ever in an age where that privilege extends only to the elite soundmen in the business who boast Benson's versatility, the producer has strategically tried to avoid a signature sound, but I know I'm identified with a certain genre as a producer, and I'm actually extremely proud of it. We talk about that every so often in the studio, about how we got—literally from 2000 to 2008—pretty much all the rock hits were mine. I'm one of those people that doesn't feel ashamed by stuff like that. As a producer you have to stand by your work, and in the same breath as Hoobastank, I've had people say to me, "Are you the guy who produced Pretty Boy Floyd?" And I say, "Yeah! What's wrong with that?" That work is part of my career, and are things you did. Are they great records? Probably not, but we all have that.

My way of producing records is my way, I can tell you no one else produces records like me. I've talked to plenty of producers, they have their own styles, that are literally 180 degrees from mine, and yet they still work. So I think the important things in making records, to me, beyond the music, is how organized you are: you really have to be organized. Because if you think about the chaoticness of a project . . . this is how I know I don't want to produce a band: every so often, a band will call me and go, "Hey Howard, we want you to produce our record, but we want you to come to Alabama to produce it in a new studio because we want you to do something new. We want you to be in a new situation," and I'm like, "Dude, you're the ones who have to be doing that. I'm the one who has to make sure the plane doesn't crash!" And when bands think like that, what they're really trying to say is: "We don't have any ideas, you do the ideas." And I never want to be involved in that, I'm just not interested in that.

I have my process, and it's very flexible in a lot of ways, but I always tell my guys, "We're flight attendants, we're there to make the passengers happy, and when they get to the next destination, and they're stoked because they've made something great, and the plane doesn't crash, it's awesome. But we're all in the service business really, we're there to serve the artist. If the artist wants peanuts, here's the peanuts." So you have to always think like that, you can't get too above it, but you still have to be the pilot. You don't want the guys coming up to the cockpit trying to fly the plane. That happens on certain projects, and you have to be really careful about that, not because of your ego, but just because the project suffers when that stuff starts to happen too much.

While they're all his babies, and some projects proved more problem children than others, Howard found himself feeling particularly proud of the sonic imprint his sound had made upon pop culture after watching how it had filtered down into his own children's, revealing that while

I probably think the first few P.O.D. records, Hoobastank, the All American Rejects album are among my favorites, the My Chemical Romance album was a *very important record to me* because it opened up another vein that lasted almost forever, just because that record's almost a seminal record for a lot of Goth kids. It's funny, when

I made that record, I noticed the kids at the high school my kids go to all started to dress like the lead singer Gerard, and it was really weird to watch it happen in real time. So that was a great record to me. The Daughtry record, of course, and I think working with Kelly Clarkson was hugely important, to work with someone at that level. There are certain records like 10 Years and Saliva that are on the résumé which I really enjoyed making, but because of the situation maybe within the band or things like that, they don't stick as well. You're not as involved maybe because the band didn't want you as involved, something like that. You can't have every record be like that, but when I'm making them, I certainly feel like every record is the most important record I'm doing.

While many would argue that simply getting up every morning to go work in his chosen profession would be satisfaction enough for any record producer—especially against the current industry backdrop—for Benson, that thrill is made even sweeter by the fact that he achieved the ultimate dream-come-true for any producer when he opened his own studio, Bay 7, a move he acknowledged was

a huge thing for me, to own a studio. I didn't want to do it, but was forced to do it, though, because of just the way the economics of the business were, and the way we make records, the studio we were at just wasn't working anymore for us financially. It was a big risk. We found the house, bought the console, got the contractors, and I had a lot of help from my engineer Mike, and in like three months, got the place up and running, which is like record time. It was amazing we got it finished, and we're learning as we go, but it's a great place to work, that studio, it has such awesome vibes and people like to come by and really like to hang out, along with working there—so they've made it like a destination almost. So that's been a big deal for me, plus I can ride my bike over there, which is awesome, because I'm a big bike rider, and now I don't have to take the freeway, which used to be like two hours a day. So it makes my life a lot less stressful, and it's my studio, and as a producer, when you have your own studio, it's just a much cooler thing.

For Benson, owning his own studio is, in part, perhaps, a reward for a work ethic that he considers second to none in an extremely competitive business. He's proud to have continued that family tradition into the next generation, one where, no matter the trade,

what I've always appreciated about myself is that I did so much work. That's actually, to me, a trait of my whole family. Even back down to my grandparents and back in the history of my family, there's a lot of very successful people that, believe it or not, you wouldn't even expect if I told you where they all came from. But they were people who worked very hard and who were self-made, and I think that just runs naturally in my family: we don't work for other people, we work for ourselves. I would say that if you want to avoid all the recessions, work for yourself. You hear about people getting laid off and fired, even in the record business, but it's pretty hard to get fired if you have your own business, so I'm pretty lucky to have that. And I think my guys are lucky that they have me, because I always keep my guys working. That means a lot to me, that stuff. I actually treasure those feelings, almost as much as the hit records. I've been doing this so long, it just feels like it's part of my life. I can't even really separate that out from the rest of it, it's just what I do and who I am. I'm proud of my body of work, more than anything. I can't single anything out, I'm more happy that I have a family and kids, and actually have succeeded hopefully to a certain extent as a parent and a husband. That's a whole other job, and I think if that's not really good in your life, I think you're gonna not enjoy your business, so I'm very lucky that's good in my life. I'd rather have that than have hit records, and I'm lucky I have both of those things.

Closing with advice to the next generation of bands waiting in the wings, some of whom if they're lucky may catch Benson's ear and wind up working with him in the future, the producer cautions that, at the beginning or end of any record, the most important thing a band or producer can bring to the studio are

songs, songs, and songs. That's what I would say, songs and songs and songs. Great songs, with great lyrics and great melodies, especially tremendous lyrics, to me, it's all about lyrics. I'm a lyric hound. When I hear a great lyric that makes me feel something, I just can't wait to record it. That's why "The Reason" was so great, or "I'm Not Okay" or "Move Along" or "Home." Those are all great songs: you could sit there and play those on an acoustic guitar sitting on the edge of the bed, and they'd be just as when I produced them. That is important for producers to remember too, you have to keep your eye on the ball, songs and vocal performances, getting a great vocal, getting a great song. And if you have to do it all yourself, then you have to do it all yourself, and frankly you should do it all yourself in the beginning because that's how you learn. I have an engineer and all these guys doing stuff for me, but I did it all: when Protools came out, I didn't have a Protools guy. I sat there and edited the drums, edited the vocals, tuned everything, it was me doing all that stuff, so then when I got somebody, I could understand it. I could say, "Hey, I don't like that," or "I do like that," so I think you gotta do all the jobs. I also would recommend playing hits on the piano.

If you're a musician, learn how to play all the hits on piano. Sit down and get a songbook, because that was infinitely important for me, being able to play other people's songs. So if somebody said, "I have a song, these are the three chords," I could sit down and say, "Oh, I know where that could go, and that goes, because that happened on this song and on that song." Knowing music, in that way, is really important. You can draw on your experience, and what you've learned, that's an amazing amount of information you can bring to your next project. You add something important, it's not just you saying it, it's like proof. We still do stuff like that, we still put songs up and look at them on the grid, to see how certain songs were recorded, just to learn about them. I listen to the Top 40 every Sunday on Sirius to listen to pop radio and make sure I'm up on what's going on. So it's a little bit of studying, doing that stuff's very important to do. You don't have to copy it, but you should be aware of it.

Most of the time, if you have a hit record, bands will be back with you next time, they're not stupid. The bands that haven't come back to me after a hit record have been disappointing, because you know you did a great job with them. But there's not a whole lot of them for me, there's a few of those, so I feel pretty blessed that I've been able to work with a lot of the same people, and I think you have to do what you have to do at the risk of losing the client in the end. Even if you don't get the next project, you still have to do your best job, because most the time, they're going to come back if you have a hit. And if they don't, SO WHAT, you still had a hit!

CHAPTER 15

Don't Stand So Close to Me—Nigel Gray

In the opinion of the esteemed Rock and Roll Hall of Fame, who inducted the band in 2003 into its coveted club, "the Police brought bristling energy and musical sophistication to the New Wave movement. They were among the first post-punk success stories, applying the succinct and speedy strictures of that genre to more challenging material that appealed to listeners of all ages and musical persuasions . . . reggae-accented New Wave pop . . . became the group's stock in trade."

Already building a global fan base touring North America and Europe before they even had a major label deal, in the six years between 1978 and 1983, the band would carve out their own mainstream reggae-pop subgenre, based on a treasured catalog of definitive LPs that began with 1978's *Outlandos d'Amour* (which ranked #434 on *Rolling Stone*'s 500 Greatest Albums of All Time list); 1979's *Reggatta de Blanc* (which hit #1 on the UK Top 200 albums chart, and won the band their first Grammy for "Best Rock Instrumental Performance'); and 1980's *Zenyatta Mondatta* (which reached #5 on the *Billboard* Top 200 albums chart, and landed the band another two Grammys for "Best Instrumental Rock Performance" and "Best Rock Performance by a Duo or Group with Vocal").

The man behind the boards recording all of these groundbreaking albums, producer

Nigel Gray, remembered feeling something special had truly walked through the door of his Surrey Sound Studios as an unknown trio back in January 1978. A fascinating fusion of punk, reggae, and new wave, the sound that Sting, Andy Summers, and Stewart Copeland generated together would go down on tape for the first time ever when

> they came in as this completely unknown band with no budget, no record deal. They had enough money to record one song, and that turned out to be "Roxanne." When we recorded "Roxanne," that was very early on when we'd just gotten the 16-track, and at the time I was a family doctor. While I'd been in medical school, I'd played in a band and we were hopeless, and I got into suddenly recording some of my own stuff, and so I bought a couple of cheap tape recorders just to have in the back room. Then after a while, I bought a second-hand 4-track setup from a studio that was upgrading to 16-track, and I also had that in my back room but needed some space to put it in in order to record stuff properly.
>
> Well, I'd found an old village hall which was just sitting vacant because no one knew what to do with it, and I rented it very, very cheaply back in 1974. So I upgraded to a 16-track Alice desk and an Ampex MM1000 16-track tape machine, and the hall was typical, where you have an entrance foray, the auditorium where people sit, the stage, and then the backstage area, so it was perfect for me to turn into a studio. I put the recording stuff up onstage, built a partition with glass in the front so I could look out so it was like a typical studio, except primitive. The control room was the stage, and the band then played in the auditorium where the audience would sit, all the chairs had been cleared out of there and the floor was empty.

Describing the sonic architecture of what would come to compose much of the famous ambience heard throughout the Police's early hits, Gray in designing the layout for the studio's live room, remembered discovering

> luckily for me that the room was big enough to be able to put drums in without them sounding boxy, and it was a little bit too loud, so I put some acoustic tiles on the ceiling that I'd bought cheaply from some guy. I was on a very strict budget, and was only doing this for fun, so I stuck all these acoustic tiles on the ceiling, and then the acoustics—just by pure luck—worked perfect for rock bands. It was live enough to be live, but not too live to be difficult to work with. So drums always sounded good in that room, you didn't have to be a genius to make drums sound good, you just put microphones in front of them and boom, there you were.
>
> So I started doing people's demos, and never got around to recording my own music because I got too busy with the whole concept of having a studio. We used to advertise in a weekly paper called the *Melody Maker* that read "16 track studio, $11/hour," and that was it, and people would come because we were cheap. But then

when they got there, they found a big studio where most cheap studios were little backroom places, this was a big environment, so we just got lucky that way. So I was recording "Roxanne." They liked that one so a few months later and did another song, and slowly over a period of two years, recorded a song or two at a time, and we did the whole *Outlandos d'Amour* album. All that time, they were trying to get a record deal, and eventually A&M reluctantly gave them a deal for "Roxanne," a one-off single deal. They weren't very keen on the Police at the time because they weren't punk, and punk was the big thing in those days.

Led by Sting, who *Rolling Stone* correctly noted wrote songs that "are universal, you hear them on both pop and classic-rock stations, and they'll be played on the radio in Germany 100 years from now," Gray remembered that for as new to the studio as he might have been, the band's front man was already a seasoned songwriter by then, confirming that

Sting had a long history of writing songs. Most of the songs I recorded with them from even the first two albums had roots from his Last Exit days, which was the jazz band he was in before. So when he first came, he had an awful good catalog of songs he'd written or half-written that had been updated for the Police. So they had a lot of material, and they had done gigs and had rehearsed the stuff, and Andy Summers was a highly experienced guitar player, he'd been playing in local bands for years so he wasn't green, and Stewart had played with Curved Air before. So they weren't just a bunch of young kids in their first band, they were all musicians who knew the best way to get on was form a band with other good musicians, and knew they wanted to be a famous rock band. And Stewart found Sting, he saw him play and thought, "He's the guy, he's a good front man." Stewart put the band together, and knew from the start he wanted to be a famous rocker. He was focused and that's what he wanted to do.

With *Outlandos d'Amour*, we didn't do any preproduction. When they came in, getting the sound together was my job, because I knew how to make things sound good in that room, so the basic sound of the Police is quite raw on the first album. The micing was very straightforward, because the room was quite live, so I just stuck microphones over each drum, a couple of overheads, and a room mic. In the early days, we didn't have a lot of money, so I couldn't buy really expensive mics, but I do remember I'd bought a Valve Neumann U-67 for $150, and I am pretty sure I had a couple of C-451s on overheads, and I had an AKG D-12 on the bass drum. Then we had Bayer dynamic mics on the toms, condenser mics.

Tracking live off the floor together in a configuration that kept the band's members locked into one another's groove, in returning to the recording of their breakout single "Roxanne" to explore some of the technical design of the band's setup in the studio, Gray began by sharing that when we did the backing tracks, we'd do guitar, bass, and drums, the three of them together, and the guide vocal. When we'd do is, Sting would stand in the monitoring room with me, and his D.I.'d bass would go straight to the desk, and the mic we'd put through the wall into the amp. With Sting's bass, I had the D.I. on one track of the mix on the 16-track machine, and the amp on another, and then in the mix, you just played with them till it sounded right, balance them up. There's no science behind it, it's just using your ears. Remember, I was not an experienced engineer, I was a doctor, and I had never, ever in my whole life been in a recording studio. My own studio was the only one I'd ever been in, and I'd built it and taught myself how to do it just using my ears.

So he would usually, in the monitoring room, sing a guide vocal into a microphone, and in the studio would be Andy dealing with a basic rhythm guitar and the drums, and anything that spilled wouldn't matter because we were going to keep it anyway. Whatever take we liked, we were going to keep that guitar, so a little bit of spill, who cares, because you only worry about spills if you're going to replace that guitar part. So we'd keep the three of them and redo the vocal obviously, and then Andy would add more guitars for solo overdubs.

With "Roxanne," we comped the lead vocal a lot, because the melody of "Roxanne" is very like a jazz thing, so every time he sang it it was different. It was a very improvised vocal, the basic melody was there, but it was just slightly different each time, and if you listen to the melody, it does sound a little bit improvised. So what we would do was do about four versions of it, and go through the takes, and Sting would choose the actual melody line he preferred, and that became the definitive one for the song. So we just kept doing takes till we got one we liked, and because we couldn't afford 2-inch tape, we always went over the old ones. We didn't have the facility to keep a whole lot of takes, because the tape cost more than the studio.

That song's arrangement was pretty sorted out when they came in, the only thing we did was, with the backing track of "Roxanne," because there's a pause in the song, and at the end of the pause, they all come in together, BANG, and to come back in live on the beat was a problem because Sting was in the monitoring room, so I'd set the tape going, walk into the studio area, stand on a big speaker cabinet, and at the end of each verse, I would do what a conductor does, "1-2-3-4" with my arm and come down, so that's how they could come back in in time.

Impressed from lick one by lead fretmaster Andy Summers's ability, against "Sting's strong bass lines"—*Billboard* would argue—"to supply subtle sonic textures and colors on his guitar, and to experiment with various effects," Gray remembered that, due in part to the space limitations within 16-track recording,

there weren't that many guitars on *Outlandos*, maybe two or three overdubs. When

Andy was doing solo overdubs, he would often start off with a very bluesy solo, because he'd been in a bunch of blues bands before, so he'd do a solo that was pretty rock 'n' roll and bluesy, and Sting and Stewart would really sort of laugh out loud and say, "Oh, that's rubbish," so then he'd say, "Well, try this then," and would do something completely outrageous just to sort of annoy them, and they'd go, "Yeah, great!," so all the outrageous stuff came from Andy being annoyed at them saying his stuff was too bluesy. He also had done some jazz-rock fusion in his time when he'd played for Soft Machine, so he came from spontaneity where he just did it off the top of his head, and that was it, we'd keep it. Andy was the guy who was just quite happy to go with the flow.

With his guitar sound, he wanted originally quite a fat guitar sound, whereas I felt it was better to have a more clean sound, because when played it was quite precise, that music, it's not grungy music. With Andy's guitar, it would have been one mic in front of the cabinet, and then D.I. as well. What he did was: he had two amps, one was an old Ampeg, so he would put his guitar into two amps, and then I would put a microphone in front of each amp, and then one farther away, a slightly distant one, and record them in stereo. That gave me a clean guitar sound, in the room it sounds great because it's loud, and when you turn an amp up it always sounds good. But if you mic it up and record it and play it back quietly, it just sounds tiny, but if you record it in stereo with two close mics and then one further out, and you put the close mics left and right, and obviously the distant one in the middle, you get a stereo sound that just sounds fuller, and sort of fills up the mix a bit better.

As he worked the dials on his Alice desk spreading the band's instruments out among the console's sixteen tracks, he shared of the band's specific channel assignments that

the drums I'd usually put on eight tracks, bass, hi-hat, snare, three toms, and two overheads, vocals would only be one or two in those days, and then the guitars were basically on two, so that takes us up to twelve, and occasionally we'd bounce something down to make room for more tracks, say for vocal harmonies.

On *Outlandos*, because they had done these songs onstage, Stewart and Andy both did the harmonies, and so in the studio, they actually sing some of the harmonies. When they're blended into the mix and not very loud, then they don't sound too bad, but they're not really good singers, so the more we used their harmonies on the first album, from *Reggatta* onwards, Sting did all his harmonies as overdubs. Stewart and Andy recognized that Sting was the singer, that he had the voice, because he did, he was a terrific singer. He was very self-confident, which is what you've got to be to be a rock star, you can't be a shrinking violet, and he was a good songwriter and singer, so really everything about him was perfect for the Police. Some people have just got it, they have got charisma, they've got presence, I don't know what it is, but some people come out onstage and you can't take your eyes off them, and he just had that in buckets.

In those days, it was the mutual admiration society, they liked the way I worked, and I loved their music, so we were all having a really good time, and there was no real friction, because we all had the same taste in everything so we were all open to the same things. So it really worked, and that's why we did it so quickly.

As harmoniously as the band and producer had gotten on during the making of their first studio LP, discord followed once the master tapes reached A&M and the man who became Nigel Gray's arch nemesis throughout his collaboration with the Police, beginning with

the second single, "I Can't Stand Losing You." Mike Noble, the A&M A&R guy who signed the Police didn't like the band, he'd only signed them up under duress. So when "Roxanne" was a hit, the second one he got an American producer to try and come in and remix it, because he thought it sounded too raw and basic, and at the end of the day, he turned to Nobel, and said, "Look, I can't improve on this, this is the band. Nigel's created a record that represents the band, it sounds like the band, I can't make it any better, this is just what it is." So Nobel went away sort of reluctantly but pissed off.

Outlandos was the first recording that I made that ended up on vinyl in the shops. I didn't realize it at the time, because I was working all the time, and when it leaves the studio, you don't think about it, and so I remember I was shopping in London one day, and walked past a record shop and heard "Roxanne" blasting out of the door, and that's the first time I realized that anyone else in the world had listened to what I had done. That was before it went up the charts, and once it did go up the charts, I thought, "Oh, that's good!" (laughs)

Once they'd had a hit album, now they were under pressure from the label to come up with another hit album. And so when it came time to do *Reggatta de Blanc*, Nobel was adamant that the Police would not come to me, saying "Wait, you've got to have a proper record producer, a huge name." So they said, "No, we're working with Nigel," and management got that across to him because they knew I was doing a good job, it was just this one guy at A&M who didn't like it.

Fortunately for Nigel and the band, the rest of Britain did, with *Guitar Player* magazine reporting that "when the Police hit the airwaves in 1978, their music simply defied categorization. It was punky, yet it wasn't punk. It had elements of reggae and power pop, but again, it was neither. What the band had come up with was a true conglomeration of musical styles unlike anything that preceded it. Their first album is peppered with songs that begin with an intro and verse in one style, and abruptly yet appropriately shift genres for the chorus."

Hailed by *Billboard* as "unquestionably one of the finest debuts to come out of the '70s punk/new wave movement," Gray's debut collaboration with the Police would produce smash hits including the timeless "Roxanne" (#8), "So Lonely" (#6), and "Can't Stand Losing You" (#2). Heading into their highly anticipated sophomore LP, the BBC would put those expectations in context with their conclusion that *Reggatta de Blanc* is to many "seen as Sting, Stewart Copeland and Andy Summers' best album . . . is more atmospheric than the band's debut; less punky and more controlled." Producing some of the band's biggest hits, including #1 hits "Message in a Bottle" and the seminal "Walking on the Moon," Nigel Gray recalled heading into production that he was feeling considerable pressure from the fact that

> I recorded *Reggatta de Blanc* in four weeks, working 10-8, and in four weeks, it was all recorded and mixed. On the second album, unlike *Outlandos*, a lot of the songs they had never played together before, and only knew two or three of them, I think "Walking on the Moon" and "Message in a Bottle" they had played live on tour, but that was about it. I think Sting's songs were all ones they'd played before. Sting's songs were always the first ones they would do, and then that's when Stewart's songs would come out. Stewart had written a couple of songs and the guys had never heard them. So Stewart would play them on a cassette player, they'd jam it around a bit and cut it. Sting didn't like a lot of Stewart's songs, he thought they were a bit schoolboyish, but they worked well, I liked the ones we did. As time went on, that became less and less.

With Sting clearly the John Fogerty of the band where his status as lead songwriter was concerned, Gray understandably focused on Sting's compositions, especially "Walking on the Moon." Though it would go on to become among the band's most popular and enduring hits, at the time they were tracking the song in the studio, the producer recalled that

> when we recorded "Walking on the Moon," we thought, "This is either going to be a hit, or people are going laugh at it and it's going to flop." But we liked it, and it's an unusual song, everything about it is unusual, and it became a #1.

Focusing on the recording process for the song's instantly recognizable bass line, Gray revealed that for as outer-space-esque as the song's production sounded,

> there's no special effects on that, there's just a mix of the D.I. and the amp and a bit of spill maybe, but he plays his bass with a plectrum. Most bass with their fingers, but Sting plays the bass like a guitar with a petrum. So that gives him a slightly different sound.

One corner of the song's sonic arena where effects were in full play came courtesy of Stewart Copeland's trippy drum track bouncing around throughout the tune as freely as an astronaut might across the moon's surface, a sound Gray explained the drummer achieved

> based around a repeat echo on the snare, rim shot and hi-hat, and Stewart had a little echo machine, like an Echoplex tape echo device next to him. And I'd plug the microphone that goes from the snare into that echo machine, and he turns it to be the right timing for the song, and so we had to get the timing right, so when he hit his stick on the hi-hat, you get the repeat, and what he's playing is "tick, tick, tick." Even though you hear the echo, he's not playing all that, he's only playing half of what's on the record. So playing to that repeat gives him a certain funkiness, and then when it comes to the chorus, he has to switch it off. That's a trick he does onstage, I couldn't have done that in the studio, but because he's used to doing it we actually recorded it like that with the repeat echo.

Having upgraded his studio equipment by then to allow for a greater application of console and outboard gear effects where he and the band felt appropriate throughout the album, the producer was tracking this time out onto

> an MCI console and tape machine I had upgraded to by then. We'd bought them as a package, and it was the first desk I ever had that was automated, so when I did the mix of *Reggatta*, it was an automated mix, which for me was fun. We were on 24-track then, instead of 16, so we had more tracks to play with and there was a little bit more overdubbing going on, definitely more guitar overdubs.
>
> I used to put a little bit of reverb on stuff, and with our EMT plate, one good thing about (those) days, was reverb units were very expensive, especially at my studio, but we had an EMT, which was the best of what you could buy in those days, they didn't have digital reverbs then. So if you wanted to use any reverb, you only had the one plate, so any reverb went through the same plate. You didn't have a different reverb from the drums to the bass, whereas now, people in their home studios have ten different reverbs, so I could put one reverb on the drums, a different one on the vocals, but that doesn't sound very natural. Whereas, if you've only got one to play with, you have to put everyone through the same reverb so it does make the whole thing sound more as if all the guys are in the same room playing. I still think that's a good idea even today.

One song off the album that would become among the band's most popular live staples in arena and stadium tours to follow where the EMT plate played a starring role in once again channeling the band's reggae roots through a new wave filter was "Bring on the Night." Gray was breaking a cardinal recording rule during recording by adding a lot of reverb on the bass drum. You don't normally put a lot of reverb on the bass drum because it made the mix sound messy, but the bass drum we were trying to keep fairly punchy, and because "Bring on the Night" was that reggae sort of thing and the bass drum was very important to that because the drums were really up front, we put a lot of reverb on that one. That was something Stewart encouraged me to do, because he loved a lot of reggae stuff. So that whole little rhythm with the bass drum is very important to the whole song, and there's not much else going on, and there's a breakdown in that song where everything drops out and it's really just drums and vocals, and we brought the echo up a lot.

Back then, I only had the one EMT plate at the studio, although I did have things like flangers, stuff like that, and did use a flanger on a few things here and there on *Reggatta*, and another thing I used to do quite a lot was an AMS digital delay. That was probably the most expensive piece of equipment in that studio, and it was a stereo delay that had one input and two separate outputs, so you could have one delay at 40 maybe milliseconds, and the other one maybe at 80, and you could also harmonize one of them, to give it a chorusy effect, and that would make the whole guitar sound sort of bigger because you'd pan the delays left and right and the whole thing would form a stereo spectrum but still sound clean. I remember using that quite a lot, and am sure I would have used that on Andy's guitar here or there to give it a little sparkle.

While Gray's in-house effects played into the Police's sound, much like drummer Stewart Copeland, guitarist Andy Summers had his own Echoplex gear in play, courtesy of a tape delay he plugged into his amp through the Echoplex. As it went to tape, Nigel recalled, it

was really noisy, but it gave you a tape delay which had a certain warmth to it that digital delays don't have, and you'd get an analog delay from these things because it had a loop of tape that ran round and round. And it was awful noisy, so you'd have to use a noise gate on his stuff all the time, and when he was not playing, you had to cut the background noise out quite religiously in the mix.

Whenever he was tracking guitars for that record, Andy didn't do a lot of layering. Generally speaking, every guitar is what it is, you don't have to double-track it, because Andy's style of playing is very crisp and clean, and if you try to layer those guitars, it just makes them messy. You lose that crispness.

Recording Sting's lead vocals for the album would prove the cleanest consideration from an engineering point of view, requiring neither coaching nor editing where his pro-from-the-go vocal performances were concerned; it was a part of the process Nigel remembered going so smoothly that

Stings vocals were the easiest thing anybody could ever do. Stick a microphone in front of him, say "Sing it," he sings it, it's done. He's brilliant, and I have a Grammy in my music room for "Best Vocal Performance," and Sting is the best singer I've ever recorded. I used a Valve Neumann U-67 on Sting all the time. I had a whole load of mics at the studio, a whole load, and the only two microphones I liked for vocals were the most expensive mic I had, which was a U-67, and the only other was a Shure SM-57, which is what everybody uses onstage, from the Rolling Stones downward. But for vocals, I just thought they didn't have that warmth, but those old Neumann Valve mics—which is why they're so sought after now—just give out something, I don't know what it was, but they just had it. So that's the only mic I ever used for vocals on everybody my whole career. Sting doesn't sing that loudly, he's got a strong voice but you don't need a special mic to coat the volume.

As the group raced through tracking over a record two-week recording marathon, coproducing an album with Gray that would feature their first #1 hits with "Message in a Bottle" and "Walking on the Moon," Gray felt that the band's combination of amazing talent, chemistry, and energy the band in their performances translated directly to tape. Those qualities also stemmed from the fact that

we didn't do a lot of takes for any song on the album, and if you listen to *Reggatta de Blanc*, a lot of the things are slightly out of time, whereas today, we're used to things being spot-on in time, synchronized to a click track. But if you listen carefully to *Outlandos* and *Reggatta de Blanc*, if you listen you'll think, "That guitar is a little out of time," but it doesn't matter! It doesn't spoil the enjoyment of the record, so we didn't do lots and lots of takes, which sort of fit the Police naturally.

Celebrating "the sheer energy of the band's rhythmic counter-punching," *Rolling Stone* recognized a band on the come in their enthusiastic review of the group's sophomore LP, writing that "constructing and repeating terse, rhythmic hooks, Sting, Stewart Copeland and guitarist Andy Summers set up patterns and crosscurrents like body builders training side by side. Songs, whether reggae or rock, rarely end. Instead, they build through chanty choruses, shift tempo and fade away." In a nod to Nigel Gray's creative contributions, the publication added that "each tune is honed by a distinct production."

Gray's third and final collaboration with the band was 1980's *Zenyatta Mondatta*, the record that would break the Police commercially in the United States and produce some of their biggest hits with "Don't Stand So Close to Me," "Driven to Tears," "When the World Is Running Down, You Make the Best of What's Still Around," and "Do Do Do Do, Da Da Da Da." For as successful as the end product would be, heading into production, Gray revealed that, before the band had even begun recording, everything almost fell apart. I arrived at the studio in Holland and walked in and Sting came up with some 24-track tapes, like his demos, the songs he'd written for this album he'd demoed on a 24-track machine in some studio in England, and they were very jazzy. And he said, "Well, perhaps we can just use my demos and Stewart can do the drumming on them," and I listened to them and they sounded like a nightclub band. They sounded like a jazz club late at night, and I said, "This doesn't sound anything like the Police!," and asked him, "Why don't you just go there out and jam around them, we'll rerecord them, the band can learn the songs, and you can just jam?" There was one song in particular, "Consider Me Gone," where in Sting's demo, you hear this jazzy thing going on before he sings the first line of that opening verse, and when they jammed that live in the studio, it sounded night and day different, and Sting never spoke to me again because he was outvoted.

So we rerecorded the album as the Police, and the record became *Zenyatta*, but had we done what Sting wanted, if I hadn't been there and been pushy, you would have had an album that was night-and-day different, more like Sting's solo stuff. Stewart and Andy liked that and were on my side, so it was three against one, but once he realized he had to do that, Sting came up with all these lovely bass riffs and reinvented those songs in a Police style brilliantly.

Another complication early on came with the fact that we couldn't record the album at my studio because they could only spend ninety days in England for tax reasons, so as we wanted to spend a couple of months doing the album, we did it outside the U.K. So Andy and I went to Holland together to look at three or four different studios, and we liked Wisseloord Studios, in Hilversum, Netherlands, and A&M booked us in there.

This was a record company studio, so no expense had been spared, it was a big console I'd never worked on before, and Studer A-80 2-inch tape machines, and it was a very big room, and the acoustics sounded strange, but I quite enjoyed it. I didn't have too many problems with the drum sound, but you could have got a thirty-piece group in there, and they were a three-piece. The band tracked live off the floor, just the same as before.

Chronicling the event that was the recording of the Police's breakout hit in the U.S., "Don't Stand So Close to Me," Nigel revealed a production far more involved than any of the material on the band's previous two studio LPs. Starting with the recording of the song's opening sound-effects sequence, the producer recalled that

the idea with the opening to that song was, Sting had just gotten this upright electronic double bass, like a jazz double bass, but was all electrical, and he thought that was really cool. It was called a stick bass, and was just like a double bass, and it made a nice drumbling sound, so my idea was for him to play that bass for maybe ten seconds or whatever as a drone, and then you just fade that in and then the drums would come in for "Don't Stand So Close to Me." So we did that, we did his drone, and then we did the backing track, and we kept two takes of the backing track, all going to a click by this time, so every time we'd do a take, the click was in the headphones.

So Stewart plays slightly different every time in terms of his drum fills and little cymbal crashes and stuff, so we listened to the two different takes, and he chose the bits he wanted. Then we had this backing track with the drone, and the backing track drums, bass and one guitar and a guide vocal. Then we did a whole load of overdubs, we did different guitar bits, different vocal bits, and what I would do was roll the tape back to the beginning, press play and record. So whoever was doing the overdub had to wait for this drone, and I didn't play around it to miss the drone, and so when Andy does a guitar overdub, for example, you can hear him plug his guitar in in the beginning and check the tuning with those notes you hear come in right at the top of the song, and he just plays around the chord he's going to be playing.

Then when Sting was doing his vocal overdubs, just waiting to come in, he was walking around the room and then he goes and claps his hands together. So that was how we did all the overdubs, over this drone, with loads of different funny noises which were just there, all these clicks and pops and things. So when we went to mix it, the drum was really boring when we took those out, just a drone before a song, what's the point of that? But all the clicks and pops and little bits were really interesting, so we added them back in.

Finally, on "Do Do Do" and "Don't Stand So Close to Me" in particular, I heard Stewart speed up in the choruses all the time, so I suggested we use a click, which we did, and was quite useful because he could actually comp the 2-inches of that, so we took different bits of two different tapes, and because it was done to a click, it was quite easy to do editing. If you listen carefully to "Don't Stand So Close to Me," the beginning that starts with those different funny sounds, and somewhere in there, you can hear the click track in someone's headphones.

Taking maximum advantage of the studio's expanded stock of effects vs. what he'd had to work with back home at Surrey Sound, as he spread them where appropriate throughout the mix of "Don't Stand So Close to Me" and other songs from the album, the producer was excited to have

more reverb units to choose from. They were still EMT plates, that's what the technology was in those days. An EMT basically looked like a big box, an eight-foot by four-foot box, inside of which was metal framework, and within that framework was this sheet of metal suspended to the framework by four screws, one on each corner. So it was this sheet of metal hanging on springs just standing there, and in the middle of it was this loudspeaker cone, so when you feed the signal in to it, it's like a loudspeaker, but instead of having a speaker cone, there's this great big sheet of metal which then vibrates, and then it has two censors on it that pick up the vibration, and when you put those sensors back into the mix, it sounds like echo. So that's how they got the first reverbs, and we had three of them at that studio.

When attention turned to tracking "Sting's tormented vocals" over the course of a truly theatrical performance of which the BBC said "the singer's voice ranges from teacher terse to panicky as the chorus of this track . . . (that's) menacing, funky, literary, thoroughly enjoyable and truly catchy," Gray felt equally moved on the first set of vocal tracking sessions where

> Sting sings all the lead vocals and harmonies, the other guys didn't sing at all. With his harmonies, Sting would do his lead vocal, and then overdubs, and I can remember with "Don't Stand So Close to Me" that it was late at night, and we had the lights dimmed down a bit and everything and the backing track going. And he did his lead vocal, and we wound the tape back, he did the first harmony, wound the tape back, and he did the next one, wound the tape back, and he did the next one, all first takes. And as it went on, I can remember thinking, "This is brilliant." I just loved it, and I got a Grammy for it, so it must have been good (laughs).

When working on "Driven to Tears," it was guitarist Andy Summers who Nigel remembered being more the focus in the studio, based first and foremost on the fact that

> he did layers and layers of guitars, and one of the problems with that particular track that drove me to tears was, he had a lot of guitars on there, four or five, which for us is a lot, and each was recorded in stereo, and each one with a lot of noisy effects on them, and each one of them with different parts to it, and each one dies away and another one would come in somewhere else. But each of those guitar parts dies away, and when I mixed it, I had plenty of time on my hands and used the automation and everywhere, as it died away, I'd bring the faders down so you didn't hear the hiss and the background noise, because there were four or five guitars in there. I didn't have time to fix all the automation before we had to turn the final mixes in, so on "Driven to Tears," all of those guitars, as they fade away, I didn't have time to cut all that out. So they just had to run, so if you listen to "Driven to Tears" now, it sounds like it was recorded next to a river.

In a true testament to Gray's immense talents as both producer and mixer, as the band reached the end of tracking, he discovered that what he thought were the final mixes he'd done in the Netherlands had to be completely redone under the kind of pressure that would have made most producers crack. Gray recalled that he first made the alarming discovery after realizing that we couldn't use the mixes because in Europe, they had a different EQ setting on their machines. The tape is set up in different ways in Western Europe than it is in England and the US, and because they're all different, when you played them back on British machines, they just sounded all bad, and I had to remix the whole album in one evening, because the complete bastards at A&M were on the verge of bankruptcy and HAD to have this Police album asap. They knew this would be a big seller, so I was under huge pressure to bring this in on a particular day, so I went in, worked right through till four in the morning, and mixed the whole album, bang, bang, bang, just like that.

There were some major problems in that the monitors they had were very flattering, they made everything sound really great. So when we finished mixing the stuff and I eventually took the mixes back to England and listened to the whole album, they just sounded completely different, and I wound up having to remix the whole album in the UK. It was a disaster. At the end, I was certainly pleased with the album. I was nominated for a Grammy for that album in three categories: Producer of the Best Vocal, Producer of the Best Instrumental, and Engineer, and the Engineer one I didn't get, but I think if I'd had more time, I could have mixed that album like I wanted to, and would have won that third Grammy (laughs).

Following its massive success in both Britain and the United States, the Police became bona fide rock stars, delivering a record that dazzled critics as mainstream as *People* magazine, who were impressed by the fact that the Police inside of three albums "have turned their . . . complementary talents into an intriguing sound. Copeland drums in a suitably American fluid style, the signature of Andy is his splashy chord work, while Sting's trim bass lines keep the band's reggae roots intact. His icy vocals add a modernistic touch."

Nigel Gray's touch as a producer would lead him following his three-LP collaboration with the Police to produce hit albums for Siouxsie and the Banshees, including the band's early '80s breakout *Kaleidoscope*, of which the BBC said, "with Police producer, Nigel Gray, also on board to smooth out the edges, *Kaleidoscope* was to propel the Banshees into the major league and to also prove that they had chart potential aplenty . . . Every track is taut and smoothly seductive, from the psychedelic synth swoops of 'Tenant,' to the weirdly atmospheric 'Lunar Camel,' *Kaleidoscope* was where Siouxsie came of age . . ."

CHAPTER 16

Rock the Casbah—Joe Blaney

In the annals of punk rock, only a handful of bands will truly go down as historic: the Ramones and the New York Dolls in the United States, and in the United Kingdom, the Sex Pistols and a band of brothers that, in the esteemed opinion of Kerrang!, "were one of the most important bands to ever grace the planet. While the Sex Pistols grabbed the headlines before exploding in a puff of their own myth, the Clash entirely defined UK punk—moving it from its three-chord birth to world-beating rock via reggae, dub, disco and funk." The Rock and Roll Hall of Fame would add at the band's induction that "the Clash were among the most explosive and exciting bands in rock and roll history . . . (playing) a major role in creating and defining the punk movement . . . (as) the Clash became the central voice of the punk movement and remained at the forefront." Contrasting the Clash with punk rock's other premier influence in the late 1970s and early 1980s, the Ramones, the *New York Times* would highlight the chemistry between lead vocalist/rhythm guitarist/lyricist Joe Strummer and lead guitarist Mick Jones as "one of rock's great songwriting partnerships," adding that "The Clash produced more exciting, durable music than any punk band except perhaps the Ramones, who didn't approach their ambition or reach."

When the Clash did invade the East Coast of the United States in 1981, they were already superstars internationally, but just beginning to see their tide rise over American radio waves, introducing themselves with a bold and experimental single, "This Is Radio Clash" that fit perfectly into the new wave mainstream beginning to dominate college/ alternative and rock radio at a time when a young engineer was also starting to climb the ranks among New York's recording studio scene. Starting out as a maintenance engineer, Joe Blaney would be thrown front and center into the making of the Clash's breakout single in a serendipitous turn of fate. Looking back thirty-plus years later, Blaney confessed that

> the first time I worked with the Clash, I mixed "This Is Radio Clash," and I shouldn't have been in the studio with them. I was a maintenance tech at Electric Lady, and back then, there was sort of a small crew/community of people around New York working at studios who all helped each other out. So, for example, we were just starting to use the TAD horns and drivers, and there were about four studios in New York who had it. So if one of our drivers blew up, I'd run over to Record Plant and they'd loan it to us, and vice versa. I loaned something to Electric Lady once, and met Sal Greko, their head tech, and after three or four months at Sound Mixers, he basically stole me and I went to work at Electric Lady with him as a technician. I worked the night maintenance shift, so would come in about six and usually worked till the sun came up. It was that kind of a gig, but I learned a lot.

Taking a walk further back down memory lane to childhood during the early '70s when he first discovered an interest and aptitude for electronics, at a time when the concept of home recording was first starting to take shape commercially, beginning for Blaney when

> I had an aunt who bought me one of those little battery-powered Akai reel-to-reel tape recorders, 3 and 3 quarter-inch plastic reels, and I experimented a little bit with cutting tape and editing tape, when I was about ten years old. Then, in eighth or ninth grade, I took an electronics class, and built my own stereo from like a kit, built the speakers by buying plywood at the hardware store and ordering woofers from Radio Shack. Back then, that was hi-tech, it was probably the equivalent of being a computer nerd in the late '80s or early '90s, that was cutting-edge science that would interest us. So consequently, I would listen to a lot of music on the FM. By then, I was into FM radio, and again we had only two stations in New York that played all the rock, probably one of my earliest awareness of what a producer or engineer was: one of the two New York FM stations, WPLJ, used to have these live radio concerts. This was the summer of '71 when I was around fifteen, so it would be "Live from A&R Studios with Phil Ramone," a weekly radio show, because at that time, rock still wasn't mainstream enough to where you'd see the Allman Brothers on Johnny Carson.

It was at least ten years before MTV, and a year or two later, some shows like *Don Kirshner's Rock Concert*, finally came around, and some other late-night rock shows. But before then, I had this FM receiver in my bedroom, and I could hear these shows Phil Ramone was broadcasting, and he'd have artists on like the Allman Brothers and Elton John, who did one, and his radio show was so good that the record label put it out as an album. That was where I first became aware of the personality of the engineer being presented as part of the live radio show.

In high school, I somehow lost all interest in doing any studying in school, and basically spent all my time into either listening to records or playing guitar, or fiddling with electronics. I would go to a technical high school half the day and take electronic classes, which was great, it was eight kids in the class with an ex-military guy teaching us radio and TV repair, and tube and transistor, and circuitry theory, the early era where digital was being used, like LED display. When I got out of high school, I was able to get a job fixing electronics, because unlike today where you throw everything away, back then, electronics you would buy as a consumer were serviceable and you would actually fix things. So if you were reasonably adept electronics technician, you could get a job. This was around 1974.

A couple of years later, a friend of mine named John Pace, who was an engineer, wound up working at a studio in New York called Sound Mixers, and they were always having problems finding the right kinds of personalities to be on the maintenance staff. At that time, studios needed twenty-four-hour maintenance because often, there would be a very expensive session going on with a bunch of session musicians being paid double-scale and the costs of studios then were more than they are now, and that's not counting for inflation and being in New York in the late '70s, so you might have been paying $220 an hour. So basically, if something ever broke, you had to have it fixed right away on the spot, because it could stop the whole session in its tracks, and burning money waiting around to get it fixed. So I got in studios and did that at Sound Mixers, which gave me my first exposure to learning the ins and outs of how studio gear worked.

Blaney's first big break into the professional recording world came when he was hired at Electric Lady Studios, the legendary recording facility built by Jimi Hendrix as his home base, and in the decade since, growing into one of the hottest rock studios in New York City, frequented by everyone from David Bowie and Frank Zappa to the Rolling Stones and Led Zeppelin. Even with his career at the studio beginning purely on the technical side of the aisle, Blaney knew he was onto something from the very first day

when I was first working at Electric Lady, we had a lot of major rock acts coming through there, which was also an amazing exposure, so suddenly I'd be the tech working on a Rolling Stones session doing overdubs for *Emotional Rescue*. We had the Brecker Brothers, a reggae artist named Maxwell Meo, so it just felt like there was such a good vibe there. It was also at the same time a bit of a hectic scene, because the studio had changed ownership and things had been slowing down there a bit in the later '70s because their equipment was a little outdated, then they'd bought three new Neve consoles right when I came to work there, and suddenly there was this onslaught of new clients coming through the door. They rebuilt one of the control rooms, and built a new room upstairs, so a lot of stuff was still being debugged, and the place was packed, so I was kind of thrown right into the fire, and it was good thing because I learned a lot.

Of all the clients who came through Electric Lady at that time, I would say the one who inspired me the most was Mutt Lange, who mixed AC/DC's *Back in Black* there with Tony Platt, and at the time, the whole band wasn't even there. Malcolm and the bass player were in for like one day to fix up some background vocals, and then those guys left, and then I think Phil Rudd stayed for a day or so, and then Mutt and Tony spent about a month mixing that record, and would spend generally three to four days on each song. And because the band was there, I was frequently in the room watching them, and there was something about their personalities and the way they worked that made them very meticulous and diligent. This was a basic rock band, and they were still spending three days a song mixing, and the console was a big Neve 8078 that didn't have automation on it, so they would mix sections on a quarter-inch tape for a three-and-a-half-minute song. So we'd often have several edits, because they'd be writing vocal and guitar parts and it kind of amazed me: one, how much I liked what was coming out of the speakers, because I wasn't even that big a fan of that band at the time, but I really liked what I was hearing. There was something about the sonics and the presentation that I think was where I really started to understand what record production was about.

They worked very hard, and it was funny because after the second song where they'd been working three or four days on it, I said to Mutt, "Is everything okay?," because I'd never seen anything like this where people spent this amount of time mixing a song, and he said, "Oh, it's great! We really got the sound we wanted, we're going to have to do the first one over again, but now we got the sound we want." I'd never seen anyone work with this sort of focus and diligence and put that amount of time in it to make something great, because other engineer friends of mine would argue things like, "You should be able to mix a song in an hour." But I think in that case, whatever they did, they did it right because I still hear it all the time on the radio.

While he felt his instincts as a sound engineer were beginning to awaken, Blaney's first engineering gig would come courtesy of a happy accident where the Clash were in New York recording on the same shift he happened to be working as a maintenance engineer, a coincidence that occurred in the first place because they were in there working on a break from touring and just wanted to go in and write some songs. So one night at about two in the morning they were jamming on something, and filled up a whole 2-inch tape with the jam, but there was about a two-minute section of it where they really locked into a groove. So that night the phone rang in the shop and they said, "They want to talk to you in Studio A," so I walked in there, and Bill Price was looking like the guys were definitely making him work. And he says to me, "They've got this song, and we like this two-minute section and we want to copy it three or four times and make a basic track." So I wheeled up another 24-track from Studio B and made the alignments so the transfer would work correctly, copied the song a few times, and Bill edited the pieces together. I'm pretty sure the song was "Magnificent 7," and was comprised of the basic track: the rhythm guitar, bass and drums.

So that's how I began to get to know the band just as a friend, but I think they were impressed with the fact that I could just wheel in this 24-track and make the transfer, which any other maintenance guy in New York at the time would have been able to do. But I got to be friends with them, and about a year and a half later they played some shows in New York at a place called Bond's Casino in Times Square, and it was a big event because it was supposed to be their only US appearance. They were coming over to play like a week of shows, and the place was a real huge room, but the capacity was much smaller than what the room could hold because it only had a certain amount of seats, and the promoter oversold it, so the first night, the Fire Dept. came by and closed it down.

So the band says, "Oh, we're going to just play for everyone who bought a ticket," and they wound up staying there for three weeks, and it was all over the New York local news. So I went to a show a few days into it, went backstage to say hello, and they said, "We've got this song we started in England called 'This Is Radio Clash,' and because they were held up in New York, they next asked, "Can we go up to Electric Lady at night and work on it with you?" Well, what they didn't understand was I'd never engineered before, beyond some basic tracks for a friend of mine, but I'd never mixed anything, I'd never made a record. I was hired by the studio as an electronics technician, but this was just when I was starting to realize: "Hey, maybe the job I want to do is being behind the console," and I didn't go to the show to try and get an engineering gig or anything. I'd just gone to say hello and watch the band being a huge fan of the Clash at the time.

Knowing it was the kind of make-or-break opportunity that sometimes only comes knocking and rocking for a sound engineer ONCE, Blaney decided this was his, and was ultimately forced to put it all on the line with his bosses at Electric Lady to take hold of it, recalling in a moment-of-truth memory that

when they asked if I could do this, and I said "Yeah fine," ran back to work and told the owners of the studio the band wanted me to bring the 24-track machine up and work on this song with them, and their jaws dropped! They couldn't figure out how this could be because I wasn't an engineer, and at first, they said they wanted me to let another one of the engineers working that night do it, and I don't know where I got the courage, but I replied, "All right look, if you don't want me to do it, I'll give you the keys now and take them over to the Power Station . . ."

So they relented and let me head the session, and we spent about four nights working on "This Is Radio Clash" at Electric Lady, and they were short sessions because the band was doing live shows those same nights, so we'd start around eleven or midnight and work till about seven in the morning, then go sleep and play the next show. So then we spent a couple nights doing mixes, and it was manual mixing, and Mick liked to push the buttons. The Neve console at the time had the "Send" buttons, and when you pushed them, it was on/off, so we set them at the right level to have echo available for any instrument that was on the tape, and you can hear a lot of digital delay. At the time, Lexicon had just come out with the TCM 41 and the Primetime, and we also used a quarter-inch tape slap, and plate reverb. These things were all available on send, so Mick and I were really playing the console like a couple of kids with toys, and in fact, inexperience is probably part of the reason the record's as wild as it is, because we kind of went crazy with it.

One big thing on that song was, I remember we did the handclaps and I decided to try to record those in the ladies' bathroom, which was a tiled bathroom with this weird geometry to it, and was way up the hall from the studio. We had to run about a 100-foot-long mic cable, and again, I didn't even really know what I was doing, but I probably overdrove the preamp a little and used a DDX 160 compressor, and it really was an important overdub that defined the record. That was the first time I'd ever mixed anything, and when I would hear it later on the radio or in clubs, it really held up, so I somehow kind of fell into working with the band after that.

Electrified by the freedom the band had given him to jump into the captain's chair and reciprocally by how excited the Clash had apparently been with Blaney's open mind to anything the group wished to try creatively behind the console—and the results that followed with the huge success of "Radio Clash"—the band would fully take the reins thereafter. With the capital thanks to their massive and ever-spreading popularity to write their own ticket with their next studio LP, the Clash made the bold decision to self-produce what would become their—and one of punk's—best-selling albums of all time.

The decision was totally punk rock, and made even more of a gamble because it marked Blaney's first rodeo as lead engineer on a recording session of any kind, in spite of everything he'd witnessed leading up to the start of recording on an album that *SPIN* magazine would say marked the point in the band's career where "rather than letting rock's past define the band, the band set out to expand the music's borders. They borrowed heavily from the sound and outlaw politics of reggae, yet were open to anything." An attitude that he was grateful he and the band shared, Blaney's hands-on approach to engineering the sessions began when

> in November of '81, the band booked Electric Lady, and hired me based off the success of "Radio Clash" to engineer the *Combat Rock* album they were going to self-produce. They had eighteen or twenty songs, and they wanted to make a double album because at the time, the record labels had been raising the retail price of records on a regular basis. They were so driven, I've never worked with any band before or since who was as focused and dedicated to what they do, and driven as them. There was a certain chemistry and thing that could only happen with a band that basically at that point had about six years of being together almost every day of the year, whether on a stage or in a studio. There was something about their energy where the only thing that can quite match that level of energy is when I worked with Prince, and with him, it was mostly coming from one person. As far as the band, I never worked before or after with a band who was quite as well integrated and had the chemistry of the Clash.

Exhibiting a compositional chemistry as cowriters that Blaney had never seen before or since in as potent abundance as Joe Strummer and Mick Jones displayed in the studio as the band got down to work writing and recording in real time, the producer—elaborating on what he witnessed firsthand as classics like "Rock the Casbah" and "Charlie Don't Surf" came together—confirmed that

> they had something very special about the chemistry amongst them where they really all helped each other and all contributed something so that when they worked together, I would dare say, almost telepathic, a very special creative connection. Mick had that tune and melody thing together, so a lot of times, even when Joe kind of started to write a song, Mick had a way with his chords and melody approach, helping Joe improve his idea.
>
> Joe Strummer was always walking around with a spiral notebook writing down song ideas, and the Electric Lady building had a movie theatre in the ground floor back then. And the studio was in the basement and then on the floors above the movie theatre, and the movie theatre was showing *Apocalypse Now*. And one day the band took a break, went up there and watched the movie, and afterward, Joe came back down and wrote that song "Charlie Don't Surf." So it was really like music as kind of a living art form where you're expressing the feelings and ideas and things that inspired you at moments in your life.
>
> The thing that's great about them is they didn't feel a need to stick with any plan, and would always improvise in the studio and try wacky things. They kind of treated

the studio and the tape a little bit in like a playful way, where you could improvise and try things, they weren't as sacred about recording techniques or things I found other people were that would come into work at Electric Lady. That was one of the things that set them apart as a punk band is that they were always evolving and trying new things, and recorded so many songs over the course of those sixteen years or so.

Of the in-the-moment creation of the Clash classic "Rock the Casbah," still in regular rotation on classic rock radio in the millennium's second decade, Blaney revealed that it was in fact drummer Topper Headon whose equally inspired musical genius brought the hit into existence. Taking fans inside the most intimate look at its recording ever, the producer—clearly feeling a special affinity for the drummer and his song—began with his admiration for the fact that

it just seemed like some kind of magical moment for everyone. There's a few moments on that record, one of them was the realization of "Rock the Casbah," where Topper played everything you hear in the basic tracks on that song himself, and we did everything in about four or five hours! Topper was probably one of the best drummers I've ever worked with. He was a tremendous musician, he could play jazz, all kinds of styles. What happened with that one was, originally it wasn't part of their plan for the record when they started the record.

Before "Casbah," we'd cut all of the rhythm tracks they had planned on for the rest of the songs on the record, and were doing overdubbing by this point. Well, the studio was getting a little messy because we had the two guitar amps, we had a Hammond B3 organ set up, the piano, the synths, the congas, a drum kit, etc. So I said to Mick: "Do you mind if tomorrow maybe we break down the drums and clean up the studio a little?," and he said, "Tomorrow I've got something to do in the afternoon, but Topper has this silly song he wants to record . . ." I don't know that he necessarily said silly, but it was kind of treated as sort of an aside, so he continued, "So why don't you guys do that tomorrow." And basically when we were overdubbing, Topper had been off hanging out with some friends in the East Village and someone had an upright piano in their apartment, and he wrote the music to "Casbah" on the piano, that right-hand riff that opens the song and the chords.

So the next day he comes in, and again, he was an amazing musician: the first thing he did was record the drums, and there were NO click tracks on that record, whereas Foreigner for instance had used one when they were in there the year before. He used this type of a metronome that he used to practice with, it was an electronic metronome you buy for home, the standard wind-up kind. And it made this kind of an obnoxious beat, so while you were playing your instrument, you would hear it. Then it also had a little light on it, and if you wanted to, you could turn the volume on the beat down and just have the light blinking. So we set up this metronome on a music stand right in front of his drum set, so basically did the count-off and played the whole song by looking at this flashing light on this early electronic metronome.

Then he immediately played the bass, then the piano, and on the piano, he was having a little bit of difficulty playing the figures so I suggested to him that we do the chords on one track, and then the little melody line that's sort of the hook of the song on an overdub. The piano he played on that song was an upright that I miced with in a way I'd come up with that I hadn't seen anyone do before, which I did for a specific reason. I miced it with two PZM microphones. They were kind of new at the time, and they were kind of a new phenomenon because they had this quality of getting a very natural sound if you put them on the wall, the pressure zone microphones. I put the PZM in with the gafford tape taped onto the underside of the piano, closed it, then put the regular quilted piano cover over it and a couple of blankets, and it ended up sounding very interesting. And my main reason for going that direction was to try and minimize the leakage of the drums into the piano, so when we did "Casbah," it was set up the same way. I had mics on the congas, so there was no getting sounds, and when Topper did those toms and congas, he knew exactly where all the percussion went . . . he had the WHOLE SONG arranged in his head!

Knowing they were onto something truly special, the song's instantly infectious nature soon caught on to the rest of the band, beginning with guitarist Mick Jones, who returned from his meeting to quickly discover that the song he'd begun regarding as of secondary importance was suddenly deserving of the kind of priority a hit song commands, inspiring the guitarist to the extreme that

we'd started at about noon, and then around 5 o'clock Mick Jones walks in and he hears it, and he got all excited, and got his guitar, and comes in with a Stratocaster—which he used mostly for overdubbing, on most of the basic tracking he'd played a Les Paul. So he says to me, "Give me a direct," and I plugged him in through a direct box with a compressor, and next he says, "Put some effect on it," and so I ran it through the Lexicon PCM 41—which we'd just gotten into the studio at that time—in series with the signal. That meant I used the mix knob on the PCM 41 and put a short delay with the envelope setting, so when Mick hit the guitar, it made like a little "wah" type of sound, and in about two or three takes, he had the guitar take, and Topper ran out and threw a tambourine on it too.

Then a friend of Topper's, a bass player who played for the Talking Heads, and he and Mick and Topper did the handclaps, and we did them the same way we'd done "Radio Clash" in the ladies' room. Fortunately, the control room in Studio A was a lot closer, and I'm pretty certain I used an 87 in there. There was something special about that room, it was not that big. It had a little tiny corner, then made a right turn, and the room was all ceramic tile on the floor and walls, plus you had the metal sinks and toilets, so it was very live and was really kind of similar to the way you would make a live chamber in an old-fashioned studio. Quite honestly, I'd never seen anyone else at the studio do that. I think it was something I came up with from just my knowledge that Phil Collins and Peter Gabriel records had been done in stone rooms in England, and I kind of applied the same concept to "Let's record the Clash in the ladies' room!" (laughs)

So we did the claps, and then I think Topper had the chorus written, and they sang the backing vocals with him and Mick and Busta Jones, but I believe about a month later, we redid those, the chorus vocals, but that night, around 7 or 8 o'clock, Joe came in and there was a whole finished track. Topper had some idea for verse lyrics, and someone had given Joe a typewriter, and he wrote the words the next morning in his hotel room. A lot of the beauty of that recording was that there were a lot of spontaneous things going on with it, because it wasn't like we set out to make a hit single. It was just this idea Topper had, and we were having a lot of fun with it, and I think that fun translated to the listener. So when Joe wrote the verses to the song that night, it turned out without knowing what the song was about that he had had a sheet of lyrics in the same sort of Middle Eastern theme that almost fit exactly over the verses.

Highlighting a theme throughout the song that *Rolling Stone* would praise as "a smart-alecky, funk-inflected romp complete with snappy hook and spry party piano, about the banning of pop music by Moslem fundamentalists in Iran," Blaney recalled that geographical influence as showing up topically and musically throughout the entire *Combat Rock* album, noting throughout its recording that

we had this sort of Middle Eastern theme going on through the whole record, because some of those songs had long jams and things, like on "I Know You're Right" there's like a five-minute jam. So when their manager Bernie Lord came through about a week into recording to hear how things were going, back then we'd make a quarter-inch rough of the session and make cassettes for anyone in the band who wanted to take something home to listen to. When Bernie came by to hear how things were going, he told us, "Some of these songs are just too long," and was joking with the band about why everything had to sound like a song from India where everything's a half hour long? (laughs) So there's this humor throughout the whole record about this Middle Eastern thing, and that's where Topper came up with the idea for "Rock the Casbah." While they were doing the background vocals, they were singing the line "The Shah don't like it," and Mick said, "Why don't we make it the Sharif," which is a Middle Eastern word.

So that second day when Joe did his vocals, I think the only thing we did was Mick resang his background vocals to make them a little tidier, and there were a few sound effects we added. One thing was after the jetfighters line, there was one of the earliest electronic drums, you'd hear it on late '70s reggae records, and Topper hit a few of those sounds on the record. There's also a few things we pulled from sound-effects albums. Then while we were doing these live things, Mick had just gotten this Casio digital watch, and it had a little alarm thing on it that played "Dixie," and I saw while we were doing the rough mix of the song that he was constantly fidgeting with his watch. And then he jumps up with this big smile and says, "Hey, I've got an idea!," and he had me put a mic on his watch, and there's actually a little Casio melody in the song somewhere. I'd just add of "Rock the Casbah" that of the I don't know how many songs I've recorded in my career, that was probably one of the most effortless recordings I've ever made. We certainly at the time didn't need another song to fill the record.

Taking fans back to the top of the album's recording, as the band got rolling, Blaney began by revealing that—unlike the latter "Casbah,"

most of the songs on the record are recorded live with a four-piece band, and there's a few different ones that weren't, but most were. Studio A at Electric Lady at the time was still a sort of early '70s design with a lot of carpet on the wall and insulation under it, and was a good live room, but wasn't like what people liked in the '80s with the really live drum room vibe. It was a pretty big room and had a certain amount of geometry where the ceiling was a little slanted, and had about a fourteen-foot ceiling. So I set up everybody in the same room, but the bass sort of went into this little corner which was almost like a booth, where it was somewhat isolated, and with the two guitars—Mick was playing a Mesa Boogie amp through a Marshall cabinet, and Joe had some kind of a black bass Fender amp. I basically put the guitar amps across the room from the drums and surrounded them with gobos, but they still had a little bit too much leakage, so I put some blankets and plywood over across the gobos on top, so it was almost like little cabins, but there was still leakage in the room. If you listen to the overheads, you hear the guitar and bass everything in the leakage.

Singling out another of the record's singles, the seminal "Should I Stay or Should I Go?," a song *Time* magazine would recognize for containing "perhaps one of the most recognizable song intros in rock history," Blaney—beginning with the guitar sound—revealed of its classic stereo feel that

for both guitars, I used a combination of a 57 and an AKG 451, and I'd run them on separate tracks so what you hear is a stereo pair that had two different tones, and I combined those. There was definitely leakage in the room mics that gave the guitars I think a more natural sound, as opposed to later '80s records where they would focus on one sound at a time. And we had a Neve 8078 recording console, which was one of the last ones made. They'd bought it new in 1979, and it's a really good-sounding console, some say it's the best console Neve ever made. But I think the leakage was a big factor in that sound because the guitars got in the room mics and overheads a little, and all those things added a natural ambience that's different than putting delays and reverbs on afterwards.

Mick Jones was using the Roland Space Echo at the time on a lot of things, so his guitar was very wet coming out of the amp, and that's also a very good way to do that, because when you put a delay on a guitar and then go into an amp, it's a tube amp and the speaker mixed the signal and the thing together in a good way. Whereas when you have a delay on a console, it sounds more separated and not as integrated.

Beyond their individual instrumental elements, the producer added that the sound the band produced within the sonic sum of those parts played a huge role in capturing what the Rock and Roll Hall of Fame argued with "*Combat Rock* (was) . . . the tumult of the times with unerring instinct and raw power." Blaney explained that, ahead of any fancy studio tricks, as a bottom line for any song's successful production to work,

there's also an element of performance that's important too, especially a band that's well-integrated like the Clash, who play their best when they're all playing together. So with most of the songs on the record—and "Should I Stay or Should I Go" is definitely one of them—we'd get a basic track, and then Mick and Joe would just go right out and double their guitar parts right there. I think that's brilliant because the musicians are kind of tuned into the song and the tempo and the feel of it, because you've been trying to get a take from anywhere from four to ten run-throughs, and you're kind of in the zone of that song. So if they'd just gotten the take they liked, they would all decide as a band and if they all thought they got it, and then Joe and Mick would go right out and overdub their guitars.

Applying some of the tricks he'd picked up working in the presence of producer Mutt Lange during the AC/DC mixing sessions where he utilized the studio itself as an instrument, Blaney proudly recalled that

another thing we did to get that sound was something I'd seen Mutt and Tony do when they were mixing *Back in Black* in Studio A was to send the snare drum out through the big playback speakers that were on the wall in the studio, and mic the room. And so when I was recording the Clash, for whatever reason, I decided that I wasn't hearing enough snare drum in the ambience of the live room where they'd recorded. So I sent the snare drum back out while they were playing through the speakers so the snare was being amplified in the room as well as the guitar amps and bass and everything. So the overhead mics would get a little—not a lot—but a little bit of the snare that was being sent back out through the speakers. The speakers were also a little further away from the drums and the drum mics, so you get a little decay of forty or fifty milliseconds and a tiny bit of an ambience there.

Another celebrated sound Blaney captured on the song that would influence generations of beatmakers to come would come with the micing methods the producer applied in the studio, impressively based largely on instinct vs. experience with Topper Headon's kit wherein

I would have put a 57 on the top snare, a AKG 451 on the bottom, Sennheiser 421s on the toms, and an RE-20 on the kick drum. I used a console EQ on everything, and on the kick, probably used a graphic EQ, and on the snare, added a Poltec in addition to the console EQ. Along with the ambience of the room, there were two effects we used with the drums, one being sending the snare out to the speakers, and I also put an AKG 451 as high as I could get it right over the drummer, kind of behind his back pointed at the snare, and I had it gated, and triggered the key to the gate with the snared rum.

So every time Topper hit the snare, this mic up top about twelve or fourteen feet above the snare would open up and then close that off again. I'd never seen anyone do that, and just did it because I liked the gated sound I was hearing on some of those English records coming out at the time, like Peter Gabriel's third solo record that Steve Lillywhite produced. Topper used a natural wood-finished kit we had at the studio, and I'd suggested to him we use those vs. his touring kit, and he was cool with that and sent his tech out to the store to buy all new heads, and tuned up the drums the way he liked them. They were wood shells without anything wrapped around them.

Rounding out the powerhouse pop polish to the punk-rock classic was the voice of a generation from a front man who *The Atlantic* would hail for his "mad-dog vocals, stamping left foot . . . (and) lyrics (that) were a rock-and-roll marvel—jagged, speedy playground chants apparently purpose-built to conduct the shocks of Mick Jones's guitar." Though Strummer tracked his rhythm guitar live with the band,

he didn't do any singing on the basic tracks because he really felt he could play his guitar a lot better without having to do the two things at once. I found that to be very unusual, and as a producer, I've preferred the band to have the vocal to sing along with more than anything, but the Clash knew the songs well enough that every guy in the band was kind of imagining the vocal in their head as they tracked. They knew the material well enough that they didn't need to have a guide vocal.

All the lead vocals were done in overdubs. That was where he started to have difficulty, and the vocals were harder work than the music on that record for two reasons: one, again I was a bit of a novice and hadn't done much recording at all, and two, because his voice was kind of raggedy, because this band had worked solid from their inception touring or recording. They might have added a few short breaks in there, but they were basically on a mission and had complete dedication and commitment to their art, and so Joe would just be singing endlessly.

Joe had a great voice, in terms of immediately recognizable character, and was also a great singer too, but would have problems sometimes with the maintenance of it, because he'd be out there on stages screaming. He also had just had his front teeth fixed, so he felt something sounded funny about his voice because of that, so we struggled a little bit with the vocals. I think we started out with an 87, but I felt it was distorting a little, so we did a lot of the vocals for that album with an RE-20, because it just seemed like it could take the screaming more than a condenser.

As excited as Blaney was about the sound he and the band were bringing to life, he still confessed to experiencing some serious frustration during the recording of Strummer's lead vocals for the song. Forced in a moment of crisis to flex for the first time his production muscle of objecting to the artist's desired direction for a song, knowing instinctively they were heading down the wrong road, while he was proven right in time, at the moment, Blaney remembered being at odds with the band because

I remember at the time being very worried about "Should I Stay or Should I Go." We had a few issues with that song as we went along. It was so commercial, and the only obvious radio song on the record, and at a point, the band wanted to either a) not do it, or b) they were going to sabotage it, and Joe was going to sing the whole thing in Spanish. My assistant Eddie Garcia was on the phone for two hours with his mother in Queens, who was from Ecuador, trying to get a Spanish translation of the lyrics. Joe was trying to sing the whole song in Spanish, I actually stormed out of the room and my assistant Eddie was recording it, and I really had no business doing that. I wasn't the producer on that song and was lucky to have the engineering gig at all.

Well, Strummer had this incredible sensitivity, which I guess is part of being a great artist, and he picked up on the fact that I was pissed off. So I was out in the lounge, and he comes out from the studio and goes, "Joe, Joe alright, I'll only do the backgrounds in Spanish!" There's something about that has always impressed me, after all these years, that he had this like antenna and could pick up on that. So when we finished the vocal on it, all the band members were in the control room and we did a playback and everyone had a big smile on their face.

There are still some Spanish backgrounds in the second verse. That was Joe Strummer and Joe Ely, who had done a tour with them and came by one night, and it was the two Joes singing those backgrounds in Spanish. I would add that "Should I Stay" was the only song we rerecorded. We put down sixteen or seventeen songs, and when they reviewed it, before we started the album, they came in for a couple of days and I ran live 2-track quarter-inch tape to record the rehearsal, and I thought the recorded version of "Should I Stay" wasn't as exciting as the reference preproduction demo we'd made, so after we got everything, that was the only song they decided to take another crack at, and it came out a lot better. We didn't do anything different technically.

Blaney had a much easier time working with Strummer for "Straight to Hell," a track that *Alternative Press* would declare the band's "most poignant song," and in the producer's recollection, its recording was exciting because it had

sort of a different twist to how they were done. One was "Straight to Hell." Joe didn't have a guitar part for that, it was just Mick's guitar, and when they were getting ready to track, Joe said, "Well, what am I going to play?" And I thought/said the logical thing, which was "Why don't you go in the booth and sing along with them." So Topper says, "I'm playing this pretty intricate drum part with what I'm doing with the snare and the hi-hat, you could play the bass drum," and in my head, I was thinking, "What the hell are they talking about?" So Joe wound up standing right there next to Topper with the same bass drum, and took the beater off the pedal and was holding it with the metal rod in his hand banging on the kick drum, and that's how we got the rhythm track to "Straight to Hell."

I remember at the end of the final take, he had a big blood blister on the palm of his hand from holding the metal end of the bass drum beater. What's funny about it is: when you listen to that song, there's a straight quarter-note bass pattern, but the way Joe's doing it, it's not quite as tight as if Topper did it, and a little bit behind, which makes it sound like the song has a more mysterious groove to it than if it was done straight. Because Topper was an amazing drummer, he had almost perfect time, but the band at the time felt it wouldn't be right to record the song without Joe doing something on it.

So the way "Straight to Hell" came together between Joe playing the bass drum and the way that that was the only vocal that we got, where it just all came out of him on one pass, and seemed like some stream of consciousness and expression you don't get that often. Another thing about the Clash, they were always interested in trying new toys, like I don't think there were too many other punk bands with the Space Echo. Mick used the Space Echo a lot more than a lot of other punk bands, and he got that from the reggae guys. Then when we were in the studio, he had heard about this new device that Roland had come out with, this guitar synth, and what it was was a monotonic—where you could only do one note at a time—and it had what they called pitch-to-voltage converter. It didn't have a second pickup on the guitar, so you plugged in any guitar, played one note, and it would have the oscillator and synthesizer track the guitar note, and there were problems with latency and false triggering where if you slipped between two notes, you got this weird thing.

So on a couple of the songs, including "Straight to Hell," where that other instrument on there that almost sounds like strings or synths, that's done on guitar, and it was like three or four tracks where he made the harmonies, so it sounded like he was a string quartet with this Roland box that had literally just hit the market a month or two before that. He wasn't afraid to just grab something he didn't know and start using it, and there's a certain expression on that song that wouldn't have been the same had he played it on the keyboard, and he's a very good keyboard player too. To this day, "Straight to Hell" might be my favorite song I ever recorded, because it's such a powerful song.

Collectively, the album Blaney and the band created together in the studio would go on not just to make punk rock history, but become one of the finest in rock 'n' roll albums period, as affirmed in *Rolling Stone's* conclusion that, as a highly anticipated follow-up LP to previous efforts, "*Combat Rock* is stirring, inspirational rock & roll, arranged with good pop sense and shot through in concentrated doses with the imagination and vigor that were spread throughout *Sandinista!*" The *LA Times* would make the equally important point—in the context of the impact the album would have in pushing punk rock into the mainstream charts as a permanent influence—that "*Combat Rock* made the Top 10, and its influence resonated in the music of Nirvana and the other grunge bands that shaped rock in the '90s, and today's rock radio playlists are packed with groups that follow the Clash blueprint of social commentary delivered in unvarnished, aggressive form. That's a far cry from punk's original position as a noisy irritant to the staid music industry of the 1970s, when major record companies and radio stations ignored the music. The growing popularity of the Clash was key in breaking down that door . . ."

It was key too in kicking open bigger doors for Blaney, as the album would put him on the map as an in-demand engineer and producer, working over the decade that followed with Prince, Soul Asylum, and the one and only Keith Richards, who tapped Joe to record both the Rolling Stones guitarist's solo efforts. Ahead of collaborating with Richards, in sharing his reflections on working with the Clash, the producer stated unequivocally that

I've never had any experience like I had working with the Clash, and the main things that stood out for me were the energy, and the commitment, and the focus. All they lived for was their music, that was their life.

Another highlight from Blaney's catalog to follow would come with hooking up with Keith Richards on the guitarist's first solo outing, *Talk Is Cheap*, in 1988 after *Billboard* reported that "Jagger decided to tour in support of his second solo album, *Primitive Cool*, Richards was disheartened and finally succumbed to the idea of recording without the Rolling Stones. Taking the band he had assembled to back up Chuck Berry for the 'Hail! Hail!

Rock 'n' Roll' documentary (along with longtime session player Waddy Wachtel), Richards put together an album that was straightforward, musical, and better than a good portion of the Stones' output in the first half of the '80s." The producer recalled that he was brought in to work on the album after

the record was started, and another engineer named Don Smith had recorded most of the basic tracks. I did some overdubbing and tracking and mixed the record, and right away, it started off with like a feeling of a five-piece band in the studio all playing together. It was a little bit antithetical to the later-'80s style of making a record for a lot of rock bands, where they'd go in the studio, get a good take of the drums, and then redo everything else, because it was believed that if you put the guitar amp in the big room by itself and really work with the guitar player, you'd get a better guitar sound.

So that was part of *Talk Is Cheap* is that they were all playing together, and the other thing was that Keith was very motivated and driven because Jagger made the solo record and Keith was upset about that and at the time we were making *Talk Is Cheap*, he wasn't even 100 percent sure that they were going to continue with the Stones. There was just a lot of tension between him and Mick, and he—because of that—put a lot of energy and commitment into the solo record, because, even though in the Stones he was the principal writer of the music, if he sang, he only sang on one or two songs per album, where here he had a record with ten songs.

So they started off trying to get everything with the band up in Canada with Don Smith engineering, and ended up getting five or six songs, then they had a bunch of ideas they had been working on but didn't get there. So they went to a little studio called 900 with Don again, and then did a lot of things as a three-piece, and in some cases it was just Keith and Steve cutting the basic track, and then they brought Bootsy Collins in to play the bass. There's something about the way he writes songs that the songwriting and the guitar playing are so integrated, like how many great Rolling Stones songs—"Brown Sugar" or "Can You Hear Me Knockin'"—where somehow the whole song is predefined in the guitar intro: you get the melody, the vocal, the rhythm.

Keith has a way of writing where he's really connected with the guitar figure, and the way he delivers it is a really important part of the song. I think what was good about *Talk Is Cheap* is that he finally got more of a leader role, which no one in the world expected he could ever do, making a solo album where he was singing on every song. I think it was an inspiration of being in a new situation, where he surrounded himself with very talented people.

Richards's band was hailed as "top draw players by" *Rolling Stone*, while *Billboard* added that "while Jagger's solo work sounded like Mick with some studio musicians, Keith had assembled a band, found a productive songwriting partner in Steve Jordan, and created a record that was free of frills. Simply put, Richards sounded like he was playing for himself, and playing with a certain sense of enjoyment. The new band, the X-pensive Winos, had a different work ethic than the Stones, forcing Richards to focus on the music. What resulted was a solid album built on fundamentals rather than style. It's hard not to see who the real musical force was in the Stones after hearing *Talk Is Cheap*." Blaney was equally impressed with the lineup, marveling years later that

> I think it's quite remarkable that Keith was able to assemble the people that he did for that record, and in a funny way, I think it was a relatively effortless thing. He had met Steve Jordan in New York when Steve was playing with the Blues Brothers, and Keith was friends with those guys, John Belushi and Dan Aykroyd. So it wasn't like they had to have hundreds of auditions, he had already worked with Steve on the Chuck Berry movie "Hail! Hail! Rock 'n' Roll," and so they were going, and Steve was friends with Charlie Drayton on bass, and Charlie was like Steve's protégé sort of at the time, so they had a rhythm section going together. Then Steve and Waddy had worked together on a Stevie Nicks record, and Keith and Waddy were already sort of friends, and then with Ivan Neville, the Neville Brothers had opened for the Stones on one of their tours, and Keith was very impressed with him. So he chose a group of people where it came together very easily and naturally, and turned out to be a great band to accompany his music. All of the main rhythm guitar parts on that record are Keith playing live with the band.
>
> Another reason that record's so exciting is they started out with a philosophy of doing tracks with everyone playing together in the room with no click tracks, just playing straight up like the Stones would have made a record. That record was grounded in the more old-fashioned way of people playing together, but at the same time, because of Steve's eclectic thing of playing a lot of different styles of jazz, pop, etc., it took a while for Keith and Steve to integrate well together, because Steve is a little more of a clean, session-style player, and he kind of modified what he did live to gel with Keith, and did a great job of it.

Mixing the album with Richards sitting alongside him at the console, Blaney found himself interacting with the guitar legend on a creative basis day in and out, from the playing side where "he overdubbed an acoustic" to the most specific of mixing decisions, offering "Make No Mistake" as one such magically collaborative moment where

> there are a few little fills in the intro and stuff where he played them, and I basically was focusing in on the sound of the track. That one they'd recorded in a very live room at the Hit Factory as a four-piece band of Keith with Steve Jordan, Charlie Drayton and then Bernie Worrell played organ, and they wanted that tight, R&B sound. So we mixed that at the old Atlantic Studio, and it was a Neve with moving faders, and with

the drums—I had to even let the overheads and toms—keep those mics way down, and then if there was a cymbal crash, the fader would shoot back up for that and then fade back down again, because there was way too much room ambience for the type of sound we were going for. So we had to kind of fight the room ambience on the track. But I got the mix sounding pretty good as far as the sound of it, which was a little bit of a struggle, and got Keith's voice sounding great, and then he pointed out a couple guitar licks he wanted me to turn up, but it was a huge contribution because somehow I'd mixed them. So Keith would make suggestions that were pretty key and made a difference.

After the platinum hit of *Talk Is Cheap*, on Richards's follow-up LP, *Main Offender*, Blaney was once again sitting behind the boards, this time in a full-first engineering capacity.

I started that one and did the basic tracks, and on that record, for Keith's amp, I miced it using a 57 combined with a Neumann TLM-170 and also a Beyer M160, so I had three mics, and I think Keith was using two amps—a Mesa Boogie and a Twin kind of together. The Twin was an older tweed Twin, and the Mesa sounded a little too biting or brittle by itself, but somehow when he mixed it with the vintage Twin, it all worked.

A lot of that stuff evolved in the studio, and there were some songs where they kept trying to get it for a day or two, and then they would change things up, play a different groove, until they found something that worked. So it was really about refining the song—everything from the guitar figure to the tempo to the beat to everything—and it really felt great doing that all live and human, and again, with no click tracks for those two albums. All those musicians were playing dynamically and listening to each other, and it was really about as close to any situation I've heard of where an artist hires a bunch of pro musicians and came up with a band that almost sounded like a real integrated band. It was a really great example of that.

Discussing his and Richards's coproduction rapport, Blaney observed that—much in line with his role as the rhythm anchor he'd held down for years in the Rolling Stones—out on his own and running the show in the studio,

Keith was a very patient producer. There were times we worked on the same song for two days till we got a take, but at the same time, the music came relatively easily, and when that was done, it seemed like what took longer was finishing the lyric and the singing of it. A lot of the lyrics were written in the studio while we were working, so we spent quite a bit of time on vocals on both those records, because Keith did it differently than most other people, who would have gone home with a cassette and come back in a month. We were doing a lot of that work of finalizing the songwriting and the melody and style of singing in the studio, so it went on for weeks, or a couple of months on vocals, much longer than the music did. I recorded most of the vocals on *Main Offender* with a Telefunken 251.

For Keith's acoustic guitar tracks, I often would use—it's a solo overdub, a C-12 or good condenser like that. Sometimes a smaller mic like the KM-54 or 56. And one thing I think is critical with acoustics is to—depending on the guitar and the part—move the mic around. So, for instance, if you want something that's kind of defined and not too boomy, sometimes you put it more toward the fretboard pointing toward the hole. But if you want it bigger, you might end up having it like closer to the bottom of the guitar where the strap attaches, away from the strings a little further out. Then you get a nice mix of the strings, projecting from the hole but also sort of the resonance of the body.

Entertainment Weekly would welcome *Main Offender* as "surprisingly infectious," concluding that "Richards once again proves that the fever that has been raging through his much-abused veins for three full decades shows no sign of breaking anytime soon."

A pace Blaney has kept for over forty years in the business, dizzying as it's been at times, the producer still has taken the time to begin to start picking his favorites, selecting them based on a premise that

it's sort of a mystical thing, you can't always explain or quantify, what record production is, but in the end, I think it's making people want to listen to it over and over again. "Rock the Casbah," of I don't know how many songs I've recorded in my career, that was probably one of the most effortless recordings I've ever made. We certainly at the time didn't need another song to fill the record. But when you hear a song that stays on the radio, something was done really well. I think the most important thing after the composition is to make sure you get a really good groove or feel, and whether that's with life musicians or programming, I think people respond. So an exciting performance is the most important thing, vs. any recording or sound techniques.

Striking a balance between commerce and art is an unfortunate reality of the business Blaney argues can be best met by remembering in the end that a producer's most essential purpose is focus on the song, reasoning that

in the end, as far as what a producer does, it's funny because the words *producer* and *product* have a lot of the same letters in them, and they're derived from the same thing. You're basically hired by the label to try and make a product, but I like to think in an ideal world, you're not trying to make something less genuine either. I think a producer's supposed to bring out the best in an artist.

ABOUT THE AUTHOR

Award-winning music biographer **Jake Brown** has written thirty-five published books since 2001, featuring authorized collaborations with some of rock's biggest artists, including 2013 Rock and Roll Hall of Fame inductees Heart (with Ann and Nancy Wilson), living guitar legend Joe Satriani, heavy-metal pioneers Motorhead (with Lemmy Kilmister), late hip-hop icon Tupac Shakur (with the estate), celebrated rock drummer Kenny Aronoff, late funk pioneer Rick James, superstar country music anthology *Nashville Songwriter*, and the all-star rock producers anthology *Behind the Boards*, among many others. Brown has also appeared as the featured biographer of record on Fuse TV's *Live Through This* series and Bloomberg TV's *Game Changers* series, and received national press in *USA Today*, MTV.com, and *Billboard*, etc. In 2012, he won the Association for Recorded Sound Collections Awards in the category of "Excellence in Historical Recorded Sound Research."